FOOLPROOF

FOOLPROOF

Why Misinformation Infects Our Minds and
How to Build Immunity

SANDER VAN DER LINDEN

W. W. NORTON & COMPANY

Celebrating a Century of Independent Publishing

First published in Great Britain in 2023 by 4th Estate under the title *Foolproof: Why we fall for misinformation and how to build immunity*

For information about permission to reproduce selections from this book, write to Permissions, W. W. Norton & Company, Inc., 500 Fifth Avenue, New York, NY 10110

For information about special discounts for bulk purchases, please contact W. W. Norton Special Sales at specialsales@wwnorton.com or 800-233-4830

Manufacturing by Lakeside Book Company
Production manager: Louise Mattarelliano

ISBN 978-0-393-88144-8

W. W. Norton & Company, Inc., 500 Fifth Avenue, New York, N.Y. 10110
www.wwnorton.com

W. W. Norton & Company Ltd., 15 Carlisle Street, London W1D 3BS

1 2 3 4 5 6 7 8 9 0

For Gavi

CONTENTS

PROLOGUE

Foolproof (adj.) – 'Incapable of being misused'

Kirkby is a relatively small town in the borough of Knowsley, in the northwest of England. Boasting a little over 40,000 inhabitants, it's the birthplace of poet Robert Atherton, the actor Stephen Graham – and a man you've probably never heard of, until now: Michael Whitty. Whitty is a dad of three. He volunteers for a local charity and operates an airport parking facility. He has also been developing some unusual ideas, slowly but steadily, with the assistance of a trusted friend, the internet.

On Sunday 5 April 2020, Whitty and two accomplices drove out to Coopers Lane, Kirkby, where they set fire to a phone mast owned by Vodafone. Whitty put on a pair of gloves, forced open the equipment box, and used some firelighters to set the whole thing ablaze. This wasn't a 'heat of the moment' decision; later police investigations show that the arson was carefully premeditated. Whitty was convinced that the latest 5G (fifth-generation) phone masts were somehow linked to the coronavirus pandemic that had recently seized the world in its grip. Evidence obtained from Whitty's phone suggests that he spent a considerable amount of time researching 5G technology and discussing it with others in online chat rooms. His anxiety about new technology and health, whilst perhaps understandable, is actually based on a false and debunked conspiracy theory that radiation from 5G phone masts lowers our immune systems and can thereby cause or exacerbate the spread of Covid-19.

Nearly four years earlier, in the run-up to the 2016 US presidential election, Edgar Maddison Welch, a twenty-eight-year-old father of two from North Carolina, walked into the Comet Ping Pong pizzeria in

Washington DC carrying a loaded semi-automatic assault rifle. He was under the impression that presidential candidate Hillary Clinton was hiding young children in the basement there as part of a secret child-sex-trafficking ring. Like Whitty, Welch had developed genuine concerns (in his case, about the possible abuse of children, the so-called 'Pizzagate' scandal) after reading dozens of fake news articles which had been shared widely online by celebrities and politicians.

A common response to such events is to dismiss them as the actions of single individuals. Outliers. Most people aren't fooled by fake news. But is this really the case? How confident are you that your vote wasn't influenced by micro-targeted misinformation? How much of what we read on social media is false or if not plain false, designed to make us think or feel a certain way? Whitty and Welch are not alone. The truth is that at a basic cognitive level we are all susceptible to misinformation.

A total of at least fifty phone masts have been set ablaze throughout the UK because of widespread misinformation that 5G masts are somehow linked to the spread of Covid-19. Scientific research later confirmed that belief in the 5G conspiracy is linked to violent intentions. In 2020, my Cambridge colleagues and I surveyed the population in the UK, the United States, Mexico, and Spain, and directly asked people if they believed that the 5G network was making us more susceptible to the coronavirus. The estimates from our study ranged from 10 to 17 per cent of the population in each country. If that sounds low to you, consider that even just 10 per cent means that over 7 million people in the UK and about 32 million people in the US report holding such beliefs. Moreover, if 10 per cent is all it takes for people to start setting phone masts on fire, we should be concerned about what wider spread of these beliefs might entail for society.

The 2021 attack on the United States Capitol, which sought to challenge Joe Biden's presidential victory, is a chilling reminder of the damage that a misinformed crowd can inflict. The false claim from former President Donald Trump that Democrats had stolen the election by committing widespread voter fraud, was frequently repeated on social media and conservative cable news. These bogus claims ranged from 'mysterious vote dumps for Joe Biden' and election officials pulling 'suitcases of ballots out from under a table', to 'dead people voting'. Dubbed the 'Tsunami of Untruth' by fact-checkers, Trump has made over 30,000 false or misleading claims during his presidency.

The violent riots at the Capitol may not have been a consequence of misinformation alone, but an extensive investigation by the independent fact-checker *PolitiFact*, who reviewed the files of over 400 of those arrested, showed that in at least half of the cases, misinformation shaped the defendants' beliefs and actions. Many of those arrested had been highly active on social media; several even cited being 'duped by fake news' as a defence in court. A lot of them were just like Whitty and Welch.

Take, for example, twenty-seven-year-old Anthony Antonio, a solar panel salesman from the suburbs of Chicago. Antonio had no prior interest in politics. He hadn't even voted in a presidential election before. After being laid off work during the pandemic, Antonio said that he simply got bored. He started watching Fox News on repeat, tuned into right-wing social media and became consumed with conspiracy theories that the presidential election had been rigged. On 6 January 2021 he wore a bulletproof vest with insignia of a far-right militia group. He was charged with five counts, including disorderly conduct and violent entry of the Capitol.

Referring to the torrent of misinformation that engulfed his client, his lawyer said: 'You can catch this disease.'

But the spread of dangerous misinformation is not just a Western issue. In April of 2018, false videos with warnings of local child-traffickers in southern India circulated on WhatsApp, claiming that more than fifty children had been abducted in the area. These messages incited a mob of around 200 people to attack an innocent family, dragging them from their car, beating one to death and leaving others critically injured. The messages triggered a spate of similar assaults. The now infamous 'Indian WhatsApp Lynchings' often follow the circulation of fake news videos and messages on the platform. For example, later that year, two men were beaten to death and seven others injured after fake messages about local robbers were distributed on WhatsApp. In early 2020 in Iran, hundreds of deaths and thousands of hospitalizations – including children – were attributed to mass poisonings, after people were fooled by false social media claims that ingesting toxic alcohol-based products would help 'neutralize' the coronavirus.

In short, fake news can get you killed.

Even an optimistic account of our ability to spot fake news has to come to grips with the fact that not everyone *needs* to be fooled in order for misinformation to be highly influential and dangerous. After all, major elections are often decided on small margins, and cyber propaganda is playing an increasingly important role in tearing down the fabric of our democracy. In early February of 2022, Russian propagandists flooded the media with fake videos supposedly portraying Ukrainian acts of aggression and attacks on Russian territory in order to create a pretext for the planned invasion. Some of the social media images were taken from Israeli airstrikes on Gaza; other footage came directly from the tactical shooter video game, *Arma 3*. The goal of these campaigns was not to convince foreign audiences that Russia's military invasion was somehow justified but to make it harder for people to discern fact from fiction: the hope was that political analysts and fact-checkers would be distracted by having to track down and debunk obviously false materials.

There's justifiable concern about the ways in which fake news is undermining democracy. For example, a 2016 poll by the Washington-based research centre Pew revealed that over 65 per cent of Americans report that fake news leaves them feeling confused about basic facts, and 83 per cent of Europeans think fake news is a major problem – with at least half of those polled reporting that they encounter misinformation on a weekly basis. Even conspiracy theories are no longer reserved for the 'lunatic fringe': over 50 per cent of Americans now endorse at least one conspiracy theory. These findings raise bigger questions about our ability to navigate the media ecosystem. How do people come to believe in misinformation? How and why does it spread? And what can we do about it?

In this book, I'll address all of those questions – but I should warn you that this is not a typical book about persuasion, at least not in the way you might think. I have studied the psychology of persuasion and influence my entire career. In fact, my interest in persuasion is not just professional – I have spent a good chunk of my personal life trying to understand the process by which people, including myself, become convinced of the veracity of all kinds of information, especially misinformation. Most of my family on my mother's side were executed by the Nazis in the Netherlands during the Second World War. My grandparents were able to escape – just barely – but one of their two sons, my uncle, a young boy, was shot on purpose by a Nazi soldier during a *razzia* (round-up). He was taken to a nearby hospital. The Dutch resistance managed to sneak him out and a lovely family took him in. After the war ended, my grandparents had no idea what happened to him. Although they were eventually reunited in good health, my uncle never recovered psychologically from what had happened to him as a child.

After learning about the impact of Nazism on my family, I became fascinated, from a young age, by the process through which people are persuaded of dangerous and harmful propaganda. I first got the opportunity to explore my interest in the psychology of misinformation scientifically in graduate school. I started studying persuasion not to persuade other people but rather – to reverse-engineer the process. What if a better and deeper understanding of the persuasion process could empower people to withstand malicious attempts to influence their opinion? I decided to explore the building blocks of disinformation campaigns to see if I could synthesize a 'vaccine'.

Although I had been researching the nature of disinformation campaigns long before 'fake news' became a popular term, it wasn't until a few months after the 2016 US presidential election that I received an email from the United Nations 'Special Rapporteur on the Freedom of Opinion and Expression', inviting me to attend a three-day meeting on 'fake news'. The venue was a secluded sixteenth-century estate on the south coast of England, a property owned by the British Foreign and Commonwealth Office. During this meeting, high-level representatives from governments and social media companies from around the world debated basic questions such as: 'What is fake news?' and 'What can we do about it?'

This meeting had a profound effect on me. I was fascinated to learn more about the complex legal and human rights issues that make defining and legislating fake news so difficult, and the practical challenges of identifying and prosecuting those who are intentionally spreading it. I quickly discovered that I was the only behavioural scientist in the room, and although initially my role wasn't entirely clear, the discussions quickly converged on the insight that the law and technology are blunt instruments: whatever legislation is introduced, it is not going to address the spread of misinformation in and of itself.

The discussion started to shift towards the importance of understanding human judgment and decision-making. Just how important the role of psychology was going to be in this debate started to sink in. I presented my initial findings on how people might become 'inoculated' against disinformation. This acted as the catalyst to what would eventually become an influential research programme that has formed the basis of strategies to counter fake news adopted by governments, public health authorities, and major technology firms around the globe.

So, instead of more lessons on how to effectively persuade other people, this is a book about how to fight back. How to gain resistance to persuasion by *proofing* our minds against the tactics of those seeking to deceive us with fake news and misinformation. I will share everything I've uncovered about how not to be duped by fake news and misinformation – from how the brain discerns fact from fiction, to the viral spread of misinformation, including its alleged role in the US 2016 election, Brexit, international wars, and the Covid-19 pandemic; to the future of truth in society. The misinformation virus will be placed under a microscope in order to synthesize a vaccine, focusing specifically on breaking down the mass persuasion process – from neurons to elections – in an attempt to cultivate societal immunity against it.

In an era increasingly filled with half-truths, fake news and misinformation, I am not here to tell you what to believe. Regardless of where you fall on the political spectrum, perhaps you can think of this book as a humble servant in your own search for truth. Andy Norman, a philosopher at Carnegie Mellon University, refers to me as a 'cognitive immunologist'. I quite like this description of my field of research: I study mental defences of the mind. I want to provide you with a guide to how your brain grapples with the onslaught of fact and fiction, a toolbox to help sniff out attempts to influence your opinion amidst the 'dark arts of manipulation'. A vaccine, if you will, against misinformation. Just as antigens produce an immune response in the body, *psychological* antigens can help build resistance to fake news. I offer eleven such antigens in this book to help boost our immunity.

The lawyer defending the Capitol rioter Anthony Antonio was not wrong when he suggested that people can catch misinformation much like a disease. In this book, I hope to convince you of three key propositions. The first is that there are viruses of the mind and not just the biological kind. A biological virus is a parasite that attaches itself to the surface of a host cell. It will then inject its own genetic material into the host, hijacking the host cell's machinery with the goal of reproducing itself. In a very similar way, misinformation, conspiracy theories, and other dangerous ideas, latch on to the brain and insert themselves deep into our consciousness; they infiltrate our thoughts, feelings, and even our memories. Misinformation can fundamentally alter the way we act and think about the world. The misinformation virus hijacks parts of our basic cognitive machinery. Unfortunately, just as viruses are notoriously difficult to treat (antibiotics don't work), decades of research show that once misinformation takes root in our brains, it too is extremely difficult to correct. The analogy runs deep.

The second proposition is that, just like regular viral pathogens, fake news must spread from one person to another. In fact, in 2020 the World Health Organization (WHO) declared the outbreak of a worldwide 'infodemic'. One thing to keep in mind is that, by themselves, viruses cannot survive for very long outside of the body. They need a host. The same is true of misinformation. On its own a misleading tweet or fake news headline doesn't do much – it needs a susceptible host in order to reproduce and spread. Biological viruses usually spread via contact or respiratory droplets. But viruses of the mind are even more contagious because they can be shared from one individual to the next without the need for any physical contact. As we'll find out, like regular viruses, they can have dangerous health-threatening consequences, leading to injury and even death. Moreover, the spread of fake news doesn't only threaten the wellbeing of individuals. It poses serious threats to the integrity of elections and democracies worldwide.

The third and final proposition is that we need an effective antiviral treatment – a psychological vaccine against fake news. Together with my colleagues at Cambridge University, I have been working on this issue for many years now. Luckily, the development of this vaccine does not require any needles, just an open mind, and is completely free of charge. However, the theory does follow the medical analogy closely. In the same way that vaccines train the immune system to recognize and fight off foreign invaders, often by introducing weakened or dead strains of a virus, it turns out we can inoculate the human mind too. By injecting people with a severely weakened dose of fake news (the virus) and refuting it in advance, over time people can develop mental antibodies – psychological immunity – against misinformation.

Creating a vaccine requires understanding the structure of a virus, which is in part determined by the chemicals that encode its genetic information (such as DNA and RNA). Accordingly, my research group has tried to uncover the key techniques that underpin the production of nearly all fake news, establishing a taxonomy of what we call the 'Six Degrees of Manipulation', polarizing groups in society; appealing to emotions to manipulate people; floating conspiracy theories; impersonating fake experts and official organisations; and trolling people and online conversations. You can think of these six techniques, which we'll explore in greater depth in chapter 9, as the core building blocks of the fake news virus. Our theory was that you could potentially inoculate people against these underlying techniques, and after many lab experiments, we finally achieved a breakthrough. But we needed a vehicle to deliver the vaccine – a way to translate the theory into a virtual needle.

Through a unique collaboration with game developers, we built a simulation engine. We called it *Bad News*. The first of its kind, *Bad News* is a fully interactive fake news game that mimics a social media environment. The game broke new ground but its logic remains slightly controversial: in order to confer immunity, people needed to be 'injected' with a microdose of the fake news virus. In the game, players are exposed to weakened doses of the key techniques that are used in the spread of misinformation. For a brief moment, the player is in charge of their own fake news empire.

In order to test the 'vaccine', our research group enrolled tens of thousands of people from all walks of life, from all around the world. Before they entered the simulation, individuals were asked to evaluate the reliability of a series of fake news headlines. Here's an example:

> The Bitcoin exchange rate is being manipulated by a small group of rich bankers. #InvestigateNow.

This fake Twitter post uses the 'conspiracy' technique: it casts doubt on the mainstream narrative by blaming a cabal of elites who are secretly plotting to accomplish a sinister goal (we'll examine the tell-tale traits of a conspiracy theory later in this book). After participating in our intervention (the vaccine), people are shown another series of fake headlines, including ones they've never seen before (the invaders). This time around they are less easily fooled. Psychological antibodies have started forming, which allow participants to better resist fake news because they understand the underlying tactics.

The theory of psychological inoculation has turned the world of fact-checkers upside down. Unlike fact-checking (or 'debunking') the idea here is not to issue corrections after the damage has been done. Like vaccination, when it comes to misinformation there is real value in the notion that an ounce of prevention is worth a pound of cure. We need to play 'offense rather than defence'. *Bad News* represents more than just a fun game: it marks the beginning of the new science of 'prebunking'.

Yet before we jump to potential remedies, we first need to understand how well our cognitive immune system deals with misinformation when we encounter it. Part One of this book is therefore devoted to understanding why all of us are susceptible to misinformation. Part Two details how falsehoods spread from one individual to another, from ancient Rome to online social networks. In the final part of the book, Part Three, we'll explore how to *pre*bunk and inoculate ourselves and others against misinformation.

So, let's start our journey at the beginning. How does our brain discern fact from fiction?

PART ONE

Viruses of the mind

CHAPTER 1

Illusory truth: How our brains discern fact from fiction

'There are no facts, only interpretations.'
FRIEDRICH NIETZSCHE

My office at the University of Cambridge is located in the Old Cavendish Laboratory – a famous landmark, once home to James Watson and Francis Crick, who, together with the crucial contributions of Rosalind Franklin, discovered the structure of human DNA. I mention this because tour groups gather below my office daily around lunchtime, not to see me muck about, but to hear about the rich history of the building. One thing I've noticed over the years is that some of the 'facts' about the site seem to change about as often as the tour guide. One of them even quoted Mark Twain once when he told the group, 'never let the truth get in the way of a good story'.

One rainy afternoon I was taking my lunch break in my office when I received a request from the Council of Europe, an organisation of European countries whose aim is to uphold human rights and democracy through international conventions. They'd invited me to their headquarters in France, a fortress-like building known as the Palace of Europe. They wanted me to provide testimony on the following question: Is the human brain the ultimate fact-checker?

It's a tricky question. How do our brains decide what to believe, what 'feels' true, what information to remember and process as undeniable facts and evidence, and what just sounds like a pile of rubbish?

Think about it. How good are you at spotting fake news, for instance? In public polls, large majorities of people typically claim that they are fairly confident in their ability to detect it. Whenever I give a public talk on fake news, I therefore like to warm up the audience with a little quiz. Without cheating, try to answer the following question off of the top of your head:

The stories below were all widely reported. Two of them are fake. Which one is true?

A. Putin issues international arrest warrant for George Soros.

B. A baby born in California was named 'heart eyes emoji' 😍

C. Criminal farts so loudly he gives away his hiding place.

In a study with just over 1,500 people, participants were shown six headlines much like the example above, three of which were false, and three of which were factual. Although about 50 per cent of respondents were 'fairly confident' in their ability to tell which was which, only 4 per cent identified all headlines correctly! Perhaps the human brain isn't the ultimate fact-checker after all.

If you're curious to know the right answer to the quiz, it's C. While most people tend towards option A or B, sometimes the truth is smellier than fiction. A man in Missouri was wanted for possession of drugs and decided to hide from the police. Unfortunately, he broke wind so loudly that he gave his own position away. The Clay County Sheriff's office tweeted: 'If you've got a felony warrant for your arrest, the cops are looking for you, and you pass gas so loud it gives up your hiding spot, you're definitely having a shit 💩 day! 😆 #ItHappened.'

If you didn't guess right, don't worry. Everyone is susceptible to fake news, including trained experts such as myself. In February 2021, my wife showed me a tweet with breaking news footage from Mars. We knew that NASA's Mars rover *Perseverance* was going to land on the planet near the end of February, so we watched the video with much enthusiasm. There was even sound – mostly wind – accompanying the footage. We looked at each other full of wonder, and I asked: 'Is this what Mars sounds like?' I was blown away.

A few hours later I wanted to show the video to a friend and after some extensive googling I discovered that in fact the footage was fake – a very sophisticated fake. The video had combined real footage from another Mars rover mission with real audio from a seismic instrument on NASA's robotic lander *InSight*. So, although the footage and Martian wind sounds were real, they weren't live, and they didn't come from the microphone of the *Perseverance*. I felt hoodwinked. But I wasn't the only one; the video was viewed over 25 million times and shared by many academics, journalists and celebrities, including Stephen King. The video's creators had taken explicit advantage of the fact that people were anticipating the footage: our brains had expectations of what we wanted to see. In short, if you think you're immune to fake news, think again.

The kids aren't all right

In fact, adults aren't the only ones duped by fake news. It might be tempting to reason that our kids are much more resilient to misinformation – after all, they're 'digital natives': they've grown up with Twitter, Tik-Tok, and the internet. And yes, although it might be true that the average digital literacy level of a teenager is higher than that of some elderly individuals, it is important to note that their brains are just as easily fooled.

To find out how easily, Stanford University Professor Sam Wineburg and his team spent a year gathering data on nearly 8,000 students in the US on fifteen different kinds of media literacy assessments. As part of one of these tests, they asked a couple of hundred middle-schoolers to evaluate the home page of the current affairs outlet *Slate Magazine*. Specifically, the students were asked to identify which bits of information were news stories and which were simply adverts. Rather worryingly, over 80 per cent of the students falsely believed that so-called 'native ads' were real news stories.

Native ads are a relatively new type of ad that mimic editorial material though are clearly labelled 'sponsored content'. For example, one post about global climate change featured a pie chart and data. Despite the ad being clearly sponsored by an oil company, and prominently featuring their logo, 70 per cent of students still selected the oil company ad as being more reliable than a traditional scientific news story on global warming. Another example concerned the resignation of the police chief of Ferguson, Missouri, following a federal report which identified widespread racial bias in his department. Students were asked which, out of the four tweets below, was the best source of information about the event. Fewer than half of the students identified National Public Radio (NPR) as the most trusted source of information. As one student put it: 'The best tweet for information is the first one because it actually shows him resigning in a picture.'

Although Professor Wineburg and I focus on different kinds of interventions, there is no doubt that we agree on the bottom line: the problem is much bigger than just fake news. We are increasingly dealing with viral half-truths, deeply partisan agendas, and constant media manipulation. It is worth noting that while commentators often focus on statements that are either true or fake, this type of fake news only represents a tiny fraction of misleading media more generally. Just focusing our definition of fake news on outlets that publish totally outrageous fabrications ignores the fact that a substantial chunk of content from even mainstream outlets can be misleading without being completely false.

For example, in 2016 the British tabloid the *Sun* ran a front-page 'Exclusive: Shock Poll' headlined: '1 in 5 Brit Muslims' sympathy for jihadis'. The story was based on a public opinion poll conducted following the terrorist attacks on Paris, almost a year earlier, asking whether people had 'sympathy with young Muslims who leave the UK to join fighters in Syria'. IPSO, the UK's independent press watchdog, rated the headline as significantly misleading as the poll never mentioned 'ISIS' or 'jihadis' (people could have easily thought of rebel groups fighting *against* ISIS). Moreover, in a previous poll, a similar percentage of non-Muslims had given the same answer. So, although the numbers were correct, the way the results were framed and presented was deemed to be highly misleading. The paper had deliberately played on people's emotions by appealing to a collective fear of terrorism.

The real danger is therefore with news that employs one or several of the 'Six Degrees of Manipulation', that is, distorting a grain of truth by using one of six specific psychological techniques to try to persuade us of the 'truth-value' of a claim. I know this because my research team studies and documents these techniques and I will show you how to recognize them later in the book.

At this point, it is useful to conceptually distinguish 'misinformation' from 'disinformation' and 'propaganda'. I define misinformation as information that is simply false or incorrect, for whatever reason. People make honest mistakes. Journalists make innocent errors. Disinformation, however, is misinformation coupled with some psychological intention to deceive or harm others. When disinformation is deployed in the service of a political agenda, state-sanctioned or otherwise, we call it propaganda. What matters here is the explicit involvement of malicious intent, often with the goal of manipulating people – for example, to vote a certain way. In other words, disinformation and propaganda are the more dangerous subsets of what everyone generally refers to as 'fake news'. Unfortunately, intent is difficult to prove, at least in a legal sense, so throughout this book I will mostly use the broader term 'misinformation' so as to remain agnostic about intent unless I specifically refer to well-documented disinformation and propaganda campaigns.

*

I had never been to Strasbourg. I was sitting on a giant staircase looking out over the Palace of Europe, which is right next to the European Parliament, flanked by the flags of all of its member states. As I was going over my presentation, I realized that policy-makers often want a short answer to their question – and (spoiler alert) the answer was no. As much as I would like to think so, the human brain is not the ultimate fact-checker.

I say this because I know how easy it is to fool people – I do it for a living! We do it because it helps us understand how the process works. But I'm not the only one. The strategic use of misinformation is widespread throughout the animal kingdom and can be advantageous from an evolutionary standpoint. For example, prey will often use (sensory) misinformation tactics to make themselves less attractive to predators by feigning death or mimicking inedible objects such as leaves. Because we either lack the skills to spot the manipulation attempt or don't have the time to figure it out, biases in our cognitive system can be exploited by others. In order to synthesize and develop a psychological vaccine, we therefore need to understand not only the virus but also how our cognitive immune system operates.

Accordingly, it's helpful to answer a more basic question first: How does the brain process and store information? This is a question that gets at the heart of the nature of reality.

The predictive brain

For all its flaws, the human brain is a remarkable information processor. Although the popular idea of the brain as a supercomputer is an oversimplification, the metaphor works on a basic level: the brain processes input in the form of signals and information it receives from your body and senses. The tissue in your brain has nearly 100 billion nerve cells called 'neurons' and each individual neuron can form thousands of links with other neurons, jointly composing a hugely complex neural network. To give you a sense of scale, the brain of a fruit fly is about the size of a poppy seed and contains around 250,000 neurons. This represents just about 0.00025 per cent of the number of neurons of an average human brain. That's a lot of neurons.

Bigger isn't always better, though. When it comes to human perception, the truth of the matter is that there's quite literally more than meets the eye. We often take for granted that, on the most fundamental level, what we see with our own eyes must be 'real' or 'true'. But how do you know that anything you see (or, indeed, hear) is real? You might say: it's just optics; light bounces off an object, hits the retina in your eyes, a signal is transported along the optic nerve, via the thalamus, into the visual cortex, and voila – an image appears. It's not that simple, however. In fact, much of human vision is probabilistic – in other words, the brain uses cues in the environment to provide a best guess of what is there.

If that's true, that must also mean that it is possible to fool the brain with 'false' information. Let me illustrate this problem to you with a simple optical illusion known as the Kanizsa triangle.

If you are like most people, you will see an upright bright white triangle shape on top of an inverted triangle. But the triangle doesn't actually exist. The *Pac-Man*-like configuration merely triggers the perception of an illusory contour. The basic process of human vision I described above starts with a chain of events initiated by an external stimulus; this is called 'bottom-up' cognition. But the visual cortex also receives input from other areas of the brain when we perceive something familiar (such as a triangle). This is called 'top-down' cognition – top-down because information travels from higher cortical structures down to the visual cortex. It's an internal process and, as such, it is literally 'all in your head'.

Nietzsche famously claimed that 'there are no facts' and so our subjective interpretations of the world are all we have. It turns out that whilst Nietzsche and I probably have different views about the nature of truth, he wasn't entirely off the mark when it comes to the role of interpretation. The major benefit of top-down cognition is that it helps the brain fill in gaps in your visual field by drawing on prior experiences and expectations of what the world *should* look like. In fact, the brain is generating an image of what it *expects* to see. It makes inferences, a best guess of what should be there, based on cues in your environment combined with things you know to be true. In this case, you'd expect to see a triangle.

Most of the time these two processes complement each other perfectly. Our brains are predictive, which is 'why yuo can raed this'. But it only takes one optical illusion to reveal how easy it is to trick your brain into seeing something that isn't there, simply because you expect to see it. Importantly, these optical illusions aren't just for fun, they actually help our understanding of how reality is constructed.

In a recent study, researchers were able to measure neuronal activity in the visual cortices of mice by momentarily 'silencing' the internal pathway when the mice looked at moving lines that represented edges. They determined that this path (the brain trying to make sense of the lines as an object with definable boundaries) contributed about 20 per cent of what the mice were actually seeing. In other words, although 80 per cent is more or less a direct response to observing the external stimulus (moving lines), about 20 per cent represented a response from higher-order areas of the brain itself, trying to make sense of things.

The role of 'top-down' processing will become more important once we start exploring how people perceive facts and evidence. If, based on our expectations, the brain is already filling in gaps when it comes to the basic visual perception of innocuous objects, how much of this is going on when we perceive potentially contested facts, science, and evidence based on our deeply held values and prior beliefs about the world? The fact of the matter is that the brain does a lot of top-down interpreting and not only when it comes to vision.

Is truth illusory?

In 1977, psychologists Lynn Hasher and David Goldstein asked a group of college students how certain they were that sixty general-knowledge trivia-like statements were either true or false. (An example would be a statement such as: 'The thigh bone is the longest bone in the human body', or 'Lithium is the lightest of all metals.') The students were asked to evaluate the sixty statements three times, at two-week intervals. Crucially, only twenty of the statements were repeated each time; the other forty were new. The researchers then compared the 'truth-ratings' of the repeated versus non-repeated statements. What they found was astonishing. Regardless of whether the statement was true or false, belief in the truth of the claim went up as a function of repetition. In other words, the more often you hear a statement, the more 'true' it sounds. This became known as the illusory truth effect.

It's worth thinking about the implications of this. 'Mass immigration is hopelessly out of control.' 'Women don't have the ambition to get to the top.' 'Global warming is a hoax.' Rinse, repeat. Does repeating a lie really make it seem more true? Perhaps unsurprisingly, propaganda experts intuited this insight long before psychologists had experimentally verified it. In fact, Paul Joseph Goebbels, Nazi Germany's infamous minister of propaganda, is often associated with writings on the 'Big Lie' rule: 'If you tell a lie big enough and keep repeating it, people will eventually come to believe it.'*

Former US president Donald Trump knows this all too well. He has repeatedly claimed that the 2020 election was rigged and stolen from him – it has become his favourite 'Big Lie'. But surely, repeating a completely outlandish claim doesn't make people more likely to believe it? A 2022 YouGov poll highlights the power of repeating the Big Lie: despite overwhelming evidence to the contrary, about 75 per cent of Trump voters continue to believe that the 2020 election was rigged. Psychological research affirms the effectiveness of the Big Lie rule.

In 2015, Lisa Fazio, Associate Professor of Cognitive Psychology at Vanderbilt University, conducted a fascinating study. Not only did she replicate the illusory truth effect, but her study also revealed an addi-

---

* Ironically, it was Hitler not Goebbels who first described the Big Lie rule. In *Mein Kampf* Hitler explains it as follows: 'In the Big Lie there is always a certain force of credibility; because the broad masses of a nation are more easily corrupted in the deeper strata of their emotional nature than consciously or voluntarily; and thus in the primitive simplicity of their minds they more readily fall victim to the Big Lie than the small lie.'

tional insight: prior knowledge does not protect against illusory truth. Participants in the research were more likely, for example, to think that 'saris are the skirts that Scottish men wear' after repeated exposure to this claim, *even* when they had correctly stated at the outset that 'kilts are the skirts that Scottish men wear'.

In other words, simply knowing that something isn't true is no guarantee that you won't be duped by a false headline when it's repeated over and over. Here's another way to think about it: have a second look at the visual illusion earlier in this chapter. Is the triangle still there? Knowledge of the illusion does not fix the bias in your perceptual system.

A few years after Fazio's study, colleagues at the Massachusetts Institute of Technology (MIT) confirmed that previous exposure to a whole range of fake news can indeed increase its truth-value, even when the stories are flagged as 'contested' by fact-checkers. Their experiments included a wide range of outlandish headlines in the context of the 2016 US presidential election, including 'BLM Thug Protests President Trump with Selfie . . . Accidentally Shoots Himself in the Face', and 'Mike Pence: Gay Conversion Therapy Saved My Marriage'. These statements were rated as more accurate after repeated exposure, regardless of an individual's political affiliation.

I know what you're thinking: there must be a limit to what people will believe? There is. Interestingly, the MIT researchers found that some claims are just too ridiculous, no matter how often you repeat them, most notably: 'The earth is a perfect square' (though even flat-earthers are on the rise; but more on that later). It's also important to keep in mind that we're not talking about fully converting people from believing that something is completely true to believing something is completely false. Typically, these illusory truth effects represent small to moderate increments on a scale of how likely it is that a statement is true or false.

What about the role of education? It is true that many studies, including much of my own work, have found that as education increases, the propensity to believe in fake news and conspiracy theories decreases. However, this doesn't mean that education necessarily protects you from illusory truth, because the underlying psychological mechanism that's at play is so basic it affects nearly everyone. Estimates suggest that up to

75 per cent of people show evidence of being susceptible to illusory truth from as young as the age of five.

The illusory truth effect works psychologically because when you see or hear something repeatedly, your brain becomes faster at responding to the claim – it *feels* familiar. This is what we call 'fluency' and, unfortunately, our brains often misinterpret fluency as a signal for truth. In other words, the brain will imbue claims that we know or have seen before with a higher truth-value. Research finds that one problematic consequence of being repeatedly exposed to fake news is that, over time, people find it less unethical to share misinformation because it starts to *feel true*. This subjective feeling of something being true, without having any objective proof to substantiate it, is what *The Late Show* host and comedian Stephen Colbert jokingly referred to as 'truthiness'. When defining the term, he said: 'I am no fan of dictionaries or reference books, constantly telling us what is or isn't true.' Instead, he challenged the viewer to 'try looking it up in your gut, this is truthiness: truth that comes from the gut, not books'.

All joking aside, there is some relationship between fluency and what we refer to as an individual's 'cognitive style'. People who have a more 'intuitive' – (fast, automatic) as opposed to a 'reflective' (slow, deliberate) – style are more likely to go with what feels familiar. Take this item from the popular cognitive reflection test:

A baseball *bat and a ball* cost $1.10 together, and the *bat* costs $1.00 more than the *ball*. How much does the *ball* cost?

Most 'intuitive' thinkers respond with $0.10, as that seems like the obvious answer. But it is also the wrong answer. The correct answer is that the ball costs $0.05. If the bat costs $1 more than the ball, then the bat must cost $1.05, which jointly, makes for $1.10. Although studies show that intuitive thinkers are more likely to fall for fake news, your cognitive style isn't set in stone and going with your gut can be useful in other settings. What's more important is that under conditions of limited time and attention we're *all* more likely to rely on our intuition and mistake fluency for truth.

The misinformation effect

Of course, having known or seen something before implies we might have a memory of it. Because much of our knowledge about the world is stored in our long-term memory, it is crucial to examine the extent to which our memories are susceptible to misinformation. Can fake news make us remember things that have never happened?

Before we answer that question, let's return to the contested computer metaphor, where your brain is the hardware and 'thinking' is the software running the program. Have you ever wondered how much a typical brain can remember? This question has puzzled cognitive scientists for decades. Modern science has provided some impressive estimates.

One of the field's most prominent theories suggests that long-term memories are stored in synapses – the connections between two neurons. Synapses allow neurons to communicate and thus control the flow of information in the brain. Given that the brain has about a billion neurons – each of which are connected to thousands of other neurons – the total covers trillions of connections. This amounts to a storage capacity of well over a million gigabytes. So how come we don't remember everything? To paraphrase cognitive neuroscientist Paul Reber, the problem is not so much with the hard drive as it is with the downloading speed. Because the rate at which we can commit information to long-term memory is relatively slow, our memories are selective; we tend to keep the memories that we like, we think about them frequently, we cherish them, and perhaps even embellish upon them along the way. We often forget the rest.

But what about memories of events that never really happened?

Elizabeth Loftus, Distinguished Professor of Psychology at the University of California, Irvine, is a controversial figure in the field, mostly because of her testimonies on the (questionable) reliability of human memory. She has consulted on hundreds of legal defence cases, including the Ted Bundy and Harvey Weinstein trials. But controversial or not, Loftus is the world's expert on 'the misinformation effect': the robust finding that exposure to misleading information after people experience an event can significantly alter our memories of what really happened.

In one of her well-known studies, 'the Bugs Bunny study', she exposed people to a fake Disneyland pamphlet entitled, 'It's time to remember the magic.' The point was to activate childhood memories of a visit to Disneyland. However, there was something odd about the pamphlet: it featured a message from Bugs Bunny – a Warner Brothers cartoon character that couldn't possibly have been present at Disneyland. After exposure to the ad, about 25 to 35 per cent of participants claimed to have met Bugs Bunny at Disneyland. People offered up specific details too; about 60 per cent of those who claimed to have met Bugs remembered they hugged him, and one individual even recalled Bugs holding a carrot.

This misinformation effect is highly pervasive, from inducing false memories about crimes and alien abductions to political fake news. In 2021, a clever group of researchers examined false memories in the context of the 2016 Brexit referendum. In the experiment, about 1,300 participants from the UK were exposed to six stories, two of which were fake – one involving local election tampering and the other a fabricated WikiLeaks report about illegal campaign donations from foreign entities. Although the stories were identical, there were two versions: one blamed the Leave campaign and the other accused the Remain campaign. Although each participant read six stories, for the two fake stories, participants were randomly assigned to view either the Leave or Remain version. The authors found that each false story was remembered by 22 to 35 per cent of participants, with 44 per cent claiming to have remembered at least one of the false articles. Importantly, Remain voters were more likely to recall fake stories that blamed the Leave campaign of wrongdoing and Leave voters were more likely to remember fake news that implicated the Remain campaign. For example, one fifty-four-year-old Remain voter (in the Leave condition) reported remembering the (fake) WikiLeaks story about foreign donations to the Leave campaign. When asked to elaborate, she said: 'It confirmed in my mind that outside interference in British politics is now deeply entrenched.'

There are plenty more real-world examples of this. Consider media coverage of the 2003 War in Iraq: studies show that repeated exposure to suggestive headlines reporting the 'possible discovery of weapons of mass destruction (WMDs)' led to persistent false memories about the war among a notable segment of the US population. Here, too, an important link with ideology emerged: about 60 per cent of Republicans falsely believed in the discovery of WMDs in Iraq, compared to 20 per cent of Democrats. The key take-away is that, during emotionally charged political events, our memories of facts become more open to suggestion.

The concept of 'fluency' doesn't just apply to vision and memory. It extends to all kinds of judgments of truth. To illustrate, statements that are more visible and thus easier to process (more fluent) are deemed more likely to be true. Consider the following example:

Osorno is a city in Chile

Osorno is a city in Chile

Despite the fact that these are identical statements, University of Southern California psychology professor Norbert Schwarz – who has pioneered some of the early research on 'truthiness' – repeatedly found that the sheer visibility of a claim can actually increase (or decrease) its fluency, and thereby the extent to which it is experienced as familiar and judged to be true. Eryn Newman, a Senior Lecturer in Psychology at the Australian National University has also consistently found evidence of this. In one experiment, people were shown names of unfamiliar celebrities with the claim that either 'this famous person is dead' or 'this famous person is alive'. Adding a photo to the name, compared to just a name on its own, led people to be more likely to judge the claim as true, regardless of whether the celebrity was presumed dead or alive.

You could think of fluency as the brain's attempt at making a fast and intuitive truth-judgment as opposed to a more deliberate, analytical assessment. Of course, the fact that the brain processes familiar things more fluently isn't a bad thing in itself. In fact, in all likelihood it's probably a useful and adaptive heuristic, or rule of thumb, in many situations. It would be absolutely exhausting for your brain if you had to process every bit of information completely anew. You know that $2 \times 2 = 4$ when you read it – this has been repeated to you many times, you can process it fast and fluently. The real problem is that something can be true or false for many reasons *other* than familiarity. If I were to ask you, for example, how many animals of each kind Moses took with him on the Ark, most people would say 'two', despite the fact that in the biblical story it wasn't Moses on the Ark, it was Noah. This doesn't matter to your brain though; it's just predicting familiar answers.

There's a crucial lesson to be learned here: if false claims are often repeated and made easier to digest than true ones – which can be long, messy, and complicated – why not make the truth more fluent? Although making facts more accessible and relatable and repeating them more frequently is helpful in countering misinformation, it is often, as we'll discover in the next chapter, not enough.

FAKE NEWS ANTIGEN 1
Make the truth more fluent

— The human brain uses rules of thumb to make predictions about what it sees.

— One of these rules is that repeated (false) claims feel more familiar and therefore must be more likely to be true.

— This phenomenon is known as the *illusory truth effect*.

— For the truth to 'stick' it therefore needs to be processed *fluently*: the more familiar a claim becomes, the easier it is to process.

— Whereas lies and fake news tend to be simple and sticky, science is often presented as nuanced and complex.

— The easier it is to process and repeat a factual claim, the more familiar it will become, and the more likely it is that the brain will use it as a signal for truth.

CHAPTER 2

The motivated brain:
What you want to believe

'People almost invariably arrive at their beliefs not on the
basis of proof but on the basis of what they find attractive,'
BLAISE PASCAL, *On the Art of Persuasion* (1658)

Making the truth more 'fluent' is easier said than done when our brains
are motivated to reject the truth. The seventeenth-century mathematician
Blaise Pascal noted this nearly 400 years ago. Pascal made tremendous
contributions to the study of probability and even laid the foundations
for the modern calculator. Although he was a man of science, his final
words were about his faith: 'May God never leave me.'

What's particularly interesting here is that Pascal never appeared to
have had a deep affinity with religion until, one night, when he experienced an episode featuring flashes of bright light which led to a devout
religious conversion.* Pascal later came up with a famous game-theoretic
puzzle, known as Pascal's Wager, which aimed to prove that belief in God
is a rational consequence of considering our options. He liked gambling
problems: 'God is, or He is not. But to which side shall we incline?'

Pascal assumed that either God does or does not exist and either you
believe in God, or you do not believe. If you wager that God exists and
you believe, then you will be rewarded with eternal life in heaven. If God

---

* Some neurologists believe that Pascal may have suffered from migraines with aura
(sensory disturbances).

exists and you do not believe, then there will be suffering and eternal damnation. If God does not exist and you still believe, then perhaps you've wasted some time; but if God doesn't exist and you do not believe either, then nothing is lost anyway. So overall, the cost–benefit analysis clearly suggests that while little is lost by believing in God, there is everything to be gained. Or in Pascal's own words: 'If you gain, you gain all, if you lose, you lost nothing. Wager then, without hesitation that God is.'

In mathematical terms, believing in God is the 'super-dominant' strategy. After all, even if you are a sceptic and assume that the probability of God existing is tiny, tiny times infinite heavenly benefits is still an infinite benefit, which looks rather attractive compared to infinite hellfire. But did Pascal sincerely believe in his own logical proof, or did he recruit his remarkable appetite for maths to justify a new – more religious – view of the world that he deemed much more appealing? Pascal's wager appeared about three years after his sudden conversion and the presumed gains and losses are clearly derived from a Christian understanding of God. Pascal was in fact known to be a Christian apologetic – that is, someone who worked on the intellectual justification of religion.

Of course, we may never know the true state of Pascal's own beliefs. But this constant tension between our search for the truth and what we want to believe about the world is the focus of this chapter. Why do some people deny climate change? Refuse to eat genetically modified (GM) foods? Or think vaccines can cause autism? Do they have a different understanding of the truth, or are they motivated to reject it because they find it unappealing?

The Bayesian brain

When the English economist, John Maynard Keynes, was once challenged for changing his position on an issue, he reportedly replied: 'When the facts change, I change my mind. What do you do, sir?' Scientists argue a lot over models that convincingly explain how the human brain reasons about evidence. If the brain were optimally attuned to processing evidence, many of us think the brain would be 'Bayesian'. Bayes's theorem was named after the eighteenth-century English mathematician

Reverend Thomas Bayes and his work on conditional probabilities. In its simplest form, Bayes's rule can be thought of as a formula for how to update probabilities that certain hypotheses we might have about the world are true, given the available evidence. In other words, you might have established some prior beliefs about an event (for example, that NASA faked the moon landing). You then encounter a piece of evidence – such as a statistic or fact – which strongly contradicts this belief (such as the 300 kilos of verified moon rock that the astronauts brought back). Following a Bayesian approach, you would update your new (formally called 'posterior') belief in accordance with this evidence.

So, is the human brain 'Bayesian'? It's an attractive model that fits quite naturally with the way that people update their beliefs about the world. It's how scientists (should) conduct their experiments: we have a hypothesis about the world, we go out and observe the evidence, and we change our beliefs about the likelihood of various hypotheses accordingly. You might mistakenly believe that putting your hand on a hot stove will not cause a burn, until you find out first-hand (pun intended) that it does, and you update (change) your beliefs in light of the irrefutable evidence from the school of hard knocks. We all navigate our environments with prior expectations about how the world works (remember 'top-down cognition'), then we observe the evidence, correct, update, and change course accordingly. We mistakenly thought we had observed a triangle in the optical illusion but, following the evidence that our brains were being misled, we no longer think that the triangle is there. We can still see it, but at least we now know we're dealing with a visual illusion.

So far so good.

It turns out, though, that in many instances people seem to be doing the complete opposite of what the good reverend Thomas Bayes would have predicted: instead of updating toward the evidence, people either do not update their beliefs, or actually update away from the evidence. The 'post-truth' era has fundamentally challenged the notion that the brain is fully Bayesian, or the ultimate fact-checker for that matter. How is this possible? Let's consider the 'contested' fact that many (more) people attended Donald Trump's Presidential inauguration than President Barack Obama's inauguration.

One way to make the truth stand out more is via the use of images. Images can help make the truth more fluent* – for example, by highlighting what we intuitively recognize as big and small numbers. This is justified when the images help represent the magnitude of the actual numbers. Let's have a look at an image which heavily featured in the world media.

Donald Trump himself claimed that 1.5 million people attended his inauguration, whereas experts have calculated a turnout anywhere between 300,000 and 600,000. Sean Spicer, then White House Press Secretary and Communications Director, claimed on 21 January 2017, that *Trump* drew 'the largest audience ever to witness an inauguration, period'. The photos above illustrate the turnout for President's Obama inauguration in 2009 (on the left) and Trump's inauguration in 2017 (on the right) and quickly (read 'fluently') invalidate this claim.

If Sean Spicer were, for the sake of argument, Bayesian, he would have updated his beliefs in light of the overwhelming evidence to the contrary. Instead, when questioned by reporters a few days later, he doubled down on his initial statement. In other words, his posterior belief, as he expressed it, did not move closer towards the evidence. If anything, it seemed to move further away from it.

---

* Importantly, as we've seen in the previous chapter, they can also be used to make lies and fake news more fluent.

Of course, we cannot be certain as to whether Spicer truly believed the claim (misinformation) or whether he was intentionally and knowingly deceiving his audience (disinformation). We may lean towards concluding the latter in this case* but it is often difficult – psychologically – to disentangle whether someone is fighting for a sincerely held belief or motivated to arrive at a particular conclusion. We'll unpack this dilemma later on, but for now, let it suffice to say that making the truth fluent is therefore not always enough in the face of what we call 'motivated cognition'. That is, our beliefs are not driven by the evidence, but rather by an underlying (political) motivation that leads us to (willingly) distort our perception of the evidence to fit our worldview, rather than the other way around.

In fact, it wasn't just Sean Spicer. Two researchers surveyed over 1,000 Americans showing them the exact same two photographs, but with one twist: this time they did not reveal which image belonged to which inauguration. One group was asked to identify which image belonged to Trump's inauguration and which belonged to Obama's. On this question, 41 per cent of Trump voters gave the wrong answer (compared to 8 per cent of Hillary Clinton voters). Perhaps they just assumed the turnout for Trump was bigger than it really was. Yet, another group was asked a much simpler question: which photo has more people in it? Still 15 per cent of Trump voters said there were more people present in the right-hand image (Trump's inauguration) than the left-hand image, compared to 2 per cent of Clinton voters. The researchers were so stunned by this result that they concluded that something else must be going on. You cannot look at these images and conclude with a straight face that the image on the right has more people in it than the left. The answer is politically motivated.

I like to think that nobody is completely immune to evidence, at least in the long-run. After he vacated his post, Sean Spicer eventually admitted to regretting having made these false claims, and even joked about them at the 2017 Emmys, saying: 'This will be the largest audience to

---

* A counsellor (advisor) to President Trump later clarified that Spicer was simply providing 'alternative facts'.

witness an Emmys, period – both in person and around the globe.' Of course, such confessions are too little too late; illusory truth has set in after countless repetition, and much of the damage has already been done.

Why your brain is motivated

So, back to the motivated brain. Like the Bayesian model, the motivated brain hypothesis has a lot going for it. The essential idea is that our basic cognitive processes – including our memory, perception, attention, and especially our judgments – are coloured by our own motivations. Rather than just seeing the evidence for what it is, you can think of it as strong top-down interference. Your brain is filling in the gaps for you based on what you would like to be true. Why do you choose to read one news article but not another? Unlike low-level perception, in which the brain is trying to lend a hand but sometimes fails (think of the optical illusion), the motivated brain selectively and often consciously seeks out or rejects evidence in a way that supports what you already believe.

This is not so strange when you think about the fact that (a) a lot of our everyday reasoning is motivated, and (b) there are different kinds of motivations, some of which are good, and some of which are not so noble. Like fluency, motivation isn't an inherently bad thing in itself. In fact, it's quite essential.

Why do you get out of bed in the morning? You're probably motivated by *something*, whether it's an appointment, your job, your parents, you name it. Similarly, our thinking and reasoning processes often start out with a goal. For example, you might be trying to figure out who to vote for, or what college to apply to, or whether or not to vaccinate your children. In those instances, your thoughts are often inevitably guided by your pre-existing beliefs or motivations to help you achieve that goal. There are exceptions of course; sometimes our minds simply wander and there are no motivations. But when we're faced with something we value, enjoy, or care deeply about, goals and motivations often come into play.

One such basic guiding motivation is the desire to be acquainted with the facts – to be accurate. Everyone has the capability to be motivated by accuracy: we just want to know the truth, discover how something really works, or uncover the best available evidence on a topic. What psychologists call 'accuracy motivation' is a fundamental force that drives much of human cognition. We can all think of a time when we used all of our mental resources to find out the 'cold hard truth'.

But the situations in which we find ourselves – especially online – aren't always conducive to eliciting accuracy motivations. We are constantly bombarded with information – from the stories we hear on the TV and radio, to social media and online news sites. It's impossible to pay attention to everything; we have to choose. Perhaps unsurprisingly, our attention and perception are therefore selective; we can only process so much information. Under these conditions, we are more likely to process information that we are motivated to consume.

Human attention is selective for a good reason. When I was a postdoctoral researcher, studying with Eldar Shafir, currently Professor of Psychology and Public Affairs at Princeton University, I learned a lot about the idea of 'cognitive bandwidth'. Eldar studies decision-making in the context of poverty and wrote an entire book about how the circumstance of poverty can be detrimental to adaptive decision-making. Here's the basic idea: if you're relatively poor, your attention is occupied with working out how to pay the bills, putting out fires, and making ends meet, leaving much less brainpower to dedicate to planning and anticipating future problems. It turns out that this principle generalizes fairly well. If I stress you out, your mental bandwidth for other things will steadily decline.

When under stress, the brain resorts to relying on short-cuts (also known as heuristics or rules of thumb). We can't escape the concept of fluency here either, because our brains process information that we like or agree with faster than information which conflicts with our preconceptions about the world. This short-cut or heuristic is called *confirmation bias*. We are biased in the sense that we are quicker to confirm and accept evidence that fits with our worldview than evidence which contradicts it. Information that challenges what we know to be true about the world is cognitively much more taxing to deal with. People have a strong desire to hold internally consistent beliefs, so evidence that challenges some of these beliefs will result in a state of having to deal with conflicting thoughts, or what we call 'cognitive dissonance'. This dissonance can be resolved by either updating one's beliefs or by rejecting the evidence instead. Unfortunately, the latter is often much easier.

There are interesting examples of the way our brains can selectively shape how we pay attention to evidence. In 2019, two Canadian researchers decided to evaluate how people attend to evidence about global warming – a very politically polarized issue, especially in the United States. To do so, they had liberals and conservatives look at the same graph of annual global temperature change, while recording their gaze. Participants were asked to sit about 50cm from a computer screen whilst hooked up to a mobile eye-tracking device. The researchers then generated a heat map that showed the amount of time participants spent dwelling on a section of the curve.

What they found was that liberals – who are more likely to believe in climate change – spent more time than conservatives looking at the rising trend. In other words, the pattern of their attention was motivated by their prior understanding of the evidence. Importantly, when the researchers specifically drew attention to the rising trend (from 1990 onwards) as opposed to the flatter phase (1940–80), liberals were more likely to perceive rising temperatures and sign a petition to act on climate change. In contrast, this was not the case for conservatives. Political ideologies can thus shape our basic attention.

Crucially – and this nuance often gets lost, even in the scientific literature – there's an important difference between selectively attending to evidence (or being quicker to accept evidence that fits your worldview) and a deep motivation to actively reject evidence because it doesn't fit with your personal or political beliefs. Some people might even become more extreme in their beliefs after being exposed to evidence that disconfirms their beliefs (think back to Sean Spicer doubling down on his initial position after fact-checkers challenged him on the inauguration turnout). This tendency is commonly known as the worldview 'backfire-effect' or 'belief polarisation'. All of these terms, including confirmation bias, motivated reasoning, and polarisation often get mixed up, both in the popular media and in the scientific literature, but they actually mean different things.

In the diagram below, I've placed these terms on a spectrum using traditional warning signs as a barometer for the degree of post-truth danger.* These transition from the more 'common' (milder intuitive heuristics such as selective perception, and confirmation bias) to the 'rare' (relatively infrequent but more deliberate biases such as motivated reasoning, and belief polarisation) to full alert mode (full-blown 'conspiracy-level theorizing').

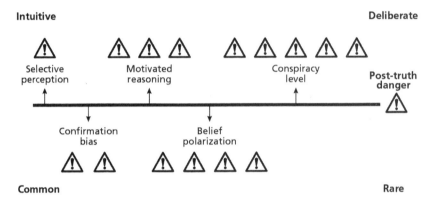

The social context

Some situations decrease 'accuracy motivation' in favour of other kinds of motivations. Yet, these other motivations do not always need to be political or deliberately malevolent or nefarious. Sometimes we willingly distort our perception of the evidence for social purposes because we have a deep need to belong and identify with like-minded others. This can often be a far more powerful and adaptive motivation to navigate the

---

* This is just a helpful schema, not everything is fully intuitive or deliberate. Sometimes you consciously direct your attention towards a conspiracy theory and sometimes you may buy into a conspiracy without realizing it. The general idea is that some of these processes are fairly common and automatic, whereas others require more effort and deliberation.

world. In fact, one key insight from social psychology is that we derive part of our identities from the groups that we belong to. Thus, we often need to balance social motivations – such as the need to fit in – against our desire for accuracy.

Solomon Asch was one of the first social psychologists to demonstrate the power of group pressure on individual perceptions of evidence. In 1955, Asch asked 123 male participants to be part of a 'visual judgment' study, or so they were told. Each person was part of a small group that mostly consisted of 'confederates' (a research term for people who secretly know the true goal of the experiment). In each trial, Asch had about six men sit next to each other. All the men were confederates except for one. They were then all asked to answer a deceivingly simple question aloud: what line on the right (A, B, or C) best matches the line on the left? This is not an optical illusion. The correct answer is C. Asch was interested in what people would do when a majority of the confederates deliberately gave the wrong answer. Would people still give the correct answer or distort the evidence in front of their eyes to conform to the group?

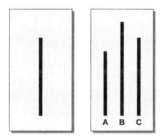

Participants in the seminal 'line-judgment' experiments were asked to evaluate which line on the right best matches the line on the left.

Probably to Asch's own surprise, 75 per cent of participants gave the wrong answer at least once over the course of twelve trials; that is, they looked at the evidence and decided to jump on the bandwagon instead. Here social motivations overrode accuracy.

This finding was so shocking that it has populated psychology text-books for decades. In fact, when I interview students for admission to Cambridge, it's still one of the key experiments they will bring up for discussion. Curiously though, they often don't seem aware of the critiques. I mention this because Asch's findings, whilst undoubtedly important, have also been exaggerated. An analysis of twenty major psychology text-books found that most of the descriptions leave out the fact that only a small minority, 5 per cent, were *always* swayed by the crowd, whereas 95 per cent challenged the majority at least once. This illustrates that extreme distortions of evidence are (still) relatively infrequent and that they take place in the context of an internal struggle between a desire for accuracy and other, competing motivations. Qualitative interviews with participants from Asch's conformity experiments revealed that some of them just weren't sure what the most accurate answer was, and therefore looked to others for guidance. This 'informational' motivation runs contrary to the classical 'conformity' explanation. Sometimes the motivation to be accurate and the motivation to be liked are difficult to disentangle for an outside observer.

So, which is it? The honest answer is that our best guess is both: Asch's participants were likely motivated by a need to be accurate (looking for the right answer by observing the judgments of others) as well as a need to be social (conforming to the behaviour of others). Psychological motivations are hard to isolate.

My good colleague Jamie Druckman, a Professor of Political Science at Northwestern University, Illinois, refers to this as the 'observational equivalence problem'. Just by looking at someone's behaviour it is difficult to know what motivates them. Is it accuracy or something else? To illustrate Druckman's point, here's an alternative explanation that makes this puzzle clear. Rather than some deliberate motivation to willingly distort evidence, it could be that people are misinformed due to selective exposure. Especially in hyper-partisan and polarized media landscapes such as in the United States, you're more likely to be exposed to only one or a few sources of information about a topic (think CNN or Fox News). How are you to know any different? It may very well be that people believe that their attitudes are based on accurate information. Think back to the inauguration photos: perhaps Trump supporters believed the larger turn-out image belonged to Trump's inauguration because that's what they'd been told was true from a source they deemed credible. At the same time, many like-minded friends and family may have also endorsed the same belief. Knowledge is community-based. In other words, you may endorse a false claim because you deem the source to be credible.

That's exactly what my graduate student, Cecilie Traberg, found in one of our studies. We exposed both conservatives and liberals to a set of false and true headlines (see the example headline below), but randomly varied the source so that the same headline would either come from a conservative news source (say, *Fox News*) or liberal source (say, the *Washington Post*). We would then ask a participant how accurate they found the headline. The results were overwhelmingly clear: conservatives were more likely to rate the same misinformation as true when it came from a conservative rather than liberal source, and liberals were more likely to rate misinformation as true when it came from a liberal versus a conservative source. Both rated politically congenial sources as more credible.

Although we experimentally manipulated the source in our study, we didn't activate people's motivations to be accurate. It turns out that economists have found a rather amusing way to do this. One way to incentivize accuracy over social motivations when it comes to matters of fact is to pay people for the correct answer. That's right: facts are for sale. In these experiments people are often told that the more answers they get correct (including political questions), the higher the pay. So, what happens when money is on the table? Well, more people answered the factual questions correctly. We have replicated these findings in our own lab as well. When you offer partisans (committed members of a political party) a monetary reward for giving correct answers, they make fewer errors, and this reduces political bias on both sides. This implies that at least *some* people initially answered based on their *political* motivations, but that doesn't mean they don't know the actual answer.* When properly incentivized, people are willing to temporarily forego their ideological commitments. But paying the whole population to be accurate could get quite expensive, so how about just using evidence?

Why scientists are poles apart on the evidence for polarisation

The now widely popularized idea that people will become further entrenched in their worldview if you repeatedly try to challenge their beliefs with factual evidence, finds its roots in a clever Stanford study. This study has been cited over 5,000 times in the scientific literature (that's a lot). In a nutshell, whilst at Stanford University, psychologists Charles Lord and Lee Ross asked a bunch of students to give their opinion on capital punishment – then (and still) a controversial issue in the States. A few weeks later, they invited a group of 'opponents' and 'proponents' back to the lab to consider two pieces of evidence, one confirming and one disconfirming their beliefs about the efficacy of the death penalty. As the researchers predicted, students rated results that confirmed their own opinions as more accurate and more convincing. The net effect of the exercise was that both groups strengthened their initial beliefs, thus ending up with more polarized attitudes (and drifting further apart) than before they were presented with the evidence. For example, a proponent of capital punishment would claim that the supporting study was 'well thought out and valid' but the disconfirming evidence had 'too many flaws'. Surprisingly, the facts *backfired*.

Dan Kahan, a Professor of Law and Psychology at Yale University, is a big proponent of what he calls identity-protective or 'cultural' cognition. Essentially the argument goes like this: people are motivated to protect the kind of values and beliefs that define their commitments to

---

* Related research finds that people often deny science not because they don't accept the science, but rather because they are averse to the associated policy implications (for example, saving energy or wearing a face mask).

important groups with whom they identify and affiliate. What's more, Dan and his group suggest that people actively recruit their reasoning abilities to distort the evidence. The more numerate, science-literate and educated you are, the better you can direct those skills at defending your beliefs. For example, in one study they found that if you zoom in on those with the highest scientific literacy scores, the opinion gap between liberals and conservatives on climate change doesn't get smaller, it gets bigger! Other studies have also found that people with the greatest level of science education are the most polarized on issues such as human evolution and climate change. These findings imply that, on average, those who are the most ideologically committed *and* the most scientifically literate, show the greatest level of polarization on contested scientific issues.

It's an interesting idea and some scholars find it a compelling version of the 'motivated brain' hypothesis. However, I see Dan's 'motivated numeracy' model as the most extreme version of the motivated brain. If true, it describes a reasoning process suggestive of the alarming end of my post-truth danger spectrum and in many ways almost defies the purpose of education. Accordingly, there's a heated scientific debate about the motivated versus the Bayesian (accuracy) brain hypothesis.

Admittedly, I have been one of the leading opponents of Dan Kahan's cultural or motivated cognition theory (and recent replications have largely failed to reproduce his most extreme claims). We get along great on a personal level at academic retreats; for example, I have fond memories of hiking through the beautiful Swiss mountains together. But as soon as we start talking about work, we firmly disagree. 'It's not that people don't know the evidence,' Dan would say slightly raising his voice. 'They do know it, but why would they want to accept a scientific consensus that runs contrary to their political identity?' He just doesn't think it's a realistic prospect.

Dan has written some passionate blog posts on his Yale website about our differences. I think the disagreement largely boils down to the fact that I am much less committed to a singular explanation than Dan is. Broadly speaking, there are two competing camps. One side – including Kahan's group – argue that people are inherently tribal and motivated to reject inconvenient evidence and that, the smarter you are, the better you can twist the facts to fit your worldview. The other side argues that most people aren't that political at all and that better critical thinking and reasoning skills make you *less* likely to fall for fake news and can actually help you control your biases. Dan often quotes the maxim: 'Many more explanations are plausible than true', by which he likely means that there can only be one correct account. Yet, I find this to be a rather narrow view of truth as many plausible explanations are not mutually exclusive. Each are pieces of a complex puzzle. My own theory sits somewhere in the middle: people do not mindlessly follow their tribe, but we are not natural-born fact-checkers either.

When reviewing the Asch, Stanford, and other oft-cited psychology studies, it is important to keep in mind that a lot of them were done a long time ago. Our culture has changed, and science has moved on. In many aspects we now have better ways of conducting such experiments. We also use much larger and more diverse samples than before. For example, an examination of 133 studies that have used an Asch-type experiment show that conformity with the line-judgment task in the US has actually been declining since the 1950s. Moreover, a lot of studies back in the day were exclusively done on small and homogenous student samples. More contemporary studies, using larger and more diverse samples, have found that 'belief polarization' or 'backfire effects' are much rarer than initially thought, and that even when people are motivated, there's a limit: like Sean Spicer, people do (eventually) succumb to repeated corrections about their beliefs. In one recent study, called the 'elusive backfire effect', researchers enrolled over 10,000 subjects and tested factual corrections on fifty-two contentious issues, including immigration, abortion, gun violence, and the Iraq War. The authors could not replicate a single instance of backfire. They concluded that, 'by and large, citizens heed factual information, even when such information challenges their ideological commitments'.

All this appears to support the Bayesian brain. But it's not so simple. In my own research, I've come to the conclusion that both sides are correct, but misleading on their own. Motivated reasoning – and even belief polarization and backfire effects – do occur. These are real processes. What's important to know is that in the seminal studies, these effects were often confined to those individuals who held the strongest or most extreme beliefs on an issue – and that's probably right. But they don't describe the *average* individual in an *average* situation. It's not our default state. There often needs to be some contextual trigger that decreases people's motivation to be accurate and increases their motivation to belong, affiliate, and prioritize political commitments. That's a positive thing. On the negative side, there are more and more situations which ramp up these motivations quickly, including divisive social contexts such as online echo chambers, filter bubbles, and digital wildfires (but more on these in chapter 6).

Perhaps a good explanation of the debate is illustrated by a study I conducted with my colleagues at Yale University and George Mason University. We examined the case for 'backfire' in the context of global warming. Given that climate change is such a polarizing issue in the United States, we hypothesized that if 'backfire' or 'motivated reasoning' is likely to occur anywhere, it would be in the context of global warming.*

To understand how our study arbitrates between these competing explanations of how people reason about evidence, we have to return to Jamie Druckman's 'observational equivalence' paradox. In other words, we need to disentangle two competing explanations: either people are motivated by accuracy but they've been duped by misinformation (or selectively exposed to just one line of evidence) and would change their beliefs if given the opportunity to do so, *or* people are *not* motivated by accuracy and as a result will reject and discount evidence that is not con-gruent with their personal or political beliefs.

In a large sample of 6,000 Americans, representative of the population, we find evidence of both accounts: if you were politically conservative, you were significantly less likely to acknowledge the scientific consensus on climate change (this is well known). However, importantly, if you were conservative *and* higher educated, you were even less likely to accept the scientific consensus! This evidence is in line with Dan Kahan's motiv-ated numeracy hypothesis. So, people do come to the table with prior

---

* The topic of climate change did not, however, feature in any of the fifty-two issues examined in the aforementioned backfire study.

motivations and political identities. But this in itself doesn't disentangle the observational equivalence problem. So, here's the real insight of our study: we then randomly exposed half of the sample (3,000 Americans) to the following factual statement: '97 per cent of climate scientists have concluded that human-caused climate change is happening'.*

So, what happened? Did conservatives and liberals polarize further once exposed to the (dis)confirming evidence, like in the Stanford study? No. Conservatives, including highly educated conservatives – as well as liberals and moderates – all updated their beliefs about the scientific consensus on climate change towards the evidence. No backfire. In fact, highlighting the strong scientific consensus led to more political agreement on the issue rather than polarization. Importantly, research in the context of the 2021 US Capitol Hill attack has found similar results: after exposure to a fact-check about false claims of 'voter fraud', the most analytical and reflective Republicans expressed greater confidence in the legitimacy of the election results.

What I take away from this is that people do walk around with their preferred beliefs about the world, but they are also open to considering evidence, even when it conflicts with their worldview. We have to consider the equivalence paradox: perhaps people want to be accurate but were simply duped by fake news or bad sources of information. In fact, influential disinformation about climate change has been weaponized to undermine accuracy-based motivations and polarize voters on the issue (something we'll explore in more detail in chapter 7).

To be clear, I am not suggesting that selective perception, confirmation bias, and motivated reasoning – the left-hand side of my post-truth danger spectrum – aren't commonplace. People can do at least three things in response to evidence:

(1) update their beliefs in the direction of facts and evidence
(2) not change their beliefs at all;
    or,
(3) update their beliefs in the opposite direction away from the evidence.

* The other half were given a boring word puzzle to solve.

What I am suggesting is that (3) is the most extreme reaction but also the most unusual. Although this is good news, the bad news is that we're heading in the wrong direction, fast.

Welcome to the age of conspiracy, where the earth is flat, global warming is just an elaborate hoax, and Satan-worshipping lizard politicians are secretly pulling the strings.

FAKE NEWS ANTIGEN 2
Elicit accuracy-driven motivations

— Although we all have a basic motivation to hold accurate views about the world, people have other social and political commitments that they need to balance, too.

— Yet, having such competing motivations does not always mean that people are unwilling to update their beliefs in light of the evidence.

— What matters is how people decide to trade-off their desire to be accurate against their need to be liked and accepted by members of their own social network (a need to be socially 'accurate').

— One way to try to resolve the tension between these competing motives is to make them one and the same. In other words, we need to counter and prevent the politicization of science, for example, by communicating scientific and bi-partisan consensus on facts and evidence.

— Unfortunately, as the recent Covid-19 pandemic has illustrated, eliciting an appetite for accuracy is easier said than done when the science itself becomes highly politicized.

CHAPTER 3

The conspiracy effect: The truth is out there

'Mulder, the truth is out there. But so are lies,'
DANA SCULLY, *The X-Files*

When I was a kid, I absolutely loved *The X-Files*. FBI special agents Mulder and Scully exposing vast government conspiracies about aliens and cover-ups, noticing hidden patterns everywhere. But although Mulder was motivated in his search (remember the infamous phrase 'I want to believe'), he did at least attempt to critically appraise evidence, and he updated his theories, every now and then, when Scully challenged him about the intensity with which he endorsed conspiratorial beliefs.

Although many of us might marginally entertain some alien conspiracies (between 11–44 per cent to be precise) – what about a more extreme proposition, such as the idea that the earth is flat?

Flat-earthers believe that the earth is shaped more like a plane or disc, not round, but flat like a pancake. There is even an official annual gathering known as the Flat Earth International Conference. (I first heard about it through a colleague who attended – or rather, infiltrated – the event as a neutral scholarly observer to study the mind of the 'flat-earther'.) The popular 2018 Netflix documentary *Behind the Curve* followed key figures in the flat earth movement. One of my favourite moments is when Bob Knodel, host of a popular flat earth YouTube channel, walks the viewer through a basic scientific experiment using a gyroscope to help determine the earth's orientation. If the earth is indeed round and rotates once every twenty-four hours, there should be about a 15-degree drift in the gyroscope every hour. Unsurprisingly, that's what Knodel's gyroscope found. Directionally motivated reasoning kicks in when we start with a conclusion of what we want to be true and then work backwards to arrive at that conclusion. Knodel's response was telling:

> Now, obviously we were taken aback by that. 'Wow, that's kind of a problem.' We obviously were not willing to accept that, and so we started looking for ways to disprove it was actually registering the motion of the Earth.

This is textbook motivated reasoning. Bob Knodel has been researching conspiracies for over twenty years and is an active member of the 'truther' community. He is as motivated as it gets.

As one journalist put it, perhaps 'flat earth is the ultimate conspiracy, a rejection of the very ground we walk on'. So how many people subscribe to the flat earth theory? According to YouGov, about 2 per cent of Americans say the earth is flat. That may sound small – and it is in absolute terms – but out of about 327 million citizens, that's still 6.5 million people. And among those 6.5 million people are celebrities such as US rapper Bobby Ray Simmons Jr, also known professionally as 'B.o.B' (you may remember his hit single 'Nothin' on You' featuring Bruno Mars). In January 2016, he took to Twitter wondering why the horizon in his Instagram pictures always look flat rather than curved. Astrophysicist Neil deGrasse Tyson quickly joined the conversation to answer his question, 'small sections of large curved surfaces always look flat to little creatures that crawl upon it . . . and by the way, this is called gravity'. The tiff quickly escalated into a rap battle with B.o.B releasing a diss track called 'Flatline' to which Tyson responded with his own rap recorded by his nephew Stephen Tyson, entitled 'Flat to Fact'. Despite Tyson's best efforts to debunk,* B.o.B. joined the Flat Earth Society later that year.

---

* Although a remarkable exchange, arguing over specific facts is often not the most effective way to debunk a conspiracy theory (but more on that later).

People who are so deeply motivated to hold a certain view that they will deflect away from the evidence like Knodel and B.o.B have, typically, been few and far between. It's a reflection of the larger population: most people are not extreme. At least not yet. But conspiracy theories are no longer reserved for those operating on the fringes of society. A 2014 study revealed that over 50 per cent of Americans endorse at least one type of conspiracy theory and in 2021, a poll from the Washington-based Public Religion Research Institute found that about 15 per cent of Americans believe in the 'QAnon conspiracy' – the bizarre idea that 'the government, media, and financial worlds in the US are controlled by a group of Satan-worshipping paedophiles who run a global child sex-trafficking operation'. The notion that climate change is a hoax or that Covid-19 is a bioweapon engineered by a military lab in Wuhan, are receiving an even more worrying degree of endorsement from large segments of the population – up to a third of those surveyed in some countries. It's therefore worth examining in close detail what's so attractive and dangerous about the psychology of conspiratorial thinking.

The conspiratorial worldview

In January 2019, Buckey Wolfe, a twenty-six-year-old man from Seattle, was accused of shoving a four-foot-long sword straight through his brother's head. According to the police, he said that he'd killed his brother because he thought he was a shapeshifting lizard. Wolfe was charged with murder but ultimately acquitted by reason of insanity.

The 'reptilian conspiracy theory' was popularized by the English conspiracy theorist and former sports broadcaster, David Icke. The basic idea is that an extraterrestrial species of reptile humanoids took control of our planet a long time ago. Their genetic descendants are the 'Babylonian Brotherhood', or 'Illuminati', who currently manipulate world events to keep humans fearful. According to Icke, the reptilian bloodline includes the Rockefellers, the Rothschilds, the British royal family, and many other elites. They drink blood, engage in child-sacrificing rituals, and change their shape.

Although the reptilian conspiracy theory may seem over the top, all conspiracy theories have something in common: they are characterized by persistent beliefs about secret and powerful forces which are operating behind the scenes to implement some sinister agenda. I have studied the psychology of conspiracy theories for many years because they are a fascinating example of an evidence-resistant worldview. No matter how many scientific facts Tyson threw at B.o.B, he didn't change his mind. Of course, it's possible that a group of people with bad intentions can come together to concoct a secret plan to conspire against a potential target. That's not the issue. It is not irrational per se to think that some people are conspiring against you if you base your beliefs on good evidence. We should also hold those in power accountable by demanding transparency. Healthy scepticism is a core value of the scientific enterprise. So, then, what exactly *is* the problem with conspiracy theories?

There are three key ways in which conspiracies deviate from scientific theories. The first and most crucial point is that the conspiratorial worldview is not characterized by belief in a single conspiracy. It's what we call a 'monological belief system', where belief in one conspiracy serves as evidence for another. For example, what's of interest is not necessarily Wolfe's belief in the lizard conspiracy per se, but the fact that Wolfe also espoused several other conspiracy theories. He was a known member of the Proud Boys – a far-right neofascist male organization that promotes political violence based on conspiratorial narratives that Western culture is under siege. Wolfe was also an avid QAnon supporter. Similarly, B.o.B. doesn't just think the earth is flat, he also believes that the moon landing was faked and that the government is secretly cloning celebrities. The key point is that people can become fully enthralled by the conspiratorial worldview.

The second issue is that, mathematically, many conspiracy theories are completely implausible due to the sheer number of people involved who all need to work together to keep the conspiracy a secret. Model estimates from physicist David Grimes suggest (based on known scandals) that for conspiracies which involve more than a thousand individuals, 'intrinsic failure would be imminent'. For example, if NASA had faked the moon landing, it would have required over 400,000 employees to have been complicit in the conspiracy. Even the most generous model assumptions suggest that at this rate, the conspiracy would easily have broken down within a few years. In short, many popular conspiracy theories are thus completely implausible.

Thirdly, conspiracy theories are also not really 'theories'. At their core, they incorporate the most fundamental motivated reasoning principle: they start out with the premise. For example, there must be an individual or entity (often the government or evil corporation) intentionally plotting a nefarious scheme and it's up to the truth-seeker to uncover evidence of the conspiracy. This is also known as the fundamental attribution error: we mistakenly attribute evil intent to random coincidences. In addition, contrary to scientific theories, beliefs are not updated in light of new evidence which might cast serious doubt on the conspiracy. Instead, disconfirming evidence is seen as a further attempt to cover up the conspiracy as the premise is already known: someone is plotting something. For this very reason, it is difficult to argue with a conspiracy theorist: any attempt to discredit the conspiracy is just more evidence that the conspiracy theory must be real!

Conspiracy theories are therefore at the extreme end of our spectrum. They are far beyond simple motivated reasoning. Richard Hofstadter, an American historian, captured the essence of the conspiratorial worldview well in his 1964 essay on the topic:

> Let us now abstract the basic elements in the paranoid style. The central image is that of a vast and sinister conspiracy, a gigantic and yet subtle machinery of influence set in motion to undermine and destroy a way of life.

In a series of studies, my colleagues and I wanted to test Hofstadter's observation and examine the link between political ideology and belief in conspiracy theories. What we found is that two key factors shape the way in which political ideology influences people's tendency to engage in conspiratorial thinking: paranoia and distrust of officialdom. We couldn't exactly disentangle whether these two variables cause conspiratorial thinking or whether people who already believe in conspiracy theories become more paranoid and distrustful over time, but one thing is clear: they are central components of the conspiratorial worldview.

Research has shown that conspiracy theories fulfil at least three basic psychological needs. The first is *epistemological* – or the desire to make sense of the world around us. Conspiracy theories offer simple causal explanations for what otherwise seem to be chaotic and random events; it's much easier to believe that global warming is a hoax (a simple explanation) than to engage with scientific predictions about its consequences. But conspiracy theories also have a way of making people feel unique and 'in the know', separating them from the regular 'sheeple'.

The second function of conspiracies is to offer *existential* relief. People worry about the uncertain nature of our existence and so conspiracy theories establish a sense of agency and control over the narrative and world events.

Lastly, conspiracy theories serve basic *relational* needs. They give people who feel marginalized in society an opportunity to affiliate and belong to a community with a common cause.

Because belief in conspiracy theories is associated with a host of closely related psychological motives, such as perceived control, paranoid ideation, politics, magical thinking, and superstition, the conspiratorial worldview is a fascinating beast.

At a fundamental level, conspiratorial worldviews are self-sustaining quasi-religious* systems. Karen Douglas, Professor of Social Psychology at Kent University, and her colleagues conducted a clever experiment in which they asked students whether they believed in several conspiracy theories, some of which were clearly mutually inconsistent. For example, agreement with the conspiracy that Diana, Princess of Wales, was murdered in Paris in 1997 was related to belief in the conspiracy that she faked her own death. Similarly, the belief that Osama bin Laden was already dead when US special forces arrived at his Abbottabad compound in 2011 correlated with belief in the – clearly contradictory – conspiracy that he is still alive.

---

* Quasi because they are not institutionalized.

My colleagues and I have found similar results. In one study we discovered that belief in the conspiracy theory that Covid-19 was bioengineered in a lab in Wuhan was linked to an entirely different conspiracy that 5G phone masts are responsible for the virus, and both were correlated with the conspiracy theory that Covid-19 is part of a global plot to force vaccinations on people. Other research has found that you get the same network of relationships with belief in completely made-up conspiracy theories. In other words, if people believe in several existing conspiracy theories and you offer up an additional, unrelated fictional conspiracy theory, they will often welcome that one too.

What could possibly explain this rather bizarre observation? The cognitive error that's being committed here is called the 'conjunction fallacy'. Psychologists Daniel Kahneman and Amos Tversky first discovered this error in another context. They presented a scenario to participants which included a description of Linda. Linda is a thirty-one-year-old woman, single, outspoken, and very intelligent. She majored in philosophy. As a student, she was deeply concerned with issues of discrimination and social justice, and also participated in anti-nuclear demonstrations. Now, which of the following options is more likely?

A) Linda is a bank teller (bank cashier),
or
B) Linda is a bank teller and active in the feminist movement?

A majority of people tend to say B because the option sounds more 'representative' of Linda. However, if we follow the rules of probability, then the probability of a single (constituent) event – that she is a bank teller – is always equal to or higher than the probability of two events occurring together or 'in conjunction' – that Linda is a bank teller AND a feminist. After all, being a feminist bank teller is a special subset of all regular bank tellers.

You can see this clearly when we do the maths. Let's say that Linda is a bank teller with a probability of 0.05, and a feminist with a probability of 0.99. According to the rules of probability, the likelihood that Linda is both a bank teller AND a feminist is given by the product of the two probabilities or 0.001 (that is, 0.05 × 0.99), which is necessarily lower than the probability of each event considered on its own.

Researchers at the University of Graz in Austria presented people with a very similar puzzle in the context of conspiracy theories. For example, they would mention that the Bill and Melinda Gates Foundation fights against Covid-19, and then asked people which claim was more likely?

A) The Gates Foundation strives for high vaccination rates

or

B) The Gates Foundation strives for high vaccination rates and thus wants to increase its wealth?

It turns out that people who were more likely to endorse a range of conspiracy theories made this type of conjunction error more often than people who were less likely to believe in conspiracy theories. What I didn't mention is that these rules of probability assume that the events in question are independent of one another, meaning that the one event (vaccinating people) doesn't impact on the other (generating income).

This makes sense, as fact-checkers have found that the Gates Foundation is a nonprofit organization that does not hold any stock in pharmaceutical companies that sell Covid-19 vaccines, and thus it does not stand to profit. The only way that you can get around this error is if you assume that the events are not independent (it's all connected). Put another way, belief in the QAnon and lizard politician conspiracies should be independent *unless* you assume that there is a larger conspiracy at play that connects both events.

A consequence of this type of reasoning is that the specifics of the conspiracy don't matter; as long as the explanation is sufficiently conspiratorial in nature, it still provides a sense of global, higher order 'coherence'. Remember, the point is that some evil group is plotting something somewhere. As long as there's potential for a superordinate conspiracy, then espousing contradictory beliefs is still consistent with the underlying worldview, even when lower-order explanations don't always add up. That's why Neil deGrasse Tyson was fighting an uphill battle: any inconsistencies in B.o.B's beliefs were justified by larger suspicions that NASA was hiding the truth. There is no psychological cure (that I know of) that unravels or counteracts the fully developed conspiratorial worldview. And it's highly contagious.

In a key experiment after which this chapter takes its title, I exposed just over 300 regular people (not conspiracy theorists) to a two-minute video clip of a conspiracy movie about global warming, *The Great Global Warming Swindle*. Shockingly, I found that even after brief exposure (compared to various control videos) people were significantly less likely to support the scientific evidence on climate change and much less willing to sign a petition to help stop global warming. People also tended to be less civically minded in general after exposure, as indicated by a reduced willingness to want to volunteer and donate to charities in the near future. I described this as the 'conspiracy effect'; even just brief exposure to this dangerous form of thinking decreases science acceptance and civic engagement. The first step to countering the conspiracy effect is to be able to identify it.

The seven traits of conspiratorial thinking

On 30 March 2014, I received an email from one 'Alan Tarica'. He had been reading my work on the psychology of conspiracy theories and decided to send me a link to his detailed website uncovering patterns of a vast conspiracy to conceal or ignore the fact that Shakespeare's famous sonnets were written by somebody else. Who might this be? According to Tarica, all signs point towards the Earl of Oxford. In several conversations, Alan tried to convince me that when you read the *Sonnets* from end to beginning, starting with the last poem and working your way back to the first poem, hidden truths are revealed.

Most of my colleagues don't typically respond to such emails, but I often feel a strong pull – like a deep desire – to learn more about what exactly motivates belief in these type of conspiracy theories. After a few emails, I sent Alan Tarica a paper about how illusory pattern perception is linked to belief in conspiracy theories. After I googled his name and discovered that TARICA is an anagram for 'ART CIA', I quickly realized that he had been obsessively emailing and attacking scholars across the board. I told him that this was not my area of expertise but that I'm sure that 'the truth is out there'.

One of his emails to me read as follows:

> Thanks for response but really have to wonder if you find the behaviour of your fellow academics even remotely acceptable. Of course, the truth is out there but without a conversation how are we supposed to get at it?
>
> I can assure you I will make this ultimately about the contemptible behaviour of those that should be able to make informed comments. And I expect far greater participation from everyone despite their discipline.
>
> But if you do nothing else, please pass that along.
> All the best, Alan.

The truth is out there, but that wasn't enough for Alan. He kept emailing and his last email to me read: 'Why don't you try and refute my "conspiracy theory" you useless and outrageous asshole.'

It may be that Alan feels marginalized: his views are not being heard and the scientific community is ignoring him.

What Alan doesn't know is that his behaviour fits exactly with what we found in one of our latest studies: an investigation into the language of conspiracy. Most studies in this field of research just ask regular people questions about the extent to which they endorse a myriad of conspiracy theories. But we wanted to do something novel – to examine the language used by actual conspiracy theorists, to see if there are particular patterns – or psycholinguistic features – that make conspiracy theorists distinct in the way that they express themselves online. By analysing the language used in hundreds of thousands of tweets from the most popular conspiracy theorists on Twitter, we found that they express much more negative emotions – particularly anger – compared to their popular-science counterparts. They also swear and talk much more about other groups and power structures. All of which is reflected in Alan's language: he's angry, he's swearing at others, and he's dismantling what he perceives as unfair power structures.

But Alan isn't the only conspiracy theorist who has harassed me or my colleagues over the years. For example, my close colleague Stephan Lewandowsky (Professor of Cognitive Science at the University of Bristol) and his co-authors wrote an article in which they analysed conspiratorial discussion in the blogosphere about one of their past papers on the psychology of conspiracy theories. Their paper had the wonderfully apt title 'Recursive fury: Conspiracist ideation in the blogosphere in response to research on conspiracist ideation.' Lewandowsky found that many of the online arguments against the research in his first paper were also highly conspiratorial in nature. For example, sceptics would accuse him of having a hidden agenda that involved a deliberate attempt to silence the debate.

The researchers identified several recurring themes which together with our own research seemed to indicate that, in addition to linguistic markers, conspiratorial reasoning has a very predictable signature. If you start examining conspiracy theories, you will notice recurring commonalities in their narrative. For example, conspiracy theories mostly assume evil or nefarious intentions. The story is typically not that a group of people are colluding – in secret – to throw you a surprise birthday party. There are virtually no *positive* conspiracy theories.

To help people spot the conspiracy effect in everyday life, my colleagues Stephan Lewandowsky, John Cook, Ullrich Ecker and I like to use a guideline that ties everything we've just learned about the conspiratorial worldview together into the 'seven traits of conspiratorial thinking', using 'CONSPIRE' as an acronym – which stands for **Co**ntradictory, **O**verriding suspicion, **N**efarious intent, **S**omething must be wrong, **P**ersecuted victim, **I**mmunity to evidence, and **Re**-interpreting randomness.

We can see each of these traits at play in the now infamous viral conspiracy theory video '*Plandemic: The Hidden Agenda Behind Covid-19*'. The film premiered on YouTube on 4 May 2020, and featured an interview with a discredited medical researcher, Judy Mikovits, who advances all sorts of conspiratorial claims about the pandemic, including that the virus was bioengineered and the false notion that, 'Wearing the mask literally activates your own virus.' The video garnered millions of views in the two days it was online before YouTube officially took it down. Studies show that exposure to the video damaged public support for vaccination programmes. It's the conspiracy effect in action, where even brief exposure to conspiracy theories can harm public debate.

Plandemic exhibits all the classic CONSPIRE traits. First, conspiracy theories are nearly always characterized by internal Contradictions. In the *Plandemic* narrative, the logical inconsistencies emerge quickly, as the film advances two false origin stories at the same time. The first describes Covid-19 as having been bioengineered in a lab in Wuhan whilst the second explanation comes from the fact that everyone apparently already had the virus from earlier vaccinations and that by wearing masks, they are activating it! Which is it? This is clearly Contradictory.

Next, by their very nature, conspiracy theories are deeply wary of the official narrative. An Overriding suspicion is advanced in *Plandemic* that casts doubt on mainstream science and just about anyone who is involved in the official explanation, including the World Health Organization (WHO) and the US Centers for Disease Control and Prevention (CDC). Question everything.

But the conspirators in question must also have sinister intentions. Nefarious intent is an explicit theme that characterizes most conspiracy theories and much of *Plandemic*. For example, according to the film, evil scientists – including Anthony Fauci, who leads the White House's Covid-19 task force, apparently created the pandemic for profit, and by extension, killed hundreds of thousands of people in the process.

When challenged, conspiracy theorists have no problem abandoning specific aspects of their theory – yet Something must be wrong (which fits with the possibility of an even larger conspiracy that could explain the inconsistency). For example, when the *Plandemic* filmmaker Mikki Willis was asked if he honestly believed that Covid-19 was engineered for profit he replied: 'I have no idea.' All he knows is that *something* is not right.

A good conspiracy theory must also feature a Persecuted victim. In particular, conspiracy theorists have a tendency to view themselves as marginalized victims of a conspiracy concocted by powerful elites. Alan is the victim of a powerful cabal of humanities scholars protecting the false origins of Shakespeare's sonnets. In the *Plandemic* video, the creators even go as far as suggesting that the whole world has fallen victim to a vast web of deception that is the Covid-19 pandemic. If you think about it, if someone is plotting to do harm, then there must be a potential victim as well, the two often go hand in hand.

Unfortunately, conspiracy theorists are often entirely Immune to evidence. I know I said earlier that almost nobody is immune to evidence – but conspiracy theorists might just be the exception. When you ask why there is no proof for the conspiracy, they will usually say that's because the conspirators did such a good job of covering it up. What's more, challenging the conspiracy is just further evidence that you must be part of it all.

The last trait involves illusory pattern perception: Re-interpreting random events and imbuing them with substantive meaning. I sent Alan Tarica the article on the link between illusory pattern perception and conspiratorial thinking because I honestly felt he was seeing patterns in the sonnets where there are none. The *Plandemic* video is no different: it mentions (in a suggestive tone) that the US National Institutes of Health (NIH) funded the Wuhan Institute of Virology in China. Hmm, coincidence? Yes, in fact, as it is well known that the NIH funds many labs around the world. The 5G conspiracy displays a very similar tendency, where coronavirus hotspots and the location of 5G masts are suddenly causally connected as part of a sinister plot, even though a third factor can readily explain the increased presence of both phone masts and disease outbreaks: population density.

You can even see the same patterns in action when you ask people to make up conspiracy theories on the spot. In our 'CONSPIRE' study, we tasked people in the US state of Georgia to come up with their own conspiracy theories about the increase in Covid-19 cases following the relaxation of lockdown measures in May of 2020. Conspiracies ranged from: 'The government elite wants to kill as many people as possible' (*nefarious* intention), to: 'The Democrats have invented the coronavirus so that they can eliminate wealthy older voters' (*persecuted* victim).

The reason why conspiracy theories spread so easily is because they are psychologically attractive; they offer simple explanations for complex events; they restore a sense of agency and control in a world increasingly filled with chaos and uncertainty. Demand for the kind of narratives that Knodel, B.o.B, Tarica, and Mikovits have to offer is increasing. Importantly, what's so dangerous about this is that once the conspiracy effect takes hold, it won't let go: it latches on like a real virus and reproduces fast and efficiently. Before you know it, you no longer believe in one conspiracy theory but two or three and you start to see the larger picture; it's all connected. Moreover, we don't need the whole population operating on the extreme side of the post-truth danger spectrum in order to undermine the status of 'facts' in democracy. This is a common misperception. Many influential elections are decided on narrow margins. Fake news just needs to dupe a few people. Study after study has shown that the people who spread the most fake news are highly politically active: they're extreme, they're motivated, they're super-spreaders. They are not most people.

But what if conspiracy theories *are* becoming more common? In May 2022, I was asked this question by members of the subcommittee on intelligence and counterterrorism of the US Congress House of Representatives. I told them that we know that extremist organizations are more likely to use conspiratorial narratives in their writings to attract new followers, and that more studies are documenting a link between belief in conspiracy theories and the endorsement of political violence. But is it true that more people than ever are embracing them? In 2021, over 20 per cent of those polled in over twenty countries think that a single group of people control world events.

However, such information by itself doesn't tell us whether that is high or low, at least historically speaking. Unfortunately, it's a difficult question to answer as very little global trend data is available. We have only reliably – but often not consistently – tracked public belief in conspiracy theories for a few decades.

A colleague of mine, Joseph Uscinski, Professor of Political Science at the University of Miami, used to visit me in Cambridge with his summer school students to discuss the latest research on conspiracy theories. He often notes that every few years the media declares another 'golden age of conspiracy'. Joe is sceptical. After all, did conspiracy theories not lead people to burn 'witches' at the stake for being in cahoots with Satan? Or cause the persecution of millions of Jews during the Second World War? Are things *really* worse now? He makes a valid point. In one study, Joe examined public belief in about thirty-seven conspiracy theories between 1966 and 2020 and finds that while endorsement of some conspiracy theories has increased, belief in others has decreased or remained fairly stable over time.

Joe has an interesting theory, though, namely that conspiracy theories are for 'losers'. What he means is that those out of (political) power are typically more likely to espouse conspiracy theories about those in power and, indeed, empirical research across many countries shows support for the idea that conspiratorial thinking, on average, is higher for supporters of political parties who are currently not in power (especially on the far-right). Several scholars, including myself, think that although this is definitely a piece of the puzzle, the trend is much broader so that endorsement of conspiracy theories seems to fluctuate more generally as a function of societal and political unrest.

For example, Gallup has been tracking the JFK assassination conspiracy since 1963, when it found that 52 per cent of people believed in the conspiracy that others were involved. This number rose to 81 per cent during most of the 1990s, when the popular Oliver Stone film *JFK* was released, before dropping off again to 61 per cent in 2011.

A recent Cambridge–YouGov poll surveyed people about the same conspiracy theories for three consecutive years. For example, at the start of the Covid-19 pandemic, anti-vaccination conspiracies were endorsed by about 13 per cent of the population in the United States, whereas this number jumped to a concerning 33 per cent in 2020, when coverage about the Covid-19 vaccines started to take off.

The basic theory is that whenever we feel uncertain and powerless due to a global crisis or socio-political turmoil, people are more likely to turn to conspiracy theories for psychological comfort and reassurance. These narratives then become part of history through social and cultural transmission.

If this is correct, then the massive global challenges we're facing represent the perfect breeding ground for conspiracy theories. In fact, what *is* clear is that the internet and social media have allowed the social transmission of conspiracy theories to flourish, enter the mainstream, and spread in new and unprecedented ways. When asked during an interview on *Hot Ones* (the YouTube show where celebrities answer questions while eating increasingly spicy chicken wings) whether more and more people believe in conspiracy theories, Neil deGrasse Tyson replied: 'I think that number of people may be the same over time, they just now can write a blog that the whole world has access to via a search engine.' Although the hot sauce was clearly getting to him, Neil's observation is spot on: many more conspiracy theories are now available, they can spread much faster, and reach larger audiences than ever before. For example, the conspiracy theory that Russia invaded Ukraine in 2022 to take down secret US-funded biological warfare labs started out as a fringe theory announced by the Kremlin, but was subsequently amplified by China's foreign ministry and then gained popularity within the United States after Fox News host Tucker Carlson, repeated the misinformation on his show. Similarly, conspiracy theories that start in the States – such as those espoused in the *Plandemic* video – can garner millions of views and make their way around the world via the internet in a matter of days. The rise of digital media has ensured everyone can now fall prey to the conspiracy effect.

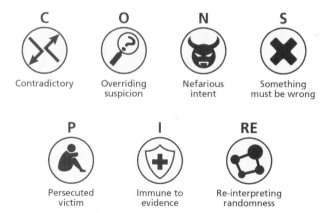

Identify and resist the seven traits of conspiratorial thinking

— Conspiracy theories are psychologically appealing because they offer certain and simple explanations of otherwise seemingly random and complex events. They also help restore a false sense of control.

— Conspiracy theories are highly contagious: their effects rub off on people even after a single exposure.

— Identifying them is the first step to building resistance.

— You can use the CONSPIRE test to your advantage. Look out for: Contradictory logic, Overriding suspicion, Nefarious intentions, Something must be wrong, Persecuted victim, Immune to evidence and RE-interpreting random events into a connected story.

CHAPTER 4

Why the virus won't leave your mind:
The continued influence of misinformation

'For the grossly impudent lie always leaves traces
behind it, even after it has been nailed down, a fact which
is known to all expert liars in this world and to all who
conspire together in the art of lying,'
ADOLF HITLER, *Mein Kampf* (1925)

In 2016 I was living and working in Princeton, New Jersey. Princeton is
not too far from Woodbridge Township, a bedroom suburb of New York
City about an hour to the northeast of Jersey. The town is home to the
Woodbridge High School, an average US public high school. I wouldn't
have heard about the place were it not for a local story about a history
teacher, Jason Ali, who was fired after it became clear that he had his students question the Holocaust.

Through presenting a series of essays with titles such as 'A Gas Chamber
Full of Lies', Ali believed that he was motivating his students to engage in
critical thinking about historic events. The lawsuit that followed included
excerpts of pieces written by students under his instruction, including one
which struck me in particular. The student explained how they had been
taught that Hitler's actions against the Jews were brutal and occurred for
no apparent reason, but should they not question the idea that Jews were
totally innocent? The student asked, in a rhetorical tone, whether Jews
did not crash Germany's economy? Did they not criticize Christianity?
Introduce pornography to the world? The rather harrowing conclusion of

the student's essay was that, although nobody deserves to die, the Holocaust wasn't unjustified either. Apparently the 'Jews' had it coming.

From our discussion in the previous chapter, we're able to recognize this as a clear conspiracy theory – one that dates back to the Second World War itself. Although conspiracy theories seem more relevant than ever in today's post-truth media environment, they were also extremely popular during the war. One of the most common (and outrageous) conspiracy theories is that Jews started the war in an attempt to destroy Germany. This theory formed the basis of a widespread propaganda campaign which claimed that Germany was under siege by a dangerous 'international Jewry', and that the country therefore had no recourse other than to defend itself by going to war. The poster below, from 1943, vividly illustrates this idea – it was designed by Hans Schweitzer, who was hired by Joseph Goebbels as the 'Reich Commissioner for Artistic Design' to produce Nazi propaganda. The poster blames Jews for the war and reads: 'The war is his fault'.

Unfortunately, Hitler was not wrong when he wrote in *Mein Kampf* that 'the grossly impudent lie always leaves traces behind it, even after it has been nailed down'. As Jason Ali's case illustrates, the false conspiracy theory, or 'colossal untruth', is still with us today, and remains popular with many modern-day Holocaust deniers.

But it's not just Holocaust denial: we now know that misinformation lives on and leaves observable traces behind in the brain's memory network. We call it the *continued influence of misinformation*.

The continued influence of misinformation

We'll return to the continued influence of Nazi propaganda on modern-day attitudes, but first, to grasp the basic psychology at work, let's consider a completely fictional example. Imagine for a moment that you turn on the news and hear about a local fire:

BREAKING NOW: On January 25th, at 8.58 p.m. an alarm call was received from the premises of a wholesale warehouse company. A serious out-of-control fire was reported in the storage hall, requiring an instant response. Immediately after, at 9 p.m., a fire engine was dispatched. It turns out that the alarm was raised by a night security guard who had smelled smoke and decided to investigate the matter. In the morning of January 26th at 4 a.m., the attending fire captain suspects that the fire was started by a short circuit in the wiring of a closet in the main storage hall.

Update: 4.30 a.m. Police investigator says that they have reports that cans of oil paint and pressurized gas cylinders had been found in the closet before the fire. Firefighters on the scene reported thick oily smoke and sheets of flames hampering their efforts. Intense heat made the fire particularly difficult to control. Several explosions occurred during the blaze, endangering firefighters in the vicinity. No fatalities were reported, but two firefighters have been taken to the hospital as a result of breathing in toxic fumes. Reports say that a small fire had been discovered on the same premises six months prior but local workers were able to contain the incident at the time. Although the premises were insured, the owner says that damages will exceed hundreds of thousands of dollars.

Update: 10.40 a.m. Police investigator Lucas has more information regarding the investigation of the fire. The closet reportedly containing the cans of oil and paint gas cylinders had actually been empty before the fire. The shipping supervisor had disclosed that the storage hall contained bales of paper, mailing envelopes, pencils, and other school supplies.

Update: 11.30 a.m. The fire captain reports that the fire is out, but the storage hall has been completely gutted.

Now let me ask you this: What is the most likely cause of the fire? What was in the storage hall? How was the fire started?

This is what participants were asked after reading the above story in a seminal misinformation experiment conducted by two psychologists at the University of Michigan in 1994. Having read the story in thirteen staggered messages, like a breaking news report, participants were invited to freely write out their thoughts to answer these as well as some other factual questions. However, in just one of the conditions – the correction group, who were presented with the story exactly as it appears above – the participants learned that the 'closet reportedly containing the cans of oil and paint gas cylinders had actually been empty before the fire'. No reference whatsoever was made to this incorrect claim in the control group; it was simply stated that the closet in the warehouse hall was empty. In other words, only the correction group were provided with updated and new information about the oil and gas cans.

The researchers then tested people's episodic memory ('episodic' refers to memories of everyday events, such as time and location, that people can consciously retrieve). In order to do this, the researchers coded people's written responses. For example, memories were evaluated based on how often people made reference to the correction, or how often they invoked themes about the origin of the fire in their answers as well as direct references to the stored chemicals. The findings were striking. In several experiments, 91 to 95 per cent of participants in the correction group made at least one direct and undisputed reference to the chemical materials from the storage room when questioned about the event, despite the correction issued.* Yet, when asked directly about the main cause of the fire, the majority of participants (75 per cent) did not mention the chemicals. In addition, over 90 per cent of subjects also accurately recalled the correction.

What's interesting therefore is that, despite this explicit awareness of the correction, the misinformation virus had already infected other memory representations of the event. For example, when asked what might have caused the toxic fumes, some participants mentioned 'burning paint'. Similarly, when queried about why the fire might have been so intense and difficult to put out, answers included 'oil fires are hard to put out'. For what reason might an insurance claim be refused? 'Because flammable items were not kept in a safe place.' In other words, although participants were clearly aware that the cause of the fire was not the chemical materials, misinformation had already started to take root in their memory; participants were relying on the misinformation when asked about the event.

Jury trials are a helpful context in which to understand this phenomenon. Imagine that false media reports are widely circulated about a defendant and the judge orders the jury to disregard what they may have heard (despite being sequestered). As much as we would like to, the continued influence of misinformation makes it hard not to use information when forming judgments once we've committed it to memory.

In fact, judges and courts were keenly aware of this fact over a hundred years ago. In 1912, using the wonderfully apt analogy that 'you cannot unring a bell', the Oregon Supreme Court concluded the following when referring to an improper testimony during an arson trial: 'While in some cases an express instruction to the jury to disregard testimony injuriously admitted is properly held to cure the error, yet the courts are cautious in the application of this rule. It is not an easy task to unring a bell, nor to remove from the mind an impression once firmly imprinted there . . .' Studies with mock jurors have shown that despite clear instructions to

---

* Interestingly, although it was never mentioned in the control group, about 27–30 per cent of people still made reference to similar (negligence-based) themes.

do so, inadmissible information is rarely disregarded by the jury when making verdicts.*

More generally, the continued influence of misinformation has been demonstrated across a wide variety of issues, not just fires in warehouses. A recent meta-analysis (a study which pools findings from many individual experiments) looked at thirty-two experiments involving over 6,000 people across four decades and found evidence for a modest but consistent continued-influence effect. In other words, when we look at this effect across many people and situations, we find that corrections do help reduce misinformation but they do not fully eliminate it: people continue to retrieve false details from memory once exposed to a falsehood. The effect appears to get more pronounced the more misinformation is repeated and the longer it is held in memory without correction. The infection worsens.

Of course, findings elicited under controlled laboratory conditions are one thing. What about evidence for the continued influence of misinformation in the real world?

The virus lives on

In 2016, the conspiracy movie *Vaxxed: From Cover-Up to Catastrophe* was scheduled to be released during New York's Tribeca Film Festival with support from actor Robert De Niro. The film's director was Andrew Wakefield, a discredited British anti-vaccination activist who lost his medical licence in 2010 due to ethical violations. To understand why he lost his licence we need to go back to 1998, when Wakefield and his colleagues published a paper in the highly prestigious medical journal *The Lancet* claiming that, based on a case study of twelve children – and no control group – they had discovered a link between the MMR (measles, mumps, and rubella) vaccine and autism. This paper became arguably one of the most serious frauds in the history of medicine.

---

* An exception occurs when the jury is made suspicious of the motivation for why the information was introduced (but we'll get to the power of unveiling motivations as an inoculation strategy later in the book).

Specifically, the paper concluded that 'we have identified a chronic enterocolitis in children that may be related to neuropsychiatric dysfunction. In most cases, onset of symptoms was after measles, mumps, and rubella immunisation.' In other words, after receiving the MMR vaccine, children supposedly experienced gastrointestinal inflammation and this was somehow related to the onset of autism. However, what Wakefield failed to disclose was that the patients had been recruited by a compensation lawyer as part of an effort to file lawsuits against MMR manufacturers. Wakefield received hundreds of thousands of pounds in compensation for his work (all undisclosed). Moreover, some of the children in the study did not actually have an autism diagnosis and despite claims that the children were neurotypical, almost half had pre-existing developmental issues. As a gastroenterologist, Wakefield specifically focused on a gut link in his paper, coining a new condition called 'autistic enterocolitis'. His idea was that the vaccine somehow damaged the intestinal lining, which supposedly caused the colitis, which in turn impacted brain development. Yet eleven out of the twelve children had normal colonoscopy results which were later changed to 'non-specific colitis', or general inflammation of the colon, by the authors themselves to justify a link between bowel inflammation, the MMR vaccine, and autism.

In short, the case study was fraudulent. Subsequent reviews of the medical literature from the Centers for Disease Control and Prevention (CDC), the American Academy of Pediatrics (AAP), the National Academy of Science (NAS), the UK's National Health Service (NHS), and the World Health Organization (WHO) have absolutely found no evidence for a link between autism and vaccination. Moreover, by 2004, ten out of the original thirteen authors had already issued a retraction notice and no other team around the world has been able to replicate the results.

Unfortunately, it wasn't until 2010, almost twelve years after its original publication, that *The Lancet* officially retracted the bogus paper, with the journal's editor-in-chief describing it as 'utterly false'. Wakefield was struck off the medical register after having been found guilty of misconduct by the UK's General Medical Council, who concluded that he abused his position and acted without ethics approval and with callous disregard for the wellbeing of the children in the study. But twelve years is a very long time for the continued influence of misinformation to fester. Although the incubation period for misinformation pathogens is currently unknown – and probably quite variable – I think it's safe to say that twelve years is more than sufficient to do some serious damage.

Indeed, parents grew increasingly concerned about the safety of the MMR vaccine. The misinformation not only affected their attitudes, but also their actions: vaccine coverage in the UK dropped to its lowest point since the vaccine was introduced in 1988. Specifically, coverage decreased from about 92 per cent in the years prior to the Wakefield paper (1995–6) to 80 per cent in 2003–4, with drops as low as 58 per cent in some areas such as London – well below the recommended 90 per cent coverage level required for 'herd immunity'. As a consequence, the number of measles cases in the UK rose sharply, and although rates have improved in recent years, they still haven't fully recovered to pre-scare levels.

Of course, the causal relationship between the conclusions of the paper and public health outcomes isn't entirely direct. For example, the media has played an important mediating role in amplifying the paper's false conclusions. Long after Wakefield's paper had been discredited, the media continued to adhere to norms of 'false balance' – that is, representing an issue as having 'two sides' despite an overwhelming scientific consensus. For example, national surveys in 2002 revealed that over half of the UK population thought that 'there is equal evidence on both sides of the debate', about a third of the population reported that they would follow Wakefield's televised recommendation to get three separate vaccines (instead of one single MMR shot), and 67 per cent of the public reported awareness of a potential link between autism and the MMR vaccine.

The ensuing vaccine hesitancy also spilled over to the United States, where coverage of the MMR vaccine has generally been closer to the 90 per cent target. Yet, in 2011, at least fifteen states had immunization coverage below 90 per cent and some national surveys reveal that about 30 per cent of parents with young children mistakenly believe that vaccines cause autism. The States has also witnessed a resurgence of measles outbreaks – an otherwise preventable disease – due in part to growing vaccine hesitancy and refusal. In several studies I have conducted since

2015, my colleagues and I found that the false belief that vaccines can cause autism is still a strong predictor of people's attitude towards vaccinating their children.

Back to Robert De Niro. In the period following the scandal, Wakefield doubled down on his media profile as a prominent voice of the anti-vaccination movement, by directing the conspiracy movie *Vaxxed*. De Niro, who co-founded the Tribeca Film Festival, initially supported the film in 2016 (before eventually pulling it). The question is why?

To understand this, we need to bring back the role of pre-existing worldviews and motivations. Robert De Niro has a child with autism. In response to the controversy surrounding the festival's planned screening of *Vaxxed*, De Niro commented on Facebook: 'Grace and I have a child with autism and we believe it is critical that all of the issues surrounding the causes of autism be openly discussed and examined.' The observational equivalence paradox strikes again: was De Niro honestly motivated by a search for accuracy and truth and just poorly informed about the movie's agenda, or were his opinions distorted by a deep-seated personal desire to understand the world in a certain way?

Although De Niro clarified that he is not anti-vax and did not personally endorse the film, many people were (rightly) outraged that such an influential celebrity was giving a platform to what is essentially a baseless conspiracy movie. Although the film was ultimately pulled from the festival, this did not stop its continued influence. It received a private screening the following year during the 2017 Cannes Film Festival, and shortly afterward another public figure (Robert Kennedy Jr*) served as executive producer on the sequel, *Vaxxed II: The People's Truth* (2019).

The misinformation virus lives on.

Vaccination isn't the only example of how misinformation continues to influence people many years later. Another illustrative case is the many false reports around the alleged existence of Weapons of Mass

---

* Notably, Robert Kennedy Jr is an environmental lawyer, environmental justice advocate, and prominent Democrat. Anti-vaccination conspiracy theories can reach across the political spectrum (at least among elites).

Destruction (WMDs) in Iraq following the events of 9/11. Both the Bush and Blair administrations suggested that Saddam Hussein was secretly hiding nuclear weapons. Initial media reports often followed suit, suggesting that WMDs could be present, only to be repeatedly corrected and disconfirmed later. For example, one *New York Times* headline from 2001 announced: 'Iraqi tells of Renovations at Sites for Chemical and Nuclear Arms'. Other headlines claimed that WMDs 'may have been found'. No evidence of WMDs was ever found at these sites. In 2004, *The New York Times* issued a public apology for its coverage of the war, concluding that: 'We consider the story of Iraq's weapons, and of the pattern of misinformation, to be unfinished business. And we fully intend to continue aggressive reporting aimed at setting the record straight.' Although the public apology and effort to set the record straight is certainly laudable, much of the damage had already been done.

A study by Stephan Lewandowsky nicely illustrated this effect several years later. Steve and his colleagues asked around 900 people whether a number of statements about the Iraq War were true or false. Participants were recruited from countries that were allies in the war, including Australia and the United States, as well as countries such as Germany whose media coverage was consistently sceptical of the motives for the war. They asked about three categories of statements: some that were deemed true; some that were initially presented as true but subsequently retracted (for example, 'Allied prisoners of war were executed by the Iraqis after being captured'); and others that were completely fictional. Participants were first asked to report on their memory of all statements in the study and whether they thought the statements were true or false. Later in the survey, people were presented with the same items again and asked how certain they were a particular claim had later been retracted. The main idea here is that if people are open to corrections of misinformation, then acknowledgement of having seen a retraction of a false claim should lead people to be less likely to rate false items as true.

The results – across all country samples – revealed that whether people thought a particular claim was true or not was strongly predicted by how well they recalled the initial claim. Remember that for the false items specifically, we would expect that knowledge of the retractions should matter so that people are less likely to endorse false statements for which they remembered having seen a retraction notice. Interestingly, this pattern was confirmed in all countries except the United States, where awareness of the retractions had no effect on participants' truth ratings of the false claims.

This next finding is more suggestive. When asked about the motivations behind the war, US participants rated the 'to destroy WMDs' explanation as the most important reason, whereas this motive was of little importance for Australian and German respondents. In other words, Americans had a stronger prior motivation to latch on to the WMDs narrative, even in the face of explicit corrections. The take-away here is that not only does misinformation linger despite repeated corrections, it does so more easily when the misinformation fits with what people want to be true about the world.

To truly understand the powerful role that prior beliefs can play in the continuation of misinformation, let's return to the example that motivated the opening of this chapter: Nazi propaganda – one of the most extensive and concerted real-world attempts to indoctrinate millions of people with disinformation.

During the Third Reich the entire German school curriculum, as well as many extracurricular activities, was harnessed in the service of Nazi ideology. Young Germans were forced to join the Hitler Youth movement, whose handbook devoted more than half its pages to racial ideology, which was further reinforced in books, films, and adverts. In 2015, two researchers set out to determine the effects of Nazi propaganda on modern-day beliefs about Jews some fifty years after the war. The researchers looked at two waves of the 'German General Social Survey' – an important national poll of social attitudes – which, among many other topics, asked 5,000 people seven questions about attitudes towards Jews across 264 German cities, once in 1996 and then again ten years later in 2006. The combined data shows that about 17 per cent of Germans thought that Jews themselves were to blame for their own persecution, and about 22 per cent still believed that Jews should not have equal rights.

These numbers are shocking, but notably the national averages mask large regional variation in the endorsement of these beliefs. For example, the percentage of the population who believed that Jews should not have equal rights dropped to 10 per cent in Hamburg but rose to about half the population (48 per cent) in Lower Bavaria. Next, the researchers identified a narrower group of what they called 'committed anti-Semites'. This group answered strongly in the affirmative to the following three questions specifically about Jewish people: 1) Whether they are responsible for their own persecution, 2) Whether they have too much influence in the world, and 3) Whether they exploit their 'victim status' for financial gain. Although the absolute incidence rate of 'extremists' in the sample was quite low (4 per cent), the authors found that there were clear generational trends. On average, younger Germans were found to be less anti-Semitic; specifically, individuals born in the 1930s were two to three times more likely to be anti-Semitic than those born later in the century. This finding remained stable even when taking into account other factors such as levels of education and perceptions of the economy.

In the final part of the study, the authors wondered what could have caused these attitudes. Combining historic voting data with survey responses for all 264 German cities offered some interesting potential explanations. For example, Nazi indoctrination appears to have been particularly effective in regions with a history of voting for anti-Semitic parties. Looking at the share of the vote that anti-Semitic parties won in each region between 1890 and 1912, the researchers found that regions that ranked in the top third showed four times the share of committed anti-Semites in 2006 than did regions in the bottom third. This suggested that the Nazis' propaganda had been especially effective on those populations who already harboured anti-Semitic sentiments in ways that persist to this day. The authors' statistical model confirmed that the effect of propaganda – or growing up under the Nazi regime – on voting for Nazi parties was influential – even in regions with no prior anti-Semitic history. However, the effect of propaganda was further enhanced if people already held negative views towards Jews. Nazi propaganda was able to persist for so long in the German population because it had efficiently tapped into pre-existing prejudices – thus reinforcing Goebbels's original hypothesis that propaganda can only be truly effective if it is in line with people's prior attitudes.

Why does the influence of misinformation continue?

Prior motivations aren't the only explanation for the continued-influence effect. Although we don't (yet) know all of the factors that can fully account for why people continue to retrieve false information from memory, we do know that misinformation and corrections coexist in our brains and compete with each other for attention.

One explanation is rooted in what we call the 'selective retrieval model'. According to this theory, accurate information and misinformation are stored in our memory simultaneously and when a correction is issued, the misinformation is automatically activated but not properly suppressed. This can happen when people are not paying sufficient attention to the correction, or discount the correction because it happens to conflict with their personal beliefs.

The alternative, 'model updating account' (or 'integration account') assumes that – like good Bayesians – people have a mental model of how something works and update it as new information becomes available. But something goes wrong in linking the correction to the misinformation. When misinformation is corrected without being replaced by a credible alternative explanation, this leaves a gap in people's mental model. For example, think back to the warehouse fire scenario. If the fire wasn't started by paint cans, then what could have started it? In the absence of a clear alternative explanation, the theory goes that people prefer to stick with a coherent yet incorrect model over an incoherent but correct mental model.

The latest research has tried to probe what is going on in the brain when we experience the continued influence of misinformation. Using scenarios very similar to the warehouse fire example, researchers from the University of Western Australia asked twenty-six healthy volunteers to undergo functional magnetic resonance imaging (fMRI) – or a brain scan – while listening to narratives that either featured a retraction or not. Although there was no overall increase in neural activity, whether the information was presented as a retraction (or not) did appear to matter for how the information was encoded in the brain. For example, participants would see a story about the evacuation of a plane. In the misinformation condition they were told that the plane evacuation was due to a fire whereas in the control group, they were given no information about its cause at all. A later sentence would then explicitly correct the misinformation for all by stating that there was no evidence of a fire. This allowed the researchers to test whether earlier exposure to the misinformation (that the crash was caused by a fire) impeded processing of the correction.

The authors found that the retractions elicited less activity in the right precuneus, an area of the occipital lobe. Because this brain region has previously been implicated in memory processes and difficulties in integrating information, the authors concluded that basic integration and coherence mechanisms are less active when new information challenges people's previous understanding of an event that requires encoding, consistent with the 'model-updating' explanation. Of course, it's good to keep in mind that the study only included twenty-six volunteers and initial support for one account doesn't rule out other plausible theories. In fact, a follow-up study from the same research team suggests that the problem also likely stems from the challenge of having to hold both correct and incorrect information in memory concurrently (which is more aligned with the 'selective retrieval model').

Although these distinctions matter for our understanding of how misinformation impacts the brain, practically, the implications are clear either way; both theories suggest that if you are to correct false information, it is especially prudent to make the correction stand out relative to the misinformation to avoid accidentally strengthening people's memory of the myth (rather than the correction). In addition, it is important to offer a credible alternative causal explanation for the events to replace the gap in people's mental model. For example, subsequent studies of the classic warehouse fire experiment have shown that if people are made aware of an alternative cause of the fire involving lighter fluid and accelerant, they are less likely to retrieve false explanations involving the paint and gas cans. Similarly, returning to our jury verdict analogy, studies with fictional murder trials have shown that, compared to defence strategies which merely attempt to explain why the defendant isn't guilty, accusing a plausible alternative suspect of the murder reduced the number of guilty verdicts to a much greater degree.

Correcting misinformation without continuing its influence

Yet, given the potential role of prior motivations, a simple alternative isn't always enough. It would therefore be ideal if the alternative explanation doesn't explicitly conflict with people's pre-existing beliefs.

This principle is well-known to social media companies. In 2020, I helped Facebook design their 'Climate Myth Buster' Information Center. As part of this new effort, Facebook's algorithm now tags posts related to climate change (including misinformation). In particular, Facebook uses what they call 'neutral information treatments' (NITs) to connect people with factual information about climate change. For example, if a user posts misinformation about climate change, Facebook will tag the post with a label that says: 'See how the average temperature in your area is changing. Explore Climate Science.' This NIT avoids challenging the user too directly and encourages others who may be exposed to the misinformation to visit the information hub, where credible scientific explanations can be found about climate change.

One Facebook post our team designed informs people about the scientific consensus on climate change – the fact that over 97 per cent of climate scientists agree that humans are causing global warming. This is based on our own academic research, where we have found that emphasizing scientific consensus can be a powerful way to avoid having to repeat influential misinformation.

Although debunking influential climate myths has been a step in the right for direction for Facebook, unfortunately, repeating misinformation remains common practice in the (mainstream) media. Poorly crafted fact-checks often repeat key aspects of the misinformation in an attempt to debunk them, which could inadvertently strengthen memory associations that people hold with the myth in question. For instance, the statement 'Vaccines do not cause autism' may just strengthen the association people have between the words 'vaccine' and 'autism'. In one experiment, our team exposed people to a post stating that over 90 per cent of medical scientists agree that approved vaccines are safe and that parents should vaccinate their children. We didn't mention or repeat the false autism link at all. Importantly, we found that compared to the control group (who received no information), treatment group participants were significantly and substantially less likely to believe in the false autism–vaccination link. Specifically, endorsement was about 30 per cent lower in the treatment group.

Of course, it isn't always possible to provide a credible alternative explanation on an issue and sometimes you may have to repeat a false claim in order to correct it. So, if you're forced to debunk, better to do it right. With about two dozen other misinformation experts, we've come up with a format of how to debunk effectively: it's an approach Berkeley linguistics professor George Lakoff refers to as 'the truth sandwich'. The idea is to layer the falsehood with the truth, in both the opening as well as the ending of the fact-check, which should include an alternative explanation for the myth. The 'meat' of the sandwich should consist of explaining why the myth is misleading (without repeating it).

Facts
- Lead with the facts
  (make them simple and sticky using expert sources)

Warn about the Myth
- Warn your audience about the myth
  (just once)

Expose the Manipulation Technique
- Explain how and why the myth is misleading
  (e.g. a conspiracy theory)

Facts
- End by reinforcing the facts along with a credible
  alternative explanation

Effective debunking: The truth sandwich

Ultimately, debunking only stands a chance of setting the record straight if people share the corrected information widely enough. If misinformation continues to circulate at a high rate, this will only boost its familiarity and might therefore simply reinforce the continued-influence effect. Which leads to our next question: how does misinformation spread online?

FAKE NEWS ANTIGEN 4
Minimize the continued influence of misinformation

— Once exposed, misinformation is difficult to correct because it takes root in our memories and continues to influence our judgments, even when we are aware of a correction.

— The longer misinformation sits in our brains and the more it coheres with people's pre-existing beliefs, the more influential it can become and the more difficult it can be to correct.

— For example, despite repeated corrections, some people continue to believe that vaccines cause autism, that WMDs were found in Iraq, and that Jews were to blame for the Second World War.

— A timely correction that provides a credible alternative without repeating the myth might have some chance of reducing people's continued reliance on misinformation.

PART TWO

Infodemic: How the misinformation virus spreads

CHAPTER 5

Misinformation pathogens:
From ancient Rome to social media

'We're not just fighting an epidemic; we're fighting an infodemic,'
TEDROS ADHANOM GHEBREYESUS,
director general, WHO

Excited about the prospect of proclaiming his great military victory over the last of his political rivals, Julius Caesar led the march back to Italy, where he re-entered the city of Mediolanum (modern-day Milan) in 45 BC. On the horse right beside Caesar sat his trusted lieutenant, Mark Antony. Strong, confident, and athletically built, some people likened Antony to Hercules; indeed, he claimed to be from the demi-god's bloodline. He was a gregarious character, known for socializing with his soldiers and drinking loudly and publicly. As the two men emerged before the public, eager to bask in their glory, they must have imagined a great future together. After all, Caesar was to become dictator for life, and Antony a Roman consul, the highest-ranking public official after Caesar.

But with the Ides of March approaching, it turned out that more nefarious plans were afoot. On 15 March 44 BC, Antony hurried to the Theatre of Pompey to warn Caesar that he'd heard of a plot to assassinate him involving at least sixty Roman senators who had grown increasingly uncomfortable with Caesar's dictatorship in the Roman Republic. Despite his best efforts, Antony was intercepted on the steps of the theatre before he was able to reach his friend. Given that he had refused to participate in previous plots to thwart Caesar's rule, the conspirators had anticipated Antony's arrival. Caesar was stabbed twenty-three times and died on the floor of the theatre.

Following the assassination, Antony fled the city but later returned to manage Caesar's will and safeguard his legacy. To his surprise he found that Caesar had left his title and wealth to Gaius Octavian (later Augustus). Octavian, twenty years Anthony's junior, was Caesar's adopted grandnephew and, despite his young age, Caesar looked at Octavian much like a son, prizing him for his intellect and political shrewdness. Although Antony was not keen to share power with anyone else, he, Octavian, and Lepidus (a lesser rival), decided to form a united front known as the Second Triumvirate in an attempt to defeat their political opponents. But as time passed and rivalries and tensions rose; Lepidus was exiled from the triumvirs, and things soon got out of hand between Antony and Octavian. Their armies clashed. So began the last war of the Roman Republic.

The story would be told many times over the centuries, including by Shakespeare. But what is perhaps less well known is that Octavian was a master of the dark arts of manipulation, launching a highly influential (and one of the oldest) disinformation campaigns on record. These events have been referred to by modern commentators as the 'Infowars of Rome'.

Antony was a charismatic general and Octavian knew that if he were to establish himself as the new leader of the Roman state, he would need more than sheer military force and victories in battle: he needed to have the popular vote too. After the triumvirs disbanded, Antony married Octavian's sister, Octavia, in order to solidify political unity, but the marriage did not last. Antony had been responsible for managing Rome's affairs in the eastern Mediterranean, including its relationships with client kingdoms such as Egypt and, over the years, Antony had grown increasingly close to Egypt's queen, Cleopatra. They eventually married and had three children.

Mark Antony's affair with Cleopatra antagonized Octavian further and provided the perfect basis for his disinformation campaign. He claimed that Antony was an adulterer who defiled traditional Roman values, a brute who was unfit to lead because he cared more about drinking and debauchery. Octavian publicly denounced the Romanesque ceremonies that Antony and Cleopatra organized in foreign lands, and accused Antony as having forsaken Rome. 'This man,' he thundered in public speeches,

> has now abandoned all his ancestors' habits of life, has emulated all alien and barbaric customs . . . he pays no honour to us or to the laws or to his fathers' gods, but pays homage to that wench [Cleopatra] as if she were some Isis or Selene . . .

He also claimed Antony had been,

> bewitched by that accursed woman . . .; her slave, he undertakes a war and its self-chosen dangers on her behalf against us and against his country . . . Therefore let no one count him a Roman, but rather an Egyptian.

Portraying Antony as a 'barbaric foreigner' tapped into existing anti-Eastern prejudices. Most Romans were especially suspicious of powerful foreign women (you might notice a striking parallel with modern-day Western politics, where the growing influence of women and foreign culture is often construed as a threat to traditional values). Meanwhile, Octavian took this opportunity to push the message that, unlike Antony, he was the perfect embodiment of everything good and traditional that the Roman Republic stood for.

Of course, the propaganda was not one-sided. Antony retaliated with a counter-campaign smearing Octavian's family affairs. Both parties tried to secure the allegiance of the troops. Yet, Octavian was extremely careful in the framing of his propaganda. He consciously avoided suggesting that two legitimate Romans were engaging in civil war. Instead, he portrayed the war as being international in nature, to ward off a dangerous foreign queen. He claimed that Antony had simply been enchanted by Cleopatra and was no longer in control of himself. Notably, the war was declared against Cleopatra (not Antony). But Octavian knew that Antony would not leave Cleopatra's side and so the war would look as though Antony had chosen to fight against his own people.

At this point, you might ask whether this isn't just your average political smear campaign. In fact, it was much more than that. Octavian had coins minted with catchy slogans to spread his message – an archaic form of a tweet, if you like. The coin below depicts the head of Octavian with the tagline '*CAESAR DIVI IVLI*' or *Divi Filius* ('Son of the Divine'). This was meant to sell his legitimacy as the heir of Caesar, the first Roman to have received divine honours.

In a final blow, Octavian claimed to have gained access to a document that contained Mark Antony's final will, which supposedly said that Antony intended to leave his legacy to his children with Cleopatra and that he wanted to be buried with Cleopatra in Egypt. These wishes were so offensive to Romans that Octavian could make a convincing case to the Senate that Antony needed to be stripped of his military power. Interestingly, whether or not the claims surrounding Antony's final will constituted 'fake news' is hotly debated. Some scholars believe it is authentic, as neither Mark nor his followers ever publicly refuted it; others maintain that because the document was so detrimental to Antony's reputation, Octavian likely completely or partially forged it.

Regardless of its authenticity, Octavian used the will to convince the Senate to turn against Antony. To further ensure public support for his campaign, he spread the news of Antony's betrayal far and wide, throughout the Republic.

We know how the story ends: during the Battle of Actium, the last war of the Republic, Antony and Cleopatra both died by suicide. After the battle, Gaius Octavian became Caesar Augustus, the very first, and perhaps most powerful, Roman emperor in history.

Scholars have pointed out that Antony and Octavian used pretty much every propaganda trick in the book, and disinformation was even spread somewhat efficiently via coins, texts, and messengers. The parallels between what happened over 2,000 years ago and modern-day political propaganda are striking. So, if disinformation has been around for centuries, what's all the fuss about, you might ask? What's changed, if anything?

That is exactly the key question I want to tackle here. Although social media clearly did not invent propaganda or polarization, it has changed the nature of the game. Social media has fundamentally reshaped the flow of information in society. Specifically, it has changed the speed with which information can travel, the number of people that can be reached with a single click of a button, as well as the social context in which information is delivered and manipulated. What we know now is that misinformation spreads and replicates much like a virus. Indeed, I have witnessed first-hand how social media companies struggle with containing the viral spread of life-threatening misinformation on their platforms.

Silicon Valley here we come

Jon Roozenbeek was about to board a plane to California. Originally from the Netherlands, in 2018 he was a graduate student at Cambridge and a researcher in my lab. Jon's razor-sharp brilliance is cloaked by a wonderful head of big curly hair, an unassuming attitude, and a strong dose of humour. Most people do not forget an encounter with Jon (among other things, he is known for Rickrolling* our colleagues at social media companies). After his plane touched down in California, Jon headed straight into the heart of Silicon Valley, to Menlo Park, Facebook (now Meta) headquarters.

Jon and I had been awarded a grant to do some research with Whats-App. We were excited but I had a busy teaching schedule that week, so we agreed that he would go down to scout out the scene. Once he arrived on the Facebook campus, Jon made a beeline for the offices of WhatsApp Inc.

Facebook had acquired the WhatsApp messaging platform in 2014 for nearly $20 billion, its largest acquisition at the time. But in early

---

* A Rickroll is a bait-and-switch internet prank whereby people think that they click on a legitimate link but are then unexpectedly confronted with a music video of the popular Rick Astley song 'Never Gonna Give You Up'.

2018 something bad had happened. WhatsApp was in trouble, and they had reached out to the research community for help. At the time, we met with Mrinalini Rao, one of WhatsApp's first research hires (she now works at Google). Mrinalini was quickly establishing a new research team and they were keen to get unbiased outside assistance to gain a better handle on the problems they were facing and how we might go about tackling them. I was impressed by their open-minded approach. The first news I received from Jon revolved around the steady supply of doughnuts he was being offered on campus. Somewhat jetlagged, they were keeping him awake with a solid sugar boost. We were one of several teams from around the world who were invited to come down to Silicon Valley to see if we could help WhatsApp with their misinformation problem.

I was connected virtually, but for some reason my face was being displayed on a massive LCD screen that covered nearly half the room. As I tried not to embarrass myself too much while on full display, we all eagerly awaited a keynote address from Chris Daniels, then freshly appointed CEO of WhatsApp. Unfortunately, I cannot tell you everything that transpired, but I can tell you that there was evidence to suggest that misinformation disseminated via the platform was getting people killed in India.

The village of Athimoor in Tamil Nadu is a sleepy temple town, with fewer than 3,000 inhabitants, that lies within the southernmost part of India. On 8 May 2018, sixty-five-year-old Rukmani and her family were travelling to the district from the state's capital, Chennai, to visit their family temple. At one point, they stopped the car and decided to give out chocolates to some local children. As they looked around, they asked an elderly lady for directions. Unbeknownst to them, the woman subsequently told the rest of the village that Rukmani and her family must be the child traffickers they had all been warned about.

Shortly after, an angry mob of over 200 villagers gathered, flipped over the family's car, beat them, killing Rukmani and critically injuring the remaining family members. The following day, about 120 miles from Athimoor, ninety villagers attacked a thirty-year-old homeless man in Pulicat also on suspicion of child kidnapping. The mob gouged out one of his eyes, tied a noose around his neck, and strung his dead body from a local bridge. Similar mob lynchings started to erupt across the country; well over two dozen people died as a result of mob violence that year alone. Of course, the million-dollar question is where in the world these child-trafficking rumours originated from, and how they were able to spread so fast, far, and wide? You probably guessed it: WhatsApp.

A deluge of fake messages was circulating on the platform – often accompanied by audio and video material – warning people about local child traffickers. These messages started spreading like wildfire about a month before the attacks took place. In one popular example, an unknown man, supposedly from Vellore, alleged that 400 people had come to Tamil Nadu to abduct children. An accompanying audio recording claimed: 'I live in Vellore and two kilometres from my house, a child was abducted by a Hindi speaker.' In the nearby district of Kancheepuram, residents were targeted with a similar message: 'Don't allow your children to leave the house alone. Till today, fifty-two children have been abducted in the district. There are complaints in every police station.' Media interviews with local villagers revealed that concerned young males were gathering in groups to go on patrols looking to find anyone suspicious who might fit the kidnapper profile described in the WhatsApp messages.

WhatsApp was growing increasingly concerned and were under severe pressure from the Indian government to do something about the problem. Globally, WhatsApp has over 2 billion users, but India is by far its single biggest market, with close to 350 million active monthly users. As one local interviewee, Raju, an eighteen-year-old from the Vellore area, put it: 'We wake up to WhatsApp messages. We sleep after reading WhatsApp messages. For us WhatsApp is our life, our Facebook, our Twitter.'

Following our initial meeting with WhatsApp, we decided to try to help them counter the spread of misinformation on their platform. Our primary remit was to conduct original research which could help inform WhatsApp's policies to help reduce the spread of harmful content, particularly in India.*

---

* Importantly, as part of our agreement to conduct independent research, they would not have direct access to our data, and likewise we would not have access to any WhatsApp user data (this data is encrypted anyway).

Our first step was to go out to the villages ourselves to ask people about their opinions and how they use the WhatsApp platform. With the help of the Digital Empowerment Foundation, a local media literacy agency in India, we were able to distribute our survey to over a thousand local citizens, including those living in remote areas. More than 60 per cent of those surveyed indicated that they use WhatsApp at least once a day or more. Worryingly, a similar percentage (63 per cent) said that they frequently received information that required urgent sharing and about 50 per cent stated that they never or rarely assess the veracity of the information they receive before forwarding it on to others.

We also asked people if they'd ever, knowingly, shared 'fake news' on WhatsApp. When we looked at the factors that were most predictive of people's self-reported sharing of fake news, three stood out: being exposed to urgent messages that contain threatening or harmful information; pretending to agree with a message because of group pressure; and not fully assessing the content of the messages before sharing them. WhatsApp was right to be concerned: these data were revealing a dangerous pattern.

But rumours have been getting people killed since the dawn of time. So, let us return to the point of what is different now? Clearly social media has not invented the practice of disinformation – but it does offer dangerous new ways for it to spread and dupe people. There are three core differences that we should consider in particular: speed; reach; and the medium itself, including how it shapes perceptions of media content.

WhatsApp is an especially interesting case in point to illustrate the unique aspects in which social media has fundamentally altered the way that misinformation propagates.

Falsehood flies, and the truth comes limping after it

The first point of difference has to do with sheer speed. For example, shortly after his victory over Mark Antony, Emperor Augustus created the *cursus publicus*, the premier courier system of the Roman Empire, comprising a series of stations, or outposts, along the extensive major road network that connected different regions of the Roman Empire. A relay service of horses and carriers would dispatch riders between the stations, transferring messages back and forth on a regular basis. Historians calculated that for an average trip, the relay teams travelled about fifty miles a day (estimates range anywhere between 38 to 62 mph) – though in emergencies the riders could cover more than a hundred miles a day. To put this into context, a message that Augustus's grandson, Gaius Caesar, had died in Limyra (now southern Turkey) is estimated to have made it to Pisa, central Italy, in about thirty-six days (covering 1,300 miles by land). But even at a much faster pace, it would have taken at least two weeks to deliver a notification by land. Can you imagine waiting for two weeks to hear about an emergency? On WhatsApp, it took less than a second for people to be notified of alarming news about local kidnappers.

But it's about more than just sheer speed. It is also about reach and diffusion. In the Roman system, a courier typically reached a single person or a small group of individuals at most, who then subsequently diffused the content of the message to the rest of the town by word of mouth. It took a while for the word to spread.

Things began to speed up from 1440 onwards with the invention of the Gutenberg printing press. By 1833 the first 'penny presses' were being produced, and one of the clearest, earliest instances of 'fake news' in the popular press followed soon after.

In 1835 the New York *Sun* – a newspaper sold on the streets for a penny per issue – falsely claimed that one of the world's leading astronomers, Sir John Herschel, had made important new discoveries about the solar system and that the findings had been published in the prestigious *Edinburgh Journal of Science*. This was all news to Herschel himself and of course, readers were unaware that the journal had actually ceased to exist two years prior. Over the course of a week, in a series of subsequent articles, the *Sun* ran exciting stories about what Herschel had discovered – from lunar vegetation, moon bison and blue unicorns, to what Herschel apparently termed '*Vespertilio homo*', or 'batman'. Yes, you read that correctly; the paper described the discovery of human-like creatures with enormous bat wings as 'moon-dwelling bat people' who were four feet tall, naked, sported curly hair and 'wings composed of a thin membrane lying snugly upon their backs'.

Many people were duped by what became known as the 'Great Moon Hoax'; circulation of the *Sun* reportedly exploded from about 4,000 to 19,000 overnight, with many newspapers reprinting the hoax story. It was never retracted.

While those numbers were impressive at the time, what's unique about WhatsApp and social media, is that you could now instantly share something like the moon hoax with a massive group of people as part of a private messaging system. You simply start a group, give it a name (for example: 'friends', 'family', or 'sports team') and add contacts to the group. When you send a message to the group, all of its members will immediately see what you posted and can, in turn, forward the message to others. There is a limit to how many people you can add to a group. The magic number is 256.* This means that when you share a message with everyone in your local group, up to 256 people will see it instantly and can in turn share it with others. Before WhatsApp implemented counter-misinformation measures, people could forward a message up to twenty times. Assuming someone is a member of twenty groups comprising 256 individuals each, this means that a single individual could expose over 5,000 people (20×256) to a message or video in just a matter of seconds. Importantly, these 5,000 recipients could each in turn expose the message twenty times to a group of 256 people. Now we have reached 2.5 million people, and we haven't even begun to consider friends of friends and their friends.

We had learned from our collaboration with WhatsApp that, unlike in most Western countries, large WhatsApp groups were far more common in places like Brazil, India, and Indonesia. This was consistent with our own findings. On average, only a minority (13 per cent) of people we sampled in India reported belonging to just 0–2 groups. Most belonged to more: for example, 30 per cent belonged to about 3–5 WhatsApp groups, about 26 per cent indicated that they belonged to 5–10 groups, another 22 per cent between 10–20 groups, and 8 per cent belonged to 20 groups or more. In contrast, in the UK, the vast majority (79 per cent) belonged to 5 groups or fewer. Most people reported that they were

---

* WhatsApp increased the limit to 256 from 100 back in 2016.

added by friends and family, but about 25 per cent of participants told us that they are sometimes added by total strangers.

The spread of misinformation via WhatsApp groups is not just a problem in India. News reports have suggested that Brazil's right-wing populist leader, Jair Bolsonaro, illegally hired organizations during his presidential campaign in 2018 to bombard heaps of WhatsApp users with fake news about his political opponents. Brazil is WhatsApp's second largest market. By using overseas phone numbers, they were able to circumvent WhatsApp's rules and reach millions of people with their propaganda. David Nemer, a media studies professor, decided to go undercover and joined several of Bolsonaro's WhatsApp groups. He reported receiving over a thousand WhatsApp messages per day. Half the Brazilian population is active on WhatsApp.

The potential for misinformation to spread is equally pronounced on other social media platforms, such as Twitter. Although Twitter has far fewer monthly active users than WhatsApp (about 330 million globally, compared to 2 billion), a single tweet can still reach a lot of people. For example, consider the fact that, as one of the highest-ranking Twitter influencers, former US president Barack Obama has nearly 130 million followers on the platform. That not only means that a potential 130 million people could be exposed to a message from him in a heartbeat (what Twitter calls 'impressions'), but the message itself can also be shared by a potential 130 million people, whose friends, in turn, can share the message with their friends, exposing it to an even wider audience, and so on.

Of course, the potential for 130 million impressions does not mean that any given tweet will reach this level of impact. One of the most liked tweets in the history of Twitter is a short tweet from the 46th President of the United States, Joe Biden, who on 20 January 2021 wrote: 'It's a new day in America.' This tweet received 4 million likes. Similarly, Obama's tweet quoting Nelson Mandela, 'No one is born hating another person because of the color of his skin or his background or religion . . .', also received 4.2 million likes. This is nowhere near Obama's 130 million potential reach. But the point is that we are often talking about hundreds of thousands, if not millions, of views, likes, and shares, all within the blink of an eye. For example, the top 25 per cent Covid-19 videos containing misinformation on YouTube collectively received over 60 million views. Remember that the *Plandemic* video alone received about 8 million views across social media platforms in just a couple of days, before being removed. In other words, both the speed at which information travels and the number of people it can reach in an instant is unprecedented.

These numbers are useful for thinking about the basic reproduction number – or infectiousness – of a virus. The R_0 (reproduction) number is a mathematical term that represents the average number of people an infected person will transmit the virus to in a population with no prior immunity. So, for example, an R_0 of 10 suggests that an infected individual will, on average, infect ten other people. In other words, the higher the R_0, the more difficult it is to control the virus in a population.

Its calculation depends on at least three main factors: the infectious period (how long an infectious person remains contagious); the mode of transmission (how the virus spreads, for example, airborne versus physical contact); and the contact rate (or how many infected people a person is expected to come into contact with). For example, although Ebola is deadly, it spreads primarily via bodily fluids, whereas measles is much more infectious because it's airborne and can spread via droplets. Measles's R_0 is estimated to be between 12 and 18 – one of the highest reproduction numbers on record.

When we apply the biological analogy to misinformation pathogens, we can think of R_0 as the number of individuals who will start posting fake news following contact with someone who is already posting misinformation (the infectious individual).* Moreover, although the 'infectious period' – during which people are contagious and actively share content – may vary from story to story, it can last longer than that of a biological virus. Asymptomatic individuals also likely represent a big vector of spread here, as people often share fake or misleading content without realizing it. In addition, people do not even need to be true believers

---

* But as we'll see in chapter 7, exposure does not always equal infection. Sometimes people need to be exposed repeatedly before they buy in to or start sharing misinformation.

themselves; they sometimes share misinformation because they find it entertaining or think it might be relevant to their audience. Misinformation also spreads more easily because of the mode of transmission: fake news can spread online without the need for any physical contact. Finally, although partially influenced by the structure of a social network,* the number of people an 'infected' person can come into contact with virtually, is entirely unprecedented. Millions of people can be exposed to viral misinformation in a matter of days if not minutes.

In March 2020, in light of the viral spread of (mis)information, the World Health Organization (WHO) declared a worldwide 'infodemic' (one indicator of the infodemic was that a Covid-19 related tweet appeared every 45 milliseconds in 2020). Moreover, this isn't just a metaphor; we can apply models from epidemiology to study the spread of 'information pathogens' on social media. When doing so, it becomes clear that basically all major platforms have infodemic-like spread potential. Having said that, there is no formal R_0 known for specific misinformation viruses; figuring out how social media dynamics influence the spread and diffusion of true and fake news online is deceptively difficult. For starters, it requires a lot of data – including social media data that is not always publicly available. So, what do we know about how much social media contributes to the spread of false news online?

You may be familiar with the famous quote: 'Falsehood flies, and the truth comes limping after it', or one of its popular variants, 'A *lie* can travel *halfway round the world* while the truth is still putting on its shoes.' It turns out that we can empirically evaluate this prediction on social media. In 2018, three researchers from the MIT (Massachusetts Institute of Technology) Media Lab published a landmark study where they were able to track the diffusion of all verified true and false news stories on Twitter between 2006 and 2017. They were able to do this because their MIT lab was given access to the full historical Twitter archives, which means that the researchers could retrieve all tweets ever posted,

---

* For example, consider that Facebook is an 'undirected' network (if I follow you, you follow me); whereas Twitter is a 'directed' network (If I follow you, you need not follow me).

including the very first tweet (posted by then Twitter CEO Jack Dorsey in 2006).

The team were looking for all English-language tweets that constitute a 'rumour cascade'. On Twitter, a cascade is initiated when a user makes a claim about a topic, which could involve, say, a short text message, a video, a photo or a link to an article. Other Twitter users then propagate the claim by retweeting it. People often reply to tweets and sometimes these replies include links to third-party fact-checking organizations that either debunk or confirm the rumour in the original tweet. The research team collected headlines from the databases of six prominent fact-checkers (such as *Snopes*) and matched them to the Twitter data, finding approximately 500,000 tweets that contained a link to one of the fact-checking websites. They included these tweets as well as all subsequent retweets. Each of these retweet cascades count as a 'news rumour' on Twitter – fact-checked as either true or false – for a total of 126,000 rumours tweeted by approximately 3 million people over 4.5 million times.

The researchers were then able to look at the dissemination or '*diffusion*' process of true and false news on Twitter. For each rumour cascade, they looked at depth (the number of unique retweets), size (the total number of users involved in the cascade over time), and breadth (the maximum number of users in a cascade at any given depth). The results were shocking.

Falsehoods diffused significantly faster, deeper, and more broadly than true claims in all categories of information, meaning false news reached far more people than true news. (For example, true claims rarely diffused to more than 1,000 individuals, whereas the top 1 per cent of false claims frequently diffused to between 1,000 and 100,000 people.) Also, many more people retweeted false claims than true claims. In particular, the spread of false news was aided by a viral process so that false claims do not typically spread in the form of a single large broadcast but rather through a branching process of peer-to-peer diffusion. The researchers calculated that, on average, it took the truth about six times as long as a falsehood to reach 1,500 people. In other words, lies had literally made their way halfway around the world before the truth had time to get its shoes on.

In total, falsehoods were 70 per cent more likely to be retweeted than true claims. This was particularly the case for political fake news, which proved most popular as a category (compared to other news, such as finance or natural disasters) and peaked around the time of the 2016 US presidential election. Using a bot detection algorithm, the MIT researchers also reran the analyses excluding cascades started by bots (automated accounts). Importantly, the results remained the same, suggesting that humans (not bots) are more likely to spread the misinformation 'virus'. An analysis of the text used in the tweets suggested that falsehoods tend to diffuse faster because they appear more 'novel' and often inspire negative emotions such as fear.

In an ironic turn of events, Daniel Engber, an editor at *The Atlantic*, tweeted out on 24 March 2022 that the conclusions from the MIT study had been debunked by new research, which had re-analysed the MIT data. Engber's tweet went viral. After all, a study on misinformation potentially being 'fake news' is rather alarming. It turns out that the newer research actually replicated and confirmed the results of the original MIT paper, whilst adding an important clarification as to why fake news travels faster, deeper, and further, because of its overall 'infectiousness'. Fake stories are more infectious than true stories. Unfortunately, with about thirty-five retweets, the corrections and apologies didn't garner much attention. In a follow-up piece, Engber wrote: 'Sorry, I lied about fake news. A false tweet really does move faster than the truth.' Sinan Aral, one of the original MIT authors, added: 'Just as we predicted.'

So fake news really can propagate faster, deeper, and further than true news. But that isn't the end of the story: there are other important differences to consider that relate to the medium itself.

When the medium becomes the message

For example, during the Roman era, you often needed certificates from the emperor to be able to use the courier system. Of course, fraud existed then too, but you could at least document and trace the sender of the message. Similarly, the source of the 'Great Moon Hoax' was easily identified: the New York *Sun*. However, unlike Twitter, WhatsApp uses end-to-end encryption, which means that they cannot (or do not) read or moderate user messages. When a WhatsApp message is forwarded, any metadata about the sender is automatically stripped and removed. In other words, WhatsApp does not engage in content moderation and cannot identify the sources of misinformation.

The Indian government repeatedly tried to get WhatsApp to allow them to trace harmful and problematic content but, to their dismay, WhatsApp did not agree to do so. The reasons are likely to be partly political (WhatsApp might worry about becoming a tool for governments to hunt down individuals), and partly driven by the fact that privacy is key to the platform's popularity.

So, how do you stop content from spreading when you cannot trace messages or intervene on the platform directly? It is a big problem. After reports of the Indian mob lynchings, WhatsApp reduced the rate at which you can forward group messages (up to five people at a time), but there is no current restriction on how often you can forward links individually, so people have found easy ways around these stricter limits. This is also partly why technology-based solutions that do not tackle the underlying psychology are rarely sufficient to stem the flow of misinformation (but more on that later).

A final point of difference is that on WhatsApp, the messages you receive often come from people within groups you know well, such as friends and family, so you're more likely to trust the information. I often get forwarded messages in my friend groups asking me to look at (bogus) content. What this signals to me, is that people automatically imbue the messages they receive with some degree of credibility because they come from a closed private group, even though its content may appear to be fake news. But it's not only about credibility; there's also social pressure to comply with forwarding requests, which we know can interfere with our motivations to be accurate. For example, in India, WhatsApp messages about the kidnappings would often be accompanied by explicit social pleas such as: 'Share this video in all your WhatsApp groups. Anyone who does not, is not his mother's son.'

This process further interacts with the fact that technology has greatly altered the content of the messages themselves, now often involving audio or manipulated film or images. Timestamped videos are regarded as highly trustworthy forms of evidence – seeing is believing after all. One thing we've found in our work with WhatsApp is that digital literacy levels in rural India are very low. Although many people are not familiar with the internet or social media, they know that they can watch videos on WhatsApp. There is one video, in particular, that has been linked to multiple deaths. In this viral video – which looks like grainy CCTV footage – two young boys are playing cricket near a driveway alongside a fairly empty street. After a short while, a black motorcycle appears with two individuals wearing black helmets. They approach the group of children but then suddenly make a U-turn and disappear from the frame. They reappear a few seconds later and this time the motorcycle stops next to a young boy. The boy was simply a bystander watching the other boys play cricket. The passenger then snatches the kid and wedges the boy between himself and the other passenger while quickly driving off. The other children notice and pursue the motorcycle, albeit unsuccessfully. The video ends with the children returning to the driveway conversing and expressing panic. For all intents and purposes, this looks like a genuine kidnapping.

Karen Rebelo, a fact-checker in Mumbai, decided to investigate the video. She noticed something unusual. At the end of the clip, the boys are joined by two girls who are wearing headscarves that don't appear to be of Indian origin. The style was suggestive of an Islamic country. Rebelo decided to go down the rabbit hole, tracing the origins of the video on YouTube, where she stumbled upon a longer version. Here, the motorcycle returns, stops, and lowers the boy while the youngsters celebrate the return of their friend. The motorcyclist unfolds a banner for the camera that reads: 'It takes only a moment to kidnap a child from the streets of Karachi.' It turns out that the video was created in 2016 by a marketing firm to support an anti-kidnapping awareness campaign in Pakistan. As opposed to a sophisticated deepfake, this is known as a shallowfake: a simple video cut using basic video-editing software and presented completely out of context.

But what are people supposed to think when they receive such doctored videos in an urgent message from a friend? In the Athimoor case and the murder of Rukmani, the WhatsApp video featured a car and a woman handing out chocolates. The victim and her family fitted the profile. Neela, a local resident, stated in a media interview: 'Of course, we had to suspect her. She came in a car, like it was shown in that WhatsApp video. What if she had taken those children away?'

Don't shoot the messenger?

It would be a mistake to blame it all on WhatsApp. In fact, although WhatsApp and other instant-messaging platforms act as important amplifiers, they are not in and of themselves the root cause of the problem. Commentators have observed something very important about the situation in India that ties back to a theme we have been discussing throughout: the dance between 'reasoning' and 'motivation'. For example, it is true that many villagers in rural India often have low levels of digital literacy. In our own study with WhatsApp only half the sample indicated that they felt confident in their ability to discern fact from fiction on the platform. In other words, there is much to be done when it comes to media literacy training, building cognitive skills, and empowering people to make informed decisions.

At the same time, however, we'd do well to remember Joseph Goebbels's writings on the dark arts: propaganda is unlikely to be effective if people are not motivated to process it in a manner that resonates with their existing beliefs and ideologies.

In India, larger tensions were afoot. You may have noticed that in many of the stories, there is an inherent 'othering' aspect to the WhatsApp messages, whether it is a kidnapper who 'speaks Hindi' or an elderly lady giving out 'Malaysian candy'. In fact, rumours of foreign kidnappers, often accompanied by gruesome (fake) video material of dead children, had been circulating in India for years. These narratives play into a complex reality, because although child-trafficking is a serious issue in India, the reports in question are clearly fake. Another polarizing example involves India's most revered animal: the cow. Cows are sacred for Hindus, who make up roughly 80 per cent of the Indian population. Minorities in India, such as Dalits and Muslims, are often accused of cow-smuggling and slaughter. Following viral misinformation about local cow smugglers, minorities are often attacked by vigilante groups, mostly consisting of nationalistic upper-caste Hindu men.

Suspicion of foreigners has flourished. One journalist noted a palpable fear amongst villagers in Vellore about north Indian migrants coming to the area to allegedly 'steal jobs' and 'commit crimes'. One of the fellow research teams that worked with WhatsApp during our tenure reviewed the content of about a thousand questionable WhatsApp messages and found a clear expression of prejudice, disgust and contempt towards various minority groups in India. This made the research team question whether it is really a lack of literacy skills that is the problem here or a deeper political, religious, and cultural motivation concerning the rising tensions between Hindus and Muslims or groups from lower and upper Indian castes. Is the medium (WhatsApp) really the message? Some social and cultural commentators have even suggested that WhatsApp has been scapegoated and that the viral spread of these fake rumours is simply providing a 'licence to kill'. There is a larger, heated scientific discussion about social media here: is fake news spreading on social media duping inattentive and otherwise well-intentioned people, or do people already have troubling motivations in place that make them receptive to the megaphone that this new technology is offering?

The fact remains that, even though WhatsApp and other social media networks may not be the root cause of larger societal tensions, they act as a massive amplifier of misinformation. The technology has fundamentally changed how information spreads and how people interact with each other online. Still, maybe there's little difference between present-day populist politics and say, the smear campaign Octavian ran and the way it tapped into prejudiced narratives about foreigners over two thousand years ago. While admittedly the parallels are striking, social media has found a new way to shape, influence, and amplify those biases too.

Welcome to the echo chamber where your biases are carefully recorded, curated, and filtered – ready to be shared with millions of like-minded individuals.

FAKE NEWS ANTIGEN 5

Limit the viral spread of fake news on social media

— Although misinformation has been a constant companion throughout human history, the rise of social media has offered unprecedented ways for misinformation and disinformation to spread rapidly to millions of people around the world.

— The speed at which misinformation diffuses, the number of global audiences it can reach, and the new ways technology can take advantage of our biases is posing a serious threat to the wellbeing of individuals and societies worldwide.

— To manage the 'infodemic' we need to control the 'R_0' value – or the number of other people an infected person can transmit the misinformation virus to.

— One way to try to break the virality of false rumour cascades is to intervene using technology-based solutions, such as limiting how often a message can be shared or forwarded. Although useful, these measures do not get at the root cause of the problem: how *people* interact with social media technology.

CHAPTER 6

Rage against the machine: Echo chambers and filter bubbles

'Move fast and break things. Unless you are breaking stuff,
you are not moving fast enough.'
MARK ZUCKERBERG, CEO, Meta Platforms, Inc.

I have always resisted new technology. I was the kid still walking around with a Walkman when all of my friends had already switched to Discmans or MP3 players. Long after DVDs had been released, I was still hanging on to my VHS collection. Today, I'm still rocking a ten-year-old iPhone. I'm wary of new technology; if it's not broken, why replace it? New innovations are known to diffuse in stages and I'm what marketeers call a 'late adopter'.

I've only made one exception in my life: I was an early adopter of the internet. I was a bit of an angry teenager – rebelling against the system – so I immediately recognized the potential to connect with like-minded others online. This was long before YouTube, Facebook, Twitter and Google. I grew up in the nineties, with AltaVista (an early search engine) and a Hotmail email address, exploring the first 'modern' chatrooms, where I found others who shared and reinforced my opinions about the world. They listened to the same punk music and were equally ready to 'stick it to the man'. I had found *my people* – my very own 'echo chamber'. Luckily for me, my echo chamber resulted in little more than the formation of what was possibly the worst punk band of the early 2000s (we self-recorded one album, before disbanding). But hey, at least I made friends and we had fun.

Over the years, I remained fascinated with the internet but struggled to keep up. As soon as I had mastered a new piece of software or programming language, a completely new update arrived. Sometimes the whole interface just changed entirely. Things were moving fast. In many ways, I hadn't even fully digested the potential psychological consequences of hanging out online for so many hours.

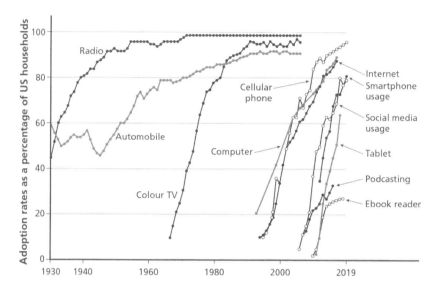

Have a look at the chart above which depicts the innovation of major new technologies in the United States between 1930 and 2019. It took radio, cars, and television several decades to be adopted by the majority of the population – plenty of time to get used to the concept and to study and explore the social consequences that these new technologies might have for both individual and societal wellbeing. But now look closely at the diffusion curve for social media. The gradient is incredibly steep by comparison. In fact, the rate of adoption is nothing like we've ever seen before. Social media use increased from covering about 5 per cent of the US population in 2005 to a whopping 79 per cent in 2019. The largest social media platform is Facebook, which covered only 1.5 per cent of the world's population in 2008, but now has over 35 per cent of the world's population active on its platform.

Inside the echo chamber: is anyone listening?

When I joined the internet craze in the 1990s, my early experience with the echo chamber was fairly innocent, but others weren't so lucky. Take Caleb Cain. Like me, Caleb was fond of counterculture, growing up and fascinated by what the internet had to offer. Though the age difference between us spans less than a decade, internet culture and technology had already changed radically by the time Caleb connected to the internet.

As a teenager, Caleb was hanging out in places like YouTube where – over a relatively short period of time – he fell into a rabbit hole, watching close to 12,000 videos containing mostly right-wing extremist content. Caleb was pulled into an echo chamber perpetuating blatant conspiracy theories, misogyny, and racism. But after several years at the epicentre of this rabbit hole, he finally started denouncing extremist content on his own YouTube channel in 2019. This is when he caught the attention of the mainstream media. Subsequent analyses of his YouTube search history by the *New York Times* revealed everything from videos proclaiming that global warming is a hoax to the idea that Western society is under attack by legions of minority immigrants, feminists, and left-wing Marxists

In February 2021, I was invited to a virtual event with Hollywood screenwriters to talk about how insights from my research could potentially help popular show-writers counter misinformation on TV. That's where I met Caleb. He was there to share his story. During the event, I had the opportunity to sit down with him to learn more about his journey. Caleb told me that he'd grown up in the Appalachian region of West Virginia and had a troubled childhood. He didn't go into the details, but said that this experience caused him to develop a deep sense of distrust of authority and institutions.

Caleb dropped out of community college and things went downhill from there. He would lie awake thinking about death and his uncertain future. He felt what could only be described as the presence of a gigantic 'God-shaped hole' – a choice of words that reflected his Christian upbringing. He went on to explain that, at the time, left-wing politics had little to offer him besides more guilt and responsibility for all the bad things that are happening to other people in the world. He told me that he understood the importance of a social justice agenda – he'd grown up knowing lots of racist people – but it wasn't comforting to him. It wasn't focused on solving *his* problems as a 'disenfranchised white male'. *His* trust issues. *His* deep feelings of loneliness.

In 2014, Caleb went online to look for help. YouTube weighed in and made a casual recommendation: Stefan Molyneux's YouTube channel. Molyneux is a far-right Canadian white supremacist, peddling 'white genocide' conspiracy theories, scientific racism, and other extremist content. He is currently banned from YouTube and other social media channels for systematically violating their hate speech policies (notably he sees himself as a philosopher and men's rights' activist). Caleb explained that he had never heard someone address the issues he felt young men face in such a persuasive manner before. He started following other YouTube recommendations, and the many extremist online personalities he came into contact with addressed all the right anxieties he was experiencing about the world. He discovered a whole universe of like-minded people. His very own echo chamber.

Near the end of our conversation Caleb explained to me that he eventually found his way out of the echo chamber. It wasn't easy, but he slowly started to expose himself to other viewpoints. Initially he dismissed most other perspectives as 'left-wing propaganda', especially when they would refer to his views as 'racist'. But then he stumbled upon a lighter-touch YouTube channel called ContraPoints, run by transgender influencer Natalie Wynn (known as the 'Oscar Wilde' of YouTube). Her approach is unique insofar as she creates animated and entertaining videos on the very same topics as far-right influencers specifically in an effort to debunk their claims, blow by blow. This practice is often referred to as 'algorithmic hijacking' because, by talking about the same topics, influencers enable their videos to be recommended to those who consume far-right material (and vice versa).

I suddenly heard a loud voice. There was a whiteboard behind Caleb so I couldn't see what was happening. He apologized and explained that his roommate has her own YouTube channel. What about you? I asked.

Caleb is still active on YouTube today. He's sharing his story and spreading the word about the dangers of echo chambers, filter bubbles, and YouTube rabbit holes.

At the same screenwriters event, I spoke to several other radicalized individuals, including a former QAnon follower, and a self-identified far-right neo-Nazi. There was a clear pattern to each of their journeys: they had been spending lots of time online. You may remember Bucky Wolfe from chapter 3, who thought his own brother was a shapeshifting lizard. Like Caleb, analyses of his YouTube history also revealed a concerning trajectory; although he started out with fitness and music videos, he quickly discovered 'alt-lite' content before moving on to die-hard conspiracy theories, white nationalism, and finally, QAnon videos. Yet, although nobody doubts or discounts the importance of these experiences, you can't help but wonder if they are the exception rather than the rule. After all, lots of frustrated people go online but do not become extreme or radicalized. As my sceptical colleague Joe Uscinski likes to put it: 'People often say, "Oh, my God, this thing just happened to my cousin." Well, no, it didn't just happen. Your cousin was always a wackadoo. I'm sorry.'

It's an important question. Some say social media is melting our brains – and democracy. Others say it's all overblown. As over 70 per cent of Americans use platforms such as YouTube and Facebook, how we measure the societal impacts of echo chambers and filter bubbles remains one of the most controversial – and urgent – questions facing scientists today. But it's not just research: understanding whether you find yourself in a polarizing echo chamber is key to unlocking insights about your own beliefs and media diet. As we'll see later on, echo chambers aid the viral spread of misinformation. Knowing how they work empowers us to gain back control over the kind of information that we're exposed to on a daily basis.* But to do that, we first need to get our lingo straight and distinguish 'filters' from 'chambers'.

---

* If you're on Twitter, you can check out the composition of your own echo chamber via our app, *Have I Shared Fake News?*

Not all echo chambers are filter bubbles

The term 'echo chamber' follows a metaphor derived from the acoustic echo chamber – an enclosed room where sounds reverberate and become amplified via sound-reflecting walls. In a similar vein, a social media echo chamber is usually thought of as a situation in which beliefs and opinions are amplified and reinforced within a closed media system. In other words, by entering an echo chamber people are able to selectively seek out information that reinforces their pre-existing views about the world, whilst avoiding exposure to counter-content that may question these beliefs in potentially uncomfortable ways.

Echo chambers are commonly thought to fuel confirmation bias, group polarization, the spread of misinformation and in some cases – such as Caleb's – radicalization and extremism. Cass Sunstein, a law professor at Harvard, provided early warnings of the insidious effects of echo chambers in his book *Republic.com*. Over twenty years ago he wrote of a then seemingly dystopian future 'It is some time in the future. Technology has greatly increased people's ability to "filter" what they want to read, see, and hear.' That future is now.

Sunstein's main concern was that in order for democracy to function, people should be exposed to a wide range of ideas, even if they would not have personally chosen to expose themselves to such opinions or ideas in advance. Though the two are closely related, it's useful to distinguish between echo chambers and filter bubbles. The latter term was coined by internet activist Eli Pariser. In his book *The Filter Bubble*, he describes how, based on your personal online search history, your unique click behaviour and other digital footprints, algorithms produce a pretty good guess of what you would like to see and tailor content accordingly.

In some aspects, Google is amazing. Every day millions of people are looking for honest answers to burning questions, whether it's the lyrics to their favourite song or how many planets occupy our galaxy. Yet, although it may seem that everyone should get the same search results when they google something, since 2009 Google's rank algorithm has been using digital traces – including your browser history, logins, prior searches, and much more – to customize personal search results for every user. There is no longer a universal 'google'. It's the very personalized form of democracy Sunstein has warned us about. Pariser argues that our computers are becoming one-way mirrors, no longer reflecting objective facts, but more and more of what we would like to see.

So, why should you care about filter bubbles? Well, the algorithmic filtering of search and news results is highly relevant to the global consumption of misinformation, which is closely tied to its popularity rank in search engines and social media feeds. For example, consider that a massive 2022 audit of millions of shared news articles by Twitter's own research team uncovered that the personalized home feed – compared to the chronological timeline – was amplifying biased media content, especially from right-wing sources and politicians.

But is that enough to undermine democracy?

Two psychologists conducted a fascinating experiment to help answer this question. They asked a group of US participants to read biographies about two candidates who were running for prime minister of Australia and how likely they were to vote for them. The researchers created a (fake) search engine (called 'Kadoodle') and asked participants to use it for about fifteen minutes to learn more about each candidate. The fake search engine would display several pages with six clickable results about each candidate per page. What people didn't know is that the researchers had manipulated the search results to be either neutral or biased in favour of one of the candidates. Following the search, people were asked again what candidate they would like to vote for.

The results were shocking: whereas there were no differences in voting preference between the treatment and control conditions before the 'Kadoodle' search, after viewing the biased search results the number of people who said they would vote for the favoured politician increased between 37 and 63 per cent – a statistic the team referred to as the 'VMP' or 'voter manipulation power'.

Of course, this is all hypothetical. But here's where things get really interesting: the researchers subsequently repeated their experiment during the high-stakes 2014 national Lok Sabha election in India. The process was the same as before: undecided voters were recruited and asked to use the fake Kadoodle search engine to learn more about one of the three main candidates. Their results proved consistent, this time during a real election: following the web search, votes for candidates that the biased search favoured increased between 8.3 and 10.7 per cent.

What's even more alarming is that between 75 and 85 per cent of people showed virtually no awareness of the manipulation. The researchers termed this the 'search engine manipulation effect' (SEME).

Of course, as far as we know, Google isn't actually manipulating global elections with their search engine, but since Twitter has already admitted that its recommender system is amplifying biased political content, the possible societal consequences of algorithmic filtering are concerning.

To understand how the echo chamber and algorithmic filter bubble work together to maximize their persuasive power, let's return to Caleb's story for a moment. Caleb didn't fall into the echo chamber by accident: he received a 'recommendation' from YouTube. Like other social media companies, YouTube makes money from advertisements on their platform, so their main concern is to maximize engagement – that is, having users watch more and more videos. Their proprietary artificial intelligence algorithm is tweaked frequently and reported to be responsible for as much as 70 per cent of watched content. The algorithm is based, in part, on prior user behaviour as well as viewing times.

It's easy to see how this supposedly 'neutral' process of optimizing user engagement can lead people astray. In fact, at a presentation in 2016, Monica Lee, a leading data scientist and machine-learning expert at Facebook, mentioned that internal research had determined that '64 per cent of all "extremist-group joins" are due to our recommendations tools', including the 'Groups You Should Join' and 'Discover' algorithms. When you are watching a video on YouTube, recommendations are made in a sidebar. Imagine you're tuning into a conspiracy theory; this may lead the algorithm to suggest similar content and ignite a feedback loop where more extremist videos are recommended and subsequently consumed. This is what happened to Caleb: his search was supported by a powerful recommendation algorithm that provided an easy gateway to extremism. Of course, at the time, Caleb was likely to be more susceptible to this kind of content too. A dangerous cocktail.

Yet, YouTube has repeatedly contested such claims and even dismissed them as 'myths'. For example, YouTube's chief product officer, Neal Mohan, has suggested that extremist content does not generate higher engagement than other types of content. He added: 'I can say categorically that's not the way that our recommendation systems are designed.' But these claims seem inconsistent not only with user experiences and the many case studies reported by the media but also with the reports of other social media companies. For example, in 2018, the *Wall Street Journal* reported that a slide from an internal Facebook presentation warned that 'our algorithms exploit the human brain's attraction to divisiveness'. In 2018, Mark Zuckerberg himself published the following graphic in a public post, noting that engagement with content on Facebook dramatically increases as it approaches the 'policy line' of what's allowed. He specifically mentioned: 'our research suggests that no matter where we draw the lines for what is allowed, as a piece of content gets closer to that line, people will engage with it more on average, even when they tell us afterwards, they don't like the content'.

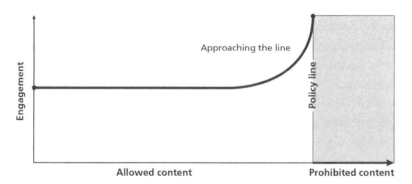

These conclusions were reinforced when whistleblower Frances Haugen released thousands of internal Facebook documents ('The Facebook Files') to the *Wall Street Journal* in February 2021. Haugen, a former Facebook product manager, argues that the company continually chose to maximize profits over what was in the public interest. Of course, Zuckerberg denied these allegations. Why, he asked, would the company employ so many people to help fix these issues if they only cared about profit margins?

One possible answer is that Facebook was only reacting because of mounting media pressure. So, scientists such as myself have been keen to do our own independent research to try to find out what exactly is going on here. Who is telling the truth? Are social media algorithms really providing a gateway to misinformation, polarization, and extremism? Because most public research is not able to directly access people's personalized feeds or viewing history, we've only began to scratch the surface of the problem – but the results so far are troubling.

Down the rabbit hole

So, let's start with YouTube's 'rabbit hole' problem. About 62 per cent of US adults say they encounter false content on YouTube, but that doesn't tell us whether it's a rabbit hole. A rabbit hole is a specific kind of filter bubble where algorithmic viewing recommendations encourage users to watch more extreme content over time. In one study, researchers looked at 8 million YouTube recommendations over the course of fifteen months from YouTube's 'watch-next' algorithm (which, in the sidebar, recommends what video a user should watch next when autoplay is enabled). The team trained an algorithm to detect and classify conspiratorial content in the videos. For example, the algorithm would classify words such as 'deep state', 'hoax', and 'illuminati' as conspiratorial. The researchers collected the first twenty recommendations from a set of over a thousand popular information channels.

What they saw was evidence of a clear filter bubble: there was a very strong relationship between the number of recommendations to dodgy content made by YouTube and the likelihood that the original video was conspiratorial. For example, for the period between October 2018 and January of 2019, if you had watched a conspiracy video, the likelihood of getting a recommendation of another video about a conspiracy theory was about 70 per cent. To be fair, this number went down the closer we get to 2020, consistent with claims from YouTube that they have started to implement countermeasures, such as deleting millions of problematic videos and making tweaks to their algorithm. This is especially interesting because none of the recommendations featured misinformation about the coronavirus despite plenty of Covid-19 conspiracy theories floating on the platform. This reveals that YouTube can help prevent misinformation from spreading, as long as they consider it a priority. A letter signed by thirty-seven Members of the US Congress was sent to the CEO of YouTube confronting the company with the study's findings.

Other recent research has found similar results. For example, another study found that nearly 50 per cent of content from political gurus was conspiratorial in nature. This is important as the type of material that drew Caleb and others like him deeper into the rabbit hole was exactly the type of extremist content produced by self-proclaimed political 'gurus' on YouTube.

When you search YouTube, the algorithm aims to provide you with the most relevant results – in terms of maximizing your viewing time – which is determined by your digital footprint. For example, a 2018 audit by Pew found that YouTube progressively recommends longer and longer videos. An important limitation of existing studies is that the researchers all accessed YouTube with an IP address that had no prior cookies stored. The results are therefore based on the general recommendation algorithm and not the personalized 'recommended-for-you' videos. This matters because if you are a regular consumer of conspiratorial content, you're much more likely to be presented with similar recommendations. So, if anything, these results may be underestimating the true state of things.

US researchers from Dartmouth College in New Hampshire, and Northeastern University in Massachusetts, recently sought to solve this issue in a novel way. Through tracking people's online behaviour they matched the recommendations YouTube made to each user with an individual's actual viewing choices. They sourced a panel of 4,000 US citizens, including 'frequent' YouTube viewers (who were more likely to be younger and male) and people who, on a pre-test, had already expressed negative views on race and gender. Overall, about 900 of these individuals agreed to take part in the study. They asked participants to install a special browser plug-in extension that recorded data from websites they visited, including their browser history. The team then looked at visits to about 200 well-known 'alternative' YouTube channels – which often provide a gateway to more extreme content – as well as various outright 'extremist' or white supremacist channels. Overall, the researchers were able to extract about 800,000 YouTube visits which resulted in over 4 million recommendations that were made by the YouTube algorithm for each user.

Interestingly, results revealed that, in general, people followed a recommendation about 20 per cent of the time. In terms of average content exposure, about one in ten (9 per cent) people viewed at least one video from an extremist channel and two in ten (22 per cent) a video from an alternative channel. Now consider that YouTube has over 2 billion monthly users worldwide. This finding points to the risky nature of YouTube's architecture; anyone can now upload extremist content and compete with the mainstream media. Moreover, when people watched such content, almost 40 per cent of recommendations from alternative and about 30 per cent of the recommendations from extremist channels went to other videos of the same category – despite the fact that YouTube claimed to have made over thirty changes to their algorithm to reduce recommendations of harmful content.

That's the filter bubble at work.

Of course, you could argue that if someone clicks on extremist content on the platform, 100 per cent of the recommendations should go towards similar channels if YouTube were truly optimizing for extremism. That's clearly not the case. In fact, the study also revealed that extremist recommendations were very unlikely to occur if people were watching mainstream content. Moreover, just a small group of users (11 per cent) appeared responsible for about 80 per cent of the alternative videos watched.

So, who were these 11 per cent of potentially motivated users? Over 90 per cent of them were those individuals previously identified as harbouring serious feelings of racial resentment. I can't speak for Caleb, but our conversation made me think he may well have scored high on 'prior susceptibility' to this type of content at the time.

In short, these findings illustrate that, although social media may not be the root cause of our problems, its algorithmic filtering can create an echo chamber that amplifies and exacerbates existing biases, especially amongst those individuals who may be more open to considering alternative or extremist content in the first place.

One of the issues researchers face in this area is having to deal with a moving target: YouTube regularly tweaks its algorithm and uploaders often tailor their content in response. Conducting research on filter bubbles is an incredibly dynamic and fast-moving process. Nonetheless, a systematic review conducted in 2020 assessed the conclusions of twenty-three academic studies. At least fourteen of them (61 per cent) clearly found the YouTube recommender system to be a gateway for problematic content. So, at the very least these findings cast serious doubt on YouTube's claim that this is not how their recommendation engine works. Although YouTube may no longer be recommending conspiracy theories outright, once you start watching questionable content, its algorithm does maximize engagement by skewing recommendations towards similar videos. It's a filter bubble.

But maybe the filter bubble is partly of our own making? After all, we make choices too.

It's you, not me

Although Facebook admits that 'provocative content' leads to more engagement on the platform, like YouTube, they are sceptical about how much this actually contributes to the formation of echo chambers and filter bubbles. In fact, a couple of years ago, Facebook decided to weigh in with their own study, published in the prestigious journal *Science*. Eytan Bakshy (a Facebook data scientist) and his colleagues looked at a set of 10 million active US Facebook users who self-reported their political ideologies and shared about 7 million distinct URLs (web links) over a six-month period. They determined whether a news story was congenial to a particular ideology by averaging the ideological affiliation of all people who shared a given story. So, for example, a story from Fox News would most likely be shared by conservatives and would thus receive a high alignment score with conservatism as opposed to liberalism, and vice versa for a story from CNN.

Now remember that Facebook is a social network, so the amount of diverse or cross-cutting ideological content you are exposed to very much depends on who your friends are and what information your friends share. The key question is how the structure of your social network interacts with Facebook's algorithmically ranked newsfeed. On Facebook, people often post news stories and Facebook's algorithm is there to try to separate the wheat from the chaff for you: it ranks content according to what the algorithm thinks you might like to engage with. The algorithm takes many things into account, including how much time you spend on Facebook, how much you interact with certain friends, and what kind of links you typically click on in your feed. The newsfeed then provides a customized ranking for you: your personal newsfeed.

To try to figure out how much Facebook's algorithm is messing with your potential to be exposed to opposing or cross-ideological content (which would counteract the echo-chamber effect), you can think of the process in three different stages – ranging from pure potential, to actual exposure, to the eventual choices we make about what news articles we decide to click on. I visualize this process in the figure below, where the grey bubble represents the gradually decreasing proportion of media content that is ideologically diverse.

The filter bubble process.

Potential: This is based on your social network. How many connections do you have available that share cross-cutting content?

Exposure: What is the effect of algorithmic filtering in reducing your exposure from full potential? This is what actually appears in your newsfeed.

Choices: What content do you actually select and click on?

Your exposure potential depends on how many friends you have in your network from the 'other side'. Before calculating this for the individuals in the sample, Eytan Bakshy and his colleagues first came up with a baseline estimate. They wondered what would happen if we optimistically assume that people get their information from random others (so the flow is not determined by your specific network). Under those conditions, Facebook estimates that, depending on whether you are conservative or liberal, about 40 to 45 per cent of the major news people are exposed to would be 'cross-cutting'. But of course, people do not get their information from random others in the network. Looking at the actual links that were shared by self-identified liberals and conservatives, Bakshy and colleagues noted that liberals were connected to fewer friends from the other side. On average, this reduced diversity in the network of liberals meant that only 24 per cent of news stories presented to liberals had a conservative leaning whereas 35 per cent of the stories shown to conservatives had a liberal leaning.

In the next stage, they wanted to figure out how much Facebook's algorithm is harming your potential. Facebook concedes that after doing its magic ranking of your newsfeed, the probability that you'll see cross-cutting content is reduced. But by how much, exactly? They calculated that the likelihood of seeing ideologically diverse versus congenial content is reduced by about 5 per cent for conservatives and 8 per cent for liberals. Overall, a relatively small reduction, the researchers argue. What's more, in the final stage of our process, we need to look at what people actually click on (not only what is recommended). Here Facebook makes an interesting argument about the power of personal choice. They estimate that the likelihood of clicking on ideologically uncongenial versus congenial content is reduced by about 17 per cent for conservatives and 6 per cent for liberals. Thus, although conservatives have more opportunities than liberals to engage with cross-cutting content, given their slightly more diverse social network, conservatives were less likely to follow through and engage with opposing viewpoints. The larger takeaway is that the impact of individual choices may exert a bigger influence on exposure than the algorithmic ranking of the newsfeed.

It's you, not me. How convenient!

But not so fast. First, for liberals the impact of algorithmic filtering (8 per cent) is actually higher than that of individual choice (6 per cent). Second, the study has a number of serious limitations. For example, the study only sampled individuals who *self-declared* their ideology – a tiny fraction of all Facebook users (9 per cent) – so these findings may not hold for the larger Facebook population. Moreover, given the dynamic interplay between our choices and the algorithm's recommendations, the assumption that our choices are somehow independent of exposure seems tenuous. Your 'freedom to choose' may well be biased by the content that the algorithm selects for you. Think about it this way: what if in one scenario I present you with five conservative- and five liberal-leaning news stories, and in another you get eight conservative and two liberal news stories? Would you make the same choice in each scenario? Maybe you always go for a conservative or liberal story, no matter what is selected for you. Maybe it depends on the content. But it seems likely our choices are shaped – in part – by the options available to you when you log on to Facebook.

Still, Bakshy and colleagues argue that in contrast to some 'Brave New World' visions of the future of the internet (such as the 'personalized democracy' Cass Sunstein has warned about), the single most important determinant of anyone's potential to be exposed to views from the other side on Facebook is simply the structure of their own social network, rather than the algorithmic filtering of your newsfeed.

How many friends from the other side do you have on Facebook?*

Before you take these results at face value, you should know that Facebook designed an internal playbook, 'What We Know About Polarization', which was posted to the company's internal workplace discussion group in March 2021. The purpose of this playbook is to help its employees fight off claims that Facebook is to blame for societal divisions. The document cites a range of social science research to buttress the idea that social media companies are not the root cause of the issue. I know this playbook well. When our team published an op-ed in the *Washington Post* in July 2020 about how our research revealed that highly divisive content elicits more engagement on their platform, Facebook went on the defensive, putting out a press release which recycled the exact same arguments from their playbook: namely, that there are many studies which show that polarization and extremism existed before Facebook (with which I agree); that they have employed 35,000 people to keep their services safe (which is good); and lastly, that contrary to our claims, 'extremism is actually bad for business'. Hence we are 'simply wrong'. Notice that Facebook used very similar language when counter-

---

* The average in the study was about 20 per cent, if you're curious.

ing the claims made by whistleblower Frances Haugen as well. She was 'simply wrong' too. I will come back to their claim that extremism is bad for business (which is not what we find in our own research), but their first argument is worth examining in more detail.

Facebook's own study generated lots of controversy not only because it was led by a Facebook scientist but also because these results contradicted commonly held assumptions among journalists and scientists about the negative impact of echo chambers. Even Eli Pariser himself was surprised that the effects of the filter bubble were much smaller than he thought they would be. Accordingly, the Facebook study fuelled much scepticism about whether or not 'echo chambers' and 'filter bubbles' are a real concern. Facebook is not wrong about the social science research cited in their report per se. There is scholarly debate about the extent to which social media companies are to blame. Moreover, although the Facebook team didn't think that their algorithm was that consequential for people's exposure to diverse news sources, they do recognize the issue that the networks of conservatives and liberals – by and large – consist of fellow liberals and conservatives. It's an echo chamber.

But is this really Facebook's fault?

A key distinction between filter bubbles and echo chambers is that echo chambers aren't always the result of filter bubbles. Although social media plays a prominent role in the formation of echo chambers, it's important to emphasize research that reveals that echo chambers exist offline too.

Let's take this offline

For example, research shows that people are more likely to move to neighbourhoods that match their personalities and political preferences. A large study that geo-located 180 million registered voters in the US found extreme partisan-sorting at the state and county level. In fact, the researchers found that even in the same neighbourhoods, Republicans and Democrats cluster away from each other. In short, Facebook is right to say that people sort into echo chambers offline too, without the help of social media. This finding raises the distinct possibility that online echo chambers are not a consequence of online social media but in fact motivated by offline echo chambers.

In 2018, some clever Italian researchers decided to try to disentangle this question by looking at Twitter posts and hashtags during the UK's heated 2016 Brexit referendum. They scraped over 5 million tweets between 15 April and 24 June 2016 (the campaign period) using keywords and hashtags such as 'referendum', 'no2eu', 'iwantout', and 'lovenotleave'. Through geocoded tweets, locations that were visible in a user's profile, and location information that appeared in a user's tweet, the researchers were able to link online tweets to a geographical location. Users were then classified as either part of the 'Leave' or 'Remain' campaign based on the hashtags they used. If online and offline echo chambers have nothing to do with each other, then someone's physical location is not going to be related to their online activity. This is our baseline assumption.

The results were fascinating. First, regardless of location, a stunning 69 per cent of messages tweeted by those who affiliated with the Leave campaign were 'in-bubble', that is, directed towards other Leave campaigners. Only 9 per cent of messages were directed towards Remainers, and so 'cross-bubble' communication was minimal. The same phenomenon was visible on the Remain side, with only 10 per cent of users tweeting messages to Leave campaigners whereas 68 per cent of messages went to fellow Remainers. In other words, there is strong evidence of an online echo-chamber effect.

But how about geographic distance? To evaluate this, the researchers looked at the geographic proximity of online interactions. They found that, overall, 'in-bubble' Leave campaign messages indeed travelled shorter average distances than 'out-bubble' messages. Moreover, looking at the average distance between sender and receiver, about a quarter of all Leave interactions took place within 100km (62 miles) of each other – that's relatively close. When you overlay these online communications on a map of the UK, it becomes clear that most Leave interactions on Twitter took place in the 'Brexit heartlands' – such as the English Midlands. While not a true experiment, the authors argue that such spatial patterns suggest that offline echo chambers could play a role in motivating online echo chambers.

Although it is interesting that offline echo chambers exist and seem to coincide with online echo chambers, this doesn't mean that Facebook is off the hook. They can still cause or exacerbate echo chambers. Moreover, filter bubbles only happen online. So where does that leave us? Well other research generally suggests that we can expect clear online echo-chamber effects for politically contested content (such as elections) but that such effects may not exist for other types of content (such as, say, the NFL Super Bowl or St Patrick's Day). I think this is probably a fair characterization of the debate: echo chambers and filter bubbles exist, but their frequency and severity depend on the platform and the issue at hand. When you zoom in on contested issues specifically, echo-chamber effects are more likely to emerge.

To illustrate: a few years ago, my team mapped out a small piece of the social network of the top-ten most popular conspiracy theorists and scientists on Twitter. The whole social network of the five most influential conspiracy theorists (think Alex Jones, founder of *Infowars*) and the five most influential popular scientists (think 'Bill Nye the Science Guy') and all of their followers comprise more than 8.5 million users. What I am showing in the graph overleaf is just a tiny snapshot of this network. The bubble on the top-right indicates followers of conspiracy theorists, the bubble on the bottom left indicates followers of popular science accounts, and the grey shaded middle area highlights overlap (some people follow both popular scientists and conspiracy theorists). The larger nodes (dots) are the top influencers. If you are wondering why the bottom bubble is so much bigger than the top bubble, that's mainly because, in absolute terms, the top popular scientists have many more followers than the top conspiracy theorists. But even from this snapshot, you can clearly see that both networks form relatively homogeneous 'information bubbles' or 'enclaves'. Conspiratorial and scientific narratives mostly operate in their own bubble, speaking to their own respective audiences without much interaction. This clearly suggests evidence of a potential echo chamber. In fact, although images like these have been visualized many times across different social networks – especially among partisans during elections – people have increasingly asked the question: so what?

*Snapshot of the echo chamber effect on Twitter:
the top bubble comprises the network of conspiracy
theorists and the (larger) bottom bubble represents
the network of popular scientists. The dots are
the top influencers within each network.
Both groups mostly reside within their
own respective 'bubbles'.*

Why online echo chambers amplify the spread of misinformation

At this point, you might wonder how everything we've discussed so far is related to the spread of misinformation? Well, if you compare the spread of misinformation on social media to a virus, then an echo chamber acts like the perfect host: it dampens our immune response and becomes a hotbed for replication. One major concern is that being stuck in an echo chamber leads to selective exposure, selective attention, and selective retention of information – a process which can ultimately lead to group polarization. For example, studies find that fake news is believed more when it is presented in a context that reinforces rather than challenges people's own political views. Moreover, when people are stuck in a situation where they just echo their own opinions and narratives, it can move the whole group towards more extreme positions and lead people to reject information from other sources.

Classic research in psychology has revealed what happens when you put like-minded people together in a group to discuss a contested issue –

a phenomenon sometimes referred to as the 'law of group polarization'. For example, say we invite people who are pro-death penalty to discuss the issue with each other at length. We then invite another group of people with anti-death penalty attitudes to do the same in another room. Importantly, the groups do not mix, they remain in their own echo chambers. Many studies show that both groups typically emerge with more extreme positions on the topic than they had going into the experiment. In other words, following deliberation with like-minded peers, people become more convinced of their own arguments and polarize away from each other.

Similarly – like the Twitter users in our graph on p. 122 – if you are mostly exposed to conspiratorial narratives, you become less and less likely to be exposed to, attend to, and share other types of content. If the same happens to the other group, then the net result is that both groups drift further and further apart and become more extreme in their beliefs. We have already talked about how this process occurs at an individual level in chapter 2, but it is important to recognize that this can also happen on a collective level when we aggregate the opinions of an entire group together.

At the same time, deliberation in and of itself doesn't always, of course, lead to polarization. In fact, we now know that there are specific conditions that facilitate group polarization. These assumptions are of crucial importance to our discussion here because they are often more likely to occur online in social media settings.

One of the scientists who arguably knows most about this topic is my colleague, Walter Q.

Walter Quattrociocchi is an Italian computational scientist who has been studying the echo-chamber effect for many years. Walter and I are both part of a research coalition that advises the UK government and his speciality is looking at the ways in which misinformation spreads on social media. To address the question of platform dependency, Walter and his team recently conducted one of the largest cross-platform comparisons of the echo-chamber effect.

To understand the study, we first need to settle on what an echo chamber is exactly. The first ingredient is what we refer to as 'homophily', or the tendency for 'birds of a feather to flock together', so that users with similar views are more densely connected with each other than with the rest of the network. The second ingredient is a bias in the diffusion of information so that similar content is also more likely to reach like-minded peers. It is often thought that, jointly, these processes assist the spread of misinformation and give rise to group polarization.*

In the study, Walter and his team looked at more than 100 million stories – from gun control and vaccination to abortion rights – on various social media platforms, including Facebook, Twitter and Reddit. Reddit and Facebook are different in that Reddit is more of a discussion forum structured around communities of common interest, whereas Facebook is a peer-to-peer social network. In other words, this analysis allowed the researchers to understand echo-chamber effects across very different social media outlets.

Across all platforms, the researchers found clear evidence that users are surrounded by peers with similar leanings on a topic and thus have a higher probability of being exposed to content that is consistent with their views on an issue. Interestingly, this tendency was much stronger on Facebook and Twitter than on Reddit.

But what about the diffusion of information? To understand how information diffuses, Walter and his team borrowed a model from epidemiology that is used to model the spread of a virus. In the so-called 'SIR' (susceptible-infection-recovered) model someone can take on one of three potential states: you are either unaware of (mis)information circulating online (and thus 'susceptible'); you are aware and actively spreading (mis)information ('infectious'); or you are in a recovered state where you are still aware of the (informational) virus but are no longer spreading it.

The basic idea is that when you are surrounded by many infected individuals, the probability that you will become infected too goes up rapidly. This is exactly what the researchers found: people with a given leaning

---

* Keep in mind that the emergence of echo chambers is a dynamic process, so that polarization can sometimes be a cause and at other times a consequence of echo chambers.

on a contested issue were much more likely to receive information from individuals with similar views. In other words, the information diffusion process was biased towards like-minded peers. An important caveat is that this was again mostly true for Facebook and Twitter but less so for other platforms such as Reddit. What could explain this discrepancy? Well, one of the differences the authors note is that, unlike Facebook and Twitter, people can tweak the news-feed algorithm themselves on platforms like Reddit. This evidence thus suggests that filtering algorithms on social media platforms might be reinforcing echo chambers.

You may have noticed that the SIR model allows for the possibility for individuals to 'recover' from their infection. It turns out that filter bubbles and echo chambers have important implications for the spread of misinformation because of the fact that users tend to share information in a manner that is biased towards others with similar views. So, aside from the general effect of distorting people's social reality, the overall likelihood that you will be exposed to biased or misinformation is in part determined by whether or not you find yourself in an echo chamber. The echo-chamber effect I visualized earlier (between 'conspiracy theorists' and 'popular scientists') was inspired by Walter Q's earlier work.

Walter had been studying how conspiratorial and scientific narratives propagate on Facebook. Back when Facebook still allowed people to retrieve data from its public API (Application Programming Interface), Walter and his colleagues were able to download data from public Facebook pages over a span of five years. In total, they collected data from 54 million Facebook users across: 330 well-known conspiracy pages (with names such as 'The Truth About Vaccines' and 'Illuminati Mind Control'); 83 science pages (such as 'Armed with Science'); and 66 pages explicitly debunking conspiracy theories (such as 'Refutations to Anti-Vaccine Memes'). On Facebook, you can either like a post (representing positive feedback), share a post (increasing its visibility), or leave a comment (engage in debate).

To understand the consequences of echo chambers for the spread of misinformation, consider that out of the 10 million users who mostly interacted with conspiratorial content, only 1 per cent engaged with a debunking post, insofar that they commented on it at least once. Overall, only 6.5 per cent of likes and 3.9 per cent of comments on debunking posts came from conspiracy users, compared to 27 per cent and 44 per cent of science users, respectively.* Thus, the circulation of corrections was mostly confined to the 'science' echo chamber. Interestingly, out of the small number of conspiracy users who did interact with the debunking pages, a text analysis revealed that the majority engaged in a negative manner and showed increased activity in the conspiracy echo chamber following a previous interaction with a debunking post. The existence of echo chambers means we are dealing with online enclaves and biased (selective) patterns of information exposure, which impedes the ability of corrections to spread and reach anyone beyond those who are already aware of its content.

One more dramatic consequence of this is the explosion of 'science denial' on social media platforms. A recent system-level analysis of the 'anti-vax' landscape on Facebook mapped out the views of 100 million users. Specifically, the researchers looked at how people interact with Facebook pages such as 'Rage Against the Vaccines' (which has about 40,000 members). They classified these pages as either 'anti-vaccination', 'pro-vaccination' or 'undecided'. Findings showed that although anti-vaccination groups are currently still in the minority (being smaller in size), they turn out to be much more centrally located in the network compared to pro-vaccination pages, which operate more on the edges. Moreover, contrary to the commonly held view that there is an ongoing information war to win the hearts and minds of the 'undecided individual', those on the fence turn out to be the fastest growing segment and appear highly active, with about 50 million of them showing some form of entanglement with the anti-vax clusters.

Qualitative analyses of the content of the anti-vaccination pages suggested that they might be more centrally located because they were able to tap into a wide range of potential narratives that may pique the interest of susceptible audiences – from vaccine safety concerns and alternative medicine to conspiracy theories about Covid-19. By contrast, pro-vaccination pages were largely scientific in focus and much more

* The remainder were classified as 'other' users.

monolithic. What's concerning is that pro-vaccination clusters never grew by more than 100 per cent (most grew by less than 50 per cent), whereas some of the anti-vaccination clusters grew by more than 300 per cent. Based on their model and various simulations, the authors predict that, without intervention, anti-vax discourse will dominate Facebook within the next ten years.

Piercing the echo chamber

You might reason that an easy solution to the echo-chamber problem is to simply expose people to opposing or more diverse viewpoints. It worked out for Caleb, after all? Unfortunately, the answer is not so simple. Chris Bail, professor at Duke University, North Carolina, and author of *Breaking the Social Media Prism*, conducted an experiment with his colleagues where they asked about 1,600 active US Twitter users whether they would agree to follow a Twitter bot for one month in return for $11. People weren't told what the bot would be posting about, only that it would be tweeting several times a day for a month. A survey asked participants about their Twitter ID, political affiliation and attitudes towards various social policies, at the start and end of the experiment. Democrats and Republicans were each randomized, separately, into a treatment and control group. Democrats in the treatment group were exposed to a month of retweets from prominent Republican accounts (including elected officials and news media) and vice versa for the Republicans. Any shift in political attitudes was assessed with an 'ideological consistency' survey (a questionnaire asking partisans about their stance on various social policy issues such as the 'government is almost always wasteful and inefficient').

So, what did the researchers find? It turns out that simply disrupting 'selective exposure' by increasing visibility of content from the 'other side' is not always a good thing! At the end of the experiment, Republicans became more conservative in their attitudes (rather than more liberal) and Democrats became more liberal (rather than conservative) albeit to a lesser extent. The end result was greater not less polarization. The researchers suggested that a multitude of reasons could help explain this surprising and rather concerning result. For example, although randomly allocated, some of the retweets from the bot accounts came from political elites which may have elicited an 'anti-elite' backlash among Twitter users. But another likely explanation comes from our own research, which suggests that the problem of echo chambers may be secondary to an even larger issue on social media.

Together with my former doctoral student, Steve Rathje, and our colleague Jay Van Bavel at New York University (co-author of *The Power of Us*), we decided to collect a large data set of over 2.7 million social media observations from both Twitter and Facebook. In particular we looked at posts from major news media accounts across the political spectrum, such as the *New York Times* and *Fox News*, as well as members of the US Congress. We classified media accounts as either liberal or conservative based on the 'All Sides Media Bias Chart' (an independent source which reports on the political bias of news outlets). We also retrieved social media posts of current members of the US Senate and House of Representatives.

Next, we wanted to identify whether any given post was talking about liberal or conservative topics, so we used several well-known dictionaries that classify words in terms of whether they are commonly associated with a particular ideology, such as 'liberal', 'leftist', 'right-wing', and 'conservative'. We also used dictionaries that automatically classify words in terms of their emotional tone to investigate whether the 'talk' about the other side (outgroup) was largely positive or negative. For example, some of the most popular posts in our liberal data set included '**Donald Trump** has lied more than 3,000 times since taking office, but **Republicans** refuse to say **Trump** is a liar. What is going on?' This post was shared about 30,000 times. A popular example from the conservative data set was: 'Every American needs to see **Joe Biden's** latest brain freeze' (shared about 15,000 times).

We know from previous research that highly emotional content such as this is more likely to go viral as it tends to cause 'moral outrage' or the tendency for people to express their anger online at offensive material (a much easier option than confronting someone face to face, in the real world).

What Steve wanted to examine here is whether derogatory language about the 'other side' is more likely to go viral as well. What we found was alarming: on average, posts about the political outgroup (so conservatives if you're a liberal and vice versa) were shared or retweeted about twice as often as posts about the ingroup. Outgroup language was also the strongest predictor of engagement (shares and retweets) on social media, much more so than emotional language. Outgroup talk was also a very strong predictor of 😡 ('angry') and 😆 ('haha') reactions on Facebook. To give you a quantified estimate, across all platforms and data sets, each word referring to the political outgroup increased the odds of a social media post being shared by about 67 per cent, nearly five times the rate of negative emotional language alone (14 per cent). Importantly, these findings were robust for both liberals and conservatives and both Twitter and Facebook.

Although echo chambers are a problem in and of themselves, these findings suggest that even when people are exposed to more cross-cutting content, this often means that we have to deal with negative and derogatory posts about the political groups that we belong to. This can help explain why the Duke University researchers found that simply exposing Democrats and Republicans to opposing views increased rather than decreased polarization. How would you feel about having to deal with a large onslaught of negative posts about your political party on a daily basis?

The perverse incentives of social media

Social media seems to offer perverse incentives by rewarding negative engagement. In fact, according to the *New York Times*, in 2020, internal research from Facebook revealed that posts which users rated as 'bad for the world' generated more engagement. This aligns with our finding that negative and divisive content maximized engagement on two of the biggest social media platforms, Facebook and Twitter. I should say that although criticizing or 'dunking' on the other side systematically coincided with higher rates of sharing, our study does not provide causal evidence of polarization. But recent randomized trials *have* revealed causal evidence: asking people to discontinue using social media for a month actually reduces polarization.

These findings may also have implications for why and how people share misinformation on the platform. For example, even though a story might be false or of questionable accuracy, if it offers up an opportunity to 'stick it' to the other side it is likely to gain traction and engagement, thereby rewarding and reinforcing polarizing patterns of information-sharing. Filter bubbles can further enhance and amplify these tendencies by prioritizing, ranking, and recommending similar content. In fact, when Facebook pilot-tested tweaks in their algorithm to down-rank content rated as 'bad for the world', they found that engagement on the platform decreased. This posed a problem for the business. A second version that down-ranked such content less strongly did not seem to hurt the number of times a user logged on to Facebook and was ultimately approved for implementation. But other solutions weren't.

The online magazine *Gizmodo* thought it was funny to comment on our findings with the following headline:

Researchers Produce Obvious Study on Dunking Because They're Nerds . . .

A new report out from the University of Cambridge confirmed what many of us have known for years: being a contrarian asshole on social media is a great way to get people clicking on your posts.

An excellent illustration of the type of headline that is more likely to go viral.

Yet, a bunch of good studies show that when you ask people to install a browser plug-in to record their internet activity over a period of several weeks, it turns out that most of us don't actively seek out polarizing content. In fact, the everyday news diet of many liberals and conservatives seem to overlap quite a bit. So, do we live in echo chambers or not?

It depends: regular non-curated browsing does not provide the same perverse incentives as social media. A key study that looked at the browsing activity of about 50,000 active US news readers (which culminated in over 2 billion page views) directly compared how polarized users were when they accessed content via social media versus direct browsing activity. This study confirmed that news content accessed via social media and search engines is associated with greater polarization.

It may therefore very well be the case that, without incentives which make group identities salient, people do their best to find factual and unbiased news, not thinking much about politics. To put it another way: social media often provides an environment which reduces people's inclination to be accurate and heightens our social and political motivations. It provides the perfect environment for people to flock together in echo chambers around hot-button issues. Importantly, algorithmic filter bubbles then further exacerbate these tendencies by recommending content that keeps us engaged in ways that elicit division, polarization, and selective sharing of (mis)information. This makes it much harder for fact-checks and corrections to spread across the population.

Zuckerberg was right – that's what happens when you move fast: you break things.

Of course, we should all recognize our individual responsibility for the content that we share, and social media companies have taken every opportunity to remind us of this. But equally, social media companies should be held accountable for what happens on their platforms. Simply exposing people to more diverse views is not enough, especially when most of the views that are being promoted elicit negative engagement.

What we really need is to move slow and fix things – a radical rethinking of the incentive structure of social media. We don't need to maximize engagement – perhaps we should maximize accuracy and constructive debate instead? What would such a social media landscape look like? At present, their revenue is heavily tied to ads, which require engagement. This brings us to our next issue.

So far, we haven't even touched on how social media is being weaponized to deceive people at scale. We are being targeted on social media with political ads without our awareness and approval. It's big business. Echo chambers and filter bubbles are only the tip of the iceberg. I am much more concerned about disinformation campaigns that micro-target users based on their digital footprints.

This leads to one of the key questions that everyone has been debating for years: Has the spread of misinformation on social media disrupted democratic elections? How do you know whether your vote was targeted? While scores of articles have been written on how Facebook data about your personality has been stolen and sold to nefarious political campaigners, few have actually dissected the science behind micro-targeting models.

In the next chapter we will take a deeper look at these new 'weapons of mass persuasion'. It all started with a strange chance encounter I had in 2016 with the man who would soon find himself in the midst of a worldwide scandal. His name? Dr Aleksandr Kogan.

FAKE NEWS ANTIGEN 6
Avoid the echo chamber and don't feed the algorithm

— Although there are various 'offline' causes of echo chambers, studies have shown that social media plays a prominent role in their formation.

— Algorithmic filtering of content, based on user behaviour and recommendation engines, can act as a funnel and nudge people down a path of polarization and extremism.

— Echo chambers and filter bubbles pose serious challenges to the dissemination and uptake of fact-checks and debunkings of misinformation.

— Inside echo chambers, people propagate information in a biased way towards like-minded others.

— Piercing the echo chamber is not simply a matter of exposing people to more diverse views from the other side; social media disproportionally incentivizes *negative* engagement (such as moral outrage) which can further polarize people.

— The incentive structure of social media thus needs be changed so that polarizing, extreme, and false content is no longer rewarded and recommended.

CHAPTER 7

Weapons of mass persuasion

'In psychological warfare, the weak points are flaws in how
people think. If you're trying to hack a person's mind, you need
to identify *cognitive biases* and then exploit them,'
CHRISTOPHER WYLIE, Cambridge Analytica whistleblower

It was sometime in August 2016 that I received an enthusiastic email
from Alex Kogan – better known as Aleksandr Spectre at the time. He
had received word that I would be arriving in Cambridge soon to take up
a new faculty position, so he graciously offered to take my wife and me
around town for a tour. It would be his last day in town – he was getting
ready to move back to the United States.

Later that week, we met Alex in the historic part of Cambridge, near
King's College – a beautiful and giant edifice which resembles an ancient
medieval castle and is often regarded as a prime example of English
Gothic architecture. I immediately sensed that Alex was friendly and full
of energy, with a contagious sense of enthusiasm. He was dressed casually,
had a bit of a goofy disposition, and talked loudly while making lots of
gestures as he showed us around town. At the time, I had no idea who
Alex was (aside from being a new colleague), and remember thinking to
myself how nice he was, taking time out of his busy schedule to welcome
us in such a warm manner. After the tour, we went our separate ways but
made plans to meet up for dinner and drinks in a local pub later that
evening. I was intrigued.

After a few pints at the pub, I wanted to know more about his story.
He told me that he had just completed a temporary lectureship at the

university and was now focusing on 'big data', in the hope that he could use machine learning algorithms to predict people's personality based on the digital traces they leave behind on social media. I was fascinated. I told him that I had been studying people's beliefs about climate change for some time and that we'd been building statistical models to understand how national public opinion data could be broken down reliably at smaller geographical subunits, such as the state or county level.

After I told Alex about our climate models, he immediately switched the conversation to his new career plans. He told me he had left academia because he found the pace rather slow with too little reward. I wasn't surprised; he struck me as an ambitious start-up type, looking for the next big thing. His plan, he explained, was to harvest big data and go into consultancy – in fact, he had already set up shop back home in the United States. He wondered why I bothered with surveying people; he could get me tons of predicted climate opinion data from Facebook, based on what people put in their profiles and the pages they 'liked'. Millions of datapoints. But it wasn't going to be free.

This suggestion triggered some alarm bells for me. Why would I buy Facebook data? Who would use that, I wondered, and how did he obtain so much of it – and for what purpose? I kindly thanked him for the offer but declined. My wife and I both left the pub with a rather strange feeling about that conversation.

I never saw Alex Kogan again after our meeting, but it wouldn't be the last time I would hear of him. A few months later he made worldwide headlines for allegedly selling Facebook data on 87 million individuals to Cambridge Analytica – a British political consulting firm. He had collected this data through a Facebook app he developed called *This Is Your Digital Life*. Cambridge Analytica used it to micro-target voters online with political advertisements, providing data science services to the campaigns of Donald Trump, the Texan senator Ted Cruz, and possibly the Brexit Leave campaign. Some commentators have even suggested that Cambridge Analytica influenced elections and undermined the functioning of democracy. From CBS's *60 Minutes*, to British parliamentary hearings, the scandal turned Kogan's and everyone else's life upside down. Yet a rigorous assessment of how these models work and direct evidence on whether micro-targeting can influence our voting preferences has remained elusive. Until recently.

The Kogan files

So, what actually happened? In 2014, Kogan developed a Facebook application called *This Is Your Digital Life*, which was basically a 'fun personality quiz'. The test was based on what psychologists call the 'Big Five' personality traits, or the OCEAN model (which stands for Openness, Conscientiousness, Extraversion, Agreeableness, and Neuroticism). Since the 1980s this has probably been the most widely accepted model of human personality in psychology. Instead of sorting people into distinct types, like other personality tests, the OCEAN model assumes that personality operates on a spectrum. In other words, you are not binned as either 'extraverted' or 'introverted', but rather placed somewhere on a spectrum for each trait, determining your level of, say, Openness or Neuroticism. Questions on this test might ask you to what extent you see yourself as 'getting nervous easily', an indicator of Neuroticism; or as 'someone who likes to think and play with ideas', an indicator of Openness. Your answers are then used to calculate an overall score for each trait. People who score high on Extraversion are typically talkative, energetic, and outgoing whereas people who score high on Conscientious tend to describe themselves as 'organized', 'thorough', and 'hard-working'.

Decades of research suggests that these traits remain relatively stable throughout life and are known to be heritable (studies show up to 50 per cent heritability). They correlate with numerous important life outcomes, such as career satisfaction, mental health, political attitudes, education, and most recently – your propensity to share misinformation.

So why did Kogan create this Facebook quiz? Well, he wasn't just interested in getting personality data from people via a survey. He wanted to match people's responses to their online activity. Before they participated, the app would ask users to consent to having public information scraped from their Facebook page, including their profile, page likes, birthday, city of residence, and sometimes even their newsfeed, posts and messages. To be fair to Kogan, this was common practice among app developers at the time; it was a standard Facebook feature that did not violate their terms of service. Facebook likes were considered public data, up for grabs for anyone interested. To help ensure that people would take part and answer all questions, Kogan paid about 270,000 people to participate in this quiz.

Here's where the controversy kicks in. What many of these people likely did not know is that the same information would also be automatically obtained from their friends – a feature Facebook technically allowed at the time before updating their developer policy in 2015. This seems like a clever, if highly unethical, trick from a data-gathering perspective: you pay 270,000 people – the 'seeders' – a few bucks ($3 or so each) to consent to sharing their data, and by automatically scraping the profiles of the friends of those individuals as well you can quickly turn this into a much larger data set.

Facebook estimated that Kogan's data set likely contained information on up to 87 million people worldwide (270,000 multiplied by an average of about 322 friends per user). In the UK, a couple of thousand initial participants ultimately yielded data on about 1 million UK residents. The 270,000 paid participants returned data on up to 70 million Americans specifically – 30 million of which were shared with Cambridge Analytica, who paid Kogan about £800,000 to get the data.

Around the same time, Kogan set up a private firm called Global Science Research (GSR) to house the data. Although Kogan did all of this in a private capacity, the app nonetheless mentioned that the data would only be used for 'academic purposes'. The fact that Kogan subsequently sold the data set to Cambridge Analytica for commercial interests clearly violated Facebook's terms of service, which at the time stated: 'You will not directly or indirectly transfer any data that you receive from us, including user data or Facebook User IDs to any ad network, ad exchange, data broker or other advertising or monetization related toolset.'

You can read rather conspiratorial accounts of Kogan on the internet. For example, he has been accused of being a 'Russian spy' because he gave guest lectures on social media at a Russian university in 2014, was born in Moldova (former Soviet Union), and changed his name to 'Spectre' after his marriage. (This also happens to be the name of the global criminal organization in the 2015 James Bond movie of the same name.) Although Kogan may not have been fully aware of what Cambridge Analytica would ultimately use the data for, he has at least acknowledged publicly that he knew it had to do with elections, and US Republican campaigns in particular, but did not care to investigate much further.

This is important because some of the principal investors in Cambridge Analytica were the American alt-right hedge-fund billionaire Robert Mercer and former executive chair of Breitbart News, Steve Bannon, who also served as Donald Trump's 2016 presidential campaign manager. Investigative journalist Carole Cadwalladr, who broke the Cambridge Analytica story in a 2017 *Guardian* feature, has detailed the personal connections between Cambridge Analytica's campaigns and the far-right political interests of Mercer, Bannon, Trump – and former leader of the UK's Brexit Party, Nigel Farage – in detail. But more on that later.

A key character in our story is whistleblower Christopher Wylie, an eccentric late-twenties Canadian data consultant and ex-Cambridge Analytica employee, who ended up creating what he called 'Steve Bannon's psychological warfare mindfuck tool'. In his book *Mindf*ck*, Wylie says that he came up with the plan to harvest data on millions of Facebook users and to leverage their online data to build psychological profiles that could then be used to target people with political ads that matched those profiles. Wylie refers to this as a modern adaptation of military 'Psyops' (psychological operations). But he needed help. Enter Kogan.

According to Kogan, Wylie got in touch to discuss turning this into a corporate project for Cambridge Analytica's parent company, 'SCL Elections Ltd'. SCL – which stands for 'Strategic Communications Laboratory' – is a military contractor founded in 1990 that engaged in psychological warfare on behalf of the US and UK governments and claims to have been the first private sector company to have offered 'influence operations'. Already back in 2005, the magazine *Slate* reported that the company had been influencing elections in developing countries by targeting voters and manipulating public opinion – often through disinformation.

Cambridge Analytica originally came about because Wylie wanted to understand why Canada's liberal democrats were losing elections and he had become intrigued by the new science of micro-targeting. The name 'Cambridge Analytica' arose purely because Bannon believed that the false association with 'Cambridge University' would make the whole operation sound more academic and scientific. According to Kogan, Wylie renamed his Facebook app and rewrote the terms of service for commercial purposes, assuring him that everything was legal and above board (though Wylie states it was ultimately Kogan's own responsibility to make sure his app was compliant with Facebook's terms). The harvested data was later sold to Cambridge Analytica via Kogan's new company, GSR, set up specifically for this project (which the UK's data protection authority verifies took place on 4 June 2014).

Wylie later found out that Bannon was intrigued by the idea of starting a culture war to change the course of US politics. Specifically, he discovered that Cambridge Analytica was going to use psychological targeting to start racial tensions in America and disengage voters during the 2016 US presidential election. After Wylie got wind of this, he left the company. Eventually, Cadwalladr convinced Wylie to blow the lid on the whole operation.

According to the signed contract, Kogan provided Cambridge Analytica with Facebook data on at least 30 million US citizens. This was not the full data set because Cambridge Analytica was specifically interested in personality data on Americans that they could match to other data they had gathered on US voters. The company's CEO, Alexander Nix, has repeatedly denied that they used Kogan's data in any way to target people with political messages when they were hired by the Trump presidential campaign. But in a public talk in 2016, Nix boasted that Cambridge Analytica could 'predict the personality of every single adult in the United States of America'. He went on to explain that they could then tailor ads to people's personalities. For example, someone 'high in Neuroticism' would need a fear-based message, such as an ad with an image of a scary burglary that reads: 'The second amendment isn't just a right. It's an insurance policy.' Conversely, someone 'high on Agreeableness' would see an ad based on tradition and family – with an image of say, a father teaching his son how to shoot, which reads: 'From father to son: Since the birth of our nation.' Another ad attacking same-sex marriage could feature a picture of a dictionary with the words: 'Look up "marriage" and get back to me. Because tradition is not old fashioned.' Dictionaries represent a source of order and structure which would appeal to someone high in 'Conscientiousness'.

Of course, the million-dollar question is whether any of this stuff actually works. Perhaps all the uproar over Cambridge Analytica and its putative influence on the 2016 US election is widely overblown? The whistleblower, Wylie, has certainly popularized a scary version of the science. Big claims have been made in the media about how so-called 'psychographic' data on people's personalities allows politicians to micro-target their messages to influence your vote. News headlines have blared 'Your Data and How It Is Used to Gain Your Vote', and 'Global Manipulation Is Out of Control'.

But I still remember something interesting that Kogan said to me during that conversation at the pub, back in the summer of 2016, long before the story broke. After I declined his offer to sell me data, he told me that his models were not very accurate anyway. The timing here is important: he told me this in private, long before all of this became public knowledge. Kogan never changed his story in the media and his testimony before the UK Parliament in 2018 reiterated that the modelling he did on the data did not prove useful in terms of predictive analytics. Indeed, respected researchers – including my own colleagues – have questioned the accuracy of these models and the science behind them.

So how do we know what's bullshit and what's legitimate?

On the one hand, nobody knows exactly what Cambridge Analytica was doing. On the other, a lot has happened since then. We know a lot more now. Science has progressed.

The UK's Information Commissioner's Office (ICO) spent three years examining forty-two laptops, thirty-one servers, tons of emails, and over 300,000 documents seized from former Cambridge Analytica employees and affiliated organizations, in one of the most in-depth and complex investigations ever carried out by a data protection authority on the use of personal data in a political context. The resulting report, issued in October 2020, found that 'there are systematic vulnerabilities in our democratic systems'. To understand why they reached this conclusion, we need to dive into the science behind 'psychographic micro-targeting'.

Can fake news influence the outcome of democratic elections?

As a first step towards answering this question, it's useful to take a look at what we know about whether fake news – in general – has disrupted the course of major elections. Can misinformation *directly* influence voter choices even when it is not micro-targeted? The answer might surprise you. Contrary to much of the commentary you may find in the popular media, scientists have been extremely sceptical.

Part of this scepticism stems from the fact that, although social scientists have been studying whether political campaigns have the power to persuade people to vote a certain way during elections for decades, there's been very little evidence that they do so directly. This is an important distinction. It may well be that campaigns influence public opinion, play into stereotypes and prejudices, and even shape how people feel about candidates – but the question at hand is whether they influence voting decisions directly. For example, one study, conducted ahead of the 2016 presidential election, found that when false claims Trump had made were corrected, Trump supporters were less likely to believe them, but it didn't change their voting preferences at all.

So, do campaigns have the power to change who we vote for? A 2016 analysis of forty field experiments by American political scientists Joshua Kalla and David Broockman estimated the average persuasive effect of traditional campaigns (including TV, radio, and canvassing) on voting decisions to be close to zero. To be precise, the researchers estimated that 'campaign contact' persuaded about 1 in 800 voters (0.13 per cent) – hardly enough to sway an election.

The same year, economists Hunt Allcott and Matthew Gentzkow were the first to try to quantify the effect of fake news on the 2016 US presidential election. The duo put some facts together to paint a persuasive picture of why we might be concerned about the role of fake news during major elections. For example, they stated that a majority of US adults (62 per cent) now get their news from social media. This is potentially problematic because the spread of fake news can outpace mainstream news on platforms such as Facebook; people often report that they believe such fake news stories when exposed to them; and the most viral fake news stories favoured Donald Trump over Hillary Clinton.

But did fake news swing the 2016 US presidential election? Their answer is a firm no.

As part of their investigation, Allcott and Gentzkow created a database of 156 news stories relevant to the election, categorized as either true or false by three independent online fact-checkers (*Snopes*, *PolitiFact*, and *Buzzfeed*). An example of a fake news entry in their database is a story from 'wtoe5news.com' with the following headline: 'Pope Francis Shocks World, Endorses Donald Trump for President'. They then figured out how often each story was shared on Facebook in the three months before the 2016 election. In total, the 156 stories were shared about 38 million times and the team could confirm that most fake stories were, indeed, pro-Trump (115 stories, shared 30 million times versus 41 pro-Clinton stories, shared 7.6 million times). So how do we get from this information to an estimate of how often each American was exposed to fake news?

Based on known social media estimates, they wagered that a typical share on Facebook generates about twenty page visits. Given the known 38 million shares of fake news stories in their database, that amounts to about 20 × 38 million, which equals 760 million page visits. If we divide 760 million by the adult US population in 2016 (about 248 million Americans) we arrive at about three visits to fake news websites per adult. That's not much.

To get another estimate, the researchers also conducted a post-election survey with about 1,200 Americans. As part of the survey, the researchers asked people whether they remembered hearing about or seeing a set of fifteen articles in the months leading up to the US election and whether they believed that the articles were true or fake (some of the fake articles were placebos made up by the researchers themselves). What they found was peculiar: people reported having seen the placebo and fake articles at about an equal rate (14 versus 15 per cent). Assuming that the rate at which people remember the placebos is a good estimate of false recall, the differential (+ 1 per cent) must be the true exposure rate. Combined with how often the stories in their survey were shared on Facebook, the researchers could now calculate the likelihood that the average adult saw a fake news article during the 2016 US election.

The result? A single fake headline.

I must admit that I was fairly dismissive of this estimate, if not solely based on my personal experience of definitely seeing more than one fake news article during the 2016 presidential election. The economists based their model on a lot of assumptions, and it's up to the reader to decide how reasonable these are. For one, is their list of 156 fake news stories representative of the full universe of fake news stories? Probably not as it contains only a subsample of fact-checked headlines that mostly excluded manipulative and biased news media, which are much more prevalent. We can also question whether people can accurately remember what fake news they were exposed to, or whether the researchers' quiz of fifteen items was a good representative test of that.

Allcott and Gentzkow do confirm that most fake news was indeed pro-Trump in its orientation and more likely to reach people via social media. However, they do not think that these facts necessarily mean that fake news had the ability to meaningfully interfere with the election. On the contrary, based on their estimates, exposure to fake news couldn't have amounted to much during the 2016 presidential election. For example, they reason that a single exposure to the most persuasive political campaign ads on TV have been shown to influence vote shares by only about 0.02 per cent. Assuming that exposure to a single fake news article is as persuasive as a TV ad, that's not enough to swing an election in key states, not even close. Other studies have corroborated these findings by analysing people's browser data during the final weeks of the 2016 election, estimating that just under half of American adults visited about one untrustworthy website.

I was still sceptical. While this work was a good first attempt at analysing the problem, the studies do not fully account for filter bubbles and echo chambers, which we know from the previous chapter play an important role in the diffusion and upranking of fake news. In fact,

Allcott and Gentzkow note that the estimates were larger for people with more ideologically segregated networks.

A number of recent studies have tackled some of these limitations by looking at social media data. One influential study by David Lazer's lab – a computer science group at Northeastern University – was able to link official US voter registration records to Twitter accounts to form a panel of 16,442 individuals that was fairly reflective of the US population. Overall, the team found that while the frequency of fake-news sharing fluctuated during the 2016 presidential election season, they also discovered something fascinating: just 0.1 per cent of the panel accounted for almost 80 per cent of all fake-news sharing. Similarly, about 1 per cent of the panel consumed nearly 80 per cent of it. Lazer and colleagues refer to these individual accounts as 'supersharers' and 'superconsumers'.

They calculated that on average, a panel member had the potential to be exposed to about 204 fake news stories during the last month of the election campaign. Assuming that about 5 per cent of these potential exposures are actually seen or remembered, that comes to about ten fake news stories for that month. That estimate is higher than Allcott and Gentzkow's but, given the widely different methodologies, Lazer and his team interpret their results to be in the same order of magnitude: on average, people were exposed to a relatively small set of fake news articles during the crucial months of the 2016 election campaign.

The added nuance that Lazer's team brings to the table is the finding that most of the fake news content was being driven by a minority of 'super-spreaders'. So, who are these people? Lazer's investigation found that a majority of the content came from the far right and was pro-Trump. Less than 5 per cent of people on the left (or centre) shared any fake news at all, whereas that number was about four times higher (20 per cent) for people on the extreme right. In fact, a growing number of studies have now all converged on the finding that – at least during the 2016 presidential election – fake news formed a relatively small (0.15 per cent to 6 per cent) part of people's overall media diet and was much more likely to be shared by older, predominantly white, male, and conservative Trump supporters who were politically active on social media, especially Facebook. Because most people are not highly politically active, some colleagues have therefore dismissed the idea that fake news has directly influenced election results.

However, all of these studies still run the risk of severely underestimating the problem. According to a national survey from Pew, in December 2016, 32 per cent of Americans said they often encountered political fake news online; 51 per cent said they often see inaccurate news; and 23 per cent self-report having shared fake news. In Europe, 68 per cent of those surveyed report seeing fake news on a weekly basis. Something doesn't add up. Either people's memories are suspect, or the models are way off.* For example, if you closely inspect the paper published by Lazer and his team, you'll find a somewhat peculiar definition of how they classify fake news. They do not pay attention to the stories themselves but determine 'fakeness' solely based on the credibility of the publisher. This makes some sense – for example, *Infowars* would be flagged for having a flawed editorial process – but focusing solely on the publisher could lead to the exclusion of lots of other relevant news content. In addition, the assumption in Lazer's study that out of the potential to be exposed to some 200 URLs during the last month of the election, on average, only 5 per cent convert to actual views is of course subject to debate – an issue the authors recognize. For example, other papers that have analysed Twitter content – including over 30 million tweets that contain links to outside media sources – have put the exposure number on fake news at closer to 10 per cent (and 15 per cent for extremely biased news).

What concerns me even more is that people's media diet is of course not restricted to Twitter. We also receive news content from Facebook, WhatsApp, TikTok, Reddit, and so on. So, what if the actual rate is more like 25 per cent? Using Lazer's data, it means that, on average, an individual would have been exposed to fifty fake news articles in the last month of the election (instead of ten), which translates to about twelve to thirteen articles a week or at least one a day. That could be influential. At minimum, I think we need to be cognizant of the fact that these estimates are only as good as the assumptions that go into the model.

---

* A third explanation is that the mainstream media amplifies people's familiarity with fake news.

Although these global estimates are somewhat useful when trying to quantify the issue, perhaps the influence of fake news is more subtle and strategic. In fact, three researchers from Ohio State University took an entirely different approach to looking at the problem. They conducted a representative post-election survey among the American public, zooming in on the voting behaviour of 660 individuals in particular: those who had voted for Barack Obama back in 2012. The research team noticed a peculiar pattern when examining the behaviour of previous Obama voters: though the majority voted for Hillary Clinton in 2016, 10 per cent of them cast ballots for Trump, 4 per cent switched to a minor party candidate, and 8 per cent disengaged and did not vote at all. Could it be that fake news was responsible for the high 'defection' rate of previous Obama voters?

The team asked people to rate three widely circulated and influential fake news stories about Hillary Clinton. One article insinuated that she was in poor health due to a serious illness; the other alleged that during her time as US Secretary of State she sold weapons to militant groups, including ISIS; and the final headline claimed that Pope Francis endorsed Donald Trump for president. In general, about 10 per cent (Pope Francis) to 35 per cent (ISIS) of the sample thought these headlines were probably or definitely true. Moreover, amongst Obama voters who did not buy into any of these fake news stories, 89 per cent voted for Clinton – but this figure dropped dramatically, to just 17 per cent for Obama voters who were duped by at least 2 out of the 3 false headlines! Of course, there could be lots of reasons other than fake news that caused former Obama voters to defect from the 2016 Democratic ticket; an alternative explanation might be that they just didn't like Hillary Clinton.

However, in a large model that controls for many of these alternative accounts – including people's feelings about Trump, Clinton, party affiliation, gender, age, education, race, views about immigration and the economy – the researchers estimated that the probability an individual would defect from voting for Hillary Clinton still increased on average by 18 per cent the more participants believed the fake news. In other words, the influence of fake news 'survived' in the model even when accounting for these other explanations.

But was it sufficient to swing the election? The researchers argue that Hillary Clinton lost in the key battleground states of Michigan, Wisconsin, and Pennsylvania by a mere 0.6 per cent of the votes cast in those states. The researchers were not able to generate state-level predictions, but they argue that if the data for these key states resemble what they observed nationwide, then fake news might have cost Clinton the election by causing substantial defection among prior Obama voters.

Critics are quick to point out that this study was not a randomized experiment, so we cannot be sure that fake news was the root cause of the loss in votes. Others argue that the data was self-reported and gathered after the election had taken place, which could have introduced biases into some people's responses. These are fair critiques, but similar issues apply to other studies. The Allcott and Gentzkow study could suffer from self-report bias and none of the other studies constitute randomized controlled experiments either. How could they? Randomly administering fake news to half the population to see if and how it might influence their vote during a major election would be highly unethical.

Therefore, at one end of the spectrum we have results which cast serious doubt on the potential for fake news to disrupt elections, and at the other social media studies which attribute most of the problem to super-spreaders, whereas still others predict that fake news could have influenced the election but in more strategic ways by causing voter defection in key swing states. My own view is that we are likely misperceiving the real impact of fake news on elections. For starters, the lists of false content that we use to check whether people have been exposed to fake news are limited and incomplete so our estimates might be off. In addition, it's not just web browsing or WhatsApp groups or YouTube videos or Twitter posts or Facebook's newsfeed or TV or radio. It's all of it at the same time, repeatedly. But, most crucially, all of these studies have one key fact in common that could lead to a severe underestimation: none of them account for the impact of micro-targeting fake news based on the psychographic profiling of millions of voters – which brings us back to Cambridge Analytica.

The digital traces you leave behind

Cambridge Analytica was already in the business of obtaining information about voters, long before Aleksandr Kogan. In the United States, you can purchase commercial voter files. These often contain publicly available information on who is registered to vote and whether someone voted in any given election but not *who* they voted for. More recently, however, these companies have been able to integrate voter data with other information that might be available about you, such as customer data obtained from credit companies and political organizations. Typically, a commercial voter file will thus not only include your name and voter history but also information about your gender, race, education, political views, magazine subscriptions, donations to charity, and anything else they can find on you.

Voter files are therefore increasingly marketed as providing rich data on every American adult. Scientists use these files to try to predict voter turnout in elections, but you can easily see how political consulting firms might be interested in these data to try to influence election *outcomes*. Christopher Wylie has talked about how predicting people's behaviour based on socio-demographic information alone has not been particularly successful. I can attest to that based on my own knowledge from evaluating such models in the scientific literature. Knowing how often someone votes, volunteers, and so on, is not sufficient to predict their stance on a particular issue. For targeting purposes, such models rarely outperform a 50 per cent random guessing pattern. You need more. You need psychological data. Wylie realized this and that's why he got so excited about Kogan's personality data. When you combine voter files with consumer and psychological data such as personality traits, you have a potentially powerful weapon.

The plan was that Kogan was going to supply the firm with the raw or predicted personality data based on his Facebook app and Cambridge Analytica would subsequently merge the personality scores with their commercial voter registration files. Matching the data proved easy. The Facebook data resulted in an additional 253 predicted features for each individual in the database. Each feature could just be a single 'like' or a predicted trait. The point is that these extra columns were Cambridge's Analytica's 'secret sauce' – something nobody else could offer. Micro-targeting would potentially become much more accurate this way.

To get a glimpse at what this datafile looked like, David Carroll, Professor of Media at the New School, New York, was able to obtain his own data from Cambridge Analytica through a Freedom of Information (FOI) request. It included information on where he lives, whether he voted, and a predicted score on his personality traits and how much he cares about policy issues (such as the economy, immigration, and gun rights). But no information was given on how they obtained these predictions.

They were, in fact, based on models.

To understand how these predictions might have been generated, we need to demystify how these models work.

The term 'machine learning' is often thrown around in the media as a powerful example of artificial intelligence (AI), but few people have a good handle on what it means. In its simplest form, machine learning refers to the idea that computers can learn from data without being explicitly told to do so. In predictive modelling, most of the learning is 'supervised', meaning that the computer is given examples using data for which labels – such as 'extraverts' – are provided so that the algorithm can learn what patterns of data match a certain label. Basically, what happens is that algorithms are trained to detect patterns in massive amounts of data in order to make future predictions on new data. You typically have what is called a 'training' data set – the data you use to train the model on. But you often want to hold out, or separate, part of the data to test and validate the model's predictions once it's sufficiently trained – this is called the 'testing' data set.

To illustrate, let's apply this logic to the context of predicting people's attitudes about climate change. The Yale University Program on Climate Change Communication has identified six segments of the American public, which it calls 'Global Warming's Six Americas'. Each segment represents a unique community in terms of how people think, feel, and act on the issue of climate change. (For example, 'the Alarmed' segment, which makes up about 26 per cent of the US population, are generally liberal in their politics and very concerned about the issue of climate change. By contrast, the 'Dismissive', who make up about 8 per cent of the population, tend to be conservative and deny that human-caused climate change is real.) Much like the Big Five personality test, people are binned into these segments based on their responses to a long (thirty-six-question) survey covering their background and beliefs on the issue. It stands to reason that if you want to target people on the issue of climate change, it is important to tailor your message to the right audience. This is called 'audience segmentation'.

However, getting people to fill out a thirty-six-item survey is time-consuming and difficult. When I worked at Yale, we gathered heaps of data to see if we could use machine-learning algorithms to uncover the questions that seem most essential in correctly classifying people into one of the six segments. It turns out we were in luck because my wife, Breanne, happens to be a brilliant statistician and data scientist. She unleashed an algorithm on part of the data to 'train' it to predict the outcome of interest; correctly classifying people into one of the Six Americas. Once we trained the predictive model it identified four out of the thirty-six questions that proved most essential, including how worried people were about the issue and how important climate change is to them personally. We then used some of the other data sets the algorithm wasn't trained on – as well as entirely new data sets – to test and evaluate its overall accuracy in predicting these segments by comparing the model's estimates to the actual data.

What we found is that the four-item version was able to correctly classify people into each of the six segments with an accuracy rate of about 70–87 per cent, depending on the segment. So, is that good? Well, consider that with thirty-six items the model can correctly classify people in each of the six segments with 79–99 per cent accuracy. We evaluated the slight drop in accuracy favourably given that we could now identify whether someone is one of the Alarmed, Concerned, Cautious, Disengaged, Doubtful, or Dismissive with decent accuracy, using just four instead of thirty-six questions!

So far so good. But what if I were to tell you that I could predict your personality (or attitudes towards climate change for that matter) solely based on your social media data? This is a radical idea. Instead of asking people to consent to participating in a survey or opinion poll we simply scrape their digital footprints online and use that behavioural data to predict people's personality. This is the major innovation that got Wylie and Kogan excited about big data – but it was neither Wylie nor Kogan who pioneered the science.

The idea came from two other researchers, David Stillwell, Professor of Computational Social Science at the University of Cambridge, and Michal Kosinski, now Associate Professor at Stanford University. Stillwell ran a Facebook application called *myPersonality*. The app allowed users to take psychometric tests and returned a personality profile in exchange for participants consenting to share data from their Facebook profile purely for scientific purposes. At the time, it was one of the largest data sets in the history of social science with about 6 million people.

Kogan had put Wylie in touch with Stillwell and Kosinski too, but once they figured out that Cambridge Analytica was not interested in funding a grant for academic research, they backed out of the project. Kogan decided he would pursue it by himself in a private capacity. He figured he could create an app similar to the one Stillwell and Kosinski had been using on his own – which he did – and that's how *This Is Your Digital Life* was born.

To better understand how accurate Kogan's model and data were in predicting people's characteristics from their social media data, we can turn to the pioneering work that Stillwell and Kosinski published back in 2013. By looking at what Stillwell and Kosinski found in their studies, we can get a pretty good feel for what happened with Cambridge Analytica.

In 2013, Kosinski and Stillwell published a paper in the *Proceedings of the National Academy of Sciences* (a prestigious journal) which leveraged data from the *myPersonality* Facebook app. Back then, Kosinski and Stillwell were the first to match people's survey responses – including the Big Five personality test – to their Facebook data. They were able to match data on about 58,000 consenting volunteers from the United States. The digital records of online behaviour that they were after were people's Facebook profiles and their 'likes'.

At its very core, a Facebook like represents a user expressing a positive association with a particular piece of content, whether it's a photo, a status update from a friend, or a Facebook page about music, sports, culture, or science. On average, Kosinski and Stillwell obtained about 170 likes per individual. With this information in hand, they could now compare how well a model trained purely on Facebook likes could predict people's personal and psychological characteristics. They did this by comparing the model's predicted answers to the actual answers, which were obtained from information that people self-declared on their Facebook profiles (such as their gender or relationship status) as well as the answers they gave during the psychometric tests that were completed as part of the survey.

The finding that shocked the research community (and the world) was that by using just Facebook likes, Kosinski and Stillwell were able to predict your gender with 93 per cent accuracy, your politics with 85 per cent accuracy, your ethnicity with 95 per cent accuracy, and even your sexual orientation with 88 per cent accuracy. Of course, some of these findings are fairly intuitive. For example, the fact that you're likely to be a Democrat if you liked 'Barack Obama' is not overly surprising. But Kosinski and Stillwell argue that this was not always the case. For example, very few users who identified as being gay and male liked sites with titles such as 'I love being gay'. Instead, the researchers found that liking 'Wicked the Musical' was far more predictive. In comparison, they found that liking 'Shaq' (the former U. S. basketball player) and a page titled 'Being Confused After Waking Up From Naps' were good predictors of male heterosexuality. Some of the best predictors of how well people performed on a standard (non-verbal) IQ test were likes that included 'The Colbert Report', 'Science', and 'Curly Fries', whereas lower IQ scores were associated with liking pages with titles such as 'Harley Davidson', 'Sephora', and 'I Love Being a Mom'.*

But remember that Cambridge Analytica had already obtained commercial databases with information on voters that likely included actual or modelled data on citizens' political orientation, income, gender, ethnicity, and other personal attributes. What they were really

---

* Stephen Colbert was quick to point out that liking his show is associated with high IQ.

after was data on psychological traits such as people's personalities. So how well did Kosinski and Stillwell's model perform for the Big Five 'OCEAN' model?

In turns out, their model performed worse on more complex psychological traits such as personality. The correlation between the model's predicted and people's actual answers was 0.3 for Agreeableness, 0.4 for Extraversion, 0.29 for Conscientiousness and 0.43 for Openness. People high in Agreeableness tended to like the 'The Book of Mormon' (the musical), 'Mitt Romney', and 'camping', whereas people low in Agreeableness liked pages such as 'I Hate Everyone'. People high in Openness tended to like the 'Hello Kitty' brand; whereas Extraverts liked 'Nicki Minaj' and 'Lady Gaga'. Makes some sense.

But note that this finding is consistent with what Kogan told me about his own models that night in the pub: the correlations are not that impressive. A correlation in the range of 0.30 to 0.40 is considered relatively small in our field. Kosinski and Stillwell don't report this in the paper themselves, but a back-of-the-envelope calculation suggests that these kinds of correlations would translate into an accuracy rate of about 67–73 per cent depending on the personality trait in question. In predictive modelling, 70 per cent accuracy is not particularly good but generally considered 'acceptable'.

David Sumpter, Professor of Applied Mathematics at the University of Uppsala in Sweden, did his own replication of Kosinski and Stillwell's data and came to a similar conclusion. Overall, he estimated the accuracy of the Facebook likes model at about 60 per cent across the personality traits. One key take-away from these results is therefore that predicting people's personality based on their Facebook likes is not as easy as predicting other personal traits and requires many more likes – in fact, hundreds of them.

But Kosinksi and Stillwell say we should put these numbers in context. They compared how well people's friends, family, colleagues, and even their spouse can predict an individual's personality compared to the predictions of their model (which was once again based on Facebook likes). What they found was astonishing: the computer algorithm could outperform the accuracy of a work colleague's prediction of someone's personality with just ten likes. It needed just 70 likes to outperform the prediction of friends, 150 likes to outperform family, and about 300 likes to be able to outperform a spouse. The idea that a computer algorithm trained on your Facebook likes can estimate your personality with the same level of accuracy as your spouse is pretty scary.

However, the fact that Facebook likes just so happen to correlate, to a certain degree, with people's personalities does not imply that targeting people with an ad based on their personalities actually causes them to do anything. Or does it?

Kosinski and Stillwell returned for the sequel. They wanted to evaluate whether such predictions are actually accurate enough to allow for real-world micro-targeting.

Back in 2012, Facebook had already filed a patent called 'Determining user personality characteristics from social networking system communications'. Part of the patent reads: 'the inferred personality characteristics are stored in connection with the user's profile, and may be used for targeting'. So clearly Facebook had been developing a similar technology of their own which could be used for targeting people with ads based on their personality.

Kogan had expressed sceptical views about the idea that his data and models could be used for micro-targeting. For example, in his parliamentary hearing in London in 2018 he pointed out that rather than working with noisy estimates, why not go to Facebook directly and ask them to micro-target advertisements to millions of people based on a set of pre-selected criteria? Kogan has a point. For example, in 2017, Facebook got in trouble because they temporarily allowed people to target 'Jew Haters' with ads which Facebook associated with 2,774 people who listed 'Jew Hater' on their profile page. Other selection criteria included 'how to Burn Jews' and 'Hitler did nothing wrong'. Once Facebook discovered what was going on, they swiftly deleted these categories. But the point is that, although Kogan is right that it's possible to directly target people on Facebook based on a wide range of (concerning) criteria, what he left out is that you cannot target people based on known psychological traits. So, Cambridge Analytica could not simply have gone to Facebook to select 'Neuroticism' or 'Openness' as potential categories for targeting ads.

So, what, if anything, could Cambridge Analytica have done with Kogan's personality data?

Because you cannot target people directly based on their personality on Facebook, Sandra Matz (now Associate Professor of Business at Columbia University) together with Kosinski and Stillwell came up with a very clever workaround for their follow-up study. It turns out that you *can* target people on Facebook based on their likes. So Matz, Kosinski, and Stillwell were able to draw on their previous research to figure out what likes were most strongly associated with different personality traits. They decided to focus on Extraversion and Openness for the experiment because their past models achieved the highest accuracy in predicting these traits from Facebook likes. In particular, the researchers looked at likes associated with the highest and lowest levels of Openness and Extraversion. (For example, target likes for introversion included 'computer' and '*Battlestar Galactica*', while target likes for high levels of Extraversion included 'Parties' and 'Making People Laugh'.)

In the first experiment, Matz, Kosinski and Stillwell selected women as their target group for a UK-based beauty retailer. They designed several ads. Some were meant to speak to individuals high on the scale for Extraversion – for example, one featured a young energetic female dancing and laughing with the text, 'Dance like nobody is watching (but they totally are).' Conversely, the Introversion (or low Extraversion) ad portrayed a young shy female doing her make-up alone at home with the text, 'Beauty doesn't have to shout.' In a nutshell, they designed two versions of the same ad, one to appeal to people high and the other to people low in Extraversion.

The team subsequently went to the Facebook advertising platform and under 'Interests' entered the relevant page likes (such as 'Making People Laugh' for Extraversion, and '*Serenity*', 'Computer', etc., for introversion). Facebook then returned the number of people who liked these relevant pages. For the first study, the team also selected some other targeting criteria, such as females aged 18–40 living in the UK. The ad campaign was real and featured on people's Facebook pages for about a week.

After a week the ad campaign reached over 3 million people who clicked on the ads over 10,000 times with nearly 400 actual purchases from the beauty retailer's website. But did the ads perform better when they were targeted at a user's personality traits? They clearly did: people were much more likely to purchase a product when they viewed an ad that was consistent with their predicted personality trait. For example, Facebook users higher in Extraversion were 50 per cent more likely to make a purchase if the ad was correctly targeted at extraverts versus not (117 versus 62 purchases).

But Matz, Kosinski and Stillwell did not just stick to the beauty store. In a second version of the experiment, they decided to use the exact same approach but now target people to download a crossword puzzle app based on 'Openness', that is, how open people are to new experiences. This time around, the campaign reached 84,176 users who clicked on the ads 1,130 times culminating in over 500 downloads. Once again, the researchers found that, across the whole campaign, if the ad shown to people was congruent with their predicted personality trait, this increased the odds of clicks by 38 per cent and app installations by 31 per cent (compared to users who received an ad that conflicted with their personality).

In a final and third study, the research team decided to look at a real-world context where a marketing strategy was already in place. Specifically, they selected a bubble shooter game and followed the company's marketing strategy, which was to target it at those individuals who'd previously shown interest in similar games (such as *Farmville*). By comparing these likes with data from their *myPersonality* app, the team was able to determine that people who play this game are highly introverted. Matz, Kosinski and Stillwell compared the company's standard message to a psychologically tailored version for introverts ('Phew! Hard Day? How about a puzzle to wind down with?'). Both campaigns again ran for a week on the Facebook platform. Results revealed that the micro-targeted message again significantly increased both the likelihood of people clicking on the ad (by 30 per cent) and installing the app (by 15 per cent) compared to the standard campaign.

This is pretty convincing evidence given that for these real-world experiments the researchers only used a *single* like (the most extreme one) to target people on Facebook. In a simulation buried in the technical appendix, the researchers make an important observation. Although the average accuracy of their prediction model varies, it depends on the discriminatory power of the 'like' in question. By that, we mean that some likes are more predictive of, say, 'Openness' than others. If you can find the likes that are most predictive of a given personality trait (and thus have high discriminatory power) you can boost the model's accuracy substantially. (For example, the average accuracy across all traits for likes with a low discriminatory power is just 58 per cent – barely above chance – but it can improve to close to 70 per cent for likes with high discriminatory power.) The team estimated that for specific traits such as Openness, the model's accuracy could be as high as 82 per cent, whereas Agreeableness seems to max out at about 61 per cent. This leads to a few important insights.

The first is that accuracy clearly differs for different personality traits and Matz, Kosinski and Stillwell's findings may be optimistic in the sense that they targeted traits in the experiment that can be predicted with the highest degree of accuracy. But it also suggests that a trade-off must be made between accuracy and reach. If you want to be more accurate, you need a larger number of 'likes'. But when you select many likes on the Facebook advertising platform you decrease the potential pool of people you can reach. (For example, although a few million people might like 'Party' pages, fewer people are going to like 'Party' *and* 'I like to meet new people'; and even fewer people will have liked 'Party' *and* 'I like to meet new people' *and* 'Lady Gaga' and so on.) So, targeting people with the highest level of precision means that you cannot reach hundreds of millions of people all at once. So, what level of accuracy will still give a micro-targeter sufficient reach? Well, Facebook is a huge platform, so the researchers estimate that even with *eight* likes, you can still reach about 6 million people.

You might reason that downloading an app or buying a beauty product is not the same as influencing who somebody is going to vote for. Although it is true that converting 'votes' is a lot harder than converting 'clicks', it is certainly not impossible.

For example, my good Cambridge colleague Lee de Wit, Assistant Professor of Psychology and author of *What's Your Bias?* conducted a study in the context of Brexit where he first gave people a personality quiz to determine their level of, say, Conscientiousness or Openness. He specifically targeted about 400 Remain supporters and exposed them to arguments in favour of *leaving* the EU framed to appeal to either those high or low on a particular personality trait. (An example for those scoring high in 'Conscientiousness' would be a media article talking about how immigration is causing 'disorder' and the need to 'systematically regulate the influx of people'.) Results showed that convincing Remainers of Leave arguments worked better if the ad was congruent with their personality profile: they thought the arguments were more credible and they were more likely to vote for a party making those kind of claims. But Lee told me that not all of the study's findings were so clear cut. Moreover, the study was not conducted on a social media platform.

In 2020, Dutch researchers tried to address this problem. They created a fake social media platform with the feel and look of Facebook. The cover story was that participants would log on to the platform to help test a new social network for the university. In the first phase of the experiment, they were asked to fill out some profile information and write a bit about themselves (on average, people wrote about seventy-three words). The researchers then employed something called 'automated text analysis'. What happens is that a machine-learning classifier is trained on a large existing database of text from people who previously self-declared their personality profile. This classifier is then used on the writing and profile information of the participants in the experiment to automatically detect linguistic features that distinguish, say, extraverts from introverts. Out of the 230 initial participants, they were able to reliably identify about 75 introverts and 81 extraverts.

In the next part of the experiment, these individuals were targeted with an ad in their social media feed. The message was a progressive left-wing ad for the Dutch green party. The only change was the text around the ad, which was manipulated to be either extraverted ('bring out the hero in you') or introverted. They then asked whether people would vote for the party on a scale ranging from very unlikely (1) to very likely (7).

Here the results were unambiguous: voting intentions were substantially (about 35 per cent) higher if the extraverted ad was targeted at extraverts as opposed to introverts and vice versa. In a second experiment, the researchers also manipulated the emotional tone of the messages and found that fear-based messages were more effective for introverts, whereas positive enthusiasm-based messages fared better with extraverts.

To me, this is clear causal evidence that political micro-targeting works, at least in a semi-realistic social media setting. What is so concerning about this result is that, as opposed to regular political ads, people cannot reasonably defend themselves against persuasion attacks when they don't even know that they are being targeted.

But what are we to make of Kalla and Broockman's earlier claim that the average persuasive effect of a political campaign ad on voter choice is close to zero? Well, the authors point to one interesting and important exception: 'when campaigns invest unusually heavily in identifying persuadable voters'. Only by being able to identify the right audience for their message in advance and by then strategically zooming in on that audience, were studies able to achieve success. Kalla and Broockman argue that these circumstances are unusual because they require a lot of investment and sophistication and most voters do not reply to surveys. But with companies scraping every digital footprint we leave behind on the internet, they no longer need surveys. Organizations can use Facebook likes to understand people's psychological traits and what their stance on a particular issue might be. They can then invest heavily in identifying subgroups of persuadable voters and micro-target them with tailored advertisements.

After all, why would companies invest millions of dollars in advertising their products every year if it didn't work? Why bother with political campaigns if the effect is negligible?

An important metric in persuasive advertising campaigns is the 'conversion rate'. The conversion rate is the number of hard 'conversions' (whether it is a purchase or vote) relative to the number of times an ad is shown. You might be surprised to learn that average conversion rates are really low. It's therefore important for political campaigns to invest tons of money into buying ads. It's hard to get people to buy things or vote a certain way, so you have to bombard people with ads *repeatedly*. Micro-targeting can make this process much more efficient. For example, in Matz, Kosinski and Stillwell's experiment, the ads that were tailored to extraverts reached 841,308 people out of whom 117 purchased an item. That's a conversion rate of 0.014 per cent. In contrast, when the ad shown didn't match the user's personality the conversion rate was much lower (just 0.008 per cent). The micro-targeting strategy thus helped bring the cost down by a whopping 50 per cent to only about £8 ($11) per conversion. The ads themselves are pretty cheap to run, so the return on investment an organization is going to see goes up dramatically with proper targeting. What's often well understood by marketers but mis-understood by scientists is that, even at low conversion rates or 'near zero' persuasion effects, it's still very profitable to target people with ads.

Micro-targeting: a psychological weapon of mass persuasion

During high-stakes elections, thousands of variations of the same ad are often being tested on millions of users to exploit people's vulnerabilities at a highly specific level.

Let's have a look at some prominent examples where micro-targeting has been used.

Dominic Cummings, director of the UK's Brexit 'Vote Leave' cam-paign, ran *a billion* targeted digital ads and spent £2.9 million (nearly 40 per cent of the campaign's total budget) on just one firm called Aggre-gate IQ (AIQ), a Canadian political consulting firm with close ties to Cambridge Analytica. The Brexit referendum itself came down to a tiny difference of just 4 per cent (52 per cent versus 48 per cent). Shortly after the referendum, Cummings is quoted as saying: 'Without a doubt, the Vote Leave campaign owes a great deal of its success to the work of Aggre-gate IQ. We couldn't have done it without them.'

AIQ offers micro-targeting services on Facebook. In fact, the official 'Vote Leave' campaign was fined by the Electoral College for overspend-ing the official limit by about £500,000 (funds that were funnelled to AIQ via another Leave campaign, known as 'BeLeave'). Although Cambridge Analytica claimed to not have consulted on the official Leave campaign – which focused more on economic issues – they did consult with the competition: the right-wing populist Leave.EU campaign (which focused more on immigration). An investigation by the Privacy Commissioner's Office in Canada revealed that AIQ failed in its duty to verify that informed consent had been obtained to use personal data to micro-target UK citizens on Facebook on behalf of the official Vote Leave campaign.

Whether Cambridge Analytica – or AggregateIQ – used Kogan's Facebook data or his modelled predictions remains a matter of controversy. Christopher Wylie testified that the data were transferred to Cambridge Analytica and that all of Cambridge Analytica's algorithms were originally trained using Kogan's Facebook data, even if not ultimately used in the Trump presidential campaign. Cambridge Analytica's CEO, Alexander Nix, bragged that his firm held over 5,000 datapoints per individual for as many as 230 million Americans. The ICO's independent audit revealed that although this may have been an exaggeration, they did uncover multiple databases that held hundreds of datapoints on up to 160 million people. That's a lot of data that could inform micro-targeting strategies.

In the end, we will perhaps never know the extent to which the improperly obtained Facebook data were used for micro-targeting during the Brexit and Trump campaigns. However, the more important takeaway is that micro-targeting strategies were heavily deployed on Facebook regardless, by both the Trump and Brexit campaigns, and this might – and likely will – happen again in the future. Although we've seen emerging evidence that micro-targeting can persuade individuals, the question of whether it can swing an *entire* election remains.

Jens Madsen, a colleague and Assistant Professor of Psychology at the London School of Economics and Political Science, wanted to evaluate how effective micro-targeting could be during an election, based on a range of different assumptions about the electoral system. In order to do this, Madsen and his co-author, Toby Pilditch, created a simulated world with three kinds of actors: voters; political candidates who make use of micro-targeted campaigns; and political candidates who rely on traditional campaigns. At the beginning of the computer simulation, each voter is given a score that determines how credible they find each political candidate. The key question is how people's voting preferences change in response to a micro-targeted election campaign.

Crucially, the 'traditional' campaign operated more or less blindly, disseminating its message using a 'one-size-fits-all' approach that assumed no special knowledge of the electorate. In contrast, the micro-targeted campaign first segmented the voters, then contacted only those who were likely to come out to vote during the election; those deemed 'persuadable' (that is, not holding overly strong views for or against a particular candidate); and those who found the candidate in question at least somewhat credible. For the purpose of the simulated world, there were 10,000 voters, two political candidates running against each other, and the campaign period lasted just shy of about two months. In total, Madsen and Pilditch ran about 9,000 simulations.

The results were clear. Assuming both candidates had equal reach, the candidate who employed micro-targeting won every election across *all combinations* of perceived credibility of the candidate. In other words, even when the candidate who used the traditional approach was deemed more credible, the only way to beat the micro-targeted campaign was to increase the campaign's overall reach. When both candidates were generally liked, the traditional candidate needed to reach about five times as many voters to keep up with the micro-targeted campaign. In the simulated world, this implied that in order to stay ahead, the traditional campaign needed to reach about a hundred voters per day for every twenty micro-targeted voters. Moreover, even when the traditional candidate was generally preferred amongst voters, simulations suggest that they still needed to reach about twice as many voters when competing against a candidate who employs strategic micro-targeting.

Granted, this is just a theoretical simulation. But in 2022, evidence of a real-world micro-targeting experiment during an election was finally published. The experiment was conducted during the 2018 US midterm elections. By partnering with an advocacy organization in Texas, Katherine Haenschen, Assistant Professor of Communication at Northeastern University, was able to study the influence of a political ad campaign. Unlike a small lab study, she identified about 900,000 registered voters. The advocacy organization uploaded a commercial voter file to Facebook's 'Custom Audience' feature, which allowed the team to assign specific voters to either a control or different treatment conditions. There were four different treatment groups, each of which were targeted with ads about a specific political issue, including abortion rights, healthcare, gun control, and immigration.

In total, about 35–40 per cent of the treatment groups were ultimately exposed to the ads (there is stiff competition for ads on Facebook). Although Haenschen did not find that the four ad campaigns meaningfully increased voter turnout, she did detect what are called 'conditional' effects. So, for example, if you zoom in on females specifically from so-called 'competitive districts' in Texas (where election outcomes are typically decided on small margins), it was found that pro-abortion ads had a relatively big effect on voting. Among that subset of individuals, voter turnout increased by about 1.66 percentage points compared to the control group.

This study illustrates that just buying ads on Facebook isn't enough to influence an election. Context matters. The message matters. The audience matters. But by uploading information on millions of voters, Facebook's algorithm was able to micro-target and hone in on the audience most likely to be persuaded by an argument. In this case, if you wanted to increase turnout in Texas during the midterm election, then zooming in on competitive districts and subsequently targeting female voters specifically by talking about abortion rights was going to give you a significant edge. The whole campaign cost $25,000.

My verdict on the role of fake news in elections

So, can fake news influence the outcome of major elections? In the Texas study, it wasn't that expensive for the Facebook algorithm to find the right buttons to push for a highly specific audience. But what if you had millions of dollars to spend on misleading ads?

It turns out that Trump's 2016 presidential campaign – internally called 'Project Alamo' – heavily invested in millions of Facebook ads. In total, they spent over $40 million on them. In many instances, there were up to 50,000 slightly different versions of the same ad being tested to optimize the right ad for the right audience. This was often done using 'A/B' testing – randomly showing people two different versions of the same ad to see which was more effective. Sometimes it took twenty or thirty tries before someone finally 'converted' to clicking on the ad. As Wylie says, it's about finding cognitive biases and exploiting them. Many of these ads were 'dark posts'. Unlike organic ads, dark posts are targeted ads that do not appear on the advertiser's page but only feature as sponsored content on a user's feed. So, even if you don't follow a company or campaign, you might see one of their ads on your feed and the ad you see might be unique to you or people that share your characteristics.

A 2020 investigation by *Channel 4 News* in the UK reported that the Trump campaign – with help from Cambridge Analytica – specifically identified a segment of voters they classified as 'deterrence': voters who might be persuaded not to vote. Examination of the voting records revealed that Black voters formed substantial proportions of this category, representing 61 per cent of the 'deterrence' audience in key swing states such as Georgia, North Carolina (46 per cent), and Michigan (33 per cent). In total, 54 per cent of the deterrence category comprised people of colour more generally, and 3.5 million Black voters were identified specifically as targets for deterrence. As part of their investigation, *Channel 4 News* visited several neighbourhoods in Milwaukee, Wisconsin, and calculated that in many wards (electoral districts within a city) voter turnout was lower than in past elections. In one ward, out of the group marked for 'deterrence', only 36 per cent voted on election day. Overall, turnout in the district fell from 75 per cent in 2012 to 56 per cent in 2016.

Of course, there may very well be other reasons than micro-targeting that could explain low turnout. Yet many of these individuals likely voted for Obama in 2012 and we know from the Ohio study that fake news might have deterred those Obama voters from voting for Clinton, either because they abstained or switched their vote. But why would this be the case?

Although Trump's digital campaign manager, Brad Parscale, has officially denied targeting Black voters, in 2020 *Channel 4 News* uncovered confidential documents from Cambridge Analytica that refer to what they called the 'superpredator' ads. These were ads designed specifically to discredit Hillary Clinton amongst Black voters. In the ads, Clinton refers to Black youth as 'superpredators' with 'no conscience and no empathy'. This wasn't blatant fake news, as Clinton did in fact use this term in a 1996 speech in New Hampshire in the context of crime legislation around gang violence (though the quote was presented out of context and could be construed as manipulating public opinion). All in all, the fact that Black voters were disproportionately marked for 'deterrence' and targeted with ads discrediting Hillary Clinton does at least suggest that this may have been part of an overall strategy of voter disengagement in key swing states made more efficient by micro-targeting.

Two important lessons emerge from these insights. The first is that although the Trump campaign might have had access to Kogan's models, predicted personality data is not even necessary for micro-targeting. Both the Trump and Brexit campaigns heavily invested in targeting people with hundreds of thousands of ads. Anyone can go to Facebook with a list of emails and ask Facebook to find thousands of similar individuals. Based on their profile information and likes, Facebook can create what they call a 'look-a-like' audience, or new people with characteristics similar to your client base. So, if you were to go them with a list of known 'extraverts', Facebook would – much like a predictive model – use their algorithm to essentially find you more 'extraverts' without knowing it.

The second lesson is that research has shown that the addition of digital footprints, such as Facebook likes, would make such targeting attempts even more accurate and efficient. Combined with the fact that almost a quarter of national elections are decided on margins under 3 per cent, the ability to micro-target misinformation based on rich digital footprints makes for a potentially dangerous weapon of mass persuasion. As more and more digital data on people's behaviour becomes available to train these models on, the better they are going to get at identifying groups who are open to persuasion. Every website you visit is a potential datapoint in the matrix. For example, the latest research has shown the feasibility of *nano-targeting* or the ability to accurately target a *single* specific user with an ad campaign.

Twitter has already recognized the potential harm of micro-targeting millions of voters with political ads and, in a controversial move, banned political advertising from their platform in 2019. Twitter also limits micro-targeting functionality. Although this is undoubtedly a good step in the right direction, people might find creative ways to get around a ban – for example, by moving their business to other platforms that do offer micro-targeting services; by not registering themselves as a political organization; by posting on their own organization's feed; by directly messaging users; by using influencers who do not disclose campaign affiliations; or via coordinated networks of users that help spread a political message. As such, a ban doesn't fundamentally address the *psychological* problem that people may not know when and where they are being targeted with political content.

It is important to highlight that we have only examined the *direct* influence of fake news on voter choices in this chapter. As discussed in previous chapters, fake news can shape public opinion in powerful ways *indirectly* as well. In fact, targeted attempts by foreign governments to interfere with national elections often seek to amplify societal tensions and destabilize public discourse rather than target voters directly. For example, many polls have shown significant polarization among Americans on the role of Russian interference in the 2016 election. Experimental research further finds that when individuals are exposed to potential evidence of foreign interference, it decreases faith in democracy and makes people less likely to vote in the future. The real or total effect of fake news can therefore best be understood by adding up both the direct and indirect effects.

In summary, although traditional campaigns may have struggled to persuade voters, social media can now help optimize the identification and micro-targeting of those individuals most open to persuasion via their digital footprints.

In effect, in the final stage of the viral analogy, we have developed a way to administer the misinformation virus in highly concentrated form to those individuals most susceptible to becoming infected and spreading the virus further. It's the digital analogue of a bioweapon.

The Brexit and Trump campaigns were just the beginning. A 2021 report from the University of Oxford shows that private firms – much like Cambridge Analytica – are now offering digital propaganda services on behalf of political entities in at least forty-eight countries around the world.

What we need now is a vaccine – a process that can produce *psychological immunity* to protect people from malicious and harmful online manipulation.

FAKE NEWS ANTIGEN 7
Identify and resist micro-targeting attempts

— Although the persuasive effect of a single fake news story on how people vote may be limited, the ability to predict psychological traits from digital online footprints has allowed political organizations to micro-target people with increasing accuracy.

— Experimental evidence shows that campaign ads targeted at people's personality, based on their Facebook likes and other online data, can influence political preferences.

— Campaigns that can identify susceptible individuals are able to exploit small persuasion effects at scale by targeting millions of people with thousands of ads.

— In other words, social media has allowed actors to synthesize those aspects of misinformation that are deemed most persuasive to a particular group of individuals and target them accordingly.

— Being aware of this new weapon of mass persuasion is the first step in gaining immunity against it.

PART THREE

A psychological vaccine against misinformation

CHAPTER 8

The new science of prebunking

'When our side was in charge, we called them
information programs; when our opponents were in charge,
we called them propaganda programs,'
ROBERT CIALDINI, author of *Influence*

David Hawkins was a sixteen-year-old kid from Oklahoma City when he enlisted in the United States Army. The year was 1949. He was following in the footsteps of his father, Clayton Hawkins, who had left home when David was about six years old to serve overseas in the Second World War.

When the war ended, tensions started to rise between the United States and the Soviet Union. There were growing concerns about the rise of communism. Only a year later, in 1950, the Korean War broke out when North Korea decided to invade South Korea with military assistance from both China and the Soviet Union. Later that year, US President Harry Truman announced to the world that he was ordering US troops to intervene in the conflict to prevent the further spread of communism. Despite being one of the most destructive conflicts, with over 3 million casualties, the Korean War is often referred to as the 'Forgotten War' because the war received relatively little public attention, especially compared to the Vietnam War, which directly succeeded it.

David was just seventeen when he was shipped out to fight in the war, yet his tenure would turn out to be short-lived. Soon after his arrival, he was wounded in battle and captured by enemy troops. He was taken to a Chinese-run prisoner-of-war (POW) camp known as 'Death Valley' (you can probably guess why). David spent the next three years in captivity.

You might ask, what's so special about David Hawkins? Well, following ceasefire negotiations between North Korea, the Chinese, and the United Nations, an agreement was signed in 1953 to separate North and South Korea, which allowed for the repatriation of prisoners of war, also known as Operation Big Switch. Thousands of prisoners were exchanged. What made David special is that when it was his turn to choose whether to return home to the United States, he declined the opportunity and decided to stay in communist China. David was not alone: twenty-one other fellow POWs, including twenty Americans and one British, made the same choice. Some of these soldiers still had families back home that they'd left behind. On 24 February 1954, these so-called 'turncoats' boarded a train that crossed the Yalu River into China. Although some – including Hawkins – eventually returned home, others were never heard of again.

The fact that twenty US citizens had voluntarily chosen to embrace communism shocked America, particularly because it had never happened before. As Monica Kim, Professor of History at New York University elegantly describes it: 'The United States was supposed to be the power that transformed the enemy in wartime encounters, not the other way around.' So, what happened in those camps?

When David Hawkins eventually returned to the United States, he told the BBC that, as a prisoner, he had been subjected to six or seven hours of indoctrination on a daily basis about the benefits of Marxism and the evils of capitalism. His captors would ask why he had come 5,000 miles to fight a civil war that was none of his business. They told him that he didn't understand what he was fighting for, nor what communism really meant. The prisoners were exposed to many lectures, books, and pamphlets as part of a systematic 're-education' campaign. Some even started to spread communist ideals themselves. In David's own words: 'My reasoning was, they really have embraced this socialism so let me see what it is like – let me check it out' – the end result being that he was intrigued enough to stay behind and find out for himself.

But was his mind still his own? The most common and highly popularized account of what happened in North Korea is that the soldiers were 'brainwashed' by enemy troops. The term 'brainwashing' was introduced by journalist Edward Hunter in 1951 in a media article about Red China and is a literal translation from the Chinese 'xǐnǎo' (washing the brain). Some have even described the captured soldiers as being 'infected, to a degree, with the virus of communism'. Allen Dulles, then director of the Central Intelligence Agency (CIA), told Princeton Alumni the following in a public speech: 'The Communists are now applying the brainwashing techniques to American prisoners in Korea, and it is not beyond the range of possibility that considerable numbers of our own boys there might be so indoctrinated as to be induced, temporarily at least, to renounce country and family.'

As we've explored in previous chapters, persuasion is difficult – let alone convincing someone to abandon their deeply held social and political beliefs in return for a whole new foreign system of values. It requires extreme circumstances.

Many of the captured soldiers had heard horror stories about the North Korean prisoner camps but what they encountered in the Chinese-run camps was unexpected. They were greeted in a friendly fashion with a big congratulations: 'You have been liberated!', 'Join the fighters for peace!' Some scholars think that because there was already some confusion among US soldiers about their role in the war, the promise of peace was more alluring.

From the perspective of the Chinese, the American soldiers were viewed as uneducated, misguided, and confused rather than seen as a violent enemy. The Chinese had a so-called 'lenient policy': if the captives showed a genuine interest in listening to what they had to say, which included an openness to studying and engaging with communist ideals, they would be treated relatively well, even rewarded, much like brothers-in-arms. Those who resisted the education programme were typically not physically punished but asked to critically self-reflect on their attitudes and eliminate 'incorrect' beliefs that caused them to act in a 'negative' fashion. Those who continued to resist were labelled 'reactionaries' and shipped off to another camp, whereas collaborators would be referred to as 'progressives' and given extra privileges.

Of course, it wasn't all good. The Chinese captors reportedly kept nutritional conditions pretty poor (whilst claiming that the prisoners received the same diet as Chinese soldiers) and manipulated group dynamics and social order by isolating soldiers. They also employed a range of other tactics, such as only allowing POWs to receive mail that contained bad news. I can only imagine that in a continuous state of hunger, tiredness, and social isolation, the mind starts to wander. The Chinese also had unusual questioning techniques. During interrogation, they created an interactive discussion forum where the prisoners' core beliefs and values were critically examined and questioned. They were asked to find flaws in their own ways of thinking and told that any past misfortune was the result of their long-held support for a flawed capitalistic society. Lectures were followed by group discussions and if these did not take the direction the Chinese had hoped for, prisoners would have to listen to the lecture again, and again, and again.

These sessions were harnessing what are now well-known psychological mechanisms, including 'illusory truth': repeated exposure increases the truth value of a claim. More generally, this approach to persuasion was highly unusual at the time, and probably much more effective than resorting to sheer physical abuse or torture.

Nonetheless, the brainwashing accounts that permeated American consciousness have received due criticism over the years. For example, focusing on a small group of soldiers who chose to stay in China takes attention away from the thousands and thousands of soldiers who did return home despite being held and questioned in POW camps for years on end. But this story is relevant insofar these specific events piqued the interest of the late American psychologist William J. McGuire (1925–2007).

Bill McGuire was the first* to propose the idea that, just as the body gains immunity to a virus after exposure to a biological vaccine, it might be possible for people to become resistant to brainwashing after the 'injection' of a cognitive vaccine. Although he never quite got there, his story lays the beginnings of our modern understanding of the emerging science of *pre*bunking.

---

* Technically, Aristotle was probably the first to write about the value of prebunking, but we'll get to that later.

A vaccine for brainwash

In 1941, shortly before the United States entered the Second World War, psychologist Carl Hovland left academia to join a research branch of the US War Department known as the 'Information and Education Division'. As head of their experimental psychology unit, Hovland was tasked with studying the efficacy of propaganda and persuasion. Specifically, he evaluated the impact of the 'Why We Fight' (WWF) films on the morale and motivation of American soldiers. WWF was a documentary series aimed at helping soldiers (and later the public) understand why the United States had become involved in the war.

In his studies, Hovland introduced the experimental method to the study of persuasion by systematically teasing out how these films influenced people's opinions, beliefs, and their knowledge about the war. He evaluated whether it was more effective to show images or just audio; communicate one-sided or two-sided arguments; how long the effects lasted over time, and whether they were more impactful for some audiences than others. In a nutshell, he was trying to uncover the basic laws of persuasion. Hovland published his investigations in a 1949 book series known as 'Experiments on Mass Communication'.

At the end of the war, Hovland moved back to Yale, where he chaired the psychology department and established the Yale Communication and Attitude Change Program – now widely regarded as the most influential programme of research on communication and attitude change in the history of psychology. One of Hovland's students at Yale was Bill McGuire. Though McGuire claims he was only peripherally involved in the attitude change programme as a graduate student, he would later return to Yale and become one of the field's foremost experts on attitudes. Inspired by the Korean War, McGuire had a particularly interesting take on attitude change.

In response to the widespread concerns about foreign brainwashing techniques, investigations of POW behaviour during the Korean conflict led US authorities to conclude that there must have been some kind of failure to adequately cultivate 'American values'. As a consequence, the widely advocated solution was for formal institutions, such as schools and the army, to more explicitly teach and communicate 'American ideals'.

But McGuire disagreed. He had a radically different idea: why not *pre-expose* people to the propaganda itself in weakened form? In other words, rather than providing more arguments that support a particular position, expose people to a weakened dose of an attack on their beliefs. He reasoned that this should work much better as an 'immunizing' agent.

McGuire had been inspired by the research of Irving Janis, another colleague at Yale, who showed that exposing people to two sides of an argument appeared to 'inoculate' audiences much better against a counter-campaign than just hearing one-sided arguments in favour of the desired position. For example, in one experiment, conducted in the early 1950s, Janis wanted to try to convince students that the Soviet Union didn't have the capability to build atomic bombs at scale. Giving students arguments both in favour and against this claim appeared to better prepare them for a counter-message (that the USSR could easily do so) than just hearing more arguments about why the Soviet Union couldn't possibly produce many atomic bombs at scale. Janis didn't have a deep explanation or coherent theory for why this might be. But McGuire did. He started to formalize the possibility that pre-exposure to the 'virus' – the persuasive attack – seemed to stimulate people's attitudinal defences.

In the context of the Korean War, McGuire reasoned that some of the captured soldiers didn't have any pre-existing mental defences to resist persuasion attempts. After all, who would expect an attack on basic capitalist ideals? It's what he called a 'cultural truism' – a societal belief so widely held that nobody seems to question it. Rather than giving people more reasons to support a desired attitude, what we should be focusing on, McGuire argued, was exposing people to weakened doses of the persuasive attack. The analogy to how our bodies become immune to viruses quickly became apparent to McGuire.

In fact, the process of psychological inoculation follows the biomedical analogy exactly: just as exposing people to a severely weakened (or dead) strain of a virus triggers the production of antibodies to help the body fight off future infection, the same can be achieved with information. By pre-emptively exposing people to a sufficiently weakened dose of a persuasive 'challenge' – and by subsequently refuting that challenge – mental antibodies can be cultivated to help generate psychological resistance against misinformation.

Like any good experimentalist, McGuire started out in a highly controlled fashion by examining cultural truisms that he believed were suitable as test cases. He wrote about 'germ-free' ideological beliefs – in other words, beliefs not infected with or tainted by politics. As an example, he used the fact that brushing your teeth frequently is good for your health. When surveyed, nearly all of his students had the same attitude towards this belief: they agreed. It was a widely shared attitude. (In contrast, only 50 per cent of students strongly agreed with the statement that 'capitalism is better than communism'.) He reasoned that nobody would expect an attack on such a widely held belief and therefore would have little to no experience rehearsing and refuting counter-arguments. After all, if you were challenged with an article which claimed that brushing your teeth twice a day is harmful to your gums, how would you respond? Would you have a rebuttal prepared? McGuire reasoned that such unrehearsed beliefs are vulnerable to attack.

In a typical experiment, he would expose students to a weakened example of a persuasive attack on their beliefs and equip them with counter-arguments for how they might respond. A few days later, he would return and challenge them on their attitudes towards the target issue. The result? The students had become more immune to persuasion. In 1970, he summarized his findings in the magazine *Psychology Today* with the title 'A Vaccine for Brainwash'.

His experiments were clever. To simulate the recommendation that Americans should become better at defending their ideals, he would craft a so-called 'reassuring message', now often termed 'a supportive argument'. He likened this idea to giving people some vitamins or a healthy 'information' diet. To take a concrete example, one of the truisms McGuire tested was the claim that: 'Everyone should get an annual physical checkup, even when he [or she] is not bothered by any symptom of illness.' The reassuring treatment would simply bolster this cultural truism by emphasizing the benefits of early detection. It didn't raise and refute any challenges; the message (typically a 600-word essay) just provided more arguments in favour of the truism.

Crucially, however, in the inoculation condition (which he also described as a 'threatening defence') the students would receive a message that pre-exposed them to weak versions of the attacking arguments, so as to stimulate their cognitive defences. The inoculation condition ignored all arguments in favour of the truism. It started out by mentioning arguments against the truism (the threatening phase), such as the notion that annual check-ups might turn people into hypochondriacs and cause people to delay seeing their doctor until the time of their next check-up. The essay then went on to immediately refute the persuasion attempt with strong counter-arguments. Students in both conditions later faced 'the full dose': a subsequent essay that 'attacked' the veracity of the truism that health check-ups are beneficial.

The difference between the two experimental conditions is that one was merely supportive (more facts) whereas the other focused solely on raising potential future attacks in weakened form and refuting them with strong counters (the inoculation). In the control condition, no messages were shown. This was a baseline measurement of people's belief in the truism. McGuire asked his students whether they thought the claim was true or false both before and after exposure to the messages on a fifteen-point scale ranging from 'definitely false' to 'definitely true'.

So, in the end, what worked better against a persuasive attack on someone's attitude: bolstering the truism or raising and refuting weakened examples of the attack beforehand?

The results were clear. As you can see in the chart below, without any information, most students simply endorsed the belief that annual health check-ups are a good thing, with an average rating of 12.62 points out of a possible 15. But the attacks significantly decreased this belief across the conditions. In the group where no defences whatsoever were provided ('attack only'), the average truth-rating was only 6.64 out of 15. In other words, the persuasive attack was effective at getting people to question their beliefs about annual health check-ups. The supportive or 'reassuring' message had some benefit, but only very minimally, with an average rating of 7.39 (a gain of less than a point when compared to the attack-only condition, 6.64). In comparison, the 'inoculation' condition revealed much greater success – even after an attack – belief levels were close to baseline at 10.33. In other words, although the 'inoculation' did not provide 100 per cent 'immunization efficacy', 82 per cent (10.33 ÷ 12.62) protection against a persuasive attack is still pretty impressive in my book!

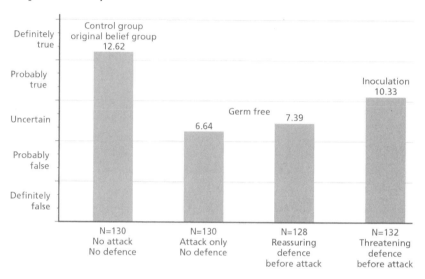

Bar graph visualizing the results from one of McGuire's initial inoculation experiments: the y axis displays whether the students rated the belief as true or false on a 15-point scale; the x axis shows the different experimental groups, including the inoculation condition.

These were the first foundations of a potential 'vaccine for brainwash'. McGuire ran a bunch of these experiments in the early 1960s, together with his (now late) graduate student Demetrios Papageorgis. Interestingly, the last thing McGuire (or Papageorgis) would ever write about inoculation was summarized in the 1970 *Psychology Today* piece. Why didn't McGuire ever test his ideas in the context of actual propaganda? Why did he stop researching it all together?

My good colleague John Jost, Professor of Psychology and Politics at New York University, was McGuire's last PhD student, as well as a close family friend. After McGuire passed in 2007, John went through dozens of files and boxes, including unfinished manuscripts, at McGuire's family home in New Haven. I figured, if anyone knew, it would be John.

John explained that McGuire felt like he had laid the groundwork on inoculation theory for others to continue. In fact, the last thing McGuire wrote on the subject is that he hoped others would explore its potential in the context of contested issues. Although McGuire's ideas remained influential in psychology, over the years and decades, the inoculation idea itself slowly faded from view. Many decades later at Yale – where it had all started – it dawned on me that, in fact, some of the most important questions had been left unanswered.

Psychological inoculation against misinformation

First and foremost, why not explore the potential of psychological inoculation in the context of real-world misinformation? McGuire offered some hints as to why he was hesitant about taking the idea of inoculation out of the lab and into the real world. Although his initial reservations seemed very sensible, as it turns out, he was wrong about them.

There was one thing in particular that didn't add up for him. At the time, he worried about the evidence for selective exposure. If it's true that people selectively attend to evidence – in the extreme sense – then they would never encounter or engage with content that might challenge their beliefs. This means that inoculation would be applicable across the board, because people would have never been challenged on any of their attitudes and thus lack the necessary mental defences in the event of an attack. But McGuire didn't buy into the theory of selective exposure, at least not in the strong form, as he often witnessed people exposing themselves to ideas that challenged their beliefs. So he reasoned that inoculation must be restricted to the subset of beliefs on which people have never been challenged. For what does it mean to inoculate someone who has already been exposed to the 'virus'?

What bothered me about this restriction is that in the real world, we cannot always know or even control the information that people may or may not have been exposed to in the past. The reason why the theory lacked further development, in my opinion, is because the 'no prior exposure' principle unnecessarily crippled its progress. In essence, McGuire argued that for inoculation to occur, people should already have the 'right', 'healthy' attitude in place and this attitude must have never been questioned before. For example, the belief that getting an annual health check-up is a good thing is shared by most people and most people have also never been questioned on this belief. It's a rare combo.

So, I started wondering what if McGuire was wrong about this assumption? The implications would be huge. But can you be vaccinated after you've already been exposed to the virus?

What wasn't apparent in McGuire's time is that the answer is actually yes. It's called 'therapeutic inoculation'. Although the classic vaccine most people are familiar with is fully prophylactic (preventative), following recent advances in medicine, we now have vaccines which you can administer after people have already been exposed to a virus. Therapeutic vaccines work by activating our immune systems to fight an existing infection. One of the first medical therapeutic vaccines was approved by the US's Food and Drug Administration (FDA) in 2010. 'Provenge' is used to treat prostate cancer and works by training a patient's white blood cells to more vigilantly attack cancer cells. Many therapeutic applications are currently being researched for other conditions, such as HIV and HPV.

I started to see a whole another dimension to the biomedical analogy. For some individuals, the inoculation would be entirely prophylactic, whereas for others it might end up being more therapeutic, but it really depends on the incubation period of the misinformation virus.

The incubation period is the time elapsed between initial exposure to a virus and the onset of symptoms. You may have been exposed to misinformation of some kind once or twice but not show any symptoms for a long period of time. Perhaps you needed to be exposed multiple times before sharing or believing it or perhaps you weren't susceptible in the first place. For biological viruses, the incubation period ranges from a few days for the common flu (influenza) to a few years for viral infections such as HIV. Similarly, for exposure to a misinformation virus the incubation period (that is, before people start to show noticeable symptoms such as believing and sharing) could be days if not years. If we use this new theoretical framework of the medical analogy, we no longer have a need for McGuire's initial restriction. In the real world, we are dealing with people in various stages of infection, and inoculation can both work as a preventative and therapeutic agent. If I ever had a 'lightbulb' moment, this was it.

Of course, these were just ideas. I needed to evaluate them empirically. What was the most polarizing issue in the United States that I could get my hands on? Something which I could almost guarantee people had entrenched and widely differing attitudes towards, perhaps caused by misinformation or selective exposure in the past. In other words, I wanted to do the opposite of what McGuire did in his initial experiments; I was looking for a 'germ-infested' ideological belief environment.

Fake news about global warming goes viral

It didn't take long to identify that one of the most hotly contested issues in the United States is global warming. The gap between liberals and conservatives on this issue has been growing since the early 2000s. Back in 2012, I was an eager graduate student at Yale University, and I had been studying the nature of disinformation campaigns about climate change together with my mentors and now long-time friends and collaborators, Tony Leiserowitz and Ed Maibach. We sat down for months to try to design the ultimate inoculation experiment on climate change.

In most social science experiments, participants are simply shown a stimulus – such as a claim or media message – selected by the researchers. The problem is that it's not always clear whether the stimuli have good 'ecological validity' – that is, whether the message is something a participant would actually encounter in the real world, outside the lab. So before doing anything, we decided to go out and conduct a nationally representative poll of the population to have the public tell us which piece of misinformation they had heard of before and found most compelling. We included many false claims about climate change (such as the idea that global warming is a hoax or that the Intergovernmental Panel on Climate Change, IPCC, is an alarmist organization). But the myth that people were most familiar with – and found most persuasive – was the claim that there is *no consensus* among scientists about climate change.

This myth is based on a bogus petition known as the 'Oregon Global Warming Petition Project', which purports to have been signed by over 31,000 'scientists' claiming that there is no convincing scientific evidence that humans are causing global warming. This petition was completely unregulated and at one point included the cast of 'M*A*S*H' and 'Ginger Spice' (listed as Dr Geri Halliwell, apparently a Boston-based microbiologist). Unbeknownst to us, this petition formed the basis of one of the most viral stories about climate change on Facebook in 2016 (just before we conducted our study), accumulating over half a million shares and likes. The fact that this petition was making the rounds on social media slightly confused us because the argument wasn't new; in fact, this specific petition dates back to 1998 and is thus well over twenty years old.

It was originally launched by Arthur Robinson, a biochemist and conservative politician who runs the Oregon Institute of Science and Medicine (which according to Google Maps appears to be a farm in rural Oregon referred to by some commentators as a 'survivalist compound'). The reason this bogus petition – and fake news stories making use of it – has been so effective over the years is because it uses a clever manipulation technique.

To understand the power of this technique, we need to travel back in time to the year 2002, when a confidential memo to the Bush administration was leaked to the public. During his presidency, George W. Bush received advice on how to 'win the global warming debate'. The advice came from Frank Luntz, an influential political consultant. Luntz recommended what turned out to be a powerful message: make sure that people think that the scientific debate remains open. Here's an excerpt of the memo: 'Voters believe that there is no consensus about global warming within the scientific community. Should the public come to believe that the scientific issues are settled, their views about global warming will change accordingly. Therefore, you need to continue to make the lack of scientific certainty a primary issue in the debate.'

Of course, we didn't take his political intuitions at face value but decided to put them to an empirical test (many empirical tests in fact).

Unfortunately, it turns out that Luntz was right. We started by reverse-engineering the message. Luntz seemed to fear the sway that a scientific consensus could hold over public opinion so instead of emphasizing disagreement, we wondered what would happen when you inform people of the fact that over 97 per cent of climate scientists agree that humans are causing global warming. For example, we know from research that people are much more persuaded by the judgment of a group of experts (a consensus) than the judgment of any single expert. This makes good sense: it's good practice to get a second opinion. The underlying intuition here is that, although individuals may be biased, it's much harder for an entire group of independent experts to get it wrong.

The gateway belief model of attitude change

This rule of thumb is adaptive given the fact that we can't all be experts in every domain of life and when confronted with limited time and resources, we rely on the expertise of others who have done the work on our behalf. Think of it this way: if 97 out of 100 engineers told you a particular bridge is unsafe to cross, you would probably just heed their advice rather than perform a structural assessment yourself (I know I would).

We discovered that people's understanding of complex science is closely intertwined with their perception of whether or not there is scientific consensus on an issue. The Gateway Belief Model (GBM) is a theory of attitude change my colleagues and I developed that is a formalization of this finding. As part of this theory, *perceived scientific agreement* (consensus) acts as a gateway because, when you visualize the mental network of beliefs that people hold about an issue, perceived consensus occupies a central position insofar as it connects to or bridges other important beliefs. In our studies, we find that when you communicate the scientific consensus to people on, for example, climate change, Covid-19, or the safety of vaccinations, this increases our perception of scientific agreement (stage 1). In turn, people's perception of scientific agreement is strongly related to other key attitudes and feelings that people hold, such as whether they *believe* climate change is happening, is *human-caused*, and how much we should *worry* about the issue. This in turn predicts the degree to which people will *support public action* on contested issues (stage 2). You can see how this mental network of people's beliefs works in the figure below.

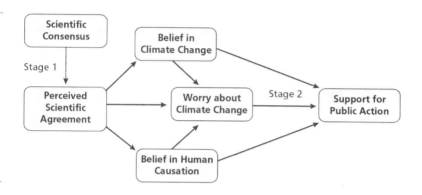

I doubt that Luntz had got this far, but his basic intuition was correct: people's perception of the scientific consensus on global warming acts as a lever for their understanding of the science, their feelings about it, and ultimately the degree to which people will support action on the issue. His advice was therefore for the Bush administration to cast doubt on the scientific consensus on climate change. Scholarly analyses reveal that this was indeed the number one myth in conservative op-eds from 2007–10. The American Petroleum Institute (the largest 'big oil' lobbying organization in the US) came up with a similar plan to introduce uncertainties into the debate about climate change. As part of their playbook, they exploited journalistic norms of 'balance' by aggressively pushing news organizations to cover 'both sides' of the debate in an attempt to confuse the public. In practice, this meant that many media articles about climate science included the opinion of a climate sceptic or contrarian. Even the BBC fell prey to this tactic by regularly featuring the opinion of climate deniers. In 2018, the BBC changed this policy and apologized for getting coverage of climate change 'wrong too often'.

The issue is that the presence of a sceptic gives people the impression that there is an even-keeled scientific debate happening. The confusion and damage caused by the popular media's use of false balance on issues such as climate change and vaccination has been widely documented. For example, as part of a national poll I conducted with *YouGov* and *The Conversation* in the UK in late 2021, we found that when asked to rate the following statement as true or false, 'Scientists disagree on the cause of climate change', 46 per cent of Brits thought this statement was true! Similar findings have been reported in the US.

The reason why Luntz's strategy is so effective is because it manipulates your perception by creating a cloud of doubt around the scientific consensus, which lowers the importance that people assign to it. For example, if I tell you that most scientists agree, but also that a few outspoken scientists disagree, you likely become more unsure. That's because your brain is counting the consensus as one voice while in fact it should be represented as thousands of voices. One way for disinformation actors to try to create this impression is to prop up the prominence of contrarian experts in the media and public debates. But another way of doing this is through petitions. The bogus 'Oregon Global Warming Petition Project' is a perfect example because although '31,000' signatories sounds like a big number in absolute terms, in relative terms, it is a tiny fraction (less than 0.3 per cent) of all US science graduates. When expert consensus is surrounded by contrarian voices, it loses its value.

It's a powerful technique.

In their book *Merchants of Doubt* Harvard science historian Naomi Oreskes and co-author Erik M. Conway uncovered striking parallels between the global warming and tobacco debates. In fact, they provide extensive historical analyses of how 'keeping the controversy alive' has been a key strategy. The same techniques were being recycled over and over again. As summarized by one tobacco executive: 'Doubt is our product, since it is the best means of competing with the "body of fact" that exists in the minds of the general public. It is also the means of establishing a controversy.' In 2006, a US court ruled that the tobacco industry had purposively lied and deceived the public for decades on the link between smoking and cancer. As part of the ruling, tobacco companies were forced to run a corrective campaign through television and newspaper ads – the language of which was only finalized in 2017. Unfortunately, corrections of 'alternative facts' don't scale in the same way as the initial misinformation: engagement with the corrective ads on social media was minimal and estimates show that they only reached about 40 per cent of smokers.

Prevention would have been much better than cure.

A psychological vaccine against misinformation

Back to McGuire. Once we'd identified our real-world misinformation campaign (the 'Oregon Global Warming Petition Project'), the question was whether we could pre-emptively inoculate people against this misinformation technique, regardless of their prior beliefs. To do so, we decided to screen participants based on their pre-existing attitudes toward global warming.

We created three groups: the first (our 'positive attitude' group) believed that global warming is both real and human-caused; the second wasn't sure about it all (our 'neutral' or 'undecided' group); and the third (our 'negative' attitude or 'sceptic' group) didn't believe in global warming to begin with. To make sure that people didn't catch on to the purpose of the experiment, we also asked participants a bunch of other questions, completely unrelated to climate change, such as what their favourite *Star Wars* movie is (spoiler alert on the consensus: *The Empire Strikes Back*!).

We then randomized participants into one of five experimental conditions. But before we did so we used some additional subterfuge by telling participants that we maintain a large database of media statements and that they would randomly be assigned a topic. As participants watched a fake count-down, a message would appear that read: 'TOPIC 10: CLIMATE CHANGE' (in actuality, all participants were assigned to read the messages about climate change). In the first condition, one group of participants was exposed to just the facts: '97 per cent of climate scientists have concluded that human-caused climate change is happening'. We'll call this the 'facts-only' or 'consensus' condition. In the second, another group of participants were exposed to just the fake news: a screenshot of the 'Global Warming Petition Project'. We'll call this the 'misinformation' condition. The third simulated the false-balance debate that often happens in the popular media, placing the facts alongside misinformation on the same screen for people: the 'false-balance' condition.

The fourth and fifth conditions both contained the psychological inoculations. In the fourth (inoculation) condition, participants were given a forewarning, after all, forewarned is forearmed! Specifically, they were warned that: 'Some politically motivated groups use misleading tactics to try to convince the public that there is a lot of disagreement among scientists.' We then reiterated that this claim was false because, among climate scientists, there is a near-unanimous consensus that humans are causing climate change. In the fifth and final condition, participants received the same forewarning, but this time coupled with a much more detailed *pre*bunk. We told participants that they might hear of some petition circulating online, but they should know that this petition was bogus and included many non-experts and even unverified signatories (including the long-deceased Charles Darwin and a 'Dr Geri Halliwell' from the Spice Girls!)

At the end of the experiment, participants in both inoculation conditions were exposed to the full dose of the misinformation: the Global Warming Petition Project website. The key outcome measure was people's perception of the degree of agreement within the scientific community about the fact that humans are causing global warming. This was measured on a scale from 0–100 per cent both before and after the participants were exposed to the messages.

To recap, the process of psychological inoculation works by: (a) forewarning people of an impending persuasion attempt (known as the 'threatening' phase), and (b) by arming people in advance with the arguments and cognitive tools they need to counter-argue and resist exposure to persuasive misinformation (known as the 'refutational pre-emption' or '*pre*bunking' phase). Or, as one BBC journalist writing about the experiment put it: 'Like Han Solo, you shoot first.'

What this boils down to is that people need both the motivation and ability to successfully identify misinformation. Specifically, the prebunking phase simulates and rehearses the attack and counter-arguing process for us, whereas the forewarning helps motivate people to start defending themselves against incoming misinformation. I've outlined the psychological inoculation process in the figure below.

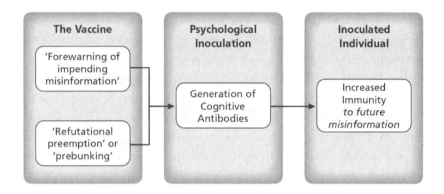

So, what did we find? When people were only provided with the cold, hard facts, they updated their perceptions of the scientific consensus by about 20 percentage points – a large margin. (If, for example, their previous estimate of the scientific consensus was about 70 per cent, they would have updated their beliefs to about 90 per cent, after learning about the actual consensus.) Although ideal, this doesn't always reflect reality, of course, as people are hardly ever exposed to just cold, hard facts.

In the misinformation condition, we saw a significant negative effect after exposure to the bogus petition, with people decreasing their estimate of the scientific consensus by about 10 percentage points.

What happened in the false-balance condition, where people were shown both the facts and the misinformation side by side, was both striking and alarming. The presence of misinformation completely cancelled out the strong positive effects of the scientific consensus. The change netted to absolutely zero . . . zip, zilch, nada. This finding really underscores the power of misinformation: its mere presence completely negates the otherwise strong and positive effect of factual information. Although 97 per cent of scientists is a strong consensus, 31,000 is a big number in absolute terms. It introduces variance around the consensus, thereby not only weakening its influence but completely eradicating it. These findings evidenced – for the first time – in a controlled experimental setting the potential threat of influential misinformation and orchestrated fake news campaigns.

Although this finding was revealing, our key question of course was whether we could prevent this from happening in the first place? Importantly, turning to the inoculation conditions, we found that both the forewarning and detailed inoculations were able to immunize people against the harmful misinformation. The forewarning by itself was able to maintain about a third of the change we observed in the facts-only condition, whereas the full inoculation was able to maintain about two-thirds of the positive effect. In other words, like McGuire's experiment, full psychological immunity was not conferred but the change in the inoculation condition was still moving in the right direction, by about 13 percentage points (versus 20 percentage points in the facts-only condition, where no misinformation was present). I have plotted the results below. The bar graph illustrates how people changed their perceptions of the scientific consensus in each experimental condition.

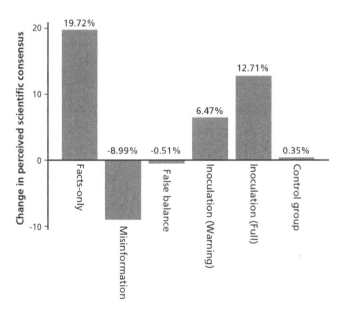

Contrary to McGuire's initial reservations, what's remarkable is that we also found the same patterns replicated in each condition regardless of what people's previous attitudes were: their attitudes were (partially)

protected from the misinformation. In other words, we were not just preaching to the converted by bolstering the attitudes of those who already had favourable or 'healthy' views towards climate change. We were also able to immunize the neutral and negative attitude groups. It is likely that the immunization acted as more of a prophylactic for the positive attitude group and became increasingly therapeutic for the undecided and sceptic groups.

It is important to note that I am not suggesting that the psychological inoculation changed the fundamental worldview of sceptics about the issue of global warming. It likely didn't – and that's not its purpose either – but it did protect them from falling prey to influential misinformation on the topic. Moreover, given the varying incubation period of different misinformation pathogens, there's a lot to be gained by inoculating the big middle. In fact, the neutral 'fence-sitter' group was by far the largest group in our study, comprising over half the sample, and arguably most susceptible to influential misinformation that aims to spread doubt about the scientific consensus.

One other notable observation is that the full inoculation treatment – which included both the prebunk and the forewarning – outperformed the forewarning-only group consistently across all conditions. This suggests that although 'forewarned is forearmed', the vaccination also needs to pre-emptively prepare people for the types of misinformation that they might come across and arm them with the facts and tools they need to confidently counter-argue and resist specific falsehoods. The mind needs specific antibodies to neutralize the threat. In other words, the prebunking component proved essential to the efficacy of the vaccine.

Although this may not seem so obvious, most of the time, scientific experiments fail pretty miserably. We do our best in the lab, but we often end up looking at a whole bunch of nothing results. The results from this experiment, however, were the most consistent I had seen in my entire academic career to that point. I remember the feeling I experienced when I first saw the results: I was ecstatic to the point where I was dancing around the room celebrating (by myself). It worked! In scientific terms, we had a relatively diverse and large sample (over 2,000 people) so the likelihood that this was a fluke or accident seemed quite small.

As exciting as the results were, many years passed before we got our results out to the public. In order to publish scientific results – no matter how convincing you think they are – its veracity needs to be assessed independently by expert colleagues through a process known as peer-review. By the time we finally got approval to publish our results, it was late December 2016 and the world was caught off-guard by the potential election of Donald Trump as president. Fake news – including Trump's climate denial – was being discussed everywhere, so in an interesting turn of events, the publication of our paper could not have been more timely.

But what happened next none of us could have anticipated.

The day our article went live it went viral all across the world. A story from the BBC led with 'Cambridge Scientists Consider Fake News Vaccine'. Even Fox News chimed in with: 'Fake News "Vaccine" Could Stop the Spread of Misinformation'. As I watched hundreds of stories around the world pop up, my phone started ringing non-stop; news media, government officials, corporations, everyone wanted me to explain the basic idea behind psychological inoculation. Before I knew it, I was talking to Ira Flatow on his nationally syndicated *Science Friday* show. It felt like I was on an episode of *The Big Bang Theory* (the one where they finally had a breakthrough discovery and were interviewed by Ira Flatow).

Not too long after the publication of our study, I received word from a team of psychologists at the University of Western Australia: Stephan Lewandowsky, Ullrich Ecker, and their graduate student at the time, John Cook, who had independently confirmed and replicated our findings. I felt reassured we were onto something important here.

We eventually replicated the study ourselves, too, with one key twist: we delayed the misinformation attack by about a week and found that those who had been inoculated earlier, before exposure, still exhibited 'attitudinal immunity' one week later. The results seemed solid.

Yet as I kept talking to journalists and fact-checkers, I noticed a sense of discomfort about the idea that you could fight misinformation with misinformation. They simply wanted to give people the facts, not a weakened dose of the virus. It was still a radical idea to put out there. It reminded me of McGuire's story that the supposed problem with the captured Korean War POWs is that society had simply failed to communicate and reinforce the importance of 'American values'. That thinking still permeates society today. Let's fast forward seventy years.

QAnon and inoculation: A missed opportunity

In 2020, the US-based furniture company Wayfair found itself in the middle of a bizarre QAnon conspiracy theory – the outlandish idea that a group of Satan-worshipping paedophiles in the 'deep state' were undermining former president Trump. One prominent Twitter user noticed that some of Wayfair's cabinets were outrageously expensive and all using girls' names. A conspiracy theory quickly emerged on social media that the furniture in question must therefore have young girls hidden in them as part of an international child-trafficking ring (of course, what else could it be?). This theory was bolstered by the fact that when typing the product's 'stock-keeping-unit' (SKU) into a Russian search engine (Yandex), images of young women would appear in the search results.

I am sharing this story because I was asked to join a select meeting with a high-level executive of Wayfair and several PR experts to discuss what exactly had transpired and what lessons were to be learned. I was surprised by what the executive ultimately took away from the conversation: that Wayfair had not sufficiently instilled their ethics and values in the minds of their customers. Like the captured US soldiers who had forgotten their American ideals, if consumers only knew that Wayfair was an ethical company, then surely they would have never believed the conspiracy theory in the first place?

I begged to differ. The problem was not that Wayfair customers somehow failed to understand that Wayfair is an ethical company. The problem is that they had no mental defences against the misinformation attack that Wayfair was involved in some sort of child-trafficking conspiracy. If Wayfair had pre-emptively warned their customers that they might hear of some ludicrous story that the company is involved in an international child-trafficking conspiracy (akin to preparing the body for invading agents) and prebunked the conspiracy by giving people the facts and arguments they needed to dismantle the conspiracy (for example, it turns out that when you enter any string of random numbers into the Yandex search engine, the same images of young women appear), then customers would have had the ability to counter-argue and resist the misinformation (akin to generating specific antibodies).

You might ask, is it not a bit far-fetched to assume that Wayfair could have somehow anticipated a story this bizarre? It may seem so at first but let's not forget Hillary Clinton and #PizzaGate. This is not the first time someone has created an outlandish child-trafficking conspiracy theory. Moreover, we know that conspiracy theories have a defined structure to them. Using the CONSPIRE guide, we can find evidence of 'Reinterpreting random events' (any random string of numbers would return the same set of images); 'Persecuted victim' (young girls); 'Something must be wrong' (those expensive and suspiciously named cabinets!), and 'Nefarious intent' – (the 'evil' company).

It is not too surprising that Wayfair was caught off-guard. Although few corporations had imagined they could be vulnerable to such misinformation attacks, the stock price of a company can easily be tanked by viral misinformation. You might rightly consider that sometimes it is appropriate to strategically monitor the risk of misinformation before getting too involved. In this case, though, the misinformation did go viral, so not inoculating customers was a missed opportunity. But even so, we now know what the virus looks like so the vaccine could be ready-made to inoculate at-risk customers. Remember that our research indicated that there may be therapeutic benefits to inoculating those who may have already been exposed – but not yet fully convinced – of the fake story.

Ultimately, our findings suggest that although McGuire was wrong about his initial assumption that inoculation only works when people have never been challenged on a given belief before, this turned out to be a good thing for the world. We discovered that inoculation could protect people against real-world misinformation.

As everyone started to wrap their heads around the new science of prebunking misinformation, I kept getting questions from journalists about how to scale the vaccine beyond specific issues like climate change. Would you have to create a weakened dose for every single myth? This nagged at me because it was a good question: even if it were theoretically possible to anticipate and prebunk a wide variety of fake news stories, there must be a better, more efficient way of doing it.

The Australian team who replicated our study provided a crucial hint: they had used the same experimental setup as us but instead of giving people – and subsequently refuting – a weakened dose of the Global Warming Petition Project, they explained the fake expert technique more generally using an example from the tobacco industry. The example featured a 1930s ad with a picture of a doctor and the accompanying text '20,679 Physicians say LUCKIES are less irritating'. Like the petition, it uses a big number (20,000 'experts') to try to convince people. The tobacco industry referred to this tactic as 'Project Whitecoat', and used spokespeople dressed up in white coats to give the appearance that they had medical or scientific expertise. What the researchers found was promising: those who were inoculated against fake experts beforehand, using the tobacco example, were much less likely to now be duped when exposed to the bogus climate petition (a different strain of the same virus).

This inspired us to sift through the scientific literature to identify the more general structure of misinformation: its core DNA. If misinformation, in general, has a common structure to it that encodes its development and spread, the possibility of a broader-spectrum vaccine could become reality. And so our search began.

I spent the next year trying to uncover the DNA structure of misinformation.

FAKE NEWS ANTIGEN 8
Inoculate against misinformation

— Exposing people to a sufficiently weakened dose of a fake news story, followed by a persuasive prebunk, helps the mind cultivate intellectual antibodies against it.

— Although there is nothing wrong with giving people more facts and a healthy information diet, if you really want to protect people from fake news it is often more effective to inoculate them beforehand.

— For example, giving people more evidence on why global warming is real doesn't really prepare them for an attack on the scientific consensus that humans are the cause. Instead, forewarning people of an impending attack on the scientific consensus, along with a weakened example of the misinformation in question and strong refutations of its claims, is going to be much more effective in generating psychological resistance against such falsehoods.

— Forewarned is forearmed but giving people the tools and mental ammunition they need – in advance – to counter-argue and understand why claims are false or misleading is what allows for the development of psychological immunity.

CHAPTER 9

Bad News:
The Six Degrees of Manipulation

'Your defences . . . must therefore be as flexible and
inventive as the Arts you seek to undo,'
PROFESSOR SEVERUS SNAPE (*Harry Potter*)

Back when I was an undergraduate student, I was assigned a book that first got me excited about psychology as a science. This book was called *Influence: The Psychology of Persuasion*, written by Bob Cialdini – perhaps now better known as the 'Godfather of Influence'.

I recently called Bob to ask him about Bill McGuire and the seminal research on the science of persuasion that he developed in the mid-1980s. He told me that on a faculty visit, McGuire had suggested that if he wanted to know about persuasion, he should go and study those who persuade other people for a living. Bob took McGuire's advice to heart and went undercover for years to study how professionals get people to say 'yes'. He signed up as a trainee for lots of different professions – from a car salesman and advertiser to fundraising for charities. What he discovered was that all of these professional influencers seemed to make use of six universal principles of persuasion.* I quickly realized that we had

---

* These are 'reciprocity', 'commitment', 'social proof', 'authority', 'liking', and 'scarcity'. Notice the fine line between persuasion and manipulation; using legitimate expert or authoritative sources to influence people's opinion is one thing but the covert use of fake experts to try to dupe people is clearly manipulation.

been on a similar journey: for over a year our lab had examined the techniques of those who practise the dark arts of misinformation. We sought to uncover the structural building-blocks of *manipulation*. We wanted to understand how professionals fool people using misinformation tactics so we can make people resistant to them.

So, what do widely different examples of misinformation have in common? Some techniques were easier to identify than others. For example, the connection between alien cover-ups in Area 51, 5G networks and Covid-19 symptoms, a secret New World Order, and lizard politicians is clear: they are all conspiracy theories. They share a common 'genetic' structure which we're familiar with from chapter 3. But other techniques are more subtle – such as the use of emotions to frame headlines and manipulate how people feel: clickbait.

The fake expert technique is actually part of a larger strategy we ended up calling 'impersonation', as it's not just experts who are being impersonated, but also politicians, celebrities, and official organizations. Other strategies include group polarization, trolling, and discrediting.

The Six Degrees of Manipulation

Together these strategies constitute the Six Degrees of Manipulation – or the 'DEPICT manipulation' framework (**D**iscrediting, **E**motion, **P**olarization, **I**mpersonation, **C**onspiracy and **T**rolling). I'll walk you through each of these techniques.

Discrediting

At one point or another, producers of misinformation have to deal with being challenged by journalists and fact-checkers on the veracity of the content that they publish. Discrediting is a technique that deflects attention away from accusations by attacking the source of the criticism. A classic illustration of the discrediting technique was employed by Donald Trump, who, on 17 February 2017, tweeted: 'The FAKE NEWS media (failing @ nytimes, @NBCNews, @ABC, @CBS, @CNN) is not my enemy, it is the enemy of the American People. SICK!' This tweet inspired our team to study a psychological bias we later termed the 'You are fake news!' effect.

The idea behind this bias is that the term 'fake news' has become a politicized rhetorical device to dismiss and discredit information that is uncongenial to our values and attitudes. Jon Roozenbeek and I, together with our colleague Costas Panagopoulos, Professor of Political Science at Northeastern University, conducted a national survey in the US where we employed an old psychological technique: we asked people to report the first thing that comes to mind when they hear the term 'fake news'.

Known as a 'top-of-mind' association, this type of study helps uncover the implicit mental representations that people have with a concept – the first thoughts, words, and symbols that pop into our head when prompted to quickly reflect on something. For example, consider that when prompted with the word 'happiness', the first thing that comes to mind for most Americans is 'smile' but for most Koreans it's 'family'. This top-of-mind technique is useful for tapping into the associative networks that exist in people's memories (that is, uncovering what concepts are semantically related to each other).

We interviewed about 1,000 Americans and then manually coded all of their responses. There were three clear associative themes that emerged around the term 'fake news':

(a) words related to the media (liberal press, Fox, CNN)
(b) the expression of negative emotions (deceit, doubt)
(c) political references (Trump, government, Russia).

Perhaps unsurprisingly, in absolute terms, most associations were about the media (44 per cent) and politics (38 per cent). But the really interesting bit is what happens when you split things up by political ideology. What's the first thing that comes to mind for conservatives when they hear the term 'fake news'? The answer was overwhelmingly – 75 per cent – a single term: CNN (the CNN association only emerged for 3 per cent of liberals). Conversely, what is the first thing the majority of liberals thought of when they heard the term 'fake news'? Fox News! – 59 per cent versus only 4 per cent of conservatives. In other words, if you're liberal, then Fox is considered 'fake news' whereas if you're conservative,

CNN is fake news. The irony is that Fox News and CNN are both rated as having 'mixed accuracy' by independent fact-checkers.

Another interesting finding is that for conservatives, the overwhelming majority of associations with the term 'fake news' were media-related (often the mainstream media), whereas for liberals the term was more associated with politics (and Donald Trump in particular). Crucially, if the mainstream media was the first thing that came to mind when hearing the term 'fake news', then people were also significantly less likely to trust the media. So the frequent discrediting of the mainstream media by Trump and other prominent politicians might well have had its intended effect.

Emotion

A second key manipulation tactic that kept coming back time and again in our research is the use of emotions to get people riled up. In 2014, Facebook published the results of a massive and controversial* experiment on their platform. By manipulating the emotional content in people's newsfeed they found that when positive news was suppressed, people posted less positive and more negative content (and vice versa when negative emotional content was reduced). The scary conclusion from this experiment is that Facebook can manipulate emotional sentiment on the platform without people's awareness.

Analyses of anti-vaccination websites have shown that about 76–88 per cent of them leverage emotional appeals. This is important because several studies have found that putting people in an emotional state can significantly increase their susceptibility to believing fake news. In fact, we know from lots of research that content which deliberately plays on people's basic emotions – such as fear and anger – gets more traction. Fearmongering and moral outrage are two particularly effective strategies. This is likely so because studies have shown that moral–emotional words such as 'hate', 'punish', and 'evil' capture our visual attention more than neutral words. Prototypical examples of stories that have elicited

---

* It was controversial ethically because people didn't have a chance to opt out of the experiment.

widespread moral outrage are the Pizzagate 'child-trafficking' conspiracy, and President Putin's bogus claim that his invasion of Ukraine was to 'de-Nazify' the country.

But can we get more specific about the added benefit of appealing to emotion in spreading misinformation? In fact, we can. In one of our social media studies looking at nearly a million posts from popular media outlets on Twitter and Facebook (see chapter 6), we find that the presence of every additional moral–emotional word in a post (such as 'murder' or 'hate') increases shares and retweets by 10–17 per cent. Our colleagues at New York University, using a different data set of about half a million posts, put that number slightly higher, at 20 per cent. This is a significant bump in terms of the diffusion of online content. Remember that in our study of the Twitter accounts of the most popular conspiracy theorists (also covered in chapter 6), we similarly found that the use of negative emotions, especially anger, was highly prevalent, amongst both conspiracy influencers as well as their followers.

This is also the reason why defining fake news in terms of whether or not the publisher is dodgy doesn't always work. A great example is the following headline from an otherwise credible and factual outlet, the *Chicago Tribune*: 'Healthy Doctor Died Two Weeks After Receiving the Covid-19 Vaccine'. Although the report was factual, the headline is highly misleading as there was no evidence that the death of the doctor had anything to do with him having received the Covid-19 vaccine. This isn't an obscure example either; the article received over 50 million views, and a report from Facebook confirmed that it was the most viewed news article on their platform in early 2021. The headline clearly uses the emotion technique to enable fearmongering about vaccinations (there are many examples like this: instead of a 'serious but rare side-effect', you could print 'a devastating and deadly blood clot'). In fact, the article was shared widely by accounts known for their anti-vaccination activity on the Facebook platform.

When you next read a news story, ask yourself whether it is trying to manipulate how you feel, especially about other groups and hot-button social, political, and scientific issues. The frequency with which this happens in all media is much higher than most of us realize.

Polarization

The use of emotions to get people agitated is followed closely by a technique which only has one singular purpose: to drive people apart. The polarization technique involves a deliberate attempt to move people away from the political centre by increasing the gap between two affinity groups, usually the political left and political right or liberals and conservatives, respectively. So how do spreaders of fake news achieve this in practice?

'False amplification' is a frequently employed tactic that blows up societal divisions by acquiring bots who tweet or retweet polarizing content to flood the discourse on a contested issue. Bots are controlled by software which contains instructions both for sending automated messages and for when to engage in polarizing behaviours, depending on the bot's level of sophistication. Of course, bots which better approximate human-like online behaviour are more likely to be able to evade detection.

For example, one big social media study looked at over 4 million Twitter posts during the 2017 Catalan referendum – an unconstitutional referendum asking citizens whether they would prefer for Catalonia to become independent of Spain. In total, a little less than 25 per cent of the posts came from bots, but almost 40 per cent of the replies came from bots. A 'sentiment analysis' of the interactions and hashtags used by individuals revealed two clearly opposing camps: 'Constitutionalists' and 'Independentists'. The independence camp revealed strong associations between terms such as 'freedom' and independence', and 'fight' and 'shame', in relation to the Spanish government. What's interesting is that the negative associations solely came from bot accounts. Moreover, although bots appear to be on the periphery of the social network, they gained influence by strategically targeting human influencer accounts, who were more centrally positioned within the network of independentists.

A similar study in 2018 found that (sophisticated) bots tweeted about vaccination at higher rates than non-bots. For example, an analysis of the Twitter hashtag '#VaccineUS' showed that they often amplify both sides of the debate using highly divisive language. Consider the following examples: '#VaccinateUS #vaccines contain mercury! Deadly poison!'

and '#VaccinateUS. You can't fix stupidity. Let them die from measles, I'm for #vaccination!' Data shows that Russian bots are known to use especially polarizing words (such as 'deadly poison', 'die', 'stupidity') and that this tendency has in fact increased over the years.

Although it is often assumed that fake news is created to dupe people into believing specific false claims, more often than not, political polarization is one of the more central aims of a well-targeted disinformation campaign. Polarization has two broad dimensions. The most commonly talked about dimension is polarization over specific policy issues (such as disagreement over Russian interference in the 2016 US presidential election). But growing concerns have been noted around what we call 'affective polarization', or the tendency for groups to dislike each other at a personal level. Research has shown that people are now less willing to date those from the other side, pay them less for the same work, and even avoid them as roommates. After all, when two (or more) political groups in society no longer get along – or even actively dislike each other – democratic discourse slowly breaks down.

Impersonation

Although we initially started out with the 'fake expert' technique, as we looked closer, it turns out that impersonation is a much bigger strategy with two key variants. The first revolves around impersonating an account or real person by closely mimicking their appearance. This could be an expert, but also a celebrity, or even a politician.

One of my favourite examples comes from Alex Jones, host of *Info-Wars*, and pedlar of the conspiracy theory that the Sandy Hook shooting was a staged event with 'crisis actors'.* He frequently promotes vitality and other dietary supplements on his show with the help of MIT medical consultant 'Dr Edward F. Group III'. Edward in fact is a naturopathic physician, chiropractor, and alternative medicine specialist who completed a non-degree management programme at the Massachusetts Institute of Technology. It's a classic example of the 'white coat' strategy

---

* During a 2022 defamation trial, Jones finally admitted that the Sandy Hook shooting was '100% real'.

used by the tobacco industry. Although selling supplements for profit is one thing, the use of fake medical experts to peddle dangerous fake cures – from gargling lemon to ingesting methanol – has exploded during the Covid-19 pandemic. Remember that the viral *Plandemic* film featured 'Dr Judy Mikovits', a discredited researcher who used her credentials to spread false claims about Covid-19, such as the myth that the flu vaccine contains the coronavirus.

Another good example is an incident in 2018, where someone impersonated the US billionaire Warren Buffett on Twitter. The account and photo looked exactly like the real thing except for a small difference: they had misspelled Buffett as 'Buffet'. Lots of people were fooled, though, and the account – retweeted by media figures and politicians – gained hundreds of thousands of followers within minutes. Fake Warren offered feel-good advice such as 'stay teachable' and 'don't spend what you don't have' – drawing inspiration from things the real Warren Buffett had said or shared before. This is important, because if, as a producer of fake news, you come off as too ridiculous, then nobody's going to believe you.

However, impersonating individuals is minor league stuff. A second variant to the impersonation technique involves posing as a legitimate organization or news outlet but without using any journalistic norms or credentials. A rather disturbing case in point was an attempt of the UK Conservative Party to rebrand their campaign account on Twitter as a fact-checking organization. During a 2019 televised debate, they temporarily rebranded their Twitter account as 'factcheckUK' with a white tick as its symbol. Twitter stated that the Conservative Party had misled the public.

Another good example is a 'scientific' paper accompanying the Global Warming Petition Project, which used the template from the *Proceedings of the National Academy of Science* to borrow credibility and dupe people into thinking the petition had come from the prestigious NAS. After many inquiries, the NAS Council had to release a public statement renouncing the petition and correcting any public confusion that had arisen from the affair.

Similarly, to anyone who has never heard of them, American Frontline Doctors (AFD) is an organization which makes it sound like they are noble doctors saving lives on the frontline of the pandemic. Unfortunately, it couldn't be further from the truth: AFD is a political organization involved in anti-vaccination activism and spreading misinformation about Covid-19.

Impersonation is also popular during wars. After Russia's invasion of Ukraine in February 2022, social media were flooded with 'shallowfakes' – that is, doctored images and videos that impersonate the presence of Ukrainian or Russian troops in attempts to dupe audiences about the state of affairs during the war.

Finally, let us not forget that I myself was recently duped by a fake video which borrowed material from a previous NASA mission, complete with Martian wind, to fool thousands of people into thinking they were listening to the actual NASA recording of the Mars rover *Perseverance* landing. The list goes on and on.

A clever impersonation technique is key to duping people with misinformation.

Conspiracy

Conspiracy theories are such a hot topic that I devoted the whole of chapter 3 of this book to the psychology of conspiratorial thinking. What's important to note here is that conspiracy theories are now part and parcel of the types of content that fringe and even some mainstream news websites are keen to offer. For example, consider that *InfoWars* – described by independent fact-checkers as 'a crackpot, tin foil hat-level conspiracy website that promotes pseudoscience and fake news' – regularly receives about 10 million visits a month. That's much more traffic than the leading US conservative magazine the *National Review*, or even mainstream news outlets such as the *Economist*. The Plandemic conspiracy film garnered many more views than Taylor Swift's 'City of Lover' TV concert special announcement, a Zoom reunion of *The Office* cast, and the Pentagon's 'unexplained aerial phenomena' videos.

Conspiracy theories have gone mainstream. A recent YouGov–Cambridge poll, for instance, found that: 37 per cent of Americans think that a single secret group of people control world events; 29 per cent think the government is secretly hiding aliens; 33 per cent think that harmful vaccine side-effects are deliberately being hidden from the public; and 27 per cent think that climate change is a hoax. This is not just the case in the States. The same survey found that well over half the population in Spain, Greece, Turkey, Mexico, and Nigeria think that a single group of people control world events. Although these estimates can vary from survey to survey, at minimum, a solid third of the population consistently endorses conspiracy theories.

In chapter 3, we used the guide CONSPIRE (Contradictory, Over-riding suspicion, Nefarious intent, Something must be wrong, Persecuted victim, Immune to evidence, and Re-interpreting randomness) to iden-tify the common structure of conspiracy theories. But our investigations revealed one additional and crucial insight: the conspiracy theories I mentioned above are all about politics or real-world societal events – things people care about.

An effective conspiracy theory leverages real events to cast doubt on mainstream and official explanations. For example, #Pizzagate rooted its false allegations in claims that 'codewords' had been found in leaked emails from Hillary Clinton's campaign manager, John Podesta, and that these codes referred to a child-trafficking ring operating out of the base-ment of a pizzeria (the apparent connection being that 'cheese pizza' is a term and emoji that paedophiles use on chat boards, 'cp' standing for 'child pornography'.) The Sandy Hook conspiracy theory uses the elementary school shooting event as evidence for a false flag operation orchestrated by the US government in an attempt to crack down on American gun rights. The *Plandemic* conspiracy theory suggests that the Covid-19 pan-demic is a hoax largely in an attempt to fuel and spread anti-vaccination sentiment. Conspiracy theories about US-funded bioweapon research in Ukraine taps into an international conflict.

What all these theories have in common is that they use a grain of truth, a real event – something people care about – in order to gain main-stream traction and appeal. The reason why you have probably never heard of Alan Tarica's conspiracy theory about Shakespeare's sonnets is because, even though it is anchored around a real discussion about authorship, most people probably don't really care that much whether or not Shakespeare wrote his own sonnets.

In 2017, twenty-something Peter McIndoe started the satirical conspiracy theory that 'Birds Aren't Real'. The theory claims that birds are in fact drones operated by the US government to spy on its own citizens. The theory can explain all sorts of interesting facts, such as the reason why birds like to sit on power lines: to recharge themselves. Supporters are known as 'Bird Truthers'. McIndoe clearly understands how conspiracy theories get traction. His theory sounds ludicrous, but its narrative touches on privacy concerns, government overreach, and real controversies. With some small tweaks, it might just capture the public imagination.

Trolling

If you're into fishing, you may know that the term 'trolling' refers to a fishing line being drawn through the water using a lure or baited hook (often from the back of a fishing boat). It's a popular method used to catch, for example, salmon or trout. Online, trolling involves using bait too, such as posting inflammatory or emotional material in an attempt to manipulate public perception or provoke a response from a user. Hence the popular advice 'Don't feed the trolls.'

We learned a lot about trolling from a special guest that one of our collaborators had invited over for one of their disinformation workshops: Lyudmila Savchuk – a former professional troll from the Russian Internet Research Agency (IRA), also known as the 'Trolls from Olgino'. Lyudmila is an internet activist and journalist in her mid-thirties who spent a few months working at one of the IRA's main offices on 55 Savushkina street in St Petersburg. She described the building as a massive warehouse filled with just offices and computers. Investigations have estimated that about 600–1,000 employees worked at the office building (and many more from home) with each worker posting content anywhere between 50–100 times a day.

Initially Lyudmila was targeted on her social media feed with ads looking for educated Russians who might be interested in joining the 'creative industry'. A friend of hers explained that it was really a secret gig at a secret location. Once she got the job, she quickly caught on to the fact that there were hundreds of people working around the clock to comment on social media, alternating between day and night shifts. The troll factory literally never closed. One of her tasks was to assume a fake identity and start posting content on a popular Russian blog. She described one example where she made up a post that a new (fictional) computer game about slavery was getting traction amongst kids. The creators? Evil Americans! The aim of the post was to fuel anti-American sentiment. About two months into the job, she started leaking documents anonymously to the press. The IRA caught on and fired Lyudmila, discrediting and accusing her of being a secret CIA operative.

The IRA conducts (foreign) influence operations on behalf of prominent Russian businesses and political actors associated with Putin. A key distinction between a bot and a troll is that the troll has a human touch and dupes people into thinking that the troll is a real and politically engaged person. There were extensive files that the trolls could pull content from, such as: 'I was in my kitchen baking, and I was thinking how Putin is doing a really good job . . .' The employees created fake profiles, videos, and images, and commented on literally everything – from European values and the US election, to pro-Putin and anti-Ukraine content.

Although the IRA's initial focus was to change public opinion in the West about Russia's military invasion of the Ukraine in 2014, they quickly turned their attention to Europe and the United States in particular. Analyses from the US Senate Select Committee on Intelligence reveal extensive evidence of a 'a sustained campaign of information warfare against the United States aimed at influencing how this nation's citizens think about themselves, their government, and their fellow Americans'. In 2018, the US Department of Justice indicted the IRA for interfering with the 2016 presidential election. Estimates show that the trolls reached over 100 million Americans on Facebook alone, with a budget that exceeded $25 million, in order to manipulate US political discourse. Examples include voter suppression tactics, such as tweets that confuse people about voting rules or tell them to stay home because their vote doesn't matter. Other instances involved sowing distrust and societal divisions by amplifying both sides of a debate, such as talking about the pros and cons of vaccination, or the secession of Texas (If Brexit, Why

Not #Texit?) and California (#Calexit), as well as influencing elections by floating pro-Trump and anti-Clinton content.

I was able to download a file with over 200,000 deleted tweets from accounts linked to the IRA. These tweets were recovered by NBC News, based on a list of just under 4,000 Twitter accounts handed over to Congress by Twitter. Examples included: 'Why can't the media talk about the real issues, the fraud, the lies, and the scandals of Clinton?? #NeverHillary', and 'Trump is the most pro-black candidate! This pic breaks all stereotypes of dishonest media! Spread it!' Although some posts didn't receive much engagement, this last one was retweeted over a thousand times. The IRA trolls were fed content through a roster of themes that emphasized divisive social and political issues, such as consistently talking about Black culture, LGBT rights, and gun control, across different social media channels. For example, the IRA operated YouTube channels with names such as 'PoliceState', 'Don't Shoot', and 'Black Matters'.

The whole IRA operation was unprecedented in terms of its scope.

Although millions of Americans were exposed to polarizing content from Russian trolls, mere exposure doesn't always translate into persuasion. For example, a 2020 study found that a sample of politically active Twitter users, who directly interacted with IRA troll accounts in 2017, did not significantly change their political attitudes over the course of a month or so. Yet, in contrast, another study found that changes in public support for Donald Trump were in fact strongly predicted by increased IRA Twitter activity in the preceding week. For example, an increase in 25,000 retweets of IRA accounts per week resulted in a 1 per cent increase in Trump's polling numbers.

In both cases, exposure to the IRA accounts was not randomized so it is difficult to draw any firm causal conclusions. But even assuming that the IRA was not as successful as commonly thought, sophisticated new troll farms are popping up every day and they won't suddenly stop trying. Trolls aim to wreak havoc by attempting to manipulate public perception.

The key is to inoculate ourselves before they wage their next attack.

Bad News

Now that our team had identified the Six Degrees of Manipulation that are used time and again to produce misinformation,* we were ready to try to generalize our inoculation. But there was another issue. How were we going to scale the production and uptake of our psychological vaccine? What was going to be our virtual needle? Jon Roozenbeek had some ideas. It turns out that this idea changed the course of our careers in ways neither of us could have ever imagined.

At the time, Jon was a newly minted graduate student at Cambridge. He and his former classmate, Ruurd Oosterwoud, who'd just started a highly innovative media group, told me that they'd been toying with the idea of creating a disinformation simulator to counter fake news. 'A *disinformation simulator*?' I asked. 'Yes,' Jon said, looking back at me with a slightly amused grin on his face.

Innovative it certainly was. I thought about the idea for a second. Either these two guys had completely lost their minds, or they were on to something. We set up weekly meetings to discuss our ideas and methodology in more detail; meetings turned into lunches, lunches turned into dinners and pub meetings and, before we knew it, we were deep into the project. Obsessed. We were often the last ones in the office – debating ideas, as we gazed out of the window.

Jon was really excited by the prospect of turning inoculation into a fake news simulator. I was excited too, because it aligned perfectly with an idea that had been brewing in the back of my mind: *active inoculation*.

---

* There are other misinformation techniques out there, but more on that in the next chapter.

In most inoculation experiments, participants receive persuasive arguments or rebuttals in the form of a short text or essay. Essentially the experimenter is providing both the misinformation and the arguments people need to resist it. But McGuire hypothesized early on that it might be more effective to let people generate their own counter-arguments, partly because this extra dose of cognitive engagement would strengthen people's memories of the material. After all, if it's your idea or argument, you're less likely to forget it! I was very much drawn to the idea of active inoculation or letting people generate their own antibodies. The question was: how?

We took inspiration from Professor Severus Snape – the infamous Defence Against the Dark Arts teacher in the Harry Potter books. Snape was right that in order for this to work, our defences needed to be as flexible and inventive as the arts we were seeking to undo. Jon and I were very conscious of the fact that, for some people, science has a yawn factor and so the intervention shouldn't feel like a boring lecture. There are already hundreds of videos out there giving people media-literacy tips (such as always checking the source of an article). We wanted to do something different. The whole experience should be fun, entertaining. Jon's major idea was to let people step into the role of a contemporary propagandist – a disinformation tycoon! Let people play the evil genius for a while.

This allowed us to test the principle of 'active inoculation': people would be producing their own media content. Although we quibbled about the exact implementation, we agreed on the most important insight: what better way is there to inoculate people against misinformation than letting them walk a mile in the shoes of a manipulator?

The logic behind this is that many decades of research in psychology shows that the human brain strongly prefers experience over analysis. Mark Twain intuitively understood this when he joked: 'A man who carries a cat by the tail learns something he can learn in no other way.' We learn by doing. I can tell you how to drive a car but that doesn't mean you know how to actually do it (let alone safely). You learn that touching a hot stove is a bad idea by burning your hand on it. The power of that experience will trump any warning that anyone is ever going to give you vicariously. I often like to use a magic show analogy to drive this point home: imagine you go and see your favourite illusionist and you are absolutely baffled by how they pulled off a spectacular magic trick. It seemed so real. How did they do it? Now, I can either give you a detailed blueprint of how the trick works at a functional level and try to engage you analytically (akin to a fact-check), or I can let you step into the shoes of the magician for a while and help you figure out how the trick works on your own. That way, I can guarantee that you'll never be duped by it again. So how could we give people a small microdose of the 'experience' of what it is like to dupe people with fake news?

By this time, Ruurd was making headway with his new organization and we all sat down to discuss how we might be able to achieve this practically. The result was to be a game. Not any game. The first of its kind: a fake news game. Jon was so enthusiastic about the whole project that he immediately started working on a physical card game with the help of Ruurd's team and a creative agency. The basic idea was a multiplayer game where people would take on the role of a particular character with the goal of creating a fake news article. The purpose of the game was to encourage players to think proactively about the methods and techniques involved in creating misleading information. In small groups, students were tasked with producing a news article that fitted the agenda of their assigned character (conspiracy theorist, fearmonger, etc.). We chose a hot-button topic – immigration – to be the centrepiece of the game. Following standard journalistic practice, the articles adhered to a fixed structure, having a title, main body, and quote from an expert. The group with the most 'correct' answers, reflecting appropriate choices of their assigned character, would win the game.

With the help of Ruurd's team, Jon and I were able to pilot-test the game with high-school students between the ages of sixteen and nineteen. We had about a hundred participants on the day, randomized to either the treatment group (who played the fake news game during class) or a control group (who just followed their regular lesson plan). To test the game's effectiveness, we assigned each group to read a fake news article we'd created ourselves on the subject of immigration. The article made use of common misinformation strategies, such as emotional manipulation and conspiracy theories. The students played for about thirty minutes, after which they were asked to read our fake news article. In particular, we were interested in how reliable and persuasive students found the article and how they'd arrived at their viewpoints. (Students in the control group were given the exact same articles and answered the same questions, but didn't play the game.)

The results were fascinating: students in the treatment group found the fake news article significantly less reliable than their peers in the control group, and as a result, rated the arguments used in the fake article as less persuasive. Looking at the written qualitative responses, many students gave explanations that fitted with the lessons they'd learned in the game. For example, students commented on how writers had employed inflammatory and polarizing language to make their points.

Now, having said this, as any good scientist, we were critical of the results too. For one, the effects were modest, the sample was small, and the signal was noisy. Jon and I were also a bit puzzled by the fact that we'd spent a huge amount of time designing a game, carefully planning and executing the study, but ultimately only had about a hundred students participate in our pilot test. That's not unusual in psychology, but we all agreed that there must be a better way to scale our intervention. We needed to reach a much larger audience. In fact, we needed a vehicle that could be employed outside the lecture theatre and the classroom. Too many initiatives focus solely on individuals within the educational system. Moreover, the biggest limitation of the game, in my mind, was the fact that it didn't feature a social media component, and so the game didn't sufficiently consider the modern environment in which people receive, select, and share misinformation.

Here's why I love working with Jon and Ruurd: about six months later, we had a prototype of an interactive engine powering an online fake news game. A full-blown social media simulation. A simulation of Twitter to be exact. We could now present people with simulated tweets, both real and fake, just as you would encounter them on Twitter, and evaluate people's ability to spot fake news before and after playing our game. The amount of people we could potentially reach was endless, from the angry teenager living in their parents' basement, to the online 'truther movement'. We no longer needed to go into schools one by one, and participants didn't have to come to our lab in Cambridge either. As long as they had access to the internet, *anyone* could participate.

We were excited to say the least. We also realized that nobody had ever attempted to do this before. We'd be introducing to the world the first fake news game of its kind. Recognizing that fake news isn't always a right-wing or left-wing issue, Jon and I figured that the worst thing would be for our intervention to become politicized so that we'd just end up preaching to the converted. Jon insisted that we make the intervention both fun and non-political, so we ended up with a slightly controversial intervention in the sense that people can make fun of climate change or view it as alarming and people can attack big government or dunk on evil corporations. For every traditional left-wing choice in the game, there is a right-wing alternative. In a nutshell, we wanted people to familiarize themselves with the techniques of manipulation on their own terms in a non-judgmental environment.

And so we did. We called it: *Bad News*.

Bad News differs from the fake news card game in many important ways. If we were going to take our efforts online, it had to be done differently. For starters, the online game simulates a social media feed, incorporates the concept of echo chambers and filter bubbles, and features the six distinct misinformation techniques ('DEPICT') that we'd recently uncovered in our research. The game has six 'badges' players can earn or levels through which they progress – mastering one misinformation technique at a time. The core philosophy remained the same though: people step into the shoes of a fake news tycoon and are exposed to weakened doses of the strategies used to mislead people online, as well as ways to spot them. By 'weakened dose' I mean that we keep the scenarios fictional and – using humour and satire – make them so ridiculous that nobody is going to actually believe them. In other words, we get the point across (stimulating the immune system) without actually duping people (in McGuire's words, triggering but not overwhelming people's immune response).

Bad News is accessible as a browser game and is entirely choice-based, so that at every juncture players are presented with a series of options about what to do next. Importantly, the choices that you make affect your pathway throughout the game. As such, it's very much a 'choose your own adventure' game. It is also highly interactive insofar as other simulated users respond to the content that you post. As you take on the mantle of a fake news tycoon, the purpose of the game is to produce media content using the Six Degrees of Manipulation and attract as many followers as possible without losing credibility. To help players keep track of their nefarious goals, follower and credibility meters are displayed on the left-hand side of the screen. We opted for an ironic 1980s arcade-style touch and feel, so the game would look ridiculously retro – the whole point being that a game about fake news shouldn't take itself too seriously. (You can play the game for free at www.getbadnews.com. I've included a screenshot of the game's interface below.)

In the game, you are tasked with creating your own news media content. You start out as an anonymous 'netizen' but gradually rise to become the master of your own (fictional!) fake news empire. You earn followers and credibility by going through the scenarios, each of which cover the main six strategies used to spread misinformation. If you fail to select options that are consistent with what a real fake news tycoon would do then you lose points and followers. You therefore have to ditch all pretence of ethical journalism and get your hands dirty. However, it's not as simple as it sounds: if you're being too ridiculous, points will be deducted. You lose the game when your credibility drops to zero. The number of followers at the end of the game counts as your final score.

One of the most frequent questions we get is about the algorithm that decides when you gain and lose points and the maximum number of followers you can obtain in the game. We've decided to keep that a secret! You can, of course, compare your score against that of your friends and family. For those who feel utterly uncomfortable duping people – even as part of a simulation – there's always the option to 'Die a Hero'.

Jon and I like to use the vaccination analogy here; just as some people temporarily feel a bit under the weather after receiving a flu vaccine, the whole point of the game is to activate our psychological immune system. In order to do that, we need to give people a little jolt.

Game on

Let's be honest, you're probably frustrated about something, right? An incompetent government? The fake news media? Or maybe the Flat Earth Society? This is how the game starts. At which point, you're encouraged to post a frustrated tweet. After you post something, let's say, 'The mainstream media is one massive conspiracy, #FakeNews', you suddenly start to gain followers . The game's narrator explains that more followers means more influence. However, they also note that you're not very credible, at least not yet. Here's where the impersonation badge comes in. The basic premise of this scenario is that the internet no longer has any barriers to entry. Anyone can start their own blog or website and publish content that looks legitimate. The goal is to illustrate to the player – in a severely weakened form – how easy it is to fake a professional look and convey a sense of legitimacy.

In the game, you can either impersonate Donald Trump (who is about to declare war on North Korea, #KimJongDone), NASA (who announces that a large space object is about to hit the West Coast, #BeSafe), or Nickelodeon (declaring the immediate and permanent cancellation of SpongeBob SquarePants, #I'mReady!). You can see a screenshot of the Trump impersonation tweet on page 215 (during the first test, most players failed to notice that we subtly manipulated the twitter handle: 'Trunp' instead of 'Trump'). Players are then encouraged to move from being an anonymous goon to the editor-in-chief of their own news outlet. (For example, with a few clicks you can launch 'The Cosmos Post: Bursting the mainstream media bubble', or 'The Honest Truth Online: What they don't want you to read'.)

So you're a big shot editor-in-chief now, but you need content! In the game, this is the first badge where you are encouraged to share content

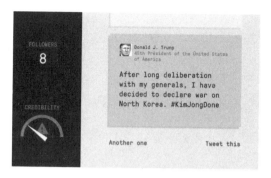

from your fictional news site. You can browse several headlines to exploit – from climate change to GMOs (Genetically Modified Organisms). The game's narrator asks for your opinion about GMOs or climate change and tells you that genetically modified food is going way too far, what's next – genetically modified pets? You're then nudged to run with the story that GMOs will bring about the Apocalypse or that climate change is a total hoax. You can pick between several attacks: for example, you can post an emotional meme that features a mother hugging their child with the line: 'Apparently I was ruining the planet . . . keeping my baby warm!' This scenario illustrates to the player that it doesn't matter what your opinion on the issue is; the same manipulation techniques are often used to attack and undermine scientific debates.

Over the course of the next five badges, the player is inoculated against the use of emotions to manipulate public opinion, polarizing audiences on hot-button issues, denial tactics, including discrediting fact-checkers, and casting doubt on mainstream narratives by concocting conspiracy theories. In the final level of the game, the trolling badge ties everything together for the player. There is only one correct option to choose from this time: a story about the mysterious disappearance of an aeroplane. Once you select the right scenario, you are prompted to sow doubt using the conspiracy technique. We put extra effort into creating the missing airliner conspiracy theory, so I am sharing the photoshopped evidence with you on page 216. After you post your theory and recruit an army of bots, a national scandal erupts and things start to unravel, fast. Like the IRA trolls, you've successfully experimented with key disinformation techniques to wreak havoc and create societal discord.

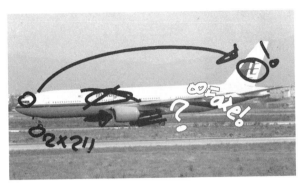

This image loosely mirrors some of the actual conspiracy theories surrounding the disappearance of Malaysia Airlines Flight 370 in March 2014.

Good news about *Bad News*

It was my first visit to London's Design Museum. An attendant passed me the special exhibit booklet and I thanked them while flipping through the pages. My wife quickly interrupted, saying that I was the artist on exhibit. Somewhat embarrassed, I mumbled that I wasn't the artist – I was the scientist, if anything – and just part of a much larger team behind *Bad News*. The real artists were three unassuming guys at the design studio, Gusmanson, who were responsible for the unique look and feel of the game.

I never thought I'd be in a museum staring at our own exhibit, listening to passers-by discuss the merits of our work. But we had finally done it. We'd created the world's first fake-news game – and it had gone viral, reaching millions of people worldwide. I was there because we'd been nominated for a Beazley Designs of the Year Award. Looking around, I felt somewhat intimidated. Our game was in competition with Elon Musk's SpaceX rocket (*Falcon Heavy*) and Fenty Beauty, a new cosmetics brand from popstar Rihanna. It felt unreal. But it was only the beginning.

Bad News moved from the Design Museum to the Australian Museum of Discovery and later the House of European History in Brussels. Before long we were on the home page of *Rolling Stone* magazine. *Bad News* was everywhere.

The game initially went viral on Reddit, trending on the main page within days. We received so much traffic that our servers flat out crashed. (The Reddit community call it the 'hug of death'; the technical term is 'the slashdot effect', where a popular website links to a smaller website, causing a massive spike in traffic.) As the game made its way all across the world, we started to receive feedback. We were nervous to say the least. Luckily, we received some favourable reviews from MIT's *Technology Review* and several other PC and design magazines. NPR's headline read: 'Spot Fake News By Making It'; CNN: 'Researchers have created a "vaccine" for fake news. It's a game'. And the *Guardian* wrote: '*Bad News*: the game researchers hope will "vaccinate" public against fake news'.

Yet the operative word for me remained 'hope'. *Had* we managed to successfully create a way to inoculate people against the techniques of misinformation? After years of development, it was finally time to put our theory to the test.

To evaluate *Bad News* 'in the wild' we programmed an in-game experiment so that players could opt-in to scientific research while playing the game. At the beginning of the game, you are asked whether you'd like to participate in scientific research and answer a few quick questions, including a fake news quiz. After about 15–20 minutes, at the end of the game, you're asked to answer the same questions again. This allowed us to examine the possibility that people have become more immune to misinformation after going through our intervention.

When we downloaded the results of our initial test over 40,000 people had taken part. Jon and I immediately realized that we would have never been able to test 40,000 people by going into schools one by one. But we also noticed that not every player had finished the test. After filtering out those individuals who'd completed both the pre and the post-test, we were left with about 15,000 valid trials (or 30,000 datapoints).

To test people, we'd asked them a few questions about themselves, such as their gender, age, education, and political affiliation. Next we administered a random selection of fictional headlines embedded in simulated tweets. We were not interested in promoting simplistic binary thinking – such as whether they are real or fake – but rather whether or not the headlines contained one of the Six Degrees of Manipulation. Some of these tweets therefore employed one of the 'DEPICT' manipulation techniques and others just contained factual or credible information without making use of any of these strategies. Importantly, we designed

217

the headlines ourselves. If we'd used a real fake news story, then people might have known whether it is true or false simply because they'd read, seen, or heard it before. By creating our own headlines, we were able to control which of the six misinformation techniques people would be shown in the post. Example headlines would be:

'The Bitcoin exchange rate is being manipulated by a small group of rich bankers. #InvestigateNow.' (Conspiracy).

'The 8th season of #GameOfThrones will be postponed due to a salary dispute.' (Impersonation).

'New study shows that left-wing people lie far more than right-wing people.' (Polarization).

We modelled our fictional items closely on actual fake news stories to offer a good compromise between realism and experimental control. Our control items referenced credible (real) headlines such as (factual information about Brexit in the UK, and Trump's intention to build a wall on the US–Mexico border), without making use of any of the misinformation strategies.

Importantly, the test items were different from the items people were inoculated against during the game. So, although the items represented the same kind of virus (let's say a conspiracy theory), the exact strain would be different. The idea behind the control items was to account for the possibility that people would start rating all news media as more manipulative post-intervention. Ideally, people would only downgrade their assessments of headlines that contain misinformation and not simply all headlines so that we know that the vaccine is targeting specific invaders instead of just attacking all 'cells.' We asked people how reliable they found each headline on a scale from 1–7 before and after playing the game.

The data revealed that the vaccine was working: there were no changes in the control items – people rated factual news as highly credible before and after the intervention – whereas they found posts containing one of the misinformation strategies as significantly less reliable. Moreover, these findings did not substantially differ for liberals or conservatives, the old or young, the highly educated or the less educated. Although there were some tiny differences, on average, everyone improved their ability to spot misinformation after playing the game. In fact, the biggest gain occurred amongst the group who seemed most susceptible to fake news at the outset: those individuals who performed the worst on the pre-test quiz.

On average, players adjusted their ratings of fake headlines downwards by about half a point (0.5) on the 1–7 reliability scale after playing (up to a whole point for those most susceptible). Relative to pre-test levels, this means that the game boosted people's immunity by about 20–25 per cent. Of course, this level of acquired mental immunity may seem small compared to biological vaccines. But psychological immunity differs from biological immunity in that it is much more variable and subject to internal and external interference. For example, our results emerge despite any strong political, social, or other worldview biases that people may bring to the table when evaluating news media content. It is also important to keep in mind that the test items are headlines people have never seen before and represent different strains of the same virus. So, unlike the climate change experiment, where people were provided with a detailed prebunk to counter a false petition they knew might be coming, people did not know exactly what type of, let's say, conspiracy theory or impersonation attempts they would encounter after playing *Bad News*. In other words, our intervention showed that when you inoculate people against one type of tactic, the acquired level of protection functions as a broad-spectrum vaccine, fighting off other unfamiliar but closely related attacks.

Although Jon and I were excited and impressed by these results, we also took turns playing devil's advocate. We still viewed these findings as preliminary. The next phase was to move to randomized controlled trials, which also allowed us to address a number of outstanding issues. For example, baseline susceptibility to misinformation was relatively low to begin with in our sample. So, who are the people voluntarily playing our game? What if our results were based on a sample of people who are very open to learning about fake news in the first place and thus are already relatively well equipped to spot misinformation? Although our sample was huge, and reasonably diverse, it was not representative of the population as a whole as it skewed towards higher educated, younger, male, and liberal audiences.

Another issue we recognized was that, although the control items were useful, it would be better to have a randomized control group. As for the fake headlines themselves, we started wondering whether people's improved post-game performance could have just been the result of the headlines that we happened to create. Because the in-game testing environment slows down the engine, we could not afford to ask people many questions in the game. We had to be quick and so we only included a single headline for several of the Six Degrees of Manipulation. What if we'd accidentally created easy-to-spot headlines? Maybe that could make the intervention look more powerful than it actually is.

A confidence boost

At this point I had taken on a new PhD student, Melisa Basol. Melisa had won some competitive funding from the Bill and Melinda Gates Foundation and was going to write her doctoral dissertation about psychological inoculation. Shortly after joining our research group, Melisa steered us in a particularly interesting new direction. One of her (many) brilliant ideas was about the role of confidence. We theorized that people are more easily influenced when they are not very confident in their ability to discern fact from fiction. After all, if you are not particularly certain about a belief, such as whether a headline is misleading or not, it might be easier for (nefarious) actors to persuade you.

This also gave us a new opportunity to test *Bad News* more thoroughly. The first thing we did differently was the way in which we collected our sample. Although, with thousands of daily players, the game website was a rich source of data, we wanted to recruit people so that they were blind to the purpose of our study. This was not entirely possible because we can't really hide the fact that the game is about fake news. However, this time people were randomly selected and paid to participate in our study. We then randomized participants into either a treatment group (who played our *Bad News* intervention) or a gamified control group. We could now also verify that players finished the game from start to finish as participants were asked to return a password that was only given out once they had finished the game.

For the control group we chose the 1980s puzzle video game *Tetris* because we wanted to make sure the control group played a game too but one unrelated to fake news. (One participant emailed us asking, somewhat jokingly, whether this is what Cambridge University has come to, paying people to play *Tetris* for twenty minutes? Well, if you were assigned to the control group, then yes, in fact!) We also increased the number of news articles, presenting people with a quiz of eighteen headlines (three headlines for each of the six 'DEPICT' misinformation techniques) to help exclude the possibility that we just got lucky the first time around.

The results of our second experiment were positive. Not only did we replicate our previous findings, but the results were even stronger, despite using a more stringent design. For each of the six manipulation techniques and for the total fake news score (the average of all eighteen items), we found that people rated misinformation as much less reliable on the post-test (as compared to the pre-test) in the treatment group, whereas there was no improvement in the control group. This finding was crucial: we could now more reliably attribute the boost in people's performance – across a larger set of headlines – to our *Bad News* intervention.

One way to think about the efficacy of our intervention is that if you were to randomly administer it to the entire population, then with some standard projections, you would expect about 73 per cent of the treated group to perform above the mean of the control group in their ability to spot fake news. For context, if you look at thousands of psychology studies, the average is about 63 per cent. Of course, this is on average, if you look at the gains per misinformation technique, then there is some variation (for example, immunity seems somewhat lower for the Polarization technique, perhaps because people have to overcome their own biases more).

Moreover, Melisa proved correct in her hypothesis: playing *Bad News* also made people significantly and substantially more confident in judging fake news headlines. The improvement in confidence only happened when people had previously correctly rated misinformation as less reliable. This is important as we did not accidentally want to make people overconfident.

Everything decays (unless you get a booster shot)

As our inoculation interventions gained more traction, one of the most popular questions we were asked – by a long shot – surrounded the longevity of the effect. How long does this newly acquired psychological immunity last? To help answer this question we can return to the biomedical analogy: Our immune systems contain memory T-cells which have been trained to recognize specific antigens. They remain in the body long after an infection has cleared up so that once the body is re-exposed to the invading antigen, the T-cells can provide a fast and strong immune response to help fight off the virus. However, the initial surge in neutralizing antibodies we receive following a vaccination, the so-called 'frontline fighters', naturally wear off over time. Given the fact that our brain's memory systems are far from perfect, and people are susceptible to social influence, political biases, and other outside forces that could counteract the mental immunization process, we would expect an even bigger drop in the efficacy of the psychological vaccine.

As our research programme expanded further, Rakoen Maertens joined the team. Rakoen had just won a national award in Belgium for his master's research, and his doctoral work was going to zoom in on why resistance to persuasion dissipates over time and whether we can model and explain the decay process of psychological immunization. At this point, we had increasing confidence that we could (at least partially) immunize people against a whole range of misinformation but we still knew very little about its long-term effectiveness. In one of our lab's discussions, Rakoen even suggested that if the effect didn't last beyond the initial intervention, then what was the point of it, practically speaking? The intervention would be much more powerful if it could withstand perhaps the toughest test of all: the test of time.

We decided to replicate the design of our previous experiments but this time with a few crucial additions. In total, we conducted three separate studies, but keeping the basic design the same. Participants, who were randomized to either a treatment or control group, rated a series of eighteen misinformation headlines before and after the intervention. What was different in Rakoen's experiment is that we decided to follow-up with people week after week for a period of two months. Every week people would be exposed to the same 'misinformation' attack. This sounds rather nefarious, but it just meant that people were confronted with the same misinformation headlines and evaluated them each week.

So what did we find? We were completely surprised by the results. As expected, on average, people rated misinformation as significantly less reliable in the treatment (*Bad News*) group versus the control group directly after playing (T2 in the graph below, T1 represents people's performance pre-intervention). However, contrary to our hypotheses, this effect persisted week on week for up to two months (T3, T4, and T5 below). The efficacy of the vaccine did not seem to decay over time at all!

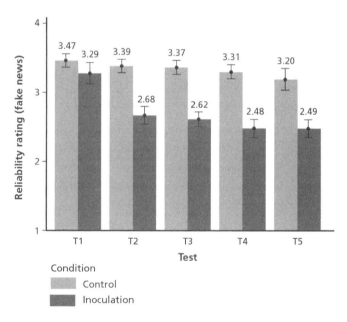

The long-term effectiveness of the Bad News *intervention: T1 illustrates no difference between the treatment and control groups before the intervention. The subsequent testing periods (T2–T5) show a stable 3-month improvement in people's ability to spot fake news so that they consistently rate it as less reliable.*

This finding baffled us. I urged Rakoen to conduct a second experiment to dig deeper. It would be fantastic to announce to the world that *Bad News* offered lifelong psychological immunity, but I felt something else must be going on here. Maybe there was no loss in immunity because people were just remembering their earlier test answers, given that we used the same fake headlines at each follow-up. To exclude this possibility, we mixed up the headlines people saw at each follow-up. The results remained the same: people also spotted misinformation when different fake headlines were presented each time. So that wasn't it.

In the final experiment, we kept everything identical to the first experiment with one crucial change: we only followed up with people at the end of the two-month testing period. This time we found what we had anticipated: although there was still improvement in people's ability to spot fake news if they were exposed to the *Bad News* intervention (versus the control group), after nine weeks there was significant decay of the effect compared to baseline. In fact, a majority (64 per cent) of the effect appeared to have decayed after two months. What happened was that unbeknownst to us, we were inadvertently 'boosting' people's immune responses by repeatedly reminding and engaging them with the issue of misinformation in the first experiment. This gave people plenty of opportunity to think about the manipulation techniques, refresh their memories of the lessons learned, and renew their motivation to protect themselves from fake news. Although we weren't able to break down exactly whether the issue is that people forget the material over time, or whether they lose motivation to stay engaged, we reckoned (and later confirmed) that it is probably a combination of both.

What we took away from the experiment is that, just as with medical vaccines, in order to maintain immunity you will often need to get one or several 'booster' shots. The same turns out to be true for psychological vaccines. In order to stay immune, people need a booster session. The booster can take various forms – whether it's re-exposure to the full intervention, a quick reminder of the six DEPICT manipulation techniques, or regularly evaluating misinformation.

Monitoring side-effects

Of course, a scientist's work is never done. One popular question we would get from fact-checkers and journalists is whether our intervention might inadvertently motivate people to start producing fake news? My first response is usually that just as you don't get influenza from the flu vaccine, you don't suddenly become a fake news tycoon after receiving a fake news vaccine. The 'weakened dose' we administer is completely attenuated.

The motivations behind why people spread fake news professionally are usually either financial or political. It is therefore important to emphasize that the game is non-political and we do not illustrate how people can profit from spreading fake news in the game. We consciously decided to eliminate these motives to make sure people don't get the wrong idea. Moreover, we are not teaching people anything new, we are merely unveiling the techniques that are already being used to fool people. Consistent with the inoculation analogy, we activate people's immune system but make sure not to overwhelm it. Of course, we don't want to accidentally give people the virus, or worse, have them spread it around. As with medical interventions, there are always benefits and risks, so it is important to monitor side-effects so we can quickly intervene and adjust the gaming experience (or dosage) when needed.

It is equally important to realize that the default response to misinformation – fact-checking and debunking – isn't completely without risk either. Although infrequent, it is possible for fact-checks to backfire and cause people to dig their heels in deeper. Debunking risks repeating the misinformation in an attempt to discredit it. Regulation needs to tread the thin line between censorship and freedom of speech and algorithms don't catch everything, often failing to identify more subtle forms of misinformation. Equally troubling, they can also incorrectly tag facts as misinformation. (For example, in 2019, YouTube inadvertently removed videos from the accounts of some British history teachers and from California State University's Center for the Study of Hate and Extremism because their educational videos featured Adolf Hitler and were erroneously classified as 'hate speech'.) The decision to implement any intervention whether social, technological, or medical needs to take risks and benefits into consideration.

The fact that *Bad News* went viral on Reddit (remember the 'hug of death') presented an interesting opportunity for us to monitor side-effects. Although this study was completely exploratory, we wondered what people talked about after playing *Bad News*. Were they sharing the lessons they'd learned or were they discussing how the game inspired them to become a fake news producer? Jon and I decided to scrape thousands of comments from the relevant Reddit forum to learn more about the conversations people were having. We were able to identify, with some degree of certainty, which users interacted with *Bad News*. We then analysed what players talked about using a machine learning algorithm (specifically a so-called 'topic model') which clusters similar words together which then get sorted into overarching topics. Perhaps what's most interesting is that when looking at the actual responses from users, we did not find any evidence that people had developed 'nefarious' intentions. On the contrary, by and large, people were enjoying the gaming experience and having productive discussions about how to best counter disinformation. For example, one user commented: 'That's a genius way to teach people. Playing as your opponent gives you a ton of insight into their strategies and how to best counter them.' Some even asked about the possibility of herd immunity.

An excellent question that we'll explore in the next chapter.

FAKE NEWS ANTIGEN 9
Inoculate against the techniques of misinformation

— Although it's possible to inoculate people against specific falsehoods, it's much more effective to immunize against the building blocks of the virus itself.

— This way individuals can gain immunity to many different strains of the same misinformation – negating the need to prebunk every single falsehood individually.

— The main underlying techniques used are the Six Degrees of Manipulation (DEPICT: Discrediting content using deflection and denial strategies; using Emotional appeals to manipulate people's feelings; Polarizing groups of people by driving two camps further apart; Impersonating people and organisations online; floating Conspiracy theories to cast doubt on the mainstream narrative; and Trolling people by falsely amplifying existing tensions, sowing societal discord, and manipulating public opinion).

— Interactive games such as *Bad News*, which simulate a social media environment, are an effective 'virtual needle' for administering a broad-spectrum vaccine, helping people to spot fake news, become more confident in their ability to discern fact from fiction, and decrease their intentions to share misinformation with others.

— Because the effectiveness of psychological vaccines wears off over time, boosting people's immune response on a regular basis will help sustain its long-term efficacy.

CHAPTER 10

Psychological herd immunity

'I hope that some day the practice of producing
cowpox in human beings will spread over the world.
When that day comes, there will be no more smallpox.'
EDWARD JENNER

Edward Jenner was an eighteenth-century English physician who created the world's first vaccine. At the time, smallpox was a deadly virus.
Believed to have originated about 3,000 years ago in ancient Egypt, in
Jenner's time smallpox killed about 30 per cent of people it infected, and
often left survivors with serious complications such as blindness and dis-
figurement. Rumour goes that Jenner had heard tales that certain farmers
seemed surprisingly immune to smallpox. In 1796, Jenner decided to
inoculate an eight-year-old boy against smallpox by exposing him to a
weakened dose of cowpox – a similar but much less virulent disease. He
reasoned that the farmers must have been immune to smallpox because of
their prior expose to the cowpox virus.

Jenner was right. After being inoculated with cowpox, the boy experienced a mild fever but subsequently proved immune to the smallpox
virus. The term 'vaccination' received its namesake from *vacca*, the Latin
word for 'cow'.

Word of his discovery soon spread around the world and he dedicated
his life to further developing the vaccine. The vaccine became mandatory
in England and was used during the Napoleonic Wars to vaccinate millions of citizens. Jenner is often credited as the individual whose work
has saved more lives than that of any other human in history. From about

1958–77, the World Health Organization launched a global vaccination campaign against smallpox that led to its ultimate eradication in 1980. It is still the only human virus to have been fully eradicated.

At the time, the WHO's strategy was to vaccinate at least 80 per cent of the population in order to achieve a level of protection that is known as 'herd immunity'. This occurs when a large enough proportion of the population has become immune to infection. The threshold for herd immunity depends on the virus's level of infectiousness (the R_0); the more contagious the disease, the greater the number of people in the population who need to be immune in order to stop its spread. (For example, measles is highly contagious and requires about 95 per cent coverage to disrupt the chain of transmission.) When this critical mass is achieved, the spread of the disease from one individual to another becomes unlikely. As a result, the whole 'herd' is protected, including more vulnerable individuals who cannot take the vaccine for medical reasons.

Although the concept of a psychological vaccine is certainly valuable at the individual level, when we push the analogy to its logical conclusion, it becomes clear that the most important implication of inoculation theory is the possibility of psychological herd immunity. William J. McGuire's initial ideas concerned achieving inoculation at the level of individual attitudes, but we can think of immunity at the group-level too, especially in online networks. If enough people are vaccinated in an (online) community, then the misinformation virus no longer has a chance to spread. Of course, we are never going to immunize everyone against all kinds of misinformation indefinitely. But the beauty of herd immunity is that not everyone *needs* to be vaccinated – just a large enough majority.

The success of the WHO's campaign against smallpox hinged on two key factors: first, the availability of a high-quality vaccine, and second, the ability to reach people with it, especially those in more remote areas who were most at risk.

Similarly, now that our lab had discovered an effective psychological vaccine, we needed to find a way to scale it across the population – to reach those audiences who needed the vaccine the most. Together with my PhD student Rakoen, we had just developed a new instrument –

the Misinformation Susceptibility Test (MIST). This test gives people an indication of how susceptible they are to misinformation, relative to others. Rakoen pioneered a novel method to develop this test: instead of coming up with the headlines ourselves, we relied on a neural network – a collection of millions of interconnected nodes or artificial 'neurons' that can learn patterns in data in a way that loosely mimics the human brain. By feeding it diverse examples of real news and fake news using the Six Degrees of Manipulation, the artificial intelligence learned from our examples and returned new headlines with similar characteristics.

The neural network performed so well in crafting hundreds of fake headlines that you wouldn't even know it was done by a computer. Examples would be: 'Government officials have illegally manipulated the weather to cause devastating storms', and 'Certain vaccines are loaded with dangerous chemicals and toxins'. We then used national samples in various countries to establish population norms for how people score on this test. It give us a sense of who might be more or less susceptible to fake news. Some general at-risk characteristics we identified included: individuals with lower digital or media literacy skills; more intuitive thinkers; people who are less open-minded; the more politically extreme; conspiratorial thinkers; and those who get their news primarily from social media.

But what percentage of the population needs to be vaccinated in order for psychological herd immunity to become a real possibility? Although the exact R_0 is not known, we know that misinformation is highly contagious and that our interventions confer at least partial immunity. But we also know that this immunity wanes over time. To formalize what we know, we ran some computer simulations with our colleagues Jens Madsen and Toby Pilditch (who designed the micro-targeting simulation described in chapter 7). In the model, we can introduce a certain part of the population who would be partially inoculated against misinformation for a certain amount of time to see whether the transmission of misinformation can be reduced via inoculation. Across a larger number of possible simulations, we found that a massive up-front inoculation campaign can significantly reduce the spread of misinformation in a simulated social network. Thus, in theory, it's possible.

But these were just predictions based on a computer model. How were we going to reach enough people for the vaccine to matter at population level?

Reverting back to the biological analogy, there are two major challenges to herd immunity. The first is logistical: you can't always reach everyone with the vaccine. We needed help. But we also discovered that the general idea of dissecting the building blocks of misinformation in specific contexts can be done systematically. By tweaking the vaccine and adapting it to new variants – say, a global pandemic, or a political election – we could scale the approach. For any given information space, the trick is to always start by asking the following questions: What are the most common techniques used to dupe or influence people? And can we pre-expose people to weakened doses of these techniques in a simulated environment?

The second challenge has to do with vaccine hesitancy: some people might not want the vaccine or the format in which you are offering it. We were facing a similar challenge: What can we do for those people who might not be open to participating in our interventions?

Let's start with the first challenge.

Spreading *Bad News* around the world

Like Jenner, we weren't going to reach everyone on our own. We needed help to mass-produce the inoculation. Not long after our research on *Bad News* was released, Jon gave a talk at a conference that elicited interest from the UK's Foreign and Commonwealth Office (FCO). A senior advisor at the Russia desk saw potential to help scale our intervention and we were intrigued. After several conversations and trips to Whitehall it became clear that the FCO had an interest in strengthening media literacy around the world. They were looking for novel interventions and we had a potential answer: a psychological vaccine that was painless, free, and easy to scale.

Our goal was for people to have access to *Bad News* for free around the globe. If the FCO could make that happen, why not? At the same time, we were also interested in finding out how well the intervention performed in non-English speaking countries. The FCO connected us to media literacy organizations who could translate and adapt *Bad News* to the local cultural context in each country.

About a year later we translated *Bad News* into ten languages, then fifteen. Today the intervention is available in pretty much every major language. For us, the benefit was not only that we were able to scale the vaccine with professional translators who knew the local media environment in each country but also that we were able to gather data on how well the intervention was performing around the world. In 2020, Jon and I, together with our colleague Thomas Nygren, Professor of Education at Uppsala University, Sweden, published a paper using the original *Bad News* methodology, replicating the effect in several different countries around Europe; by and large, we found that people improved in their ability to spot fake news in their local language. But it wasn't just Western data; an independent research team replicated our findings in India as well.

We also created a version for kids, *Bad News Junior*.* The game is the same but with more age-appropriate content. There's fake news about SpongeBob and instead of impersonating Trump, you are impersonating the high-school principal, spreading misinformation that school's out today! We started receiving emails, tweets, and letters from educators all over the world about how much their students loved playing *Bad News*, and how much they'd learned from it.

At this point, we'd reached about a million people around the world with our game intervention. Though that's undoubtedly rare for a science project, considering the nearly 8 billion people that inhabit our planet, we still had a long way to go.

Let's go viral: vaccinating against misinformation about Covid-19

As we were brainstorming about how to roll out our psychological vaccine programme further, I received a call from the UK's Prime Minister's Office. We were at the start of the pandemic and the strategic

---

* You can play the kid's version at www.getbadnews.com/junior.

communications team* wanted to have a chat about how to best counter misinformation about Covid-19. The government's strategy was still in flux and so after I told them about our theory of psychological inoculation and the importance of prebunking fake news about Covid-19, they were intrigued. To be honest, I have conversations with government officials all the time and I find that scientific evidence – while appreciated – is not always part of the policy conversation, so I didn't have high expectations from our call. But I figured I had done my job. I'd shared all the evidence our team had gathered over the years so at least they knew about the new science of prebunking.

To my great surprise, they came back to us right away. This time with a senior official of the government's communications service (GCS) on the call. Let's design a prebunking campaign together, they said. The Cabinet Office was excited about our work, and they wanted to have an evidence-based plan to counter misinformation about Covid-19. I was impressed. Although they liked *Bad News*, they wanted a new intervention that specifically targeted misinformation about Covid-19. 'A new vaccine?' I asked. How soon can you make it happen? they wondered.

With the pandemic underway, we were feeling the pressure, but they were completely on board with our request to evaluate everything empirically and scientifically. As the biomedical labs were racing to get a Covid-19 vaccine evaluated and approved, we were working around the clock to trial a psychological vaccine. I immediately brought Jon and Melisa on board, and we told the Cabinet Office that we were up for the challenge.

We had about four months to make it happen. Luckily, Cambridge University had awarded us some emergency Covid-19 research funding to allow us to conduct the research in a rapid enough fashion. At this point, the UK government had also brought in the United Nations and WHO as potential partners. This was going to be the biggest inoculation campaign we had ever conducted. By a landslide.

Jon and I quickly realized that we weren't going to be able to do this on

---

* To protect the identity of government officials, I simply refer to people's roles within government (rather than their actual names).

our own, so we were lucky that both Ruurd's *Bad News* team and the design guys at Gusmanson studio were willing to get the band back together to produce a sequel. I had been lamenting on public radio and TV about the need for government communication teams to adopt an evidence-based approach, so the likelihood that we'd get another opportunity to help design and implement the government's international campaign to counter misinformation about Covid-19 seemed small. This was it.

As the designers were storyboarding ideas for a new game with the government's communication team, Jon, Melisa, and I got to work. Our first objective in creating the vaccine was to figure out the structural building blocks of the virus – the key techniques that were being used to dupe people with misinformation about Covid-19. We would then create weakened doses of these techniques in a simulated social media environment to inoculate people against them.

The government team thought that *Bad News*, which is very general and takes about *fifteen* to *twenty* minutes to play, was a little long for a global campaign. We'd heard similar things from social media companies, so we were cognizant of the fact that on social media people have limited attention spans. We therefore needed to create a shorter intervention that could be scaled more easily across a wider audience. After scouring both the academic literature and the darker corners of the internet for examples of misinformation, we ended up identifying and prioritizing three key techniques: fearmongering (*emotion*), using fake experts (*impersonation*), and spreading *conspiracy* theories.

The game, which we named *GoViral!*, turned out much shorter than *Bad News* (five minutes to play on average) and has three chapters: 'The Fearmonger'; 'My Imaginary Expert'; and 'Master of Puppets'. Although there are many similarities in the basic concept, unlike *Bad News*, *GoViral!* simulates a direct messaging platform.

At the start of the game, you choose an avatar such as Joel (see page 235). The story is that he's bored at home in lockdown during a worldwide pandemic, but luckily the internet still works! Joel tells his audience that he could use a 'Quarantini'. The game's narrator then explains that his 'dad jokes' are not the right influencer frame. Joel starts to pick up on a heated online debate about the coronavirus and after creating an emotional stir, joins a group called 'Not Co-fraid' and starts posting material about how official stats on Covid-19-related deaths and infection rates are based on dodgy data.

The game's narrator explains that Joel's following doesn't get what he's talking about. He first needs to gain scientific credibility by impersonating a fake expert. He creates the identity of 'Dr Isley, Doctor of Natural Medicine' – a renowned health authority at the 'University of Camford'. Posing as Dr Isley, he then claims that *no deaths* have actually been caused by Covid-19! Popularity of the 'Not Co-fraid' group explodes and before he knows it, Joel is spreading conspiracy theories – from lizard people being behind the outbreak, to NGOs covering up evidence that eating kiwifruit cures the virus, to Big Pharma's secret plan to include jelly chips (fizzy sweets) in the Covid vaccine as a form of global surveillance.

www.goviralgame.com (PEGI rating of ages 3 and up).

Of course, in the game, Joel could have chosen to blame it all on the government instead of Big Pharma. It doesn't really matter; the lessons are the same. We forewarn people about the dangers of misinformation (alerting the immune system) and use humour, to expose the player to weakened doses of the techniques used to spread misinformation about Covid-19, as well as ways to spot them (motivating antibody production). At the end of the game, players receive a summary of the misinformation tactics and a final score alongside some performance data so that people can see how well they did relative to other players.

We made sure that *GoViral!* was available in different languages before the launch and could be shared on social media, so that people could easily pass on the vaccine to others within their social networks.

It is important to note once again that we do not tell people what to believe about Covid-19 in the game – we just dismantle the techniques behind the spread of misinformation. While the government did not interfere with the content of the game, they were helpful in ensuring the translations were done to a high standard and conducted some in-house user-experience (UX) testing with potential target audiences so we could get some initial feedback to help improve the gaming experience.

So far working with governments and social media companies we'd learned that they were keen on UX testing – asking, for instance, to what extent audiences like the message or game, do they have any concerns, are they engaged with the material? Although these questions are important, especially for product development, they do not answer the type of questions we, as scientists, are typically interested in: does the intervention work in helping people spot fake news regardless of how they feel about it? There is also a delicate balance here because, no matter how scientifically rigorous, if people do not seem to enjoy the interventions, it is unlikely that they will engage with them. Luckily user feedback on *GoViral!* came back positive, but we still wanted to conduct our own investigation.

We ran a large, randomized controlled trial where we randomly assigned a national sample of British, French, and German citizens to either a placebo control group (who played *Tetris*), a passive inoculation condition (more on that below), or our active *GoViral!* inoculation game. We assessed people's ability to identify and resist fake news both before and after playing the game. We included an extra comparison group because we wanted to see if actively generating your own antibodies in a simulated social media environment is more effective than passively reading infographics on social media – the default campaign of many organizations. In fact, we included a set of prebunking infographics (#ThinkBeforeYouShare) from UNESCO (the United Nations Educational, Scientific, and Cultural Organization), which showed people how to spot fake news and conspiracy theories.

At the beginning of the experiment, people were shown a series of eighteen social media posts, half of which contained one of three misinformation strategies (fearmongering, fake experts, and conspiracy theories) and the other half did not. We then assessed how manipulative people found the posts, how confident they were in their assessment, and how likely they were to share the information with others in their social network.

Here's an example of a fake expert test item which says that a 'Nobel laureate professor' has claimed that Covid-19 is a man-made virus. After people have been exposed to several microdoses of the fake-expert technique in our simulation, they should have become more immune to the persuasive power of these kind of social media messages.

And this is exactly what we found. People tested in England, Germany and France all significantly improved in their ability to discern fake from credible news posts; became more confident in their veracity assessments; and were less likely to want to share misinformation with others in their social networks.

Importantly, the UNESCO prebunking infographics were also successful, but the treatment effect of the game was bigger. One potential explanation for this difference is that the game seemed to elicit a stronger motivation from people to want to defend themselves against the threat of misinformation. This is likely so because active inoculation can simulate and actually show people how dangerous fake content spreads on social media. We also followed up with people one week after the trial and exposed them to a fresh series of twelve headlines. This allowed us to evaluate the broad-spectrum potential of the vaccine, covering different strains of the same virus. For example, the first time around we included an item about how Covid-19 testing is a secret attempt to collect people's

DNA profiles; in the follow-up we referred to a cover-up which suggested that scientists had discovered a cure for Covid-19 but were being blocked from publishing their findings. These are different variants of the same virus: conspiracy theories.

So what did we find? In the *GoViral!* group, we found no evidence that the effects on accuracy and confidence judgments had decayed over the course of a week. The immunization was still intact. In contrast, the initial gains observed for the UNESCO group were no longer significant at follow-up, which further speaks to the benefits of actively inoculating people. Of course, if the vaccine is to spread, we have to design interventions that people are keen to share. Encouragingly, we found that participants were also more willing to share *GoViral!* on their social media feed than the infographics.

A global vaccination campaign with the Cabinet Office, the UN, and the WHO

After the successful trial, we were keen to launch the intervention worldwide. The British government was too, but they just needed to get a final sign-off. A few days later we received the good news and they set a date for its official release. Unfortunately, one day before the release the Cabinet Office staff was called down to Number 10, the Prime Minister's Office, for further clarification. They had political concerns. I offered to have a conversation with the higher-ups so I could share the encouraging outcomes of our trial in case they hadn't had a chance to read the research. But the problem wasn't the research, we were told. After some back and forth, we finally received a new date. This was it: guaranteed. The software team had to stay up the night before to monitor traffic and make sure there were no technical glitches in the game. Cambridge University's press office was on stand-by. We were all ready to launch the campaign.

And then, one day before launch, we again received word that there was going to be a delay. The timing of the intervention didn't mash with the policy agenda for that week. We received a new date. By this time, I'd started to lose faith in the process. Don't get me wrong, the driven communications staff in the Cabinet Office were fantastic. They are non-political civil servants interested in research and motivated to launch evidenced-based campaigns. They were doing everything they could to make their case and I even felt bad that they had to apologize so often – but I sensed their initial optimism was being worn down as well. I should add that some pretty high-up government officials were making an urgent case for the importance of countering misinformation about Covid-19 but it struck me that 'someone' in Number 10 seemed like they had a problem with the 'fake news' topic.

I understood their political hesitation on some level. As soon as the government says something about countering misinformation, people will criticize it and say that the government itself is 'fake news'. Of course, whilst it's true that many governments have made big mistakes during the pandemic, the politicization of anti-misinformation efforts wasn't helping our case and proved to be a major hurdle to implementing our interventions. In the end, the official release might not happen, we were told. Everyone was disappointed. At this point, the university was considering releasing the game on its own.

The next day, however, the Executive Director of Government Communications tweeted out our game: 'The new phase of the UK government's public health campaign to counter misinformation with the launch of the "inoculation game" in collaboration with University of Cambridge and WHO to teach people how to identify and understand disinformation.'

I scrolled down the government's website but there was still no official announcement. Next up was the Secretary of State for Digital, Culture, Media and Sport (DCMS), who tweeted: 'GoViral! is a new game released by @GOVUK @Cambridge_Uni to help stop the spread of false and misleading information. Play #GoViralGame today to uncover tactics used to spread harmful Covid-19 misinformation. http://goviral-game.com.' After the DCMS, it was Public Health England (PHE) who tweeted out the game.

The announcement from the Prime Minister's Office never came.

To this day, I have no idea how it happened exactly, but I want to emphasize that if it wasn't for those inside government who persisted and put evidence ahead of politics, the whole thing may never have happened. I realized that launching an innovative campaign that has never been tried before is no easy feat, especially when fighting 'fake news' turns into a political debate.

Earlier that year, the United Nations had launched a campaign called 'Verified', where information volunteers deliver lifesaving, accurate and verified information to the public. The Cabinet Office arranged for us to become part of that campaign and the UN tweeted out a short video of us explaining the *GoViral!* game. We also became part of the WHO's 'Stop the Spread' (anti-Covid misinformation) campaign and they listed the game on their website to help get the word out. Upon release, the game was the WHO's second most viewed resource on Covid-19 information. As *GoViral!* made its way around the globe, the campaign would ultimately reach over 200 million views across all social media channels, earning our government colleagues a well-deserved public service communication award. Although, at least for us, this was a unique moment in history where scientists, governments, game designers, and international organizations were able to team up and produce an innovative inoculation campaign to protect people from the spread of misinformation about Covid-19 on a massive scale – it wouldn't be the last time.

In fact, it was only the beginning.

Homeland security and the war on pineapple pizza

As it turns out, on the other side of the Atlantic another potential crisis was unfolding: the 2020 US presidential election. In the run-up to the election, Ruurd had been in contact with the US State Department's Global Engagement Center (GEC). They wanted their own game too – not to counter Covid misinformation, but an intervention that would inoculate people against *'foreign adversarial propaganda and disinformation'.*

We don't conduct research with a political agenda, so we wanted to make sure this was going to be a non-political intervention, in the interest of the wider public. The point of our research is to help people spot dodgy content irrespective of who the producer is; our interventions may well lead people to discount government messages if their messages make use of misinformation techniques.

Jon and Ruurd headed off to Washington DC to meet with White House officials in person to discuss the plans. They fully agreed. The aim was to create a fun but evidence-based serious game that would inoculate people against political disinformation and foreign influence tactics. It was another big project and we wanted to test and launch the game before the election was over.

We were collaborating with the State Department and the Department of Homeland Security (DHS): specifically, the Cybersecurity and Infrastructure Security Agency (CISA), a federal unit within the DHS that aims to protect the nation's infrastructure against (foreign) threats. Although they look at physical infrastructure, such as the likelihood of outsiders hacking voting machines, they were much more concerned about another type of threat: 'the *perception* hack'.

As NPR journalist Andrea Bernstein put it in a 2022 interview with CISA's former director:

'a perception hack, a campaign of lies would basically get injected into American public discourse, and then they'd mutate and spread like a virus infecting what Americans say and think so severely, that a lot of voters would no longer be able to tell the difference between what was true and what wasn't'.

In the interest of national security, I can't tell you everything, but I can give you the official line that explained what we worked on: 'The State Department assisted in the development and tailoring of *Harmony Square* [our game] within the scope of addressing foreign adversarial propaganda and disinformation and its impact on foreign audiences and elections.' Quite the mouthful, but basically it was part of CISA's campaign to 'strengthen the national immune system' against disinformation. In fact, I *can* tell you that in her conversation with CISA's former director, Chris Krebs, Bernstein explains that Krebs's approach to securing the election was premised on finding a non-political way to introduce the American people to the tactics of how adversaries conduct a disinformation campaign so that when it actually happens, they'd be inoculated – a 'psychological vaccine against disinformation'. It was based on our research. It's important to mention that although the government provided feedback on the content of the game, they were not at all involved in the research – which we conducted independently.

Harmony Square is based on an idyllic representation of small-town America. It's a place that's known for its living statue, lots of green space and majestic pond swan (yes, that's right, a majestic swan). Every year the townsfolk gather for the annual 'Pineapple Pizza Festival'. They are also known for being obsessed with democracy: they love fair and open elections, and the town's political parties are always bickering – the perfect conditions for you to come in as Chief Disinformation Officer and mount an influence campaign to disrupt peaceful small-town America.

Image depicting how Ashley Ploog's polarizing election campaign for bear patroller is disrupting the town's pineapple pizza festival (www.harmonysquare.game).

In the game, an opportunity to create misinformation presents itself when (the fictional) Ashley Ploog is running unopposed for the community's 'bear patroller'. Although there are no bears to patrol in Harmony Square, the people love elections so much that they keep voting for a patrol person anyway. You start mounting a fake news campaign which implies that Ploog was involved in supporting animal abuse while she was in college. You watch the headlines unfold and her ratings drop as Ronald Bordeaux aka 'Ron', the town's beloved television news anchor, covers the election. The game is interactive so that you can see approval ratings change in response to your targeted disinformation campaign. A once-peaceful community quickly descends into chaos and paranoia and your disruption of the town's beloved pizza festival leaves its citizens utterly polarized, distrustful, and angry.

The *Harmony Square* game scenarios are based on a real 2019 CISA publication (entitled *The War on Pineapple: Understanding Foreign Interference*) and exposes the playbook of election misinformation campaigns in four consecutive steps:

1. You target an ostensibly non-partisan issue, such as whether or not it's acceptable to put pineapple on pizza, and then turn it into a heated and polarizing debate. The idea is to sow division on social issues.
2. The next phase involves moving bot accounts into place to amplify and manipulate the conversation.
3. You blow up both sides of the debate so you can make a mountain out of a molehill.
4. You eventually go mainstream and take the debate on the road so that the online conversation now escalates into real-world protests and disruption.

Although *Harmony Square*'s content is strictly fictional and utterly ridiculous, there are clear parallels to #Pizzagate, Russian interference and political riots. At the time, CISA was headed by Chris Krebs. In a tweet in July 2019 Chris made a case for never putting pineapple on pizza. Ironically, after our project finished, Krebs was fired via Twitter by President Trump, allegedly because of Krebs's involvement in debunking election-related disinformation – much of which was being promoted by Trump himself.

We tested *Harmony Square* by randomizing people to either a treatment or control group and asked them how reliable they found a series of headlines, how confident they were in their assessment, and how likely they were to share the news headline with others in their social network. Crucially, we exposed people to exactly the type of highly polarizing content that is characteristic of divisive social media debates in the US. Below are two examples: one shows a digitally manipulated image of two women making their case against Father's Day (meant to polarize), while the other mocks the death of a Trump supporter and his young daughter who were killed in a hunting accident.

Indeed, once again we found that after playing our intervention, people became much better at spotting such divisive content, were more confident in their judgments and less likely to indicate that they would want to share these types of posts with friends in their social network. I can't really summarize the results better than how a journalist at *VICE* magazine described the game's impact: 'People called bullshit on misinformation more often.'

More misinformation, more vaccines

But the requests to produce more and more interventions kept coming. We had ignited a whole new research field on inoculation theory and prebunking, and even inspired others to produce serious games, such as John Cook's *Cranky Uncle*, a fantastic game which inoculates players against the key techniques used in climate denial. A German research team from the Max Planck Institute found that if you pre-emptively boost people's self-knowledge about their personality (via feedback after a short quiz), this inoculated them against micro-targeted ads that seek to exploit their personality traits. This pre-treatment boosted people's ability to correctly spot micro-targeted ads by up to 26 per cent.

The potential to apply inoculative methods to different misinformation problems seemed unlimited. We decided to expand our reach horizontally and create several other games. These included *Join This Group*, which we designed with WhatsApp Inc. and which simulates their direct messaging platform. In the Middle East, we worked with our NGO partner Nudge Lebanon, to create *Radicalize*, a gamified intervention that aims to inoculate people against strategies used for extremist recruitment.

After analysing the techniques used to recruit people to extremist causes, we found that there are essentially four steps:

1. identifying a 'vulnerable' target (ideally someone who is going through a rough patch and is looking for validation).
2. gaining their trust.
3. isolating them from their friends and family.
4. activating them to do something to show their commitment to the cause.

Usually, the recruit starts out with a small task before escalating to the greater target. In the game, players join the Anti-Ice Freedom Front (AIFF), and their radical mission is to recruit people to help melt the global ice caps. The logic behind the immunization process always remains the same: what better way is there to prepare people for extremist recruitment than to expose them to a weakened dose of such an attack in a simulated environment?

Our research has found time and again that once the simulation is complete, people become better at recognizing and resisting the techniques of deception or, in the above case, knowing when they are being groomed to join an extremist cause. You can compare it to the production of memory T-cells, protecting people against future attacks that match previously encountered pathogens.

Game over: Inoculating against misinformation with Google

Although the games were a great way to take a theoretical idea and implement it as part of an interactive global media campaign, over time we realized that not everyone wants to play a game. If we really wanted to achieve herd immunity, we needed a much larger variety of 'virtual needles' to reach the population. We learned this the hard way after a visit to Google in New York.

By this stage, we were being approached by technology giants, such as WhatsApp, Facebook, and Google, on a regular basis. These organisations have many different teams, misinformation researchers, policy managers, news media and literacy programme directors – you name it. It was a different department every time, but we were happy to engage. If anything, we were just excited they wanted to learn from us. These billion-dollar companies, with arguably some of the smartest people in the world, wanted to know how our games worked, what the research showed, and how they might be able to get involved. They especially loved inoculation theory and, before long, our research papers were circulating on a regular basis in Silicon Valley. We had their attention.

In some ways, I was pleasantly surprised – even flattered – that they took the time to read research papers, let alone ours. But I was also fairly cagey about their interest in our most well-known intervention: *Bad News*. I wasn't quite sure of their intentions, and because we hadn't copyrighted *Bad News* at that time, we were operating purely on a trust basis.

Jon decided to head down to New York to meet with Google Jigsaw, Google's technology incubator (formerly known as 'Google Ideas'). Google was intrigued but wanted to do some testing with *Bad News* on their own. Not too long after, we hosted a Google colleague at Cambridge, who presented some of the projects they were working on at Jigsaw.

I was particularly intrigued by a project called 'Redirect', which, based on interviews with many (former) members of ISIS/Da'esh, led to the identification of key search terms that vulnerable individuals used to find extremist content online. When people search for extremist content on Google (for example, 'How do I join ISIS?'), they would be targeted with ads that 'redirected' them to curated YouTube videos debunking violent extremist propaganda. A pilot study showed that about 300,000 individuals had watched the debunking videos. Whether the videos actually changed their minds remains unclear, but it seemed like a good effort.

Our team started to have bi-weekly calls with Google, keeping each other in the loop and although there was interest in *Bad News*, we didn't end up collaborating. They had done some testing with *Bad News* in rural Virginia and were not entirely convinced about the level of engagement from audiences over the age of fifty, as they suspected that older individuals were most likely to share fake news online but perhaps less likely to want to play a game. We agreed. We talked at length about ways in which we could scale and tweak the game to appeal to a larger and wider audience. They had some good ideas but nothing concrete came of it, so in the end, we went our separate ways.

A year or so passed before I unexpectedly got reconnected with Google through a mutual colleague. I was introduced to Beth Goldberg, who is currently Head of Research at Jigsaw. I immediately liked Beth; she was to-the-point, really concerned about disinformation, and seemed genuinely motivated to tackle it. She also impressed me with her knowledge of inoculation theory.

Together with our colleague Stephan Lewandowsky, we started to have regular conversations with Google once again. I'd had dealings with dozens and dozens of staff at social media companies, but I sensed that Beth was different. She was involved, didn't want to commercialize anything, had great ideas for research, and got us funding, resources, anything we needed to succeed together. But although Beth liked our games, she had a different plan in mind for our partnership, one that involved a potential solution to our 'herd immunity problem'. She was very interested in scaling inoculation via YouTube (Google owns YouTube) but didn't quite see how our games could be easily implemented on YouTube as, after all, it's a video platform. Our joint idea was therefore that it might be much easier to scale short inoculation videos on social media.

Stephan had already been experimenting with videos (with some success) and Beth had done research on what types of misinformation were common in social media videos and resonated with conspiracy believers. She very much liked our technique-based inoculation approach and was particularly interested in rhetorical techniques. Beth likes to explain it using a TV analogy. For example, when watching a horror movie, we nearly always know what's going to happen when a young couple's car breaks down late at night in the middle of the woods (don't get out of the car!). It's a predictable trope.

The same is true for misinformation. During Edward Jenner's time, rumours circulated that the smallpox vaccine would turn you into a human–cow hybrid and now Covid-19 vaccines were supposedly altering our DNA. It's the same trope just 200 years apart. Although with the Six Degrees of Manipulation we'd identified the general building blocks of a lot of misinformation, Beth was more interested in how people get convinced by misleading rhetorical strategies that are often employed by ideological extremists on YouTube. You can think of these more as 'logical reasoning fallacies'.

One of the common techniques Beth identified was scapegoating. Scapegoating occurs when a person or group is, without merit, singled out and blamed for a negative event. For example, in Europe, Jews were falsely accused of being responsible for poisoning wells and even for the Black Death. Thousands of Jews were murdered as a result. Like the plague, scapegoating survived the fourteenth century and is still very much alive, not least during the Covid-19 pandemic. For example, think of former President Trump's attempt to shift blame onto 'China' by frequently referring to Covid-19 as the 'Chinese virus' or 'kung flu', fuelling a long history of discrimination against Asian Americans. The problem with this kind of technique is not just the fact that it's false, but it also has the potential to be inflammatory and bring harm to other people.

Other related techniques we discussed with Beth included strategies such as making use of 'false dichotomies'. A false dichotomy is a manipulation technique designed to make you think that you only have two options to choose from, while in reality, there are many more. An example would be me telling you that either you finish reading this important book on fake news, or you must not care about the issue at all! The two options are not mutually exclusive of course: in other words, you can definitely stop reading this book and still care about the dangers of misinformation. I just made it seem like those are your only two options, which, without further thinking about it, may sound persuasive to some people the first time they hear it.

Because YouTube doesn't really deal in headlines or social media posts, the issue here is that these more subtle rhetorical techniques were often being used – persuasively – by bad actors in YouTube videos. From rants that spread fake news about Covid-19 and climate change to attempts to recruit people to QAnon and ISIS. For example, one ISIS recruitment video explicitly aimed at Western Muslims was titled 'There is no life without Jihad' – a clear example of a false dichotomy: either you join 'jihad' or you cannot lead a meaningful life.

To produce the vaccine, we needed to synthesize weakened doses, so we started to make our own videos – animated videos, like the games; educational but fun. Luckily Beth shared our sense of humour (for the most part!). After we'd written the scripts, we teamed up with a graphic design company to storyboard and produce them.

The videos follow the inoculation format closely and start with an immediate warning that you (the viewer) might be targeted with an attempt to manipulate your opinion. We then show people how to spot and refute misinformation that explicitly makes use of these techniques by exposing them to a series of weakened examples (the microdose) so that people can easily identify and resist them in the future. Beth's team

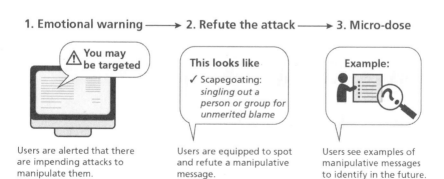

1. Emotional warning ⟶ 2. Refute the attack ⟶ 3. Micro-dose

⚠ You may be targeted

This looks like
✓ Scapegoating: singling out a person or group for unmerited blame

Example:

Users are alerted that there are impending attacks to manipulate them.

Users are equipped to spot and refute a manipulative message.

Users see examples of manipulative messages to identify in the future.

created the infographic on page 249 to explain to both colleagues at Google and the wider public how inoculation works.

For example, in the video that inoculated people against the 'false dichotomy' technique, we pulled material from *Star Wars III – Revenge of the Sith*. In particular, we show the climactic confrontation between Anakin Skywalker, soon to become Darth Vader, and his mentor, Obi-Wan Kenobi. Obi-Wan says, 'My allegiance is to the Republic, to Democracy!' to which Skywalker replies: 'If you're not with me, then you're my enemy.' This is clearly a false dilemma. We explain to the viewer that Obi-Wan is simply trying to prevent Anakin from joining the dark side; just because he disagrees with Anakin doesn't automatically make them enemies. Obi-Wan points out the fallacy in his reply: 'Only a Sith deals in absolutes.'

Although Beth had some questions about our relatively obscure *Star Wars* humour, the videos tested well. In fact, we ran several large randomized controlled trials where we either exposed people to one of our short videos or a boring control video about 'freezer burn'. We then asked people how manipulative they found a series of arguments and how willing they were to share them with others. An example of the false dichotomy quiz would be the following post: 'Why give illegal immigrants access to social services? Why should we help illegals when we should be helping homeless Americans instead?' Such provocative arguments typically receive lots of engagement, partly because they might seem to make sense when you first come across them. But when reflected upon more critically, the argument falls apart as it clearly presents a false dilemma: we can give immigrants access to social services and still help homeless Americans at the same time. The non-manipulative version of this post read: 'The debate over whether to prioritize combating homelessness or poverty among immigrants continues. Just a thought: why can't we do both?' An example of scapegoating would be: 'Well, it's pretty obvious, people of your ideology are incapable of being fiscally responsible. So yeah, the deficit and the fact that we can't pay for support for our vets is YOUR fault.' In the experiment, we asked people to rate many such misleading and control items and what we were hoping to see was that their ability to discern manipulative from non-manipulative content would improve after being exposed to the videos that inoculated people against the relevant manipulation technique.

This is exactly what we found. Unlike the control group, the inoculated groups got much better at identifying which posts contained a specific manipulation strategy and they were subsequently less likely to want to share this type of content with others in their social network. Our samples were largely representative of the US population and the effects were pretty consistent across different audiences, videos, and techniques so we were pretty confident in the results.

Introducing the vaccine to social media

Beth's idea was that we could implement and scale these videos on YouTube by inserting them in the 'non-skippable ad space' (you know, when you're trying to watch a video on YouTube and you get stuck watching an annoying ad that you can't skip? That's where our inoculation video could be placed). If the YouTube algorithm can identify, with some probability, the likelihood that someone is going to be exposed to harmful content, then it could automatically insert our prebunk video so that people are immunized before they are exposed to the misinformation.

This would help solve a number of problems. First, the intervention would no longer be opt-in, as all individuals who are about to watch a video that may contain harmful content would be exposed to the prebunk. Secondly, from a policy-perspective, an intervention such as this avoids the need for Google and YouTube to become 'arbiters of truth' and take down content entirely. Instead, they could now inoculate people beforehand. This doesn't mean that my personal opinion is that they shouldn't take down bad content: I think they should. But we considered this a small step in the right direction insofar as they were willing to do *anything* to help solve the problem. Thirdly, putting the videos in the ad space would scale our psychological vaccine across millions of users on YouTube. Beth's idea was brilliant. There was only one issue: Beth wasn't the CEO of YouTube.

It turns out that, unlike Google, YouTube rarely works with outside scientists. They also don't reveal much about how their proprietary algorithm works. Luckily, they were willing to speak to Beth about our inoculation work and were intrigued by the approach. Although they really liked the research, they wanted to do some testing of their own. This is quite typical of social media companies; they don't trust any research unless they've performed it themselves on their own platform. On the one hand, this is understandable because findings from the lab may not translate to the dynamics of specific social media platforms. On the other hand, the cold hard truth is that I've seen a decent amount of the internal research that these companies conduct, and it is not of a scientific standard (they often use small unrepresentative samples, don't have randomized control groups, and adopt lenient statistical criteria). But to be fair, they are often not trained scientists and are usually interested in a different kind of question. Whether an intervention 'works' is often secondary to the findings from their UX research (e.g., How many people click on the video and do they still like us if we show them this video? Do they trust us more or less?). In the end, we weren't made privy to You-Tube's objections. The short answer was: we needed to find another way.

Beth did find another way. We simply leveraged YouTube's ad platform to upload and target either our inoculation or the control videos to millions of users. This way we could test our intervention 'in the wild', while people were watching the videos on YouTube. Beth then got You-Tube to agree to allow us to customize their 'brand lift' survey (which usually polls people on whether they recognize a brand) for a scientific experiment. Within twenty-four hours, users would be presented with a quiz in the ad space evaluating their ability to spot the misinformation technique they had been inoculated against. We were able to reach about 5 million 'impressions' (views) with just a single campaign. After watching the 90-second inoculation video, we boosted people's ability to spot misleading content by about 5–10 per cent. That might not seem much at the individual level, but remember that this is for a single dose of a short video clip that can be scaled across potentially hundreds of millions of people.

Although Google Jigsaw is rolling out prebunking videos on YouTube, it turns out that Twitter beat us to the punch. In October 2020, they decided to prebunk false information about the US election results. They placed messages at the top of people's feeds that would warn people that they might be exposed to misinformation on Twitter (the forewarning) and pre-emptively refuted false claims about the election process. This was revolutionary for Twitter because, up until this point, they had solely engaged in debunking misinformation, after the fact.

One of Twitter's prebunking messages addressed concerns about voting by post: 'You might encounter unconfirmed claims that voting by mail leads to election fraud ahead of the 2020 US elections. Election experts confirm that voting by mail is safe and secure, even with an increase in mail-in ballots.' A button below the message encouraged people to learn more.

Twitter's prebunk is known as a fact-based inoculation; in other words, they are attempting to immunize people against a specific myth rather than a larger technique. The format Twitter adopted followed the structure of our climate-change inoculation experiment closely (a forewarning coupled with a prebunk of the myth centred around expert consensus). They implemented the approach fairly well but what's even more impressive is that Twitter scaled the inoculation message across all of its 73 million US Twitter users. It's possibly the largest real-world pre-bunking experiment a social media company has ever performed to date. Although I can't share much information from the pilot results I've seen, let it suffice to say that the effects seemed positive and that the messages appeared to reinforce trust in the US election process. Twitter is now rolling out the same approach to fight disinformation on climate change.

So, all in all, in the space of about five years, we were able to take a theoretical idea out of the lab and turn it into a global campaign, with social media and technology companies evaluating and adopting the approach on their platforms. We started out by inoculating individuals against misinformation one at a time to being able to scale the approach online to millions of people around the world. Of course, the work is far from finished. Like managing a biological virus, psychological herd immunity may require coverage of 90 per cent of the population or more and, as we've seen earlier in this book, the human brain doesn't acquire natural immunity to misinformation. But whereas herd immunity was once just a theoretical possibility, it now seems like a real option.

You might wonder whether you can apply the principles of psychological inoculation in your own life? You can and I'll be happy to show you how. The use of inoculation is not restricted to games, videos, scientific research, or formal organizations. Anyone can harness the power of inoculation through a simple conversation; every conversation has the potential to bring us one step closer to herd immunity. In fact, as we'll discover in the next and final chapter, you have the power to pass on the vaccine yourself. You can help inoculate people against misinformation.

FAKE NEWS ANTIGEN 10
Psychological herd immunity

— Vaccines protect people at the individual level but, in order for misinformation to no longer have a chance to spread in online and offline communities, enough people need to be vaccinated against the misinformation virus.

— The end goal of any vaccination programme is to protect the 'herd'. This is crucial because it's not realistic to assume that we're going to reach every single individual – plus some people might not be willing to accept the vaccine. But as long as enough people in a community are vaccinated, then herd immunity will protect others too.

— For this to happen, the vaccine needs to be able to scale and reach people around the world. Progress on this front has been made with governments, public health authorities, and technology companies.

— Since the needle is completely 'virtual', there is no limit to its potential reach. It doesn't need to be a game, video, or message. In fact, it could be a personal conversation.

CHAPTER 11

How to inoculate your friends and family

'He who speaks first should state his own proofs
and afterwards meet the arguments of the opponent,
refuting or pulling them to pieces beforehand,'
ARISTOTLE (*Rhetoric*, III, chapter XVII)

The facts of the case are this: At midnight on 6 August, the defendants went into the barracks room of their platoon-mate, PFC William Santiago. They woke him up, tied his arms and legs with rope, and forced a rag into his throat. A few minutes later, a chemical reaction in Santiago's body called lactic acidosis caused his lungs to begin bleeding. He drowned in his own blood and was pronounced dead at thirty-two minutes past midnight.

These are the facts of the case. And they are undisputed. That's right. The story I just told you is the exact same story you're going to hear from Corporal Dawson, and it's the exact same story you're going to hear from Private Downey. Furthermore, the Government will also demonstrate that the defendants soaked the rag with poison, and entered Santiago's room with motive and intent to kill.

(beat)

Now, Lt. Kaffee, is gonna try to pull off a little magic act, he's gonna try a little misdirection.

He's going to astonish you with stories of rituals and dazzle you with official sounding terms like Code Red. He might even cut into a few officers for you. He'll have no evidence, mind you, none. But it's gonna be entertaining. When we get to the end, all the magic in the world will not have been able to divert your attention from the fact that Willy Santiago is dead, and Dawson and Downey killed him. These are the facts of the case.

(beat)

And they are undisputed.

You may recognize the above scene from the 1992 Academy Award nominated movie *A Few Good Men*, written by Aaron Sorkin and starring Tom Cruise, Jack Nicholson, Demi Moore, and Kevin Bacon. The movie tells the story of two court-martialled marines accused of (accidentally) killing a fellow marine when executing an off-the-books physical punishment order from a commanding officer. I have selected this particular scene because it illustrates a perfect example of psychological inoculation. The prosecutor, played by Kevin Bacon, starts by laying out the facts, plain and simple. He then warns the jury that the opposition is going to use misleading tactics ('a little misdirection') by trying to dazzle them with big-sounding terms like 'Code Red', because they have no actual evidence (the weakened dose). He even douses the whole argument in a little bit of humour by calling it a 'magic act' that's 'gonna be entertaining'.

You might notice a close parallel with our climate change inoculation experiment, where we forewarned people that there are politically motivated actors who use misleading techniques to influence your opinion. That they might even bring up some fancy-sounding petition citing 'PhD experts' and claiming that scientists disagree on the issue. However, you should know that nearly all scientists have concluded that humans *are* causing climate change. These are the facts. And they are undisputed.

What's remarkable is that we often use elements of psychological inoculation in daily life without noticing or recognizing it as such. Lawyers use it all the time; they need to 'forewarn' the jury about the opposition's case, create a weakened dose, and pre-emptively refute it. Trade unions use it too: they train workers to recognize misleading corporate tactics which often suggest, for example, that there's no room for a pay raise. The union provides evidence to its members that the company's balance sheet shows a different story, so that when the argument comes up in negotiations the workers are prepared to resist the persuasion attempt, with counter-arguments at the ready. They've been inoculated.

Psychological inoculation is also useful in political contexts. One of my favourite examples comes from Reverend Raphael Warnock, a senior pastor at the Ebenezer Baptist Church in Atlanta. In 2020, Warnock was running for the junior senator seat in Georgia and decided to 'inoculate' his audience against persuasive attacks from the opposition. The video clip for his ad starts with: 'Raphael Warnock eats pizza with a fork and knife . . . Warnock once stepped on a crack in the sidewalk . . . Warnock even hates puppies. Get ready Georgia, the negative ads are coming. Senator Kelly Loeffler doesn't want to talk about why she's for getting rid of healthcare in the middle of a pandemic so she's going to try to scare you with lies about me. And by the way, I looove puppies!'

Reverend Warnock forewarned his audience of an impending attack, provided them with a simulation of what the attack might look like (that weakened dose) and refuted it with a dose of humour. It seems his inoculation campaign was successful, as Warnock won the election.

Even Aristotle loved a good prebunk

The point I'm making here is that, at its very core, psychological inoculation is a rhetorical strategy that can be used by anyone. By the same token, inoculation, could, in theory, be adopted by people with nefarious intentions – we could even try to inoculate people against an inoculation (call it 'meta-inoculation'). Like most tools, inoculation isn't good or bad in and of itself. It's how we choose to use it.

However, since its inception, the purpose of our approach has been to safeguard people against manipulation by helping them spot dodgy persuasion attempts. Indeed, although it was psychologists who formalized the theory of psychological inoculation, its roots date back thousands of years. It all started with Aristotle.

Aristotle's rational analysis was geared specifically at helping people identify snake-oil persuasion by exposing flawed reasoning. He argued that in order to know the true state of things we should not only consider our own facts but also any counter-arguments, including their logical flaws. Aristotle reasoned that once people were able to identify errors in reasoning, they'd become resistant to persuasive challenges that make use of them. Consider the following passage from Aristotle's *Rhetoric*, a fourth-century AD book on the art of persuasion: 'The orator should be able to prove opposites as in logical arguments; not that we should do both (for one ought to not persuade people to do what is wrong), but that the real state of the case may not escape us, and that we ourselves may be able to counteract false arguments, if another makes unfair use of them'. (*Rhetoric*, I.I. 11–14)

As is clear from the quote that opens this chapter, Aristotle discovered the process of inoculation. He calls it a 'refutational enthymeme' – a 2,000-year-old prebunk!

One of the most popular questions I get is how people can use the principles of psychological inoculation in their own lives. First, I think it's important to consider that applying insights from our research requires some caution. Our findings are based on averages of groups of people, and we cannot pinpoint with certainty how any single individual is going to respond. For example, we know that biological vaccines are highly effective, but we can't predict the exact level of protection for a specific individual. We just know that, on average, it helps people, and that the risk of side-effects is low. It's the same with psychological inoculation. It works well on average and the risks of it backfiring are low. In fact, in comparison to other approaches such as fact-checking, there is almost no record of backfire effects for inoculation interventions. As is the case with medicine, this may change in the future as we learn more and conduct more tests; however, as far as we know, people seem to respond positively to the approach. With this in mind, let's explore how the different inoculation concepts we've looked at in preceding chapters can be applied in interpersonal situations. How do you inoculate your friends and family against the viral spread of fake news and misinformation?

In considering how and when to best apply inoculation in your own life, it's helpful to distinguish between fact-based and technique-based inoculation; active versus passive inoculation; and prophylactic versus therapeutic inoculation. Different contexts may call for different types of inoculation, so to help you select which variant of inoculation will be a good fit for your own situation, I'll run through some illustrative examples that consider the relative strengths and weaknesses of each approach in turn. We'll start with the classic fact-based or 'narrow-spectrum' inoculation.

The fact-based inoculation

The fact-based inoculation tries to immunize people against a specific falsehood on a particular issue, such as the myth that NASA faked the moon landing, or that global warming is a hoax. The thrust behind inoculation is that people need to have both the motivation and ability to defend themselves against persuasion. The motivational aspect is embodied in the forewarning: you need to warn friends and family that they may be exposed to harmful misinformation. The ability part comes in the form of pre-emptively refuting the falsehood, or the prebunk. The prebunk is crucial and specific to the issue at hand, so the fact-based inoculation is sometimes also referred to as an issue-based inoculation (they are one and the same). We've seen lots of examples of fact-based inoculation throughout the last few chapters – from arguments that voting by post leads to election fraud, to bogus petitions that cast doubt on the scientific consensus that humans are causing climate change. The purpose of the prebunk is to give people the 'antibodies' or evidence-based ammunition they need to argue against the persuasive features of the misinformation.

So, let's run through a specific example. Say you've become aware of a viral online story falsely claiming that you can get influenza from the flu vaccine. You are now in a position to forewarn those in, say, your household, your sports team, or social media channels that they might be exposed to harmful misinformation which falsely claims that you can get sick with flu from the flu jab. You add that they might even try to convince you that influenza vaccines are responsible for flu outbreaks. You then explain that this isn't possible because most flu vaccines use inactivated strains of the virus which cannot cause an infection. Accordingly, it is thus not possible that the flu vaccine could cause flu, let alone an epidemic! (When some people say that they experience a mild-grade fever or sore arm after receiving the vaccine, this only indicates that the vaccine is working because it is eliciting a successful immune response, without causing an infection. People who report that they became ill with the flu shortly after getting an influenza shot must have contracted the disease before gaining their immunity or were possibly exposed to a different virus altogether.)

This is not an entirely hypothetical example. In 2018, a viral Facebook post claimed that you can get the flu from the influenza vaccine and that a 'disastrous' flu shot administered by an anonymous doctor at the Centers for Disease Control and Prevention (CDC) caused a deadly flu epidemic. If this story finds its way back to social media (and it usually does), thanks to your inoculation, your friends and family will not only have been forewarned (so they know it's coming) but they now also have been exposed to a weakened version of the story and have the right facts at hand ready to counter-argue and resist the contagious misinformation. Of course, this is just one way to go about prebunking; you can get as creative as you like, using stand-up comedy, instructional or entertaining videos, games, social media messages, have your family doctor or a public health official deliver the prebunk, or perhaps arrange an in-person conversation over dinner or drinks. The most important thing is that you give people both the motivation to defend themselves and the ability to actually do so.

The main benefit of the fact-based inoculation approach is that the vaccine is highly specific and tailored to the misinformation someone is about to be exposed to. You create (and refute) a weakened dose of the exact same virus. It's perfectly matched and thus easy for people's psychological immune system to recognize and neutralize.

The main drawback is that the issue-based approach doesn't guarantee generalized immunity on the topic – in our example, related misinformation about the flu vaccine that you didn't specifically prebunk. There is some evidence that an issue-based inoculation can create an 'umbrella of protection' against related misinformation; for example, the inoculation might motivate people to seek out more information about vaccinations or make people more likely to question other misinformation about the flu vaccine as well. However, such additional protection is not guaranteed. There's strong evidence that the vaccine will work against the specific strain of the misinformation virus but anything extra is a mere bonus. In other words, the problem with the fact-based vaccine is that you need to inoculate people (separately) against every specific myth. It's narrow-spectrum.

This doesn't mean it's not useful. You might very well identify specific falsehoods that you want to inoculate people against. The benefit is that the level of immunization is relatively high because the refutation can be detailed and targeted towards the specific misinformation at hand. Unfortunately, it is not always possible to anticipate what specific piece of misinformation is going to crop up (having said this, the same misinformation about the flu vaccine seems to surface every winter but that may not always be the case). Sometimes it's therefore more useful to take a broad-spectrum approach.

The technique-based inoculation

Technique-based (or sometimes called logic-based) inoculation borrows more generally from Aristotle's approach to identifying and exposing flawed reasoning tactics. A prime example of this technique is the Six Degrees of Manipulation (DEPICT). You can also take broad techniques, such as conspiracy theories, and break them down into their constituent tactics (think of CONSPIRE). Unlike the issue-based prebunk, the technique-level inoculation doesn't deal with specific facts but forewarns people that they may be misled by a particular misinformation technique and subsequently prebunks that technique using one or several weakened doses.

The reason why we focus so much on manipulative intent is because prior research has found that people become more resistant to persuasion when they perceive an intention to manipulate them and recognize their own vulnerability to being persuaded. For example, in one experiment, Bob Cialdini's team trained participants to recognize the fake-expert technique by asking them to pay attention to whether or not a supposed authority figure has any expertise in the area. They then went through several illustrative examples. When they later exposed people to a series of misleading ads – for example one featuring Arnold Schwarzen-egger endorsing an internet television product by saying: 'This is the most sophisticated technology currently available' – people were more resistant and less persuaded by the ads because they found them to be more manipulative. After all, we may love Arnie but he's not an expert on the topic, they're just borrowing his credibility.

In our *Bad News* game, participants step into the shoes of the manipu-lator and attempt to dupe other people precisely because it makes the point salient that there's people out there trying to fool us with misinfor-mation and that we are vulnerable to such attacks. People became more immune to misinformation after our interventions because they were able to perceive fake news as being manipulative and recognized their own vulnerability in the process. So instead of enabling people to resist and argue against a specific piece of misinformation by providing them with the refutation in advance (fact-based inoculation), technique-based inoculation works by allowing people to identify the broader misinfor-mation technique, which alerts us to the possibility that we are being misled and as a consequence enhances the likelihood that we reject false information.

So how do you achieve this in a personal conversation? Let's return to the flu jab example. Instead of focusing your efforts on prebunking the specific myth, you would now turn your attention to demystifying the relevant manipulation technique for people. For example, you would fore-warn people that there are bad actors trying to manipulate us by making use of clever techniques to spread misinformation. One such example is called 'impersonation' and often involves the use of fake experts. These are people who may seem authoritative but have no expertise on a subject. Impersonation also frequently involves borrowing the legitimacy of an official-sounding organization, such as a public health authority. Some-times these experts are completely imaginary and are kept 'anonymous'.

A great way to dispel people's illusion of invulnerability to such tactics is to give them a little quiz. For example, you might challenge a friend to tell you whether a given headline contains the fake-expert technique. You could run through a few illustrative examples such as 'prominent scientist confirms that Covid-19 virus is a hoax', or 'renowned history professor says climate change is natural and has occurred throughout the ages'. When your friend is now exposed to the story of an 'anonymous doctor at the CDC' supposedly causing a flu epidemic, they have been inoculated – even without knowing all of the details of the story – as they can identify an attempt to manipulate their opinion by appealing to fake experts.

Another example could be the conspiracy technique. You might explain that conspiracy theories are recognizable by their predictable plot: they often cast doubt on the mainstream narrative surrounding a salient political issue by suggesting that there is some nefarious group working behind the scenes – in secret – to dupe people. When your friends or family members next come across a viral YouTube video entitled *Plandemic: The Hidden Agenda Behind Covid-19*, they are going to be better able to resist and identify it as a conspiracy theory.

The major benefit of technique-based inoculation is that it's broad-spectrum and therefore not tied to any single specific issue. Once inoculated against the fake expert or conspiracy technique, people are going to be relatively more immune to a wide range of different strains, regardless of whether the conspiracy is about Covid-19, climate change, or QAnon. The protection conferred is much broader so it's more efficient insofar as you do not have to prebunk every conspiracy theory or instance of impersonation anew.

Another major advantage is that you can pivot to a technique-level approach when people are unlikely to accept the fact-based inoculation. For example, it may be the case that someone is resistant to considering the evidence on a particular issue. I've found both in our research and over the course of many personal conversations that unveiling the techniques of manipulation encounters less resistance than trying to tell people what the facts are. This works partly because it's less direct – you're allowing people to still make up their own mind, but at least now they are aware of the possibility that they might be manipulated. People all across the political spectrum really dislike being manipulated – especially individuals who consider themselves 'truthers' and 'outside of the mainstream' who often pride themselves on being independent thinkers – so they might respond well to an opportunity to resist being manipulated even when it's on an issue that may appear congenial to their attitudes.

A possible drawback of the technique-level approach is that it's not as targeted and specific as a fact-based inoculation, so the level of psychological immunity might be lower, on average, because it's more difficult for people to recognize a general tactic across a whole range of instances and it might work better for some strains of misinformation than it does for others. In short, in some ways you are trading-off breadth for depth, but the approach often scales better across different issues and tends to encounter less psychological resistance.

Active versus passive inoculation

In delivering either a fact-based or technique-based inoculation, you have the choice to do it in an 'active' or a 'passive' way. An example of a passive inoculation is the message participants read in our experiment about climate change. We told them that the petition they were about to be exposed to contained many false signatories and accounts for just a tiny proportion of scientists, most of whom had no expertise in climate science. In other words, we (the experimenters) provided participants with the pre-emptive refutation in advance. In contrast, in the *Bad News* game, people actively generate their own content. They are finding out for themselves how misinformation is produced.

My hypothesis is that active inoculation is often more effective because it is better suited to how people generally learn about and experience the world. Our research supports this. We also know from lots of research that people learn better from experience, including through games and simulations. Experiential learning theory involves 'active experimentation'. We like to use our senses to discover how something works. We learn by doing. This is important insofar as experiential learning helps us store and retrieve information from memory. We can think of human memories as having a network structure. In particular, there are spiderlike structures that reside in our long-term memory, known as associative networks. These networks contain concepts (nodes) that are connected to each other via associative links (edges). The strength of the associative linkages depend on how well-connected the nodes are and how much importance people assign to them.

A network is typically activated by a specific node which then spreads to related nodes within the network. For example, the concept 'flu' might activate related concepts in your memory such as 'vaccine' and 'fever'. The concepts of flu, vaccine, and fever also happen to be connected to each other via associative paths. The idea is that an inoculation message can help strengthen links between concepts, increase the number of concepts, or change the structure of the network altogether. For example, if there is refutational content in a fact-based inoculation that people didn't know before, a new node might be added. Where previously it may have been 'virus', perhaps there are now additional nodes such as 'inactivated' versus 'live' virus. Similarly, while previously there may have been a path from 'virus' to 'vaccine' there may now be an additional path from 'inactivated virus' to 'vaccine'. If such a path already existed, the inoculation message would have strengthened the link by activating it. The higher the density of the memory network surrounding the inoculation, the more resistant it is going to be against a misinformation attack. We think that active inoculation does a better job of strengthening the links between concepts and maybe even the importance people assign to them, because of the extra cognitive effort involved in the process of active inoculation.

So, short of building your own fake news game, how can you harness the power of active inoculation in daily life?

If you have the facts to hand, you can of course (passively) provide people with the counter-arguments they need to withstand future exposure to misinformation. But what if you took an approach much like the one we used in our gamified interventions? What if you let people generate their own mental antibodies?

One clever way to do this would be to ask people if they can come up with any counter-arguments to a fake news story themselves. For example, you could ask a friend or colleague how they would respond if someone told them they can get the flu from the influenza vaccine. What would be a good counter-argument to that? Could you think of any, you might ask? How do vaccines actually work? In the same vein, you could ask your friend to generate arguments as to why a particular conspiracy theory would be unlikely? Can you give me three reasons why the earth is not flat?

The benefit of this approach is that people will feel more ownership over the arguments and ideas (they came up with them after all) and they will exert much more motivation and cognitive effort in retrieving, selecting, and memorizing them, causing more frequent activation and strengthening of the linkages between relevant concepts in memory. Of course, not everyone is able to come up with good counter-arguments of their own, so in those cases you may still need to be ready to provide people with weakened doses and persuasive refutations.

Prophylactic versus therapeutic inoculation

The ideal application of psychological inoculation is purely prophylactic: before people have been exposed to the misinformation. We can do this under stylized conditions in the laboratory where we can ensure that people have never been exposed to a piece of false information before. However, in reality, this is often difficult to achieve without polling the entire population. We simply don't know whether people have been exposed to a piece of (mis)information before, how often, and to what extent it has influenced their attitudes towards the issue. In other words, we can't be sure about people's 'infection status'.

Luckily, as we've seen throughout the last few chapters, inoculation still works even when people have already been exposed to the misinformation virus. Therapeutic inoculation can boost people's psychological immune response even when they have already been exposed to misinformation before. For example, we were still able to inoculate climate sceptics against a false petition that tried to sow doubt about the scientific consensus on global warming. Participants in our games come from all walks of life and we know little about their previous exposure levels, but they still improve in their ability to detect misinformation techniques across a wide variety of issues, and they report sharing less misinformation with others. Therapeutic inoculation can therefore still put the brakes on, sometimes quite effectively, but that doesn't mean it is always as effective as prophylactic inoculation. There's a clear advantage to striking first.

The point is that, even if you cannot strike first or don't know for sure at which point you are entering the conversation, it is reassuring to know that inoculation can still work when people have already been infected. For example, imagine that a friend of yours has just plunged into the ocean and you notice something disturbing: they missed the shark season warning sign! You immediately warn your friend that that there are dangerous sharks out there. Just because he or she is already in the water (and thus partly committed to their goal) doesn't mean that it's too late, they can still get out. The same applies to therapeutic inoculation. Moreover, compared to, say, a public health campaign, the advantage of a personal conversation is that you can actually find out more about people's infection status. When I have conversations with people I typically ask when they came across the misinformation? I try to assess whether they are still on the fence about believing it or whether have they fully internalized it as information that must be correct. This will help me determine where in the process I am entering the conversation and adjust my strategy accordingly.

To give you an example, my family sometimes forward misinformation posts circulating in their WhatsApp groups. At first, the information might look quite credible. For example, I was sent a viral video from 'Dr Dan Lee Dimke' claiming that he'd found a cure for Covid-19 that exploits a unique vulnerability in the coronavirus. His magical elixir involved taking a regular hair-dryer and basically shoving it up your nose because the hot air treatment would kill the virus. He recommended five heating treatments a day, if your symptoms have already started, and just two per day for preventative purposes. This may sound amusing to you, but the video presented all sorts of scientific papers and used complex medical-sounding jargon.

So, what was my approach here? I still forewarned the WhatsApp group that there's harmful misinformation circulating that makes use of clever manipulation techniques. I explained to the group that Dr Dimke is a fake expert: he has a degree in business and a PhD in education and therefore has no relevant expertise in medicine. I also embedded an abbreviated version of his professional biography, including prestigious accomplishments such as being 'the world's youngest astronomy lecturer at age 10', and 'the world's youngest hypnotist at age 11'. He also invented his own education system and has been publishing since the age of fourteen. To top it all off, 'he can slice through information at 25,000 words per minute'. I added that, although impressive, unfortunately, none of these credentials have anything to do with practising medicine, and his advice is dangerous as there is a significant burn risk. I was able to inoculate the WhatsApp group against this type of content even though the video had already been circulating. (I should add that the delivery matters; you want to make sure you relate and empathize with people's concerns. We should recognize that nobody is the ultimate arbiter of truth but we can help each other spot manipulation. It should be a positive exchange and not a hostile discussion.)

Now, I could have gone for a fact-based inoculation on why using a hairdryer to fight off the coronavirus won't work from a scientific perspective (using official public health advice) but given the prevalence of snake-oil salesmen peddling fake cures during the pandemic, I went for the technique-based inoculation. So even though I'd lost the opportunity for a prophylactic dose, I knew that there was still hope for therapeutic inoculation.

Of course, there must come a point where the virus spreads so deeply that you are simply left with no options other than plain old debunking. The individual will now need to reclassify information they previously thought was true as 'false' and replace it with an alternative story. Effective debunking requires that you provide a compelling alternative explanation, and, ideally, in a way that is least likely to trigger the political or social biases that may have predisposed people to accept the misinformation in the first place. It is much harder to do. Prevention is always better than cure.

Booster shots and post-inoculation talk

As is the case with some biological vaccines, we know that psychological immunity wanes over time. We lose our immunity to misinformation. This happens because either we're no longer motivated to defend ourselves, because we've forgotten how to do it, or most likely some combination of both: a loss in motivation and ability. A good example comes from my own WhatsApp groups. Although fake cures stopped being shared for weeks – months even – they eventually returned. Here's where the importance of booster shots come in.

People need regular booster shots to preserve both the motivation to protect themselves from fake news as well as their ability to actually do so. With the *Bad News* game, we found that engaging people weekly with a fake news quiz was a good way for them to maintain their acquired immunity over time, because it motivated them to keep paying attention and also provided people with an opportunity to hone their skills. But you can get as creative as you'd like with booster shots. We have also asked people to play the game again or complete a short five-minute version of it or watch a brief video. In the case of my WhatsApp group, I briefly ran through some novel examples of the fake-expert technique to boost people's 'antigen-specific memory cells' for detecting this type of content. You could easily re-engage people with the inoculation regularly in casual conversations, however briefly.

I do think it's possible for people to acquire long-term immunity against misinformation, but it likely requires exposure to several if not many booster shots over longer periods of time. Remember that a vaccine essentially gives the body a mugshot of a potential intruder. The more mugshots (weakened examples) of the intruder you can provide over time, the more effective the mind is going to become at striking back. In a world where people are continuously exposed to contradictory information that might interfere with the inoculation process, regular boosting is critical.

One other positive side-effect of psychological inoculation is that people tend to talk about the inoculation with others in their network. We refer to this organic sharing process as 'post-inoculation talk', and it opens up the possibility that people can share the vaccine vicariously from one friend to the next within their social network. If the spread of the vaccine outpaces the spread of misinformation, then misinformation no longer has a chance to take hold. For example, we observed that after the release of *Bad News*, thousands of people were talking about it on online forums such as Reddit. They were sharing the lessons that they had learned from the game. Similarly, after you've successfully inoculated someone, they might share the inoculation with others. You might even encourage people to explicitly do so. Pay it forward.

It turns out that frequently discussing the inoculation also helps strengthen resistance to persuasion. Research shows that people who report having talked about the inoculation more frequently have acquired greater immunity than those who didn't engage with the inoculation much after having received it. We therefore need to keep the conversation going. People talk about misinformation all the time. We need to start talking about the 'vaccine' as well. Sharing the inoculation not only strengthens its efficacy but also aids the herd immunity process. Every single one of us can play an active role in getting society one step closer to achieving herd immunity against misinformation.

There you have it. These are the lessons I've learned over the many years studying why people fall for misinformation and how we can most effectively counter it. I hope this book has given you some useful tools to better discern fact from fiction in your own life and equally important, the motivation to share these insights with others. Of course, one cognitive vaccine is just a drop in the ocean but sharing the vaccine can turn a drop into a wave and transform an individual into a crowd and crowds can change the world.

The spread of misinformation starts with a single individual choosing to share it, and that is also where it will end. Let's turn individual resistance into societal immunity. Over to you. May the truth be with you.

FAKE NEWS ANTIGEN 11
Inoculate your friends and family

— When it comes to implementing psychological inoculation in our daily lives we can choose between fact-based and technique-based inoculations.

— A fact-based inoculation is a narrow-spectrum vaccine that pre-emptively refutes specific falsehoods with facts and evidence. The benefit of this type of inoculation is that it is highly specific and targeted to a specific piece of misinformation.

— A technique-based inoculation, on the other hand, is a broad-spectrum vaccine that immunizes people against the overarching tactics used to spread misinformation. A strength of this type of inoculation is that it confers resistance across a wide range of falsehoods that make use of the same tactic. It might also generate less resistance when people's attitudes are not congenial to the facts.

— Both types of inoculations can be administered in passive and active form. Active inoculation requires more involvement from the target individual: they are encouraged to generate their own antibodies (counter-arguments), which help strengthen their resistance.

— In order for the inoculation to stick and spread far and wide, people need regular 'booster' shots and to talk about the inoculation with others in their network. Because our motivation and ability to counter-argue and identify misinformation wanes over time, it is important to have regular conversations that motivate, remind, and engage people with the inoculation process.

EPILOGUE

The future of truth

'The Dark Arts ... are many, varied, ever-changing, and
eternal. Fighting them is like fighting a many-headed monster,
which, each time a neck is severed, sprouts a head even fiercer and
cleverer than before. You are fighting that which is unfixed, mutating,
indestructible ... Your defences ... must therefore be as flexible
and inventive as the Arts that you seek to undo.'
PROFESSOR SEVERUS SNAPE on the DADA (*Harry Potter*)

I return to the wise lessons of Professor Severus Snape once more, in full,
because they perfectly illustrate the challenges that lie ahead. Just as some
viruses mutate to become more contagious and cause more severe illness, I
have no doubt that the misinformation virus will continue to mutate into
more sophisticated, more contagious, and yet more damaging strains. A
key open question is whether the vaccines that we currently have available
are still going to be effective against new and potentially more contagious
strains.

It's for this very reason that our lab focused on developing broad-
spectrum psychological vaccines that protect people not only from a
single strain but a whole range of variants. Of course, there is going to be
a limit to the efficacy of such vaccines. Just as the flu vaccine needs to be
updated every year against the latest variant, we should prepare to do the
same with our psychological vaccines.

For example, a number of books have been written about the looming dangers of deepfakes. Deepfakes use artificial intelligence, or so-called
'deep learning' methods, to create highly realistic but fake videos. In a

deepfake, the body and face of a person is digitally altered so that they appear to be someone else. The way this typically works is that the creator trains a machine learning algorithm on thousands of hours of real footage of the target individual so that the programme can get a good understanding of the person's appearance from different angles and under different lighting conditions. This algorithm often uses a so-called 'autoencoder' to discover similarities between the target individual and the actor's faces. Compression and computer graphics are then used to superimpose a copy of the target individual onto a different actor – this is called a 'face-swap'. Vladimir Putin, Barack Obama, Donald Trump, and Mark Zuckerberg have all been victims of some widely shared deepfakes, where they appear to be saying things that they've never actually said. For example, in his deepfake, Mark Zuckerberg says: 'Imagine one man with total control over billions of people's stolen data. All their secrets, their lives, their futures.' In another video Barack Obama supposedly calls Trump a 'total and complete dipshit'. These videos often look highly convincing.

Although online deception is getting more sophisticated, deepfakes have characteristics that should enable people to spot them – including unnatural or lack of eye blinking, bad lip-synching, patchy skin tones, flickering around the edges of transposed faces, and badly rendered hair, teeth and lighting conditions. Some of these issues can be fixed with better technology but at the end of the day, a deepfake is just a form of impersonation. What I like about our gamified approach is that our active inoculation interventions are a 'living' vaccine. We can continually adapt it – often pre-emptively – to prepare people for novel challenges. In fact, we're currently working on integrating deepfakes as a 'new strain' under the impersonation technique. We have already integrated 'shallow-fakes', or videos that are presented out of context after editing them with basic software (for instance, a video of a 2002 riot might be repurposed to make it look like it's happening today). When the Covid-19 pandemic hit, we immediately updated the scenarios in *Bad News* to reflect the current misinformation landscape so we could inoculate people against fake news about Covid-19.

The benefit of this technique-level approach to updating the vaccine has to do with the future of truth and how we define falsehood. Our scientific understanding of the facts can evolve quickly – especially during a crisis – and often with a fair amount of uncertainty. For example, whereas news media initially claimed that taking ibuprofen could worsen Covid symptoms, this claim was based on a single study and, as more evidence came to light, was later retracted. Thus, the problem with this approach is that we're going to need to update our understanding of what's 'true' on a regular basis.

In contrast, as I have often done throughout this book, by defining misinformation in terms of the techniques that underlie its production, we arrive at a more stable understanding of falsehood. What was considered flawed reasoning over 2,000 years ago, in Aristotle's time, is still considered flawed reasoning today. Unless we fundamentally change the rules of logic or what counts as media manipulation, the techniques I have identified in this book are going to remain deceptive for a long time to come. Although they might evolve, become more sophisticated and contagious, their basic properties will remain similar, so we don't have to combat a continuously moving target.

While issue or fact-based inoculation will certainly have its place, especially for established science or urgent issues, I believe technique-based inoculation will be the way of the future in helping people discern reliable content. This is not only because it avoids having to deal with changing definitions of truth (or misinformation) but also because it targets a common understanding of what content is more likely to be manipulative. I therefore think that we need to move away from overly simplistic 'true versus false' categorizations and help each other calibrate our judgments more carefully, towards how reliable, accurate, or manipulative online content is going to be. Very little content is either completely true or false. Most media manipulation leverages a grain of truth – and occurs somewhere in the grey middle. Inoculation against the underlying techniques used in spreading misinformation will allow people to make up their own minds about how credible a piece of information is.

My optimism about the future of prebunking is reinforced by its worldwide implementation.

On 3 February 2022, for example, President Biden's administration forewarned the public that they might be exposed to a Russian propaganda attack. Specifically, they warned people that they might soon see a fake video with graphic footage of a supposed Ukrainian attack on Russian territory. The basic plot of the film would be to portray Ukrainian 'genocide' against Russian-speakers in an attempt to concoct a false pretext for a planned Russian invasion. People were told that these videos might include images of explosions and dead bodies and even actors pretending to be Russian mourners. This move from the Biden administration was highly unusual as, typically, the US sits on sensitive intel like this. Moreover, even though they had high confidence in the intelligence, they weren't sure of all of the details. But the stakes were so high that the decision was made to inoculate ahead of a possible Russian invasion of Ukraine.

The prebunk followed inoculation theory closely: people were forewarned of a propaganda attack; they explained the underlying manipulation technique, and provided a weakened dose of what the attack might look like along with a persuasive refutation.

It's been suggested that the prebunk helped prevent polarization amongst the US public, as well as NATO member states, and may have even delayed the Russian invasion. Even though the Russian propaganda may not have materialized, preparing people for the attack was the right decision in my opinion: the Kremlin uses the same manipulation tactics over and over so it is likely that the attack would ultimately have emerged in some shape or form. Inoculation offers control over the narrative and allows us to cultivate mental antibodies.

At the same time, we should keep in mind that psychological inoculation isn't going to be sufficient on its own. Although the best response we have is to prebunk false content, we need to be prepared to intervene at every stage of the 'infection' process. An effective multi-layered societal defence system against misinformation will entail prophylactic inoculation as our first line of defence, with therapeutic inoculation as a close second. If that fails, we need to have real-time fact-checking in place to tag and flag information as false as soon as it spreads. If people miss the fact-check – and a substantial proportion might – we need to implement the most effective ways to debunk misinformation after it has spread. I have visualized a timeline (page 277) for mounting such a societal firewall against the looming danger of a post-truth society. Only with rapid responses at every stage of the infection process can we reduce the likelihood of misinformation seeping its way through the system.

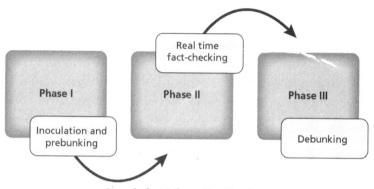

Spread of misinformation (time).

But the onus isn't on individuals alone. The system is comprised, in a large part, of social media companies that control the flow of information. Without a radical rethink of how to use these systems in the service of truth and accuracy, our individual efforts are going to be hampered. What's fascinating is that in my conversations with social media companies, they have told me, in no uncertain terms, that their platforms are not designed to promote accuracy. Although they try to help stop the spread of misinformation (through internal reviews of their policies, research funding, algorithmic tweaks, and external partnerships with fact-checkers), the goal is to promote the conversations people want to have – regardless of accuracy – as long as these conversations don't violate the company's user policies (such as hate speech). It is therefore important to realize that the social information systems controlled by these organizations are typically not incentivized to help promote more accurate, evidence-based, and constructive sharing of information. Such radical re-thinking of the incentives – and arguably the associated loss in profits – is not on the agenda. We are going to have to demand it. If we could start from scratch, how would we rebuild Facebook, Twitter, YouTube and other social media platforms to bring out the best of humanity? To make sure facts and evidence go viral? To prevent false or misleading information from being spread at all?

Although we're still a long way from answering these tough questions, I hope to have illustrated with this book that we are not defenceless in the fight against misinformation. New challenges will keep coming. A recent study showed that fake news can even influence us without our conscious awareness. In the study, people were asked to tap at their maximum speed during a reading task. In one of the conditions people read a fake article about the relationship between intelligence and tapping speed. People tapped faster in the fake news condition but showed no awareness of the change in their behaviour. How can we fight an enemy we're not even aware of? The fake news article used emotions to manipulate how good or bad people felt about the relationship between intelligence and tapping ability. The first step to countering it lies in your ability to spot and neutralize these techniques.

In the Harry Potter books, students of 'Defence Against the Dark Arts' (a mandatory subject) learned about the tell-tale signs of demons, how to counter jinxes, and cast defensive spells. Teachers who only used theory weren't effective demonstrators, as students needed to experience a weakened dose to truly understand how to counter the Dark Arts. The same goes for fake news.

What I haven't told you is that many of the Defence Against the Dark Arts teachers didn't survive for very long – a jinxed position with most suffering an unpleasant fate. Although I surely hope to remain 'Cambridge's Defence Against the Dark Arts teacher' for many years to come, I have passed on everything I know, just in case. Please treat this book as your guide to defeating the dark arts of manipulation. It is in your capable hands now. Use it wisely.

11 ANTIGENS TO HELP STOP THE SPREAD OF MISINFORMATION

1. Make the truth fluent
The more familiar a claim becomes the easier it is for the brain to process.

2. Incentivize accuracy
Create an environment where people strive to be accurate rather than political.

3. Learn the tell-tale signs of conspiracy theories (CONSPIRE)
Conspiracy theories have a predictable structure that you can learn to spot.

4. Minimize the continued influence of misinformation
The longer misinformation sits in our brains the more influential it becomes.

5. Break the virality of misinformation on social media
Limiting how often misinformation is liked and shared dampens its influence.

6. Avoid echo chambers and filter bubbles
Echo chambers bias the flow of (mis) information towards like-minded others.

7. Be aware of micro-targeting
Micro-targeting can help identify susceptible individuals open to persuasion.

8. Inoculate against misinformation
Pre-emptively refuting weakened doses of fake news can confer mental immunity.

9. Identify and prebunk the Six Degrees of Manipulation (DEPICT)
Discrediting, emotion, polarization, impersonation, conspiracy, and trolling.

10. Help spread inoculation against misinformation
When enough people are vaccinated, misinformation can no longer spread.

11. Inoculate your friends and family
Pick your method: fact-based, technique-based, active, or passive inoculation.

FURTHER RESOURCES

Want to learn more about inoculation theory?
Visit www.inoculation.science.

Want to play one of our games, inoculate your friends, or participate in our research? You can play them here for free:
www.getbadnews.com
www.goviralgame.com
www.harmonysquare.game.

On Twitter and want to find out more about your own media diet? Check out whether you have shared fake news on our app:
https://newsfeedback.shinyapps.io/HaveISharedFakeNews/.

Want to know more about the science?

S. van der Linden (2022), 'Misinformation: susceptibility, spread, and interventions to immunize the public', *Nature Medicine*, 28, 460–7.

S. van der Linden, and J. Roozenbeek (2022), 'A psychological "vaccine" against fake news: from the lab to worldwide implementation', in N. Mazar and D. Soman (eds), *Behavioral Science in the Wild*, Toronto University Press, pp. 188–206.

Assess your skills with the Misinformation Susceptibility Test (MIST). Here's a sample:
'Government Officials Have Manipulated Stock Prices to Hide Scandals'
'New Study: Left-Wingers Are More Likely to Lie to Get a Higher Salary'
'One-in-Three Worldwide Lack Confidence in NGOs'

'Certain Vaccines Are Loaded with Dangerous Chemicals and Toxins'
'Attitudes Toward EU Are Largely Positive, Both Within Europe and
    Outside It'

Three out of these five headlines are dodgy. Can you spot the
misinformation techniques? (The first headline uses 'conspiracy', the
second 'polarization', and the fourth 'emotion'.)

NOTES

Prologue (pp. 1–9)

For 5G phone mast attacks see *BBC News* (8 June 2020). For Michael Whitty see *Sky News* (10 June 2020) and the Crown Prosecution Service (10 June 2020). It is worth noting that although Whitty had positive character witnesses describing him as a committed volunteer, he also had a string of prior offences, including assault. For violence and the role of 5G Covid-19 conspiracy beliefs see D. Jolley and J. L. Paterson (2020) and F. Vegetti and L. Littvay (2022) for a general link between conspiracy theories and endorsement of political violence. For global susceptibility to misinformation about Covid-19 see J. Roozenbeek, C. R. Schneider, et al. (2020). For Trump's 'misleading' claims see G. Kessler, S. Rizzo, and M. Kelly (2020). For the role of misinformation in the Capitol riot arrests see B. McCarthy (2021) as well as D. Keppler (2021) for Antonio's story and the 'fake news defence'. For coverage of the 'WhatsApp Lynchings' in India see V. Goel, S. Raj, and P. Ravichandran (2018). See D. Funke (2022) for fact-checks on viral misinformation about Ukraine and S. Seibt (2022) and J. Roozenbeek and R. Finnin (2022) on motives behind Russian disinformation. For links between fake news and mass poisonings in Iran see *PBS Newshour* (27 March 2020) as well as H. Aghababaeian, L. Hamdanieh, and A. Ostadtaghizadeh (2020). For polling evidence on belief in conspiracy theories see J. E. Oliver and T. J. Wood (2014). For data on public confusion over facts see M. Barthel, A. Mitchell, and J. Holcomb (2016) and for reported exposure to misinformation in Europe see European Commission (2018). An account of my family history is described in R. Groenteman (2002). The UK Foreign Office meeting on fake news was held under the Chatham House Rule: this means that I can share my insights with you but not reveal the identity or affiliation of any of the attendees or speakers; for a public report see *Wilton Park* (2017). For cognitive immunology see A. Norman (2021) and for the *Bad News* game see J. Roozenbeek and S. van der Linden (2019).

1: Illusory Truth: How our brains discern fact from fiction (pp. 13–27)

For people's performance on the fake news quiz see Channel 4 (6 February 2017). For more on the suspect who had a 'shit day' see D. Evon (15 November 2019).

A good account of how many (including myself) were duped by the fake 'Wind on Mars' NASA video is provided by J. Wenz (2021). For the studies that assessed how well teens can spot dodgy content online see S. Wineburg et al. (2016) and S. McGrew et al. (2017), as featured in S. Shellenbarger (21 November 2016). For the ruling on how the *Sun*'s poll on Brits having 'sympathy' for Jihadis was misleading see *IPSO* (2016). It is difficult to know the exact number of neurons in the brain so the more *truthful* answer is approximately a 100 billion, with estimates ranging between 75 and 125 billion. For a good discussion on the number of neurons in the brain see R. Lent et al. (2012). For the role of top-down processing in vision see D. E. Pafundo et al. (2016) and for an excellent discussion of the brain as a prediction machine see A. Seth (2021). For mention that the Big Lie rule is often associated with Goebbels see J. Goebbels (1941) and J. Herf (2005). For polling data on Trump's 'Big Lie' that the election was rigged see A. Romano (2022). For the illusory truth effect see L. Hasher, D. Goldstein and T. Toppino (1977) (original study) as well as L. K. Fazio et al. (2015) and L. K. Fazio and C. L. Sherry (2020) for illusory truth across different age groups. See E. L. Henderson, D. J. Simons, and D. J. Barr (2021) for estimates on the incidence rate of illusory truth. See W. C. Wang et al. (2016) for neural mechanisms. Specifically, the perirhinal cortex (located in the medial temporal lobe) shows increased activity when judging repeated (vs novel) claims. This part of the brain is known to play an important role in memory. For boundary conditions see J. De Keersmaecker et al. (2020) and for the claim that prior exposure increases familiarity with fake news see G. Pennycook, T. D. Cannon, and D.G. Rand (2018). For research on how repeated claims seem less ethical to share see D. A. Effron and M. Raj (2020). For a popular overview on how much the brain can store see A. Hadhazy (2 April 2015). A good review on memory storage is provided by Y. Dudai (1997) and for extensive coverage of the role of synaptic plasticity see W. C. Abraham, O. D. Jones, and D. L. Glanzman (2019) and T. M. Bartol Jr et al. (2015). I should note that there is a difference between the theoretical information capacity of the brain and the amount of storage we use for everyday memory retrieval; it is likely that only a small percentage is dedicated to autobiographical memories. Moreover, we don't really know how much space a single memory requires; this likely depends on the nature of the memories (how detailed, words vs pictures), the specific memory system, the unit of measurement, and so on. For example, after viewing *thousands* of images, people can generally recognize ones they've seen with 90 per cent accuracy. This suggests we have a huge capacity for memories of visual objects (see T. F. Brady et al. 2008). In contrast to humans, chimpanzees have a much better working memory (we traded some memory space for language). There are many estimates using various techniques so perhaps the true number of memories the human brain can *theoretically* store will remain an enigma. It's also worth mentioning that although we likely forget a lot of detail, there's also the opposite problem of having memories that we cannot seem to get rid of, for example, following traumatic events. For 'Truthiness' see S. Colbert (2005) and the first episode of the *Colbert Report*. For the 'Cognitive Reflection Test' (CRT) see S. Frederick (2005) and G. Pennycook and D. G. Rand (2019) for its relation to falling for fake news. Nobel laureate Daniel Kahneman often refers to this distinction as 'System 1' vs 'System 2' in his book *Thinking, Fast and Slow* (Farrar, Straus, and Giroux, 2011). I should note that there is scientific debate about whether or not the CRT is a good measure of intuitive (System 1) and reflective (System 2) thinking and it isn't always the best predictor of fake news susceptibility – see J. Roozenbeek et al. (2022). A related measure is your receptivity to what we, in scientific jargon, refer to as 'pseudo-profound bullshit'. Here's an example from the bullshit receptivity scale: 'Imagination is inside exponential space time events.' For a review of the 'misinformation effect', including the Bugs Bunny study see E. F. Loftus (2003, 2005). I should note that Loftus received extensive criticism from students, colleagues, and the #MeToo movement for testifying on behalf of Harvey Weinstein in particular. Her reasoning seems to stem from the fact that because many people have been falsely convicted as a result of unreliable eyewitness accounts, even 'the unpopular deserve to have a defence'; see A. Marsh and S. Lorge (2012) for an in-depth interview. For the misinformation effect in the context of committing crimes see J. Shaw and S. Porter (2015), alien abductions see H. Otgaar et al. (2009); for the War in Iraq see S. Lewandowsky et al. (2005), and for Brexit see C. M. Greene, R. A. Nash, and G. Murphy (2019). For a conceptual replication during Ireland's abortion referendum see G. Murphy et al. (2019). For the role of fluency in judgment see R. Reber and N. Schwarz (1999), N. Schwarz, E. Newman, and W. Leach (2016) and E. J. Newman et al. (2012). For the Moses illusion see H. Song and N. Schwarz (2008).

2: The Motivated Brain: What you want to believe (pp. 28–45)

The 'art of persuasion' is a phrase that originates from Pascal's '*L'Esprit de géométrie et De l'art de persuader*', which was first published posthumously in the eighteenth century (see E. Ciocoiu 2019). *The Pensées* ('thoughts'), an unfinished collection written by Pascal and first published in 1670 (see P. Blaise 1941), lays the groundwork for his infamous 'wager' and intellectual defence of Christianity. For interpretations of his wager and paradoxical views on science and religion see N. Hammond (2000), J. A. Connor (2019) and D. Clarke (2015). For a neurological assessment of his visions see M. Paciaroni (2010). The Keynes quote is often attributed to Nobel-prize winning economist Paul Samuelson, though Samuelson reports that he first heard it from Keynes, see L. H. Clark Jr (13 October 1978). Bayes's theorem was published posthumously via a letter from his friend, Richard Price, to the Royal Society (see T. Bayes 1764). For a good discussion on the Bayesian brain and belief-updating, see B. M. Tappin and S. Gadsby (2019). For the role of images in fluency and truthiness see E. Fenn et al. (2013). For turnout at Donald Trump's presidential inauguration see P. Bump (23 January 2017) and L. Robertson and R. Farley (23 January 2017). For the public opinion experiment on the perceived size of the inauguration crowd see B. F. Schaffner and S. Luks (2018). For how political motivations can shape visual attention to climate-change trend data see Y. Luo and J. Zhao (2019, 2021). For the classic experiments on conformity, see Asch (1951, 1956) and R. A. Griggs (2015) for how these studies have been covered in psychology textbooks. See R. Bond and P. B. Smith (1996) for how conformity with the line-judgment task declined over time in the US. For an excellent treatment of the power of groups and identity see Van Bavel and Packer (2021) as well as Tajfel and Turner (1979) for the origins of social identity theory. There's an interesting relationship with political ideology here, too; for example, some studies find that (all else equal) liberals are higher on the need to be accurate than the need to identify with others in their group, whereas the opposite is generally true for conservatives, who are higher on the desire for a 'shared reality': see J. Jost et al. (2019). Different groups have different values and motivations. For the observational equivalence paradox see J. N. Druckman and M. C. McGrath (2019). For our study on how people are more likely to fall for misinformation when the source is politically congenial see C. S. Traberg and S. van der Linden (2022). For evidence that people deny science because they don't like the implications of the science for policy see T. H. Campbell and A. C. Kay (2014) and for the impact of financial incentives on accurate responding see M. Prior, G. Sood, and K. Khanna (2015). For the original Stanford study on attitude polarization see C. G. Lord, L. Ross, and M. R. Lepper (1979). For research which argues that more scientifically literate people are the most polarized on contested issues see D. M. Kahan, H. Jenkins-Smith, and D. Braman (2011) as well as D. M. Kahan et al. (2012), and C. Drummond and B. Fischhoff (2017). For research which is critical of this finding see E. Persson et al. (2021) and B. M. Tappin, G. Pennycook, and D. G. Rand (2021). For further research which finds that facts don't backfire, see T. Wood and E. Porter (2019). For my critical exchanges with Dan Kahan see S. van der Linden (2016) and S. van der Linden et al. (2017). For our experiment on climate change, which illustrates how people can have both strong prior beliefs but still update toward the evidence, see S. van der Linden, A. Leiserowitz, and E. Maibach (2018). For the insurrection study see D. L. Painter and J. Fernandes (2022). For politicization of science see S. Lewandowsky et al. (2022).

3: The Conspiracy Effect: The truth is out there (pp. 46–62)

The quotes from Mulder (David Duchovny) and Scully (Gillian Anderson) come from Episode 17 of the cult-classic TV show *The X-Files* (E.B.E), which premiered in 1994, see C. Carter (1994). Every episode opened with the phrase 'the truth is out there'. For public opinion data on belief in the Alien cover-up conspiracy see C. Ibbetson (18 January 2021). For the flat earth documentary see D. J. Clark (2018) and *YouGov* (2018) for belief in the flat-earth conspiracy (note that 7 per cent of Americans say that they are unsure). For the flat earth rap battle between B.o.B and Neil deGrasse Tyson see E. Brait (26 January 2016), Y. Philips (26 January 2016), and L. Said-Moorhouse (30 January 2016). For B.o.B's induction into the Flat Earth Society see J. Davis (28 July 2016). For the claim that over half of Americans believe in at least one conspiracy theory see J. E. Oliver and T. J. Wood (2014); for data on QAnon belief see Public Religion Research Institute (27 May 2021) and see J. Roozenbeek et al. (2021) for belief in Covid-19 conspiracy theories. For more on Bucky Wolfe's story see B. Montgomery (9 January 2019). For David Icke's conspiracy theories see D. Icke (1999) and BBC (20 May 2016). For mathematical models on the implausibility of popular conspiracy theories see D. R. Grimes (2016). For the paranoid style in American politics see R. Hofstadter (1964). It is useful to note that Hofstadter was very careful to make a distinction between clinical delusions and the focal interest of his essay, which was specifically about the 'paranoid modes of expression by more or less normal people'. To avoid any confusion, I echo this observation here in that although some individuals who engage in extremist acts may have underlying mental health problems, growing paranoid suspicion about the motives of other groups in society is 'what makes the phenomenon significant'. For our empirical test of Hofstadter's 'paranoid style' in explaining belief in American conspiracy theories see S. van der Linden et al. (2021), and for a general overview of what leads people to believe in conspiracy theories see S. van der Linden (2013) and K. M. Douglas, R. M. Sutton, and A. Cichocka (2017). For feelings of being 'in-the-know' see A. Lantian et al. (2017). For the 'dead and alive' study see M. J. Wood, K. M. Douglas, and R. M. Sutton (2012). I should note that one critique of this study is that because none of the students really endorsed any of these conspiracy theories, it is not entirely clear how representative these results are but see B. Franks (2017) for interviews with real conspiracy theorists and quasi-religious views. For further evidence of conspiracy theories forming a monological belief system see Goertzel (1994), M. N. Williams et al. (2022), Swami et al. (2011) for fictitious theories, and Roozenbeek et al. (2020) on Covid-19. For the 'Linda' problem see A. Tversky and D. Kahneman (1983) and evidence of the conjunction fallacy in conspiratorial reasoning see A. Wabnegger, A. Gremsl, and A. Schienle

(2021). For the Gates Foundation not having a stake in the Covid-19 vaccines see D. Funk (14 May 2020). For my research on the conspiracy effect see S. van der Linden (2015) and M. Biddlestone, F. Azevedo, and S. van der Linden (2022). For the language of conspiracy see A. Fong et al. (2021). For conspiratorial accusations against research on conspiracy theories see S. Lewandowsky et al. (2015). In fact, the conspiracy theorists were so ticked off that their online discussion had become the subject of scientific research that they sued the journal. For the *Plandemic* video (the first film) see M. Willis (12 May 2020) and C. Newton (12 May 2020) on virality. For the seven traits of conspiratorial thinking, see Cook et al. (15 May 2020) and S. Lewandowsky, J. Cook, U. K. Ecker, and S. van der Linden (2020). I credit S. Lewandowsky and J. Cook for initially developing the CONSPIRE acronym. For the link between belief in conspiracy theories and political violence see D. Jolley and J. L. Patterson (2020), F. Vegetti and L. Littvay (2022) as well as G. J. Rousis et al. (2020). For the claim that 20 per cent of populations worldwide believe a single group of people control world events see C. Ibbetson (18 January 2021). For Joe's sceptical views on claims of increased popularity of conspiracy theories see A. Morris (15 October 2021), J. Uscinski and J. M. Parent (2014), and J. Uscinski et al (2022). For the quote from Neil deGrasse Tyson see *Hot Ones* (11 May 2017). For evidence on the theory that conspiracies are for 'losers' see R. Imhoff et al. (2022), and for the idea that demand and supply of conspiracy theories follows societal unrest see J. W. van Prooijen and K. M. Douglas (2017). For longitudinal polling data on the JFK conspiracy see A. Swift (15 November 2013), and for rising anti-vaccination conspiracy theories during the pandemic, compare US data for the 'YouGov Cambridge Globalism Project – Conspiracy Theories' from 2019 to 2020.

4: Why the Virus Won't Leave Your Mind: The continued influence of misinformation (pp. 63–79)

Hitler's manifesto, *Mein Kampf* ('My Struggle'), was originally published in 1925; for the quote (translated by Ralph Manheim) see A. Hitler (1925). For the legal case against Ali, including excerpts of student essays see *Jason Mostafa Ali vs Woodbridge Township School District et al.* (2019). For a historical perspective on Goebbels's 'international Jewry' conspiracy see J. Herf (2005). For the modern persistence of these beliefs: a 2016 US national survey amongst those aged 18 to 39 revealed that at least 11 per cent think that Jewish people were responsible for their own persecution and almost half (49 per cent) have witnessed some form of Holocaust denial online; see Claims Conference (2016) for details. Although Goebbels may not have known that images can enhance feelings of *fluency* and *familiarity*, he was a big fan of visual media. When designing propaganda, he specifically wrote about the fact that visual images often have much greater credibility than the written or spoken word alone, see L. W. Doob (1950). For the original continued influence effect study see H. M. Johnson and C. M. Seifert (1994). For reviews and meta-analyses, see S. Lewandowsky et al. (2012), N. Walter and R. Tukachinsky (2020), as well as M. P. S. Chan et al. (2017). For the 'unring a bell' legal reference, see *State vs Rader* (Or. 37, 1912). For jury studies see S. Fein, A. L. McCloskey, and T. M. Tomlinson (1997). You can also find traces of the continued influence effect in popular psychology myths such as the claim that 'humans only use 10 per cent of their brain power'. When probed about this myth no tangible sources are typically offered for belief in the claim just a 'vague memory recall' (even after exposure to lectures which specifically refute these myths) – see K. L. Higbee and S. L. Clay (1998). Note that *continued-influence effects* may sometimes be partly rational if people take into account the reliability of the source of the correction. For the movie *Vaxxed*, which was scheduled to premier at the 2016 Tribeca Film Festival, see A. Wakefield (2016). For the retracted paper in *The Lancet* see A. Wakefield et al. (1998), and coverage by S. Boseley (2 February 2010). More details of Wakefield's misconduct are provided by the General Medical Council (2010) and F. Godlee, J. Smith, and H. Marcovitch (2011) in the *British Medical Journal*. For the drop in vaccination coverage and damage to public opinion see D. C. Burgess, M. A. Burgess, and J. Leask (2006) as well as J. Lewis and T. Speers (2003). For US vaccination data see M. East et al. (2012), M. Motta and D. Stecula (2021), and V. K. Phadke et al. (2016). For our research on how belief in the autism–vaccine link shapes attitudes toward vaccination see S. van der Linden, C. E. Clarke, and E. W. Maibach (2015) and H. Yousuf et al. (2021). For Robert De Niro's Facebook post see N. Rayne (26 March 2016). For the apology from the *New York Times* on coverage of the Iraq War see 'From the Editors' (26 May 2004) and for study on the continued influence of WMDs see S. Lewandowsky et al. (2005). For the study on the persistent influence of Nazi propaganda see N. Voigtländer and H. J. Voth (2015). For neurological studies of the continued influence of misinformation see A. Gordon et al. (2017) and further discussion in U. Ecker et al. (2022). For my debunking work with Facebook see University of Cambridge (18 February 2021). The evidence for the risk of repeating misinformation initially came from an advertising study which showed that repeatedly identifying a consumer claim as false surprisingly made people more likely to think it was true three days later, because of increased familiarity with the claim itself, see I. Skurnik et al. (2005). For the truth sandwich and best practices in debunking misinformation see our *Debunking Handbook* by S. Lewandowsky et al. (2021).

5: Misinformation: From ancient Rome to social media (pp. 83–102)

For my sources and historical perspectives on the propaganda campaign between Gaius Octavian and Mark Antony see Dio Cassius (n.d.), K. Scott (1933), J. Sifuentes

(2019), and J. Rich (2010). For popular and more accessible accounts see I. Kaminska (17 January 2017) and E. Macdonald (13 January 2017). For quotes from Octavian see J. Sifuentes (2019) and Book 50 of Dio Cassius (n.d.) for the original translation. For more information about the life of Augustus see A. Goldsworthy (2015). It is worth noting that starting with Augustus, the Roman Empire witnessed an unprecedented period of relative peace and stability for the next 200 years or so, known as Pax Romana. For the Roman 'propaganda' coin featuring Octavian see Classical Numismatic Group (n.d.). For the WhatsApp lynchings and Rukmani's story see the *New York Times* story by V. Goel, S. Rai, and P. Ravichandran (18 July 2018) who visited the village in India. For context regarding our research with WhatsApp see M. Burgess (13 November 2018). WhatsApp's founders, Jan Koum and Brian Acton, left earlier that year due to disagreements with Mark Zuckerberg about the fact that Facebook wanted to monetize the platform by selling business analytics and targeted ads; Chris also resigned, not too long after we met him, albeit for different reasons. For a deep dive into the socio-political context, including tensions between the Indian government and WhatsApp see T. Mclaughlin (12 December 2018). For national coverage and quotes from local villagers see D. Karthikeyan (25 May 2018) and P. Thirumurthy (11 May 2018); I should note that although there is broad international coverage of these events, there are slight discrepancies in the dates and names of places in some local publications. For travel estimates of the Roman courier system see A. M. Ramsay (1925) and C. W. Eliot (1955). For background on the Great Moon Hoax see B. Thornton (2000); the reporter responsible for the story, Richard Adams Locke, eventually admitted the story was fake. For the undercover operation in Bolsonaro's WhatsApp groups see D. Nemer (25 October 2018). Wikipedia maintains a list of the most popular tweets, see 'List of most liked tweets' (2021). The research we did with WhatsApp in India is not yet published but available upon request. For statistics on the top 25 per cent Covid-19 videos on YouTube that contained misinformation see H.O.Y. Li et al. (2020). For the WHO's declaration of a worldwide 'infodemic' see J. Zarocostas (2019) and for the claim that a new tweet appeared every 45 milliseconds see A. Josephson and E. Lambe (11 March 2020). It is worth noting that some are critical of the infodemic metaphor and claim that information doesn't spread like a virus – see F. M. Simon and C. Q. Camargo (2021). However, I think this claim is demonstrably incorrect. For example, models from epidemiology are regularly used to model the spread of misinformation media as a simple contagion, see M. Cinelli et al. (2020), R. Gallotti et al. (2020) and S. Vosoughi, D. Roy, and S. Aral (2018) and J. B. Bak-Coleman et al. (2022). The infodemic model has greatly advanced our understanding of the viral spread of misinformation. However, it *is* true that some misinformation behaves more like a *complex* contagion (where infection only results from repeated contact with close neighbours). For research on how people share misinformation because it's entertaining, interesting, or could be true, see J. W. van Prooijen et al. (2022), S. Altay, E. de Araujo, and H. Mercier (2022), and B. A. Helgason and D. A. Effron (2022). For the study which claimed that it takes the truth about six times as long as a falsehood to reach 1,500 people see S. Vosoughi et al. (2018). For the replication see J. L. Juul and J. Ugander (2021) and for the subsequent misinformation debacle about the study itself see D. Enger (26 March 2022) and S. Aral (6 April 2022); to be fair, it's a highly technical issue so I can see how the wording in the replication paper's abstract might have confused casual commentators. Ironically, there is a lot of disagreement about the 'falsehood flies' quote, which has been attributed to Mark Twain, to Winston Churchill and to Jonathan Swift. For readings on the larger social and political tensions that fuelled the WhatsApp lynchings see T. Mclaughlin (12 December 2018), P. Dixit and R. Mac (9 September 2018), and C. Arun (2019). For research on the prejudiced content of many WhatsApp messages see S. Banaji and R. Bhat (2019). It is estimated that over 67,000 children are reported missing in India a year (about 183 children a day), see National Crime Records Bureau (2019). Note that the fake news problem is not unique to WhatsApp. For example, more recently, the 'Telegram' instant messaging service (another popular social media app with end-to-end encryption) was a major source of disinformation after Russia invaded Ukraine in February 2022.

6: Rage Against the Machine: Echo chambers and filter bubbles (pp. 103–132)

For the quote from Mark Zuckerberg see interview with H. Blodget (1 October 2009). For the Oxford data on technology adoption in the US see E. Ortiz-Ospina (2020). For public accounts of Caleb Cain's story and analyses of his YouTube history see K. Roose (8 June 2019) as well as his own YouTube channel, Faraday Speaks (22 March 2019). For an informal analysis of Buckey Wolfe's YouTube watch history see T. View (10 January 2019). For Joe Uscinski's quote see A. Morris (15 October 2021). For our fake news app, see https://newsfeedback.shinyapps.io/HaveIShared-FakeNews/. For YouTube user statistics in the US see P. Van Kessel (4 December 2019) and YouTube (n.d.). For Cass Sunstein's initial predictions about personalized democracies see C. Sunstein (2001) and for the filter-bubble hypothesis see E. Pariser (2011). For biased amplification and Twitter's audit of their own personalized home feed see F. Huszár et al. (2022), and for the 'Search Engine Manipulation Effect' (SEME) see R. Epstein and R. E. Robertson (2015). These voter effects strike me as rather big but see R. Epstein et al. (2017) for a replication. For YouTube radicalization see Z. Tufekci (10 March 2018). For quotes from Facebook data scientist Monica Lee see J. Horwitz and D. Seetharaman (26 May 2020). For quotes from YouTube's chief product officer, Neal Mohan, see J. E. Solsman (10 January 2018) and K. Roose (29 March 2019). For Zuckerberg's graph on engagement see M. Zuckerberg (5 May 2018). For Francis Haugen see 'The Facebook Files' (1 October 2021). For the Pew audit of YouTube's recommendations and the number of US adults who see problematic content on the platform see A. Smith, S. Toor, and P. Van Kessel (7 November 2018). For the YouTube rabbit hole study see M. Faddoul, G. Chaslot, and H. Farid (2020) as well as coverage by J. Nicas (2 March 2020). See T. Malinowski and A. G. Eshoo for associated letter informing US Congress of the study's findings. For additional studies and evidence see M. Alfano et al. (2020). A cookie is a small piece of data stored on your computer by your web browser; when you visit a website, it sends a cookie to your computer to keep track of your activity. For the study looking at alternative and extremist recommendations on YouTube see A. Y. Chen et al. (2019). Racial resentment was measured by asking how people feel toward minority groups on a scale from 0 (cold) to 100 (warm). A systematic review of academic studies evaluating YouTube's role as a gateway to misinformation is provided by M. Yesilada and S. Lewandowsky (2022). For the Facebook filter-bubble study see E. Bakshy, S. Messing, and L. A. Adamic (2015). For Eli Pariser's critique of this study see E. Pariser (7 May 2015). For Facebook's playbook on polarization see R. Mac and C. Silverman (12 March 2021). For our op-ed in the *Washington Post* about Facebook see S. Rathje, J. Van Bavel, and S. van der Linden (13 July 2021) and for Facebook's reply see P. Raychoudhury (13 July 2021). Unfortunately, the headline, 'Why Facebook really, really doesn't want to discourage extremism', was overly hyperbolic but picked by the editors despite our objections. The WaPo replied suggesting that the headline was tongue-in-cheek, perfectly illustrating the gist of our research: extreme headlines receive more engagement. For discussions on offline echo chambers see K. H. Jamieson and J. N. Cappella (2008) as well as J. R. Brown and R. D. Enos (2021) on the partisan sorting study. For the study matching online and offline echo chambers around Brexit see M. Bastos, D. Mercea, and A. Baronchelli (2018). For evidence that echo chambers are less likely to emerge for non-controversial topics see P. Barberá et al. (2015). For the echo chamber graph and our study on conspiracy influencers see F. Fong et al. (2021). For the 'law of group polarization' see C. R. Sunstein (1999) as well as S. Moscovici and M. Zavalloni (1969) and K. Strandberg, S. Himmelroos, and K. Grönlund (2019). For systematic reviews on how social media shapes polarization see E. Kubin and V. Sikorski (2021) and J. Van Bavel et al. (2021). For comparisons of the echo chamber effect across social media platforms see M. Cinelli et al. (2021), and for research on how echo chambers facilitate the viral spread of misinformation see P. Törnberg (2018). For evidence on how filter bubbles make fake news more believable see S. Rodes (2021). For how echo chambers impede efforts to debunk and disseminate fact-checks see F. Zollo et al. (2018).

For the study which mapped the anti-vax landscape on Facebook, including predictions about future trends see N. F. Johnson et al. (2020). For the study which showed that having Democrats follow Republican accounts and vice versa resulted in more polarization see C. A. Bail et al. (2018). For moral outrage see M. J. Crockett (2017). For content rated as 'bad for the world' receiving more engagement see K. Roose, M. Isaac, and S. Frenkel (24 November 2020) and for our study on how out-group animosity predicts virality on social media see S. Rathje. J. Van Bavel, and S. van der Linden (2021). For studies that quantify echo chambers effects when comparing direct browsing versus curated social media feeds see A. Guess (2021), G. Eady et al. (2019), and particularly S. Flaxman, S. Goel, and J. M. Rao (2016). For 'Obvious Study on Dunking Because They're Nerds', see S. Wodinsky (25 June 2021). I should note that although Facebook has shared data with the research community, they announced in February 2021 that they uncovered a major flaw: previously shared datasets which they claimed were representative of all US users only contained about half the data; this lack of transparency makes independent replications difficult, see C. Timberg (10 September 2021).

7: Weapons of Mass Persuasion (pp. 133–166)

The quote from Christopher Wylie and related source material can be found in his 2019 book *Mindf*ck* see C. Wylie (2019) and his written testimony to the UK Parliament (28 March 2018). For the models on local public opinion about climate change see B. Zhang et al. (2018). For Cadwalladr's breaking story of the whole Cambridge Analytica affair see C. Cadwalladr (4 March 2017), C. Cadwalladr and E. Graham-Harrison (17 March 2018), and M. Rosenberg, N. Confessore, and C. Cadwalladr (17 March 2018). For further background see the *Guardian*'s 'Cambridge Analytica Files' (2018) and an earlier article from H. Davies (11 December 2015) for which Michal Kosinski was a key source. For a detailed history of the Big Five 'OCEAN' model of personality see O. P. John, L. P. Naumann, and C. J. Soto (2008). For heritability see C. J. Soto (2019) and for the role of personality in fake news see D. P. Calvillo et al. (2021). Big Five is not to be confused with the Myers–Briggs personality test, which has little to no scientific support: see L. Al-Shawaf (3 September 2021). For sources and details on Aleksandr Kogan, see interviews he gave, including *60 Minutes Asks* (22 April 2018) and L. Stahl (22 April 2018) as well as his written testimony to the UK Parliament, see A. Kogan (2018). Other details come from personal conversations with him. For Wylie's response to Kogan, see C. Wylie (2018). Note that Kogan was able to get data from people's friends because most people had not enabled privacy restrictions that would prevent such data-sharing. For a copy of Facebook's original privacy policy in 2013 see PIPEDA Findings #2019-002 (25 April 2019) and for data breach see Meta (4 April 2018). To find out whether your own Facebook data was shared with Cambridge Analytica see https://www.facebook.com/help/yourinfo. For additional sourcing on the Facebook controversy see S. Levy (2020). For background on the activities of SLC Elections see S. Weinberger (19 September 2005) and E. Barry (20 April 2018); see also accounts from former employees C. Wylie (2019) and B. Kaiser (2019). For evidence of bribes and entrapment see Channel 4 News Investigations Team (19–20 March 2018). I should note that Wylie and Kaiser didn't work for Cambridge Analytica at the same time (Kaiser joined when Wylie left) and they seem to question each other's credibility in their 'whistleblower' memoirs: for example, it's been suggested that Wylie had no formal training in data science and was merely an intern at the company, according to an 'internal investigation', see J. Malins and L. Hudson (13 April 2018). When he left, Wylie started his own data science company 'Eunoia'. For the behavioural targeting claims made by Cambridge Analytica's CEO Alexander Nix, see A. Nix (19 September 2016). For an official timeline of events and verification of claims and documents see Information Commissioner's Office (2 October 2020). For the review of academic studies which reports zero persuasion effects of political campaigns see J. L. Kalla and D. E. Broockman (2018). For the Trump voting study see B. Swire et al. (2017). For the study which estimates that people only saw about 1 fake news article during the 2016 presidential election see H. Allcott and M. Gentzkow (2017). Their exact numbers were (0.012 ÷ 386,000) × 38 million total FB shares = 1 article per individual. The 386,000 figure is the rate at which the fake articles in their survey were shared on social media (0.386 per million) and 0.012 is the 1.2 per cent differential recall between the placebo and fake articles. For similar estimates see A. Guess, B. Nyhan, and J. Reifler (2020). For the study on 'superspreaders' see N. Grinberg et al. (2020). For more fake news exposure estimates see A. Bovet and H. A. Makse (2020) as well as J. Allen et al. (2020). For public opinion data which suggests much broader exposure to fake news see M. Barthel, A. Mitchell, and J. Holcomb (15 December 2016) and 'Eurobarometer' (2018). For the Ohio study on how fake news about Hillary Clinton might have caused defection among prior Obama voters see R. Gunther, P. A. Beck, and E. C. Nisbet (2019). For the small margins in key swing states where Trump won see T. Meku, D. Lu, and L. Gamio (11 November 2016). For the machine-learning study on 'Global Warming's Six Americas' see B. Chryst et al. (2018). Find out what segment you belong to here: https://climatecommunication.yale.edu/visualizations-data/sassy. For David Carroll's story and his personal data file, which included predicted personality scores from Cambridge Analytica's Trump Campaign, see R. Pegoraro (8 October 2020) and K. Guru-Murthy (20 September 2020). For the original study which showed that personal characteristics can be predicted from Facebook likes see M. Kosinski, D. Stillwell, and T. Graepel (2013). The study was based on Stillwell's

2007 anonymous myPersonality database (n.d.), which was never sold. For the study which calculates how many Facebook likes are needed to outperform your spouse see W. Youyou, M. Kosinski, and D. Stillwell (2014). For an independent assessment of the predictive validity of these models see D. Sumpter (2018). For the Facebook patent on user-targeting see M. Nowak et al. (2 September 2014). For the story on how Facebook allowed anti-Semitic targeting on their platform see J. Angwin, M. Varner, and A. Tobin (14 September 2017). For causal evidence that micro-targeting people with ads based on their personality can change behaviour see S. C. Matz, M. Kosinski, and D. Stillwell (2017). If you're wondering how they know that the purchases come from Facebook, websites can install what is known as a 'Facebook pixel'. Basically, a pixel is a piece of code that you install on your website that automatically triggers cookies that track and record activity from people – including whether they were redirected from Facebook or elsewhere. In fact, it links people's browsing behaviour to their Facebook account so that this information can be used (among other things) for future targeting. Dean Eckles, a former Facebook data scientist whose name is on the aforementioned Facebook patent (Eckles still holds a financial interest in Facebook), was one of the first to criticize the study because it wasn't perfectly randomized: the Facebook algorithm prioritizes ad displays based on their performance in a way that remains unknown to the research team. Matz, Kosinski, and Stillwell (2018) replied, arguing that their experiments were conducted over at least three years using different likes and ads and the results were always the same regardless of the mysterious algorithm: targeted campaigns performed better than non-targeted campaigns; this reply struck me as pretty convincing. For the causal evidence that micro-targeting can influence political attitudes and voter preferences see C. Walker, S. O'Neill, and L. de Wit (2020), B. Zarouali et al. (2020), and K. Haenschen (2022). For the Vote Leave overspending fine and quote from Dominic Cummings before it was removed, see BBC (7 April 2018). For his own perspective on winning Brexit see D. Cummings (9 January 2017). For a detailed investigation into the link between Aggregate IQ (AIQ) and Cambridge Analytica, including its role in the Vote Leave Campaign see M. McEvoy and D. Therrien (26 November 2019) as well as DCMS (18 February 2019). For additional accounts see B. Kaiser (2019) and C. Wylie (2019). For computational studies on how micro-targeting campaigns can sway elections see J. K. Madsen and T. D. Pilditch (2018) and J. K. Madsen (2019). For Trump's digital campaign strategy see I. Lapowsky (15 November 2016), S. Frier (13 April 2018), J. C. Wong (29 January 2020), and B. Kaiser (2019). For evidence on how the Trump campaign used voter-disengagement strategies and targeted Black voters specifically see Channel 4 News investigation (28 September 2020), V. Bakir (2020), as well as testimonies from C. Wylie (2019) and B. Kaiser (2019). For the claim that a quarter of elections are decided on tiny margins see R. Epstein and R. E. Robertson (2015). For Twitter's political ads ban see J. C. Wong (15 November 2019). For nano-targeting see J. González-Cabañas et al. (2021). For research on how fake news undermines trust in democracy see E. C. Nisbet, C. Mortenson, and Q. Li (2021), B. Albertson and K. Guiler (2020), and N. Berlinski et al. (2021). For the Oxford report on the rise in digital propaganda services around the world see S. Bradshaw, H. Bailey, and P. N. Howard (2021). For the *Scientific American* article that motivated this chapter see S. van der Linden (10 April 2018).

8: The New Science of Prebunking (pp. 169–194)

For the opening quote see R. Cialdini (2016). My intent is not to make value judgments about the preference people espouse for the role of capitalism or communism in society; the reason why I quote Bob Cialdini is because he makes a great point that what one government describes as 'education' is viewed by another as 'propaganda'. Nonetheless, I note the rise of 'cultural Marxism' in modern (Western) politics, a far-right conspiracy theory – popularized by authors such as Jordan Peterson – which falsely claims that liberal arts education has been infiltrated by Marxists seeking to subvert traditional Western values. For the Korean War POWs and David Hawkins's quote and story see C. Hadjimatheou and D. Nasaw (27 October 2011) as well as V. Pasley (1955) and *The Graybeards* (July/August 2002). For a modern perspective and quotes from former CIA director Allen Dulles and historian Monica Kim see M. Kim (2019). For background and early use of the term 'brainwashing' see E. Hunter (24 September 1950) and M. Holmes (26 May 2017). For a critique of the brainwashing account see T. Melley (2008). For a scientific overview of the efficacy of brainwashing attempts see K. Taylor (2016). For the 'lenient' policy adopted by the Chinese and the culture of Chinese-run prison camps during the Korean War see studies and interviews conducted by E. H. Schein (1956). See J. Zweiback (1997) for additional context. For evidence on how torture tactics are not effective see D. Feinstein (2014). In the words of the late Republican US Senator John McCain (who himself was a POW in Vietnam): 'I know they will say whatever they think their torturers want them to say if they believe it will stop their suffering', see A. Chandler (9 December 2014). For Carl Hovland's seminal studies during the Second World War see 'experiments on mass communications' by C. I. Hovland, A. A. Lumsdaine, and F. D. Sheffield (1949) as well as C. I. Hovland and A. A. Lumsdaine (1971). For details on his career see biographical memoir from R. Shepard (1998) and personal account given by W. J. McGuire (1996). For the study on producing resistance to Russian propaganda via two-sided messages see A. A. Lumsdaine and I. L. Janis (1953). For McGuire's original formulation of inoculation theory see W. J. McGuire (1961, 1964) as well as W. J. McGuire and D. Papageorgis (1961, 1962). For the 'vaccine for brainwash' article and experiment see W. J. McGuire (1970). Additional material about McGuire was sourced from my conversations with John Jost and Bob Cialdini. I originally conceptualized the idea of therapeutic inoculation as 'reverse-inoculation' (to reverse an existing infection). This term was coined during my very first conversation on the issue as a graduate student back in 2011 with Martin Bauer (a psychology professor at the LSE). Josh Compton and I later referred to this as therapeutic inoculation; for an overview of therapeutic inoculation in medicine and psychology see J. Compton (2020) and J. Compton et al. (2021). For the Provenge vaccine see M. A. Cheever and C. S. Higano (2011). For the growing political divide on climate change see P. J. Egan and M. Mullin (2017). For the debunked petition which was rated 'pants on fire' by Politifact, see 'Global Warming Petition Project' (n.d.) and J. Greenberg (8 September 2017). For details on Arthur Robinson and the fake signatories, including characters from Star Wars and members of the Spice Girls, see J. Hebert (1998), M. Lahsen (2005), and P. Giles (31 August 2012). The petition allows anyone with an undergraduate degree to sign; fake signatories have since been removed. For the viral hoax social media story based on the petition see G. Readfearn (29 November 2016). For the leaked Luntz memo to the Bush administration see F. Luntz (2002) and coverage by O. Burkeman (4 March 2003). See also J. Cook et al. (2018). In 2019, when questioned on the memo, Luntz admitted to the US House Select Committee on Climate Change that this 'was a lifetime ago' and that 'he was wrong'; after a wildfire forced him out of his LA residence in 2017, he is now committed to pushing for action on climate change, see K. Yoder (20 July 2019). For estimates of the scientific consensus on climate change see J. Cook et al. (2016) and M. Lynas, B. Z. Houlton, and S. Perry (2021). For the 'Gateway Belief Model' (GBM) see S. van der Linden, A. Leiserowitz, and E. Maibach (2019) as well as S. van der Linden (2021). On the psychological importance of expert consensus in the context of vaccines, see V. Bartoš et al. (2022). The idea that aggregating the independent opinions of a large crowd is as or more reliable than the advice of any single individual (expert) is based on the finding that if, on average, half the group overestimates and the other half underestimates, the errors cancel out, a statistical phenomenon known as the 'wisdom of the crowd' effect see J. Surowiecki (2005). For evidence of organized climate denial see R. E. Dunlap and A. M. McCright (2011), for documentation on the 'merchants of doubt' see N. Oreskes and E. M. Conway (2011). For the federal case with the tobacco industry see *United States vs Philip Morris USA Inc* (2006) and for limited effectiveness of the correction campaign see O. G. Chido-Amajuoyi et al. (2019) and G. Kostygina et al. (2020). For false media balance (on climate change) and its effects on public opinion see M. T. Boykoff and J. M. Boykoff (2004) and D. J. Koehler (2016). For the BBC's false media balance on climate change see D. Carrington (7 September 2018). For public misperceptions about the scientific consensus on climate change in the UK see M. Biddlestone and S. van der Linden (28 October 2021) and for the US see A. Leiserowitz et al. (2020). For the Han Solo 'shoot first' quote see D. A. Ortiz (14 November 2018). For the climate change inoculation study see S. van der Linden et al. (2017). For the replication see R. Maertens, F. Anseel, and S. van der Linden (2020). For the Australian team's independent replication see J. Cook, S. Lewandowsky, and U. Ecker (2017). Note that some minor deception is often necessary in psychology experiments because if participants know what the true purpose of the experiment is then we can no longer ensure that their responses are valid. Our studies are reviewed by ethical oversight committees and participants are fully debriefed about the true purpose of the study. For a review of these studies and inoculation theory see S. Lewandowsky and S. van der Linden (2021). For a meta-analysis of inoculation theory see J. A. Banas and S. A. Rains (2010). For media coverage see 'Cambridge scientists consider fake news "vaccine"' (23 January 2017), S. Pappas (25 January 2017), and *Science Friday* (27 January 2017). For the Wayfair and QAnon story see M. Spring (15 July 2020).

9: *Bad News*: The Six Degrees of Manipulation (pp. 195–227)

For the Defence Against the Dark Arts quote from *Harry Potter* see J. K. Rowling (2005). For Cialdini's principles of influence see R. B. Cialdini (1984, 2021). For Trump's tweet calling the mainstream media 'the enemy of the American people' see N. McCaskill (17 February 2017). For our top-of-mind study on the 'you're fake news' effect see S. van der Linden, J. Roozenbeek, and C. Panagopoulos (2020) as well as C. Tong et al. (2020) for similar findings. For the Facebook experiment manipulating the emotional sentiment of people's feed see A. D. Kramer, J. E. Guillory, and J. T. Hancock (2014). For evidence that most anti-vaccination websites use emotional appeals see S. J. Bean (2011). For how reliance on emotions can increase susceptibility to fake news see C. Martel, G. Pennycook, and D. G. Rand (2020) as well as J. Han, M. Cha, and W. Lee (2020). For moral outrage see M. J. Crockett (2017) and for how moral–emotional words capture our visual attention see W. J. Brady, A. P. Gantman, and J. J. Van Bavel (2020). For estimates of the extent to which emotional words can increase engagement and sharing on social media see S. Rathje, J. J. Van Bavel, and S. van der Linden (2021) as well as W. J. Brady et al. (2017). For the use of negative emotions (such as anger) by conspiracy theorists and their followers see A. Fong et al. (2021). For the *Chicago Tribune*'s 'healthy doctor' story see A. Boryga (8 April 2021) and for its virality on Facebook see J. Benton (24 August 2021). For bots and the false amplification technique during the Catalan referendum see M. Stella, E. Ferrara, and M. De Domenico (2018). For the use of bots in polarizing online vaccination debates see D. A. Broniatowski et al. (2018). For the rise of affective polarization see S. Iyengar et al. (2019) and for evidence that trolls have become more polarizing in their rhetoric see A. Simchon et al. (2022). For Sandy Hook see E. Williamson (2022), for Alex Jones's testimony see B. Debusmann Jr (3 August 2022) and for *InfoWars* questionable business model see C. Shaffer (31 July 2017). For the flood of fake Covid-19 cures see FDA (18 November 2021), K. Srivastava (2021) and H. Aghababaeian et al. (2020). For the false claims made by Judy Mikovits see M. Enserink and J. Cohen (8 May 2020). For the Warren Buffett impersonator see BBC (28 August 2018). For the Conservative Party misleading the public with the 'FactCheckUK' account see F. Perraudin (20 November 2019). For the bogus 'Global Warming Petition' mimicking the template of the National Academy of Sciences see *NAS* (20 April 1998). For the American Frontline Doctors (AFD) see D. Funke (29 July 2020). For the description of *InfoWars* as a 'crackpot website that promotes pseudoscience and fake news' see Media Bias/Fact Check (10 April 2021). For data that conspiracy theories can gain more traction than mainstream news, see Z. Beauchamp (7 December 2016), Similarweb (n.d.), and S. Frenkel and D. Alba (20 May 2020). For global data on belief in conspiracy theories see C. Ibbetson (18 January 2021). Note that such polling can be vulnerable to wording and framing effects, see T. W. Smith (1995). For the 'Birds Aren't Real' satire conspiracy theory see T. Lorenz (9 December 2021). For Lyudmila Savchuk's 'Russian troll' story see J. Myers and M. Evstatieva (15 March 2018) and the Danish Institute for International Studies (December 2017). For the workshop see The Annual Supreme League of Masters of Disinformation (23 June 2018). For the US Senate Select Committee Report see 'Russian active measures campaigns and interference in the 2016 US election, 116th Congress' (10 November 2020). For the IRA toll campaigns see P. N. Howard et al. (2019) as well as R. DiResta et al. (2018). For the NBC dataset see B. Popken (14 February 2018). For the effect of the IRA trolls on political attitudes see C. Bail et al. (2020) and D. J. Ruck et al. (2019) for how increased troll activity predicted the 2016 US election polls. For further background on the DEPICT manipulation techniques see S. van der Linden and J. Roozenbeek (2018). For McGuire's early ideas on active inoculation see M. McGuire (1961). For research on the efficacy of experiential learning and games see D. A. Kolb (2014) and a meta-analysis from W. Mao et al. (2022). For the earliest test of our fake news 'board' game see J. Roozenbeek and S. van der Linden (2018). For exhibits of *Bad News* see Design Museum (2018), House of European History (23 July 2021), and Museum of Discovery (2020). For the *Rolling Stone* article see A. Kroll (24 February 2021), see also A. Orlando (17 May 2021) for *Discover Magazine*. For *MIT's Technology Review* see J. Condliffe (20 February 2019). For the Reddit 'hug of death' see 'fake news "vaccine" works' (20 June 2019). For media coverage see University of Cambridge (20 February 2018), NPR (18 March 2018), H. Gold (4 July 2019) and I. Sample (20 February 2018). For the 'dream vaccine' reference see J. Cohen (2021). *Bad News* is licensed under a Creative Commons Attribution Non-Commercial License. For empirical evaluation of *Bad News* see J. Roozenbeek and S. van der Linden (2019). For the confidence boost study see M. Basol, J. Roozenbeek, and S. van der Linden (2020). For the translation of effect-sizes into probability of superiority see K. Magnusson (2021). For average effect-sizes in psychological research see F. D. Richard et al. (2003). For memory T-cells see K. D. Omilusik (2017). For the long-term effectiveness of inoculation and the *Bad News* game see R. Maertens et al. (2021). For more on testing and items effects see J. Roozenbeek et al. (2021). For more on *Bad News*'s efficacy against real-world misinformation and 'cross-protection' see J. Roozenbeek, C. S. Traberg, and S. van der Linden (2022). For reviews see S. Lewandowsky and S. van der Linden (2021), J. Compton et al. (2021), and C. S. Traberg, J. Roozenbeek, and S. van der Linden (2022). For downsides of algorithms deleting content from platforms see E. Dwoskin (14 June 2019).

10: Psychological Herd Immunity (pp. 228–254)

For Jenner's story and the history of the smallpox vaccine see S. Riedel (2005), M. Bennett (2020), A. J. Stewart and P. M. Devlin (2006) and Jenner Institute (2022). Note that although the 'milkmaid' story is the most frequent explanation, this may have been fabricated; it is more likely that Jenner heard about cowpox immunity from a group of local farmers in Thornbury, see A. Boylston (2013) and S. Brink (1 February 2018). It is also important to clarify that Jenner didn't invent the process of immunization. In China and India people were long exposing themselves to small doses of smallpox in order to gain immunity through a much riskier method known as 'variolation'. For the WHO's herd immunity campaign see F. Fenner et al. (1988). Two highly secured samples of smallpox still exist (in the US and China) for research purposes. For the Misinformation Susceptibility Test (MIST) see R. Maertens et al. (2021) and J. Roozenbeek et al. (2022). For psychological herd immunity models see T. Pilditch et al. (2022), S. van der Linden et al. (2017), and J. Compton and M. Pfau (2009). For international evaluations of *Bad News* with the UK's Foreign Office (FCO) see J. Roozenbeek, S. van der Linden, and T. Nygren (2020). For the independent replication of *Bad News* in India see A. Iyengar, P. Gupta, and N. Priya (2022). For the *GoViral!* study and its evaluation see M. Basol et al. (2021). Fun fact: the original name we had come up with was 'UNMASKED' (after 'unmasking' misinformation techniques) but perhaps, unsurprisingly, our partners didn't find this name as ironic as we did. For the WHO campaign see World Health Organization (23 September 2021) and for the UN campaign see United Nations (12 October 2020). For the tweet from the Director of UK Government Communications see A. Aiken (8 October 2020). For the Secretary of Digital, Media, and Culture tweet see C. Dinenage (5 November 2020) and DCMS (12 October 2020). For impact and social media statistics of the inoculation campaign see Government Communication Service (18 February 2021). For the study evaluating *Harmony Square* see J. Roozenbeek and S. van der Linden (2020). For the manipulated images aiming to polarize see D. Evon (28 March 2016). For the pineapple pizza playbook from CISA see Cybersecurity and Infrastructure Security Agency (July 2019). For Chris Krebs being fired by Trump see A. Wise (17 November 2020) and for his pineapple pizza tweet see C. Krebs (25 July 2019). For the interview transcript between Andrea Bernstein and Krebs see *Will Be Wild* podcast (3 June 2022). For the *Vice* quote see M. Gault (11 June 2020). For our collaboration with WhatsApp see J. Roozenbeek, M. Basol, and S. van der Linden (11 January 2019). For John Cook's *Cranky Uncle* book and game see J. Cook (2020). For the study which shows that people can be inoculated against micro-targeting see P. Lorenz-Spreen et al. (2021). For our *Radicalize* intervention see N. Saleh et al. (2021). For Google Jigsaw's *Redirect* initiative see L. Dishman (28 January 2019) and Y. Green (2018). For our research with Google and Beth Goldberg see R. Diresta and B. Goldberg (28 August 2021) and *Jigsaw* (24 June 2021). For the YouTube study see J. Roozenbeek et al. (2022). For our NATO handbook see J. Roozenbeek and S. van der Linden (2021). For coverage of Twitter's prebunking during the 2020 US election see D. Ingram (26 October 2020) and on climate see A. Gregg (1 November 2021).

11: How to Inoculate Your Friends and Family (pp. 255–271)

For the screenplay of *A Few Good Men* see A. Sorkin and R. Reiner (1992). For the quote from Aristotle and the ancient 'prebunk' see a 1991 translated version of the original *Rhetoric* by Aristotle (n.d.) and discussion in J. Compton (2005). Inoculation is also related to the concept of 'stealing thunder' and 'procatalepsis' (meaning 'anticipation') and involves anticipating and refuting objections to your own arguments. For the use of inoculation in political ads see 'Reverend Raphael Warnock: "Get Ready" Campaign 2020' (5 November 2020). For the labour union example see A. Hanson (18 October 2016). For the idea of meta-inoculation see J. A. Banas and G. Miller (2013). Some of the advice in this chapter is based on an article I wrote for the *Guardian* see S. van der Linden (23 December 2021). Just for the sake of accuracy: the only (rare) situation under which it is possible to get the flu from the flu shot is when a (rare) live (attenuated) virus vaccine is given to someone who has a severely compromised immune system or underlying health condition. For more on the different kinds of inoculation and post-inoculation talk see J. Compton et al. (2021) and B. Ivanov et al. (2012). For the fake CDC outbreak story see B. Palma (17 January 2018). For the importance of 'dispelling illusions of invulnerability' in motivating resistance to fake news and the Schwarzenegger example see B. J. Sagarin et al. (2002). For evidence on the efficacy of experiential learning see D. A. Kolb (2014). For active inoculation see M. Basol et al. (2021). For Dan Lee Dimke and his fake Covid-19 cures see B. Palma (17 March 2020). For booster shots and the role of memory networks in inoculation see R. Maertens et al. (2021) and M. Pfau et al. (2005).

Epilogue: The Future of Truth (pp. 273–278)

For the DADA *Harry Potter* reference see J. K. Rowling (2005). For more on deepfakes see N. Schick (2020), R. Tolosana et al. (2020), and V. Dan et al. (2021). For how deepfakes can influence political attitudes, especially when micro-targeted, see T. Dobber et al. (2021). For evidence that training can reduce susceptibility to deepfakes see Y. Hwang et al. (2021). For the fake Mark Zuckerberg and similar deepfakes see S. Putterman (12 June 2019) and BuzzFeedVideo (17 April 2018). For the ibuprofen controversy during the Covid-19 pandemic see F. Poutoglidou et al. (2021) and J. McDonald (30 March 2020). For the claim that the Biden administration's prebunk of the Russian invasion prevented polarization and may have delayed the attack see J. Astill (26 February 2022). In conversation with Ukrainian academic colleagues, I was told that President Zelenskyy has also successfully deployed inoculation campaigns against Russian disinformation. For a good overview of problems with the social media ecosystem see P. Lorenz-Spreen et al. (2020). For an overview of the benefits of technique-based inoculation see C. Traberg, J. Roozenbeek, and S. van der Linden (2022).

BIBLIOGRAPHY

60 Minutes Asks (22 April 2018), 'Is Aleksandr Kogan a Russian Spy?' 60 Minutes, https://www.youtube.com/watch?v=WNNcfSopfc4

Abraham, W. C., Jones, O. D., and Glanzman, D. L. (2019), 'Is plasticity of synapses the mechanism of long-term memory storage?', *NPJ Science of Learning*, 4(1), 1–10

Aghababaeian, H., Hamdanieh, L., and Ostadtaghizadeh, A. (2020), 'Alcohol intake in an attempt to fight COVID-19: A medical myth in Iran', *Alcohol*, 88, 29–32

Aiken, A. (8 October 2020), 'The new phase of the UK government's public health campaign to counter misinformation with the launch of the "inoculation game" in collaboration with University of Cambridge and WHO to teach people how to identify and understand disinformation' [tweet], Twitter, https://twitter.com/AlexanderAiken/status/1314112216447188993

Al-Shawaf, L. (3 September 2021), 'Should you trust the Myers-Briggs personality test?', *Areo Magazine*, https://areomagazine.com/2021/03/09/should-you-trust-the-myers-briggs-personality-test/

Albertson, B., and Guiler, K. (2020), 'Conspiracy theories, election rigging, and support for democratic norms', *Research and Politics*, 7(3), 2053168020959859

Alfano, M., Fard, A. E., Carter, J. A., Clutton, P., and Klein, C. (2020), 'Technologically scaffolded atypical cognition: the case of YouTube's recommender system', *Synthese 199*, 835–58

Allcott, H., and Gentzkow, M. (2017), 'Social media and fake news in the 2016 election', *Journal of Economic Perspectives*, 31(2), 211–36

Allen, J., Howland, B., Mobius, M., Rothschild, D., and Watts, D. J. (2020), 'Evaluating the fake news problem at the scale of the information ecosystem', *Science Advances*, 6(14), eaay3539

Altay, S., de Araujo, E., and Mercier, H. (2022), '"If this account is true, it is most enormously wonderful": Interestingness-if-true and the sharing of true and false news', *Digital Journalism*, 10(3), 373–94

Angwin, J., Varner, M., and Tobin, A. (14 September 2017), 'Facebook enabled advertisers to reach "Jew Haters"', *ProPublica*. https://www.propublica.org/article/facebook-enabled-advertisers-to-reach-jew-haters

Annual Supreme League of Masters of Disinformation (23 June 2018), *DROG*, The Hague, Netherlands, https://wijzijndrog.nl/

Aral, S. (6 April 2022), 'Fake news about our fake news study spread faster than its truth . . . just as we predicted', *Medium*, https://sinanaral.medium.com/fake-news-about-our-fake-news-study-spread-faster-than-its-truth-just-as-we-predicted-77db6d9ca8c8

Aristotle (nd), *The Art of Rhetoric*, translated by H. C. Lawson-Tancred, Penguin books

Arun, C. (2019), 'On WhatsApp, rumours, lynchings, and the Indian Government', *Economic and Political Weekly*, 54(6)

Asch, S. E. (1951), 'Effects of group pressure on the modification and distortion of judgments', in H. Guetzkow (ed.), *Groups, Leadership and Men* (pp. 177–90), Pittsburgh, PA, Carnegie Press

— (1956), 'Studies of independence and conformity. A minority of one against a unanimous majority', *Psychological Monographs: General and Applied*, 70 (9), 1–70

Astill, J. (26 February 2022), 'Deploying reality against Putin', *Economist*, https://www.economist.com/united-states/2022/02/26/deploying-reality-against-putin

Bail, C. A., Argyle, L. P., Brown, T. W., Bumpus, J. P., Chen, H., Hunzaker, M. F., . . . and Volfovsky, A. (2018), 'Exposure to opposing views on social media can increase political polarization', *Proceedings of the National Academy of Sciences*, *115*(37), 9216–21

Bail, C. A., Guay, B., Maloney, E., Combs, A., Hillygus, D. S., Merhout, F., . . . and Volfovsky, A. (2020), 'Assessing the Russian Internet Research Agency's impact on the political attitudes and behaviors of American Twitter users in late 2017', *Proceedings of the National Academy of Sciences*, *117*(1), 243–50

Bak-Coleman, J., Kennedy, I., Wack, M., Beers, A., Schafer, J. S., Spiro, E., . . . and West, J. (2022), 'Combining interventions to reduce the spread of viral misinformation', *Nature Human Behaviour* (https://doi.org/10.1038/s41562-022-01388-6)

Bakir, V. (2020), 'Psychological operations in digital political campaigns: Assessing Cambridge Analytica's psychographic profiling and targeting', *Frontiers in Communication*, 67

Bakshy, E., Messing, S., and Adamic, L. A. (2015), 'Exposure to ideologically diverse news and opinion on Facebook', *Science*, *348*(6239), 1130–2

Banaji, S., and Bhat, R. (2019), *WhatsApp Vigilantes: An exploration of citizen reception and circulation of WhatsApp misinformation linked to mob violence in India*, Department of Media and Communications, London School of Economics and Political Science, https://www.lse.ac.uk/media-and-communications/assets/documents/research/projects/WhatsApp-Misinformation-Report.pdf

Banas, J. A., and Miller, G. (2013), 'Inducing resistance to conspiracy theory propaganda: Testing inoculation and metainoculation strategies', *Human Communication Research*, 39(2), 184–207

Banas, J. A., and Rains, S. A. (2010), 'A meta-analysis of research on inoculation theory', *Communication Monographs*, 77(3), 281–311

Barberá, P., Jost, J. T., Nagler, J., Tucker, J. A., and Bonneau, R. (2015), 'Tweeting from left to right: Is online political communication more than an echo chamber?', *Psychological Science*, 26(10), 1531–42

Barry, E. (20 April 2018), 'Long before Cambridge Analytica, a belief in the "Power of the Subliminal"', *New York Times*, https://www.nytimes.com/2018/04/20/world/europe/oakes-scl-cambridge-analytica-trump.html

Barthel, M., Mitchell, A., and Holcomb, J. (15 December 2016), 'Many Americans believe fake news is sowing confusion', *Pew Research Center*, https://www.pew research.org/journalism/2016/12/15/many-americans-believe-fake-news-is-sowing-confusion/

Bartol Jr, T. M., Bromer, C., Kinney, J., Chirillo, M. A., Bourne, J. N., Harris, K. M., and Sejnowski, T. J. (2015), 'Nanoconnectomic upper bound on the variability of synaptic plasticity', *Elife*, 4, e10778

Bartoš, V., Bauer, M., Cahlíková, J., and Chytilová, J. (2022), 'Communicating doctors' consensus persistently increases COVID-19 vaccinations', *Nature*, 542–9

Basol, M., Roozenbeek, J., and van der Linden, S. (2020), 'Good news about bad news: Gamified inoculation boosts confidence and cognitive immunity against fake news', *Journal of Cognition*, 3(1)

Basol, M., Roozenbeek, J., Berriche, M., Uenal, F., McClanahan, W. P., and van der Linden, S. (2021), 'Towards psychological herd immunity: Cross-cultural evidence for two prebunking interventions against COVID-19 misinformation', *Big Data & Society*, 8(1), 20539517211013868

Bastick, Z. (2021), 'Would you notice if fake news changed your behavior? An experiment on the unconscious effects of disinformation', *Computers in Human Behavior*, 116, 106633

Bastos, M., Mercea, D., and Baronchelli, A. (2018), 'The geographic embedding of online echo chambers: Evidence from the Brexit campaign', *PloS One*, 13(11), e0206841

Bayes, T. (1764), 'An Essay Toward Solving a Problem in the Doctrine of Chances', *Philosophical Transactions of the Royal Society of London* 53, 370–418

BBC News (20 May 2016), 'David Icke on 9/11 and lizards in Buckingham Palace theories', https://www.bbc.co.uk/news/av/uk-politics-36339298

— (23 January 2017), 'Cambridge scientists consider fake news "vaccine"' https://www.bbc.co.uk/news/uk-38714404

— (7 April 2018), 'Facebook suspends AIQ data firm used by Vote Leave in Brexit campaign', https://www.bbc.co.uk/news/technology-43680969

— (28 August 2018), 'A fake billionaire is fooling people on Twitter', https://www.bbc.co.uk/news/world-us-canada-45331781

— (8 June 2020), 'Coronavirus: Man jailed for 5G phone mast arson attack', https://www.bbc.co.uk/news/uk-england-merseyside-52966950

Bean, S. J. (2011), Emerging and continuing trends in vaccine opposition website content', *Vaccine*, *29*(10), 1874–80

Beauchamp, Z. (7 December 2016), 'Alex Jones, Pizzagate booster and America's most famous conspiracy theorist, explained', *Vox*, https://www.vox.com/policy-and-politics/2016/10/28/13424848/alex-jones-infowars-prisonplanet

Bennett, M. (2020), *War against smallpox: Edward Jenner and the global spread of vaccination*, Cambridge, Cambridge University Press

Benton, J. (24 August 2021), 'Facebook sent a ton of traffic to a Chicago Tribune story. So why is everyone mad at them?', *NiemanLab*, https://www.niemanlab.org/2021/08/facebook-sent-a-ton-of-traffic-to-a-chicago-tribune-story-so-why-is-everyone-mad-at-them/ (2021)

Berlinski, N., Doyle, M., Guess, A. M., Levy, G., Lyons, B., Montgomery, J. M., . . . and Reifler, J. (2021), 'The effects of unsubstantiated claims of voter fraud on confidence in elections', *Journal of Experimental Political Science*, 1–16

Biddlestone, M., and van der Linden, S. (28 October 2021), Climate change misinformation fools too many people – but there are ways to combat it. *The Conversation*, https://theconversation.com/climate-change-misinformation-fools-too-many-people-but-there-are-ways-to-combat-it-170658

Biddlestone, M., Azevedo, F., and van der Linden, S. (2022), 'Climate of conspiracy: A meta-analysis of the consequences of belief in conspiracy theories about climate change', *Current Opinion in Psychology*, 101390

Biderman, A. D. (1962), 'The image of "brainwashing"'. *Public Opinion Quarterly*, *26*(4), 547–63

Blaise, P. (1941), *Pensees / The Provincial Letters*, translated by W. F. Trotter and T. M'Crie, New York, Modern Library

Blodget, H. (1 October 2009), 'Mark Zuckerberg on Innovation', *Business Insider*, https://www.businessinsider.com/mark-zuckerberg-innovation-2009-10?r=US&IR=T

Bond, R., and Smith, P. B. (1996), 'Culture and conformity: A meta-analysis of studies using Asch's (1952b, 1956) line judgment task', *Psychological Bulletin*, *119*(1), 111–37

Boryga, A. (8 April 2021), 'A "healthy" doctor died two weeks after getting a COVID-19 vaccine; CDC is investigating why', *Chicago Tribune*, https://www.chicagotribune.com/coronavirus/fl-ne-miami-doctor-vaccine-death-20210107-afzysvqqjbgwnetcy5v6ec62py-story.html

Boseley, S. (2 February 2010), '*Lancet* Retracts "Utterly False" MMR Paper', *Guardian*, https://www.theguardian.com/society/2010/feb/02/lancet-retracts-mmr-paper

Bovet, A., and Makse, H. A. (2019), 'Influence of fake news in Twitter during the 2016 US presidential election', *Nature Communications*, *10*(1), 1–14

Boykoff, M. T., and Boykoff, J. M. (2004), 'Balance as bias: Global warming and the US prestige press', *Global Environmental Change*, *14*(2), 125–36

Boylston, A. (2013), 'The origins of vaccination: myths and reality', *Journal of the Royal Society of Medicine*, *106*(9), 351–4

Bradshaw, S., Bailey, H., and Howard, P. N. (2021), *Industrialised Disinformation: 2020 Global Inventory of Organised Social Media Manipulation*, Oxford, Project on Computational Propaganda

Brady, T. F., Konkle, T., Alvarez, G. A., and Oliva, A. (2008), 'Visual long-term memory has a massive storage capacity for object details', *Proceedings of the National Academy of Sciences*, *105*(38), 14325–9

Brady, W. J., Gantman, A. P., and Van Bavel, J. J. (2020), 'Attentional capture helps explain why moral and emotional content go viral', *Journal of Experimental Psychology: General*, *149*(4), 746–56

Brady, W. J., Wills, J. A., Jost, J. T., Tucker, J. A., and Van Bavel, J. J. (2017), 'Emotion shapes the diffusion of moralized content in social networks', *Proceedings of the National Academy of Sciences*, *114*(28), 7313–18

Brait, E. (26 January 2016), 'I didn't want to believe it either: Rapper BoB insists the Earth is flat', *Guardian*, https://www.theguardian.com/music/2016/jan/25/bob-rapper-flat-earth-twitter

Brink, S. (1 February 2018), 'What's the real story about the Milkmaid and the smallpox vaccine?', *NPR*, https://www.npr.org/sections/goatsandsoda/2018/02/01/582370199/whats-the-real-story-about-the-milkmaid-and-the-small pox-vaccine

Broniatowski, D. A., Jamison, A. M., Qi, S., AlKulaib, L., Chen, T., Benton, A., . . . and Dredze, M. (2018), 'Weaponized health communication: Twitter bots and Russian trolls amplify the vaccine debate', *American Journal of Public Health*, *108*(10), 1378–84

Brown, J. R., and Enos, R. D. (2021), 'The measurement of partisan sorting for 180 million voters', *Nature Human Behaviour*, *5*, 998–1008

Bump, P. (23 January 2017), 'There's no evidence that Trump's inauguration was the most watched in history. Period', *Washington Post*, https://www.washingtonpost.com/news/politics/wp/2017/01/23/theres-no-evidence-that-trumps-inauguration-was-the-most-watched-in-history-period/

Burgess, D. C., Burgess, M. A., and Leask, J. (2006), 'The MMR vaccination and autism controversy in United Kingdom 1998–2005: Inevitable community outrage or a failure of risk communication?', *Vaccine*, *24*(18), 3921–8

Burgess, M. (13 November 2018), 'After murder and violence, here's how WhatsApp will fight fake news', *WIRED*, https://www.wired.co.uk/article/whatsapp-fake-news-technology

Burkeman, O. (4 March 2003), 'Memo exposes Bush's new green strategy', *Guardian*, https://www.theguardian.com/environment/2003/mar/04/all

BuzzFeedVideo (17 April 2018), 'You won't believe what Obama says in this video', *YouTube*, https://www.youtube.com/watch?v=cQ54GDm1eL0

Cadwalladr, C. (4 March 2017), 'Cambridge Analytica affair raises questions vital to our democracy', *Guardian*, https://www.theguardian.com/politics/2017/mar/04/cambridge-analytica-democracy-digital-age

Cadwalladr, C., and Graham-Harrison, E. (17 March 2018), 'Revealed: 50 million Facebook profiles harvested for Cambridge Analytica in major data breach', *Guardian*, https://www.theguardian.com/news/2018/mar/17/cambridge-analytica-facebook-influence-us-election

Calvillo, D. P., Garcia, R. J., Bertrand, K., and Mayers, T. A. (2021), 'Personality factors and self-reported political news consumption predict susceptibility to political fake news', *Personality and Individual Differences*, *174*, 110666

'The Cambridge Analytica Files' (2018), *Guardian*, https://www.theguardian.com/news/series/cambridge-analytica-files

Campbell, T. H., and Kay, A. C. (2014), 'Solution aversion: On the relation between ideology and motivated disbelief', *Journal of Personality and Social Psychology*, *107*(5), 809–24

Carrington, D. (7 September 2018), 'BBC admits "we get climate change coverage wrong too often"', *Guardian*, https://www.theguardian.com/environment/2018/sep/07/bbc-we-get-climate-change-coverage-wrong-too-often

Carter, C. (Writer), Morgan, G. (Writer), Wong, J. (Writer) and Graham, W. A. (director), (18 February 1994), E.B.E. (Season 1, Episode 17) [TV Series]. In C. Carter (executive producer), *The X-Files*. Ten Thirteen; Twentieth Century Fox Film Productions

Chan, M. P. S., Jones, C. R., Hall Jamieson, K., and Albarracín, D. (2017), 'Debunking: A meta-analysis of the psychological efficacy of messages countering misinformation', *Psychological Science*, *28*(11), 1531–46.

Chandler, A. (9 December 2014), This is how a prisoner of war feels about torture, *The Atlantic*, https://www.theatlantic.com/politics/archive/2014/12/John-Mccain-Speech-Senate-Republican-CIA-Torture-Report/383589/

Channel 4 (6 February 2017), 'C4 study reveals only 4 per cent of surveyed can identify true or fake news', https://www.channel4.com/press/news/c4-study-reveals-only-4-surveyed-can-identify-true-or-fake-news

Channel 4 News Investigations Team (19 March 2018), 'Revealed: Trump's election consultants filmed saying they use bribes and sex workers to entrap politicians', https://www.channel4.com/news/exposed-undercover-secrets-of-donald-trump-data-firm-cambridge-analytica

— (20 March 2018), 'Exposed: Undercover secrets of Trump's data firm', https://www.channel4.com/news/exposed-undercover-secrets-of-donald-trump-data-firm-cambridge-analytica

— (28 September 2020), 'Revealed: Trump campaign strategy to deter millions of Black Americans from voting in 2016', https://www.channel4.com/news/revealed-trump-campaign-strategy-to-deter-millions-of-black-americans-from-voting-in-2016

Cheever, M. A., and Higano, C. S. (2011), 'PROVENGE (Sipuleucel-T) in Prostate Cancer: The First FDA-Approved Therapeutic Cancer Vaccine', *Clinical Cancer Research*, *17*(11), 3520–26

Chen A. Y., Nyhan, B., Reifler, J., Robertson, R. E., and Wilson, C. (2019), *Exposure to alternative and extremist content on YouTube*, ADL Center for Technology and Society, Anti-Defamation League, https://www.adl.org/media/15868/download

Chido-Amajuoyi, O. G., Robert, K. Y., Agaku, I., and Shete, S. (2019), 'Exposure to court-ordered tobacco industry antismoking advertisements among US adults', *JAMA Network Open*, *2*(7), e196935-e196935

Chryst, B., Marlon, J., van der Linden, S., Leiserowitz, A., Maibach, E., and Roser-Renouf, C. (2018), 'Global warming's "Six Americas Short Survey": Audience segmentation of climate change views using a four question instrument', *Environmental Communication*, *12*(8), 1109–22

Cialdini, R. B. (2021), '*Influence: The Psychology of Persuasion*', (New and expanded), New York, NY, Harper Business

Cinelli, M., Morales, G. D. F., Galeazzi, A., Quattrociocchi, W., and Starnini, M. (2021), 'The echo-chamber effect on social media', *Proceedings of the National Academy of Sciences*, *118*(9), e2023301118

Cinelli, M., Quattrociocchi, W., Galeazzi, A., Valensise, C. M., Brugnoli, E., Schmidt, A. L., . . . and Scala, A. (2020), 'The Covid-19 social media infodemic', *Scientific Reports*, *10*, 16598

Ciocoiu, E. (29 December 2019), 'De l'esprit géométrique-de l'art de persuader', *The Literary Encyclopedia*, https://www.litencyc.com/php/sworks.php?rec= true&UID=25055

Claims Conference (2016), 'First-ever fifty-state survey on Holocaust knowledge of American Millennials and Gen Z reveals shocking results', *Holocaust Knowledge and Awareness Study*, https://www.claimscon.org/millennial-study/

Clark, D. J. (director) (2018), *Behind the curve* [Documentary]. Delta-v productions

Clarke, D. (2015), 'Blaise Pascal', in E. N. Zalta (ed.), *The Stanford Encyclopedia of Philosophy* (Fall 2015 edition)

Clarke Jr, L. H. (13 October 1978), 'US Monetary Troubles', *Wall Street Journal*, New York, NY, p. 22

Classical Numismatic Group (n.d.), 'Roman Imperial Issues OCTAVIAN, 38 BC; AR Denarius (4.08g, 12h), Military mint moving with Octavian. [IMP] CAESAR DIVI IVLI, https://www.cngcoins.com/Coin.aspx?CoinID=76590

Cohen, J. (2021), 'The dream vaccine' *Science, 372* (6539), 227–31

Colbert, S. (2005), 'Truthiness', *The Colbert Report*, New York, NY, Comedy Central

Compton, J. (2005), 'Tracing the roots of resistance to influence: Comparison, contrast, and synthesis of Aristotelian rationality and inoculation', *STAM Journal, 35*, 1–23

— (2020), 'Prophylactic versus therapeutic inoculation treatments for resistance to influence', *Communication Theory, 30*(3), 330–43

Compton, J., and Pfau, M. (2009), 'Spreading inoculation: Inoculation, resistance to influence, and word-of-mouth communication', *Communication Theory, 19*(1), 9–28

Compton, J., van der Linden, S., Cook, J., and Basol, M. (2021), 'Inoculation theory in the post-truth era: Extant findings and new frontiers for contested science, misinformation, and conspiracy theories', *Social and Personality Psychology Compass, 15*(6), e12602

Condliffe, J. (20 February 2019), 'This video game wants to be a fake-news vaccine', *MIT Technology Review*, https://www.technologyreview.com/2018/02/20/ 145498/this-video-game-wants-to-be-a-fake-news-vaccine/

Condon, R. (1959), *The Manchurian Candidate*, New York, NY, McGraw-Hill

Connor, J. A. (2009), *Pascal's Wager: The Man Who Played Dice With God*, San Francisco, CA, HarperOne

Cook, J. (2020), *Cranky Uncle Vs. Climate Change: How to Understand and Respond to Climate Science Deniers*, Citadel Press

Cook, J., Lewandowsky, S., and Ecker, U. K. (2017), 'Neutralizing misinformation through inoculation: Exposing misleading argumentation techniques reduces their influence'. *PloS One, 12*(5), e0175799

Cook, J., Oreskes, N., Doran, P. T., Anderegg, W. R., Verheggen, B., Maibach, E. W., ... and Rice, K. (2016), 'Consensus on consensus: a synthesis of consensus estimates on human-caused global warming', *Environmental Research Letters*, *11*(4), 048002

Cook, J., van der Linden, S. Lewandowsky, S., and Ecker, U. K. (15 May 2020), 'Coronavirus, "Plandemic" and the seven traits of conspiratorial thinking', *The Conversation*, https://theconversation.com/coronavirus-plandemic-and-the-seven-traits-of-conspiratorial-thinking-138483

Cook, J., van der Linden, S., Maibach, E., and Lewandowsky, S. (2018), *The Consensus Handbook*, http://www.climatechangecommunication.org/all/consensus-handbook/

Crockett, M. J. (2017), 'Moral outrage in the digital age', *Nature Human Behaviour*, *1*(11), 769–71

Crown Prosecution Service (10 June 2020), 'Merseyside man jailed for setting fire to phone mast', https://www.cps.gov.uk/mersey-cheshire/news/merseyside-man-jailed-setting-fire-phone-mast

Cummings, D. (9 January 2017), 'Dominic Cummings: how the Brexit referendum was won', *Spectator*, https://www.spectator.co.uk/article/dominic-cummings-how-the-brexit-referendum-was-won

Cybersecurity and Infrastructure Security Agency (July 2019), *The war on pineapple: Understanding foreign influence in 5 steps*, U.S. Department of Homeland Security, https://www.cisa.gov/sites/default/files/publications/19_1008_cisa_the-war-on-pineapple-understanding-foreign-interference-in-5-steps.pdf

Dan, V., Paris, B., Donovan, J., Hameleers, M., Roozenbeek, J., van der Linden, S., and von Sikorski, C. (2021), 'Visual mis-and disinformation, social media, and democracy', *Journalism & Mass Communication Quarterly*, *98*(3), 641–64

Danish Institute for International Studies (December 2017), 'My life as a troll – Lyudmila Savchuk's story', https://www.diis.dk/en/my-life-as-a-troll-lyudmila-savchuk-s-story

Davies, H. (11 December 2015), 'Ted Cruz using firm that harvested data on millions of unwitting Facebook users', *The Guardian*, https://www.theguardian.com/us-news/2015/dec/11/senator-ted-cruz-president-campaign-facebook-user-data

Davis, J. (28 July 2016), 'The Flat Earth Society Welcomes B.O.B', *Flat Earth Society*, www.theflatearthsociety.org/home/index.php/blog/bob-bobby-ray-simmons-jr-flat-earth-society

DCMS (18 February 2019), 'Disinformation and "fake news": Final report,

London, House of Commons, Digital, Culture, Media, and Sport Committee, https://publications.parliament.uk/pa/cm201719/cmselect/cmcumeds/1791/179107.htm#_idTextAnchor034

DCMS (12 October 2020), 'Misinformation about Covid-19 is being shared far and wide, Play Go Viral!' [tweet], Twitter, https://twitter.com/DCMS/status/1315 681179157356546

Debusmann Jr, B. (3 August 2022), 'Alex Jones concedes Sandy Hook attack was "100% real"', *BBC*, https://www.bbc.co.uk/news/world-us-canada-62415376

De Keersmaecker, J., Dunning, D., Pennycook, G., Rand, D. G., Sanchez, C., Unkelbach, C., and Roets, A. (2020), 'Investigating the robustness of the illusory truth effect across individual differences in cognitive ability, need for cognitive closure, and cognitive style', *Personality and Social Psychology Bulletin*, 46(2), 204–15

Desai, S. A. C., Pilditch, T. D., and Madsen, J. K. (2020), 'The rational continued influence of misinformation', *Cognition*, 205, 104453

Design Museum (2018), 'Fenty beauty by Rihanna, the world's first plastic-free shopping aisle, and the SpaceX Falcon Heavy rocket: Design museum announces Beazley Design of the Year nominees (Sept 2018–Jan 2019)', London, Design Museum https://www.beazley.com/Documents/Beazley%20DotY%20final.pdf.

Dinenage, C. (5 November 2020), *GoViral! is a new game released by @GOVUK and @Cambridge_Uni to help stop the spread of false and misleading information. Play #GoViralGame today to uncover tactics used to spread harmful Covid-19 misinformation* [tweet]. Twitter https://twitter.com/cj_dinenage/status/1324405001222049803

Dio Cassius (n.d.), *Roman History, Volume V: Books 46–50*, trans. Earnest Cary (Loeb Classical Library), Cambridge, MA, Harvard University Press (1917)

Diresta, R., and Goldberg, B. (28 August 2021), '"Prebunking" health misinformation tropes can stop their spread', *WIRED*, https://www.wired.com/story/prebunking-health-misinformation-tropes-can-stop-their-spread/

DiResta, R., Shaffer, R., Ruppel, B., Sullivan. D., Matney, R., Fox, R., Albright, J., and Ben Johnson, B. (2018), *The Disinformation Report: The Tactics & Tropes of the Internet Research Agency*, Austin, TX, New Knowledge

Dishman, L. (28 January 2019), 'Google algorithms and human psychology: How jigsaw rescues teens from ISIS recruiters', *Fast Company*, https://www.fastcompany.com/90294876/how-jigsaw-is-using-ai-human-connections-and-adwords-to-fight-isis

Dixit, P., and Mac, R. (9 September 2018), 'How WhatsApp Destroyed a Village', *Buzzfeed News*, https://www.buzzfeednews.com/article/pranavdixit/whatsapp-destroyed-village-lynchings-rainpada-india

Dobber, T., Metoui, N., Trilling, D., Helberger, N., and de Vreese, C. (2021), 'Do (microtargeted) deepfakes have real effects on political attitudes?', *The International Journal of Press/Politics*, *26*(1), 69–91

Doob, L. W. (1950), 'Goebbels' principles of propaganda', *Public Opinion Quarterly*, *14*(3), 419–42

Douglas, K. M., Sutton, R. M., and Cichocka, A. (2017), 'The psychology of conspiracy theories', *Current Directions in Psychological Science*, *26*(6), 538–42

Druckman, J. N., and McGrath, M. C. (2019), 'The evidence for motivated reasoning in climate change preference formation', *Nature Climate Change*, *9*(2), 111–19

Drummond, C., and Fischhoff, B. (2017), 'Individuals with greater science literacy and education have more polarized beliefs on controversial science topics', *Proceedings of the National Academy of Sciences*, *114*(36), 9587–92

Dudai, Y. (1997), 'How big is human memory, or on being just useful enough', *Learning and Memory*, *3*, 341–65

Dunlap, R. E., and McCright, A. M. (2011), 'Organized climate change denial' (pp. 144–60), in J. Dryzek, R. B. Norgaard, and D. Schlosberg (eds), *The Oxford handbook of Climate Change and Society*, Oxford

Dwoskin, E. (13 June 2019), 'How YouTube erased history in its battle against white supremacy', the *Washington Post*, https://www.washingtonpost.com/technology/2019/06/13/how-youtube-erased-history-its-battle-against-white-supremacy/

Eady, G., Nagler, J., Guess, A., Zilinsky, J., and Tucker, J. A. (2019), 'How many people live in political bubbles on social media? Evidence from linked survey and Twitter data', *Sage Open*, *9*(1), 2158244019832705

East, M., America, N., America, S., Platform, G. D., Platform, A. D., Platform, A. D., . . . and Map, G. D. (2012), 'National, state, and local area vaccination coverage among children aged 19–35 months – United States, 2011', *Morbidity and Mortality Weekly Report 61*, 689–96

Ecker, U. K., Lewandowsky, S., Cook, J., Schmid, P., Fazio, L., Brashier, N., Kendeou, P., Vraga, E., and Amazeen, M.A. (2022), 'The psychological drivers of misinformation belief and its resistance to correction', *Nature Reviews Psychology 1*, 13–29

Effron, D. A., and Raj, M. (2020), 'Misinformation and morality: Encountering fake-news headlines makes them seem less unethical to publish and share', *Psychological Science*, *31*(1), 75–87

Egan, P. J., and Mullin, M. (2017), 'Climate Change: US Public', *Annual Review of Political Science*, *20*, 209–27

Eliot, C. W. J. (1955), 'New evidence for the speed of the Roman Imperial Post', *Phoenix*, *9*(2), 76–80

Engber, D. (March 26, 2022) 'Sorry, I lied about fake news', *The Atlantic*, https://www.theatlantic.com/technology/archive/2022/03/fake-news-misinformation-mit-study/629396/

Enserink, M., and Cohen, J. (8 May 2020), 'Fact-checking Judy Mikovits, the controversial virologist attacking Anthony Fauci in a viral conspiracy video', *Science*, https://www.science.org/content/article/fact-checking-judy-mikovits-controversial-virologist-attacking-anthony-fauci-viral

Epstein, R., and Robertson, R. E. (2015), 'The search engine manipulation effect (SEME) and its possible impact on the outcomes of elections', *Proceedings of the National Academy of Sciences*, *112*(33), E4512-21

Epstein, R., Robertson, R. E., Lazer, D., and Wilson, C. (2017), 'Suppressing the search engine manipulation effect (SEME)', *Proceedings of the ACM on Human-Computer Interaction*, *1*(CSCW), 1–22

'Eurobarometer on Fake News and Online Disinformation' (2018), *European Commission*, https://europa.eu/eurobarometer/surveys/detail/2183

European Commission (2018), 'Eurobarometer on Fake News and Online Disinformation', https://europa.eu/eurobarometer/surveys/detail/2183

Evon, D. (28 March 2016), 'Protests seek to #EndFathersDay?', *Snopes*, https://www.snopes.com/fact-check/fathers-day-protest-photo/

— (15 November 2019), 'Did a loud fart give a suspect's location away to police?', *Snopes*, https://www.snopes.com/fact-check/loud-fart-locates-crime-suspect/

'The Facebook Files: A Wall Street Journal Investigation' (1 October 2021), *Wall Street Journal*, https://www.wsj.com/articles/the-facebook-files-11631713039.

Faddoul, M., Chaslot, G., and Farid, H. (2020), 'A longitudinal analysis of YouTube's promotion of conspiracy videos', *arXiv preprint arXiv:2003.03318*

Fake news 'vaccine' works. [online forum post] (26 June, 2019), *Reddit*, https://www.reddit.com/r/science/comments/c5ptfz/fake_news_vaccine_works_suggests_a_large_new/

Faraday Speaks (22 March 2019), 'My descent into the Alt-right pipeline', *YouTube*, https://www.youtube.com/watch?v=sfLa64_zLrU&t.

Fazio, L. K., and Sherry, C. L. (2020), 'The effect of repetition on truth judgments across development', *Psychological Science*, *31*(9), 1150–60

Fazio, L. K., Brashier, N. M., Payne, B. K., and Marsh, E. J. (2015), 'Knowledge does not protect against illusory truth', *Journal of Experimental Psychology: General*, *144*(5), 993–1002

FDA (18 November 2021), *Beware of fraudulent coronavirus tests, vaccines, and treatments*, Washington, DC: U.S. Food and Drug Administration, https://www.fda.gov/consumers/consumer-updates/beware-fraudulent-coronavirus-tests-vaccines-and-treatments

Fein, S., McCloskey, A. L., and Tomlinson, T. M. (1997), 'Can the jury disregard that information? The use of suspicion to reduce the prejudicial effects of pretrial publicity and inadmissible testimony', *Personality and Social Psychology Bulletin*, *23*(11), 1215–26

Feinstein, D. (2014), *The Senate Intelligence Committee Report on Torture: Committee Study of the Central Intelligence Agency's Detention and Interrogation Program*, Brooklyn, NY, Melville House

Fenn, E., Newman, E. J., Pezdek, K., and Garry, M. (2013), 'The effect of nonprobative photographs on truthiness persists over time', *Acta Psychologica*, *144*(1), 207–11

Fenner, F., Henderson, D. A., Arita, I., Jezek, Z., and Ladnyi, I. D. (1988), *Smallpox and its eradication* (Vol. 6), Geneva, World Health Organization.

Finnin, R. and J. Roozenbeek (22 March 2022), 'The real goal of Kremlin disinformation isn't what you think', *Politico*, https://www.politico.com/news/magazine/2022/03/22/putin-disinformation-apathy-00018974?fbclid=IwAR0E-AOhW_uwiaqOm4QXSGwhf4kvC82SPlw68wKoT3bOnSstVY18X_2OS2A

Flaxman, S., Goel, S., and Rao, J. M. (2016), 'Filter bubbles, echo chambers, and online news consumption', *Public Opinion Quarterly*, *80*(S1), 298–320

Fong, A., Roozenbeek, J., Goldwert, D., Rathje, S., and van der Linden, S. (2021), 'The language of conspiracy: A psychological analysis of speech used by conspiracy theorists and their followers on Twitter', *Group Processes & Intergroup Relations*, *24*(4), 606–23

Franks, B., Bangerter, A., Bauer, M. W., Hall, M., and Noort, M. C. (2017), 'Beyond "monologicality"? Exploring conspiracist worldviews', *Frontiers in Psychology*, *8*, 861

Frederick, S. (2005), 'Cognitive reflection and decision making', *Journal of Economic Perspectives*, *19*(4), 25–42

Frenkel, S., and Alba, D. (20 May 2020), 'How the 'plandemic' movie and its falsehoods spread widely online', *New York Times*, https://www.nytimes.com/2020/05/20/technology/plandemic-movie-youtube-facebook-coronavirus.html

Frier, S. (13 April 2018), 'Trump's campaign said it was better at Facebook. Facebook agrees', *Bloomberg*, https://www.bloomberg.com/news/articles/2018-04-03/trump-s-campaign-said-it-was-better-at-facebook-facebook-agrees

'From the editors' (26 May 2004), 'The Times and Iraq', https://www.nytimes.com/2004/05/26/world/from-the-editors-the-times-and-iraq.html

Funke, D. (14 May 2020), 'No evidence Gates Foundation will profit from a

coronavirus vaccine', *PolitiFact*, Poynter Institute, https://www.politifact.com/
factchecks/2020/may/14/facebook-posts/no-evidence-gates-foundation-will-
profit-coronavir/

— (29 July 2020), 'Who are the doctors in the viral hydroxychloroquine video?',
Politifact. https://www.politifact.com/article/2020/jul/29/who-are-doctors-
viral-hydroxychloroquine-video/

— (22 February 2022), 'Fact check: Viral clip shows "Arma 3" video game, not war
between Russia, Ukraine', *USA Today*, https://eu.usatoday.com/story/news/
factcheck/2022/02/21/fact-check-arma-3-not-russia-ukraine-conflict-shown-
viral-video/6879521001/

Gallotti, R., Valle, F., Castaldo, N., Sacco, P., and De Domenico, M. (2020),
'Assessing the risks of "infodemics" in response to COVID-19 epidemics',
Nature Human Behaviour, *4*(12), 1285–93

Gault, M. (11 June 2020), 'Homeland security funded this game about
destabilizing a small U.S. town', *VICE*, https://www.vice.com/en/article/dyv
zm/homeland-security-funded-this-game-about-destabilizing-a-small-us-town

GCS (18 February 2021), 'GCS International joins the fight against health
misinformation worldwide', Government Communication Service, https://gcs.
civilservice.gov.uk/news/gcs-international-joins-the-fight-against-health-
misinformation-worldwide/

General Medical Council (GMC, 2010), 'Transcripts of hearings of fitness to
practise panel (misconduct) in the case of Wakefield, Walker-Smith, and
Murch', https://cdn.factcheck.org/UploadedFiles/gmc-charge-sheet.pdf

Giles, P. (31 August 2012), 'Is the word of one climate scientist worth that of 420
Spice Girls?', *RenewEconomy*, https://reneweconomy.com.au/is-the-word-of-
one-climate-scientist-worth-that-of-420-spice-girls-90361/

Global Warming Petition Project (n.d.), http://www.petitionproject.org/

Godlee, F., Smith, J., and Marcovitch, H. (2011), 'Wakefield's article linking MMR
vaccine and autism was fraudulent', *British Medical Journal*, *342*, c7452

Goebbels, J. (12 January 1941), *Aus Churchills Lügenfabrik, Die Zeit ohne Beispiel*,
Munich, Zentralverlag der NSDAP, pp. 364–9

Goel, V., Raj., S., and Ravichandran, P. (18 July 2018), 'How WhatsApp Leads
Mobs to Murder in India', *New York Times*, https://www.nytimes.com/
interactive/2018/07/18/technology/whatsapp-india-killings.html.

Goertzel, T. (1994), 'Belief in conspiracy theories', *Political Psychology*', *15*, 731–42

Gold, H. (4 July 2019), 'Researchers have created a "vaccine" for fake news. It's a
game', *CNN*, https://edition.cnn.com/2019/07/04/media/fake-news-game-
vaccine/index.html

Goldsworthy, A. (2015), *Augustus: First Emperor of Rome*, New Haven, CT, Yale University Press

González-Cabañas, J., Cuevas, Á., Cuevas, R., López-Fernández, J., and García, D. (2021), 'Unique on Facebook: formulation and evidence of (nano) targeting individual users with non-PII data', in *Proceedings of the 21st ACM Internet Measurement Conference* (pp. 464–79)

Gordon, A., Brooks, J. C., Quadflieg, S., Ecker, U. K., and Lewandowsky, S. (2017), 'Exploring the neural substrates of misinformation processing', *Neuropsychologia, 106*, 216–24

The Graybeards (July/August 2002), *Official publication of the Korean War Veterans Association, 16*(4), 1–71.

Green, Y. (2018), 'How technology can fight extremism and online harassment', *TED*, https://www.ted.com/talks/yasmin_green_how_technology_can_fight_extremism_and_online_harassment?language=en

Greenberg, J. (8 September 2017), 'No, 30,000 scientists have not said climate change is a hoax', *Politifact*, https://www.politifact.com/factchecks/2017/sep/08/blog-posting/no-30000-scientists-have-not-said-climate-change-h/

Greene, C. M., Nash, R. A., and Murphy, G. (2021), 'Misremembering Brexit: Partisan bias and individual predictors of false memories for fake news stories among Brexit voters', *Memory, 29*(5), 587–604.

Gregg, A. (1 November 2021), 'Twitter's new strategy to fight climate lies: give users accurate information first', *Washington Post*, https://www.washingtonpost.com/business/2021/11/01/twitter-climate-disinformation/

Griggs, R. A. (2015), 'The disappearance of independence in textbook coverage of Asch's social pressure experiments', *Teaching of Psychology, 42 (2)*, 137–42

Grimes, D. R. (2016), 'On the viability of conspiratorial beliefs', *PloS One, 11*(1), e0147905

Grinberg, N., Joseph, K., Friedland, L., Swire-Thompson, B., and Lazer, D. (2019), 'Fake news on Twitter during the 2016 US presidential election', *Science, 363*(6425), 374–8

Groenteman, R. (2002), *Als mijn zakdoek huilt*, Ra'anana, Israel: DocoStory Publishers Ltd

Guess, A. M. (2021), '(Almost) Everything in Moderation: New Evidence on Americans' Online Media Diets', *American Journal of Political Science 65(4)*, 1007–22

Guess, A. M., Nyhan, B., and Reifler, J. (2020), 'Exposure to untrustworthy websites in the 2016 US election', *Nature Human Behaviour, 4*(5), 472–80

Gunther, R., Beck, P. A., and Nisbet, E. C. (2019), '"Fake news" and the defection of 2012 Obama voters in the 2016 presidential election', *Electoral Studies, 61*, 102030

Guru-Murthy, K. (20 September 2020), 'It works as a suppression system, it works to subvert the will of the people' – Professor David Carroll, *Channel 4 News*, https://www.channel4.com/news/it-works-as-a-suppression-system-it-works-to-subvert-the-will-of-the-people-professor-david-carroll

Hadhazy, A. (2 April 2015), 'What's the most we can remember?', *BBC Future*, https://www.bbc.com/future/article/20150401-whats-the-most-we-can-remember

Hadjimatheou, C., and Nasaw, D. (27 October 2011), 'The American POW who chose China', *BBC News*, https://www.bbc.co.uk/news/magazine-15453730

Haenschen, K. (2022), 'The Conditional Effects of Microtargeted Facebook Advertisements on Voter Turnout', *Political Behavior*, 1–21

Hammond, N. (2000), *'Blaise Pascal'*, In A. Hastings, A. Mason, and H. Pyper (eds.), *The Oxford Companion to Christian Thought*, Oxford, Oxford University Press, p. 518

Han, J., Cha, M., and Lee, W. (2020), 'Anger contributes to the spread of Covid-19 misinformation', *Harvard Kennedy School Misinformation Review*, *1*(3)

Hanson, A. (18 October 2016), 'Inoculate your co-workers against the boss's tactics', *LaborNotes*, https://labornotes.org/2016/10/inoculate-your-co-workers-against-bosss-tactics

Hasher, L., Goldstein, D., and Toppino, T. (1977), 'Frequency and the conference of referential validity', *Journal of Verbal Learning and Verbal Behavior*, *16*(1), 107–12

Hebert, J. (1 May 1998), 'Odd names added to greenhouse plea', *Associated Press*, https://apnews.com/article/aec8beea85d7fe76fc9cc77b8392d79e

Helgason, B. A., and Effron, D. A (2022), 'It might become true: How prefactual thinking licenses dishonesty', *Journal of Personality and Social Psychology*.

Henderson, E. L., Simons, D. J., and Barr, D. J. (2021), 'The trajectory of truth: A longitudinal study of the illusory truth effect', *Journal of Cognition*, *4*(1)

Herf, J. (2005), 'The "Jewish war": Goebbels and the antisemitic campaigns of the Nazi propaganda ministry', *Holocaust and Genocide Studies*, *19*(1), 51–80

Higbee, K. L., and Clay, S. L. (1998), 'College students' beliefs in the ten-percent myth', *The Journal of Psychology*, *132*(5), 469–76

Hitler, A. (originally 1925–6, reissue edition 1999), *Mein Kampf*, translated by Ralph Manheim, New York, Houghton Mifflin

Hofstadter, R. (1964), *The paranoid style in American politics*, New York, NY, Vintage

Holmes, M. (26 May 2017), 'Edward Hunter and the origins of "brainwashing"', *Hidden Persuaders*, http://www7.bbk.ac.uk/hiddenpersuaders/blog/hunter-origins-of-brainwashing/

Horwitz, J., and Seetharaman, D. (26 May 2020), 'Facebook Executives Shut Down Efforts to Make the Site Less Divisive', *The Wall Street Journal*, https://www.wsj.com/articles/facebook-knows-it-encourages-division-top-executives-nixed-solutions-11590507499

Hot Ones (11 May 2017), 'Neil deGrasse Tyson Explains the Universe While Eating Spicy Wings', YouTube, https://www.youtube.com/watch?v=Da8-Qf Gemgo

House of European History (23 July 2021), 'Fake for Real Virtual Tour'. Brussels, Belgium, The House of European History. https://youtu.be/Z3SgE4chQME

Hovland, C. I., and Lumsdaine, A. A. (1971), '*Experiments on mass communication*', Princeton, NJ, Princeton University Press

Hovland, C. I., Lumsdaine, A. A., and Sheffield, F. D. (1949), *Experiments on mass communication, (Studies in social psychology in World War II)*, Princeton, NJ, Princeton University Press

Howard, P. N., Ganesh, B., Liotsiou, D., Kelly, J., and François, C. (2019), 'The IRA, social media and political polarization in the United States, 2012–2018', Computational Propaganda Research Project, Oxford, Oxford Internet Institute

Hunter, E. (24 September 1950), '"Brain-Washing" Tactics Force Chinese into Ranks of Communist Party', *Miami Daily News*

Huszár, F., Ktena, S. I., O'Brien, C., Belli, L., Schlaikjer, A., and Hardt, M. (2022), 'Algorithmic amplification of politics on Twitter', *Proceedings of the National Academy of Sciences*, 119(1) e20253341

Hwang, Y., Ryu, J. Y., and Jeong, S. H. (2021), 'Effects of disinformation using deepfake: The protective effect of media literacy education', *Cyberpsychology, Behavior, and Social Networking*, 24(3), 188–93

Ibbetson, C. (18 January 2021), 'Where do people believe in conspiracy theories? *YouGov-Cambridge Globalism Project*', https://yougov.co.uk/topics/international/articles-reports/2021/01/18/global-where-believe-conspiracy-theories-true

Icke, D. (1999), *The biggest secret: The book that will change the world*, Isle of Wight, David Icke Books

Imhoff, R., Zimmer, F., Klein, O., António, J. H., Babinska, M., Bangerter, A., . . . and Van Prooijen, J. W. (2022), 'Conspiracy mentality and political orientation across 26 countries', *Nature Human Behaviour* 6, 392–403

Independent Press Standards Organisation (IPSO, 2016), *09324-15 Muslim Engagement and Development (MEND) v The Sun*. https://www.ipso.co.uk/rulings-and-resolution-statements/ruling/?id=09324-15

Information Commissioner's Office (2 October 2020), 'ICO investigation into use of personal information and political influence', https://ico.org.uk/media/action-weve-taken/2618383/20201002_ico-o-ed-l-rtl-0181_to-julian-knight-mp.pdf.

Ingram, D. (26 October 2020), 'Twitter launches "pre-bunks" to get ahead of voting misinformation', *NBC*, https://www.nbcnews.com/tech/tech-news/twitter-launches-pre-bunks-get-ahead-voting-misinformation-n1244777

Ivanov, B., Miller, C. H., Compton, J., Averbeck, J. M., Harrison, K. J., Sims, J. D., ... and Parker, J. L. (2012), 'Effects of postinoculation talk on resistance to influence', *Journal of Communication*, 62(4), 701–718

Iyengar, A., Gupta, P., and Priya, N. (2022), 'Inoculation against conspiracy theories: a consumer-side approach to India's fake news problem', *Applied Cognitive Psychology*

Iyengar, S., Lelkes, Y., Levendusky, M., Malhotra, N., and Westwood, S. J. (2019), 'The origins and consequences of affective polarization in the United States', *Annual Review of Political Science*, 22, 129–46

Jamieson, K. H., and Cappella, J. N. (2008), *Echo chamber: Rush Limbaugh and the conservative media establishment*, Oxford, Oxford University Press

Jang, K. L., Livesley, W. J., and Vemon, P. A. (1996), 'Heritability of the big five personality dimensions and their facets: A twin study', *Journal of Personality*, 64(3), 577–92

Jason Mostafa Ali vs. Woodbridge Township School District et al. (Civil Action No. 17–2210, 2019), https://cases.justia.com/federal/district-courts/new-jersey/njdce/2:2017cv02210/346734/32/0.pdf?ts=1556702477

Jenner Institute (2022), *About Edward Jenner*, Oxford, University of Oxford. https://www.jenner.ac.uk/about/edward-jenner

Jigsaw (24 June 2021), 'Psychological inoculation: New techniques for fighting online extremism', *Google Jigsaw*, https://medium.com/jigsaw/psychological-inoculation-new-techniques-for-fighting-online-extremism-b156e439af23

John, O. P., Naumann, L. P., and Soto, C. J. (2008), 'Paradigm shift to the integrative Big Five trait taxonomy: History, measurement, and conceptual issues', in O. P. John, R. W. Robins, and L. A. Pervin (eds), *Handbook of Personality: Theory and Research* Guilford Press, pp. 114–58

Johnson, H. M., and Seifert, C. M. (1994), 'Sources of the continued influence effect: When misinformation in memory affects later inferences', *Journal of Experimental Psychology: Learning, Memory, and Cognition*, 20(6), 1420–36

Johnson, N. F., Velásquez, N., Restrepo, N. J., Leahy, R., Gabriel, N., El Oud, S., ... and Lupu, Y. (2020), 'The online competition between pro-and anti-vaccination views', *Nature*, 582(7811), 230–3

Jolley, D., and Paterson, J. L. (2020), 'Pylons ablaze: Examining the role of 5G Covid-19 conspiracy beliefs and support for violence', *British Journal of Social Psychology*, *59*(3), 628–40

Josephson, A., and Lambe, E. (11 March 2020), 'Brand communications in times of crisis', Twitter, https://blog.twitter.com/en_us/topics/company/2020/ Brand-communications-in-time-of-crisis

Jost, J. T., van der Linden, S., Panagopoulos, C., and Hardin, C. D. (2018), 'Ideological asymmetries in conformity, desire for shared reality, and the spread of misinformation', *Current Opinion in Psychology*, *23*, 77–83

Juul, J. L., and Ugander, J. (2021), 'Comparing information diffusion mechanisms by matching on cascade size', *Proceedings of the National Academy of Sciences*, *118*(46)

Kahan, D. M., Jenkins-Smith, H., and Braman, D. (2011), 'Cultural cognition of scientific consensus', *Journal of Risk Research*, *14*(2), 147–74

Kahan, D. M., Peters, E., Wittlin, M., Slovic, P., Ouellette, L. L., Braman, D., and Mandel, G. (2012), 'The polarizing impact of science literacy and numeracy on perceived climate change risks', *Nature Climate Change*, *2*(10), 732–5

Kaiser, B. (2019), *Targeted: My inside story of Cambridge Analytica and how Trump, Brexit, and Facebook broke democracy*, London, HarperCollins

Kalla, J. L., and Broockman, D. E. (2018), 'The minimal persuasive effects of campaign contact in general elections: Evidence from 49 field experiments', *American Political Science Review*, *112*(1), 148–66

Kaminska, I. (17 January 2017), 'A lesson in fake news from the info-wars of ancient Rome', *Financial Times*, https://www.ft.com/content/aaf2bb08-dca2-11e6-86ac-f253db7791c6

Karthikeyan, D. (25 May 2018), 'WhatsApp Rumours, Fake Videos Lead to Lynching and Deaths in Tamil Nadu', *The Wire India*, https://thewire.in/media/a-whatsapp-rumour-a-fake-video-lead-to-lynching-and-deaths-in-tamil-nadu

Keppler, D. (9 May 2021), 'Defense for some Capitol rioters: election misinformation', *Associated Press*, https://apnews.com/article/dc-wire-donald-trump-health-coronavirus-pandemic-election-2020-b7e929bb8d49b77d0922e ae7ad3794b7

Kessler, G., S. Rizzo, and M. Kelly (13 July 2020), 'President Trump has made more than 20,000 false or misleading claims', *Washington Post*, https://www. washingtonpost.com/politics/2020/07/13/president-trump-has-made-more-than-20000-false-or-misleading-claims/

Kim, M. (2019), *The interrogation rooms of the Korean War: The untold history*, Princeton, NJ, Princeton University Press

Koehler, D. J. (2016), 'Can journalistic "false balance" distort public perception of consensus in expert opinion?', *Journal of Experimental Psychology: Applied*, 22(1), 24–38

Kogan, A. (2018), 'Written evidence submitted by Aleksandr Kogan', *Parliamentary Inquiry on Fake News*. London, House of Commons. Digital, Culture, Media, and Sport Committee, https://www.parliament.uk/global assets/documents/commons-committees/culture-media-and-sport/Written-evidence-Aleksandr-Kogan.pdf

Kolb, D. A. (2014), *Experiential learning: Experience as the source of learning and development* (second edition), Upper Saddle River, NJ: Pearson Education, Inc.

Kosinski, M., Stillwell, D., and Graepel, T. (2013), 'Private traits and attributes are predictable from digital records of human behavior', *Proceedings of the national academy of sciences*, 110(15), 5802–5

Kostygina, G., Szczypka, G., Tran, H., Binns, S., Emery, S. L., Vallone, D., and Hair, E. C. (2020), 'Exposure and reach of the US court-mandated corrective statements advertising campaign on broadcast and social media', *Tobacco Control*, 29(4), 420–4

Kramer, A. D., Guillory, J. E., and Hancock, J. T. (2014), 'Experimental evidence of massive-scale emotional contagion through social networks', *Proceedings of the National Academy of Sciences*, 111(24), 8788–8790

Krebs, C. (29 July 2019), 'Definitely without. Pineapple on pizza is disgusting', [Tweet] *Twitter*, https://twitter.com/cisakrebs/status/1154462806311235584

Kroll, A. (24 February 2021), 'The Disinformation Vaccine: Is there a cure for conspiracy theories?', *Rolling Stone*, https://www.rollingstone.com/politics/politics-features/disinformation-conspiracy-theories-inoculation-edelman-corporate-america-1132325/

Kubin, E., and von Sikorski, C. (2021), 'The role of (social) media in political polarization: a systematic review', *Annals of the International Communication Association*, 45(3), 188–206

Kutner, S. (2020), 'Swiping right: The allure of hyper masculinity and cryptofascism for men who join the Proud Boys', *ICCT Research Paper*. International Centre for Counter-Terrorism. doi: 10.19165/2020.1.03

Lahsen, M. (2005), 'Technocracy, democracy, and US climate politics: the need for demarcations', *Science, Technology, & Human Values*, 30(1), 137–69

Lantian, A., Muller, D., Nurra, C., and Douglas, K. M. (2017), 'I know things they don't know!', *Social Psychology* 48(3), 160–73

Lapowsky, I. (15 November 2016), 'Here's how Facebook actually won Trump the presidency', *Wired*, https://www.wired.com/2016/11/facebook-won-trump-election-not-just-fake-news/

Leiserowitz, A., Maibach, E., Rosenthal, S., Kotcher, J., Bergquist, P., Ballew, M., Goldberg, M., Gustafson, A., and Wang, X. (2020), '*Climate Change in the American Mind: April 2020*', New Haven, CT, Yale Program on Climate Change Communication

Lent, R., Azevedo, F. A., Andrade-Moraes, C. H., and Pinto, A. V. (2012), 'How many neurons do you have? Some dogmas of quantitative neuroscience under revision', *European Journal of Neuroscience*, 35(1), 1–9

Levy, S. (2020), *Facebook: The Inside Story*, New York, NY, Penguin Random House

Lewandowsky, S., and van der Linden, S. (2021), 'Countering misinformation and fake news through inoculation and prebunking', *European Review of Social Psychology*, 32(2), 348–384

Lewandowsky, S., Armaos, K., Bruns, H., Schmid, P., Holford, D. L., Hahn, U., . . . and Cook, J. (2022), 'When science becomes embroiled in conflict: Recognizing the public's need for debate while combating conspiracies and misinformation', *The ANNALS of the American Academy of Political and Social Science*, 700(1), 26–40

Lewandowsky, S., Cook, J., Ecker, U. K., and van der Linden, S. (2020), *How to Spot Covid-19 Conspiracy Theories*, http://sks.to/conspire.

Lewandowsky, S., Cook, J., Ecker, U., Albarracin, D., Amazeen, M., Kendou, P., Lombardi, D., Newman, E., Pennycook, G., Porter, E., Rand, D., Rapp, D., Reifler, J., Roozenbeek, J., Schmid, P., Seifert, C., Sinatra, G., Swire-Thompson, B., van der Linden, S., Vraga, E., Wood, T., and Zaragoza, M. (2020), *The Debunking Handbook 2020*, https://www.climatechangecommunication.org/wp-content/uploads/2020/10/DebunkingHandbook2020.pdf

Lewandowsky, S., Cook, J., Oberauer, K., Brophy, S., Lloyd, E. A., and Marriott, M. (2015), 'Recurrent fury: Conspiratorial discourse in the blogosphere triggered by research on the role of conspiracist ideation in climate denial', *Journal of Social and Political Psychology*, 3(1), 161–97

Lewandowsky, S., Ecker, U. K., Seifert, C. M., Schwarz, N., and Cook, J. (2012), 'Misinformation and its correction: Continued influence and successful debiasing', *Psychological Science in the Public Interest*, 13(3), 106–31

Lewandowsky, S., Stritzke, W. G., Oberauer, K., and Morales, M. (2005), 'Memory for fact, fiction, and misinformation: The Iraq War 2003', *Psychological Science*, 16(3), 190–5

Lewis, J., and Speers, T. (2003), 'Misleading media reporting? The MMR story', *Nature Reviews Immunology*, 3(11), 913–18

Li, H. O. Y., Bailey, A., Huynh, D., and Chan, J. (2020), 'YouTube as a source of information on Covid-19: a pandemic of misinformation?', *BMJ Global Health*, 5(5), e002604

'List of most liked tweets' (2021), *Wikipedia*, https://en.wikipedia.org/wiki/List_of_most-liked_tweets

Loftus, E. (2003), 'Our changeable memories: Legal and practical implications', *Nature Reviews Neuroscience*, *4*(3), 231–4

Loftus, E. F. (2005), 'Planting misinformation in the human mind: A 30-year investigation of the malleability of memory', *Learning & Memory*, *12*(4), 361–6

Lord, C. G., Ross, L., and Lepper, M. R. (1979), 'Biased assimilation and attitude polarization: The effects of prior theories on subsequently considered evidence', *Journal of Personality and Social Psychology*, *37*(11), 2098–109

Lorenz-Spreen, P., Geers, M., Pachur, T., Hertwig, R., Lewandowsky, S., and Herzog, S. M. (2021), 'Boosting people's ability to detect microtargeted advertising', *Scientific Reports*, *11*(1), 1–9

Lorenz-Spreen, P., Lewandowsky, S., Sunstein, C. R., and Hertwig, R. (2020), 'How behavioural sciences can promote truth, autonomy and democratic discourse online', *Nature Human Behaviour*, *4*(11), 1102–9

Lorenz, T. (9 December 2021), 'Birds aren't real, or are they? Inside a Gen Z conspiracy theory', *New York Times*, https://www.nytimes.com/2021/12/09/technology/birds-arent-real-gen-z-misinformation.html

Lumsdaine, A. A., and Janis, I. L. (1953), 'Resistance to "counterpropaganda" produced by one-sided and two-sided "propaganda" presentations', *Public Opinion Quarterly*, *17*(3), 311–18

Luntz, F. (2002), 'The Environment: A cleaner, safer, healthier America', *Sourceatch*, https://www.sourcewatch.org/images/4/45/LuntzResearch.Memo.pdf

Luo, Y., and Zhao, J. (2019), 'Motivated attention in climate change perception and action', *Frontiers in Psychology*, *10*, 1541

Luo, Y., and Zhao, J. (2021), 'Attentional and perceptual biases of climate change', *Current Opinion in Behavioral Sciences*, *42*, 22–6

Lynas, M., Houlton, B. Z., and Perry, S. (2021), 'Greater than 99% consensus on human caused climate change in the peer-reviewed scientific literature', *Environmental Research Letters*, *16*(11), 114005

Mac, R., and Silverman, C. (12 March 2021), 'Facebook created an employee "playbook" to respond to accusations of polarization', *Buzzfeed*, https://www.buzzfeednews.com/article/ryanmac/facebook-execs-polarization-playbook

MacDonald, E. (13 January 2017), 'The fake news that sealed the fate of Antony and Cleopatra', *The Conversation*, https://theconversation.com/the-fake-news-that-sealed-the-fate-of-antony-and-cleopatra-71287

Madsen, J. K. (2019), '*The psychology of micro-targeted election campaigns*', Springer International Publishing

Madsen, J. K., and Pilditch, T. D. (2018), 'A method for evaluating cognitively informed micro-targeted campaign strategies: An agent-based model proof of principle', *PloS One*, *13*(4), e0193909.

Maertens, R., Anseel, F., and van der Linden, S. (2020), 'Combatting climate change misinformation: Evidence for longevity of inoculation and consensus messaging effects', *Journal of Environmental Psychology*, *70*, 101455

Maertens, R., Götz, F. M., Schneider, C. R., Roozenbeek, J., Kerr, J. R., Stieger, S., ... Linden, S. (2021), 'The Misinformation Susceptibility Test (MIST): A psychometrically validated measure of news veracity discernment', https://doi.org/10.31234/osf.io/gk68h

Maertens, R., Roozenbeek, J., Basol, M., and van der Linden, S. (2021), 'Long-term effectiveness of inoculation against misinformation: Three longitudinal experiments', *Journal of Experimental Psychology: Applied*, *27*(1), 1–16

Magnusson, K. (2021), *Interpreting Cohen's d effect size: An interactive visualization* (Version 2.5.1) [Web App], R. Psychologist, https://rpsychologist.com/cohend/

Malinowski, T., and A. G. Eshoo (21 January 2021), '[Letter to Mr. Sundar Pichai and Ms. Susan Wojcicki]', Washington, DC, Congress of the United States, https://malinowski.house.gov/sites/malinowski.house.gov/files/Letterpercent 20topercent20YouTubepercent20--percent20Malinowski_Eshoo_final_0.pdf.

Malins, J., and Hudson, L. (13 April 2018), '*Report to the board of Cambridge Analytica*', https://www.malinschambers.com/wp-content/uploads/2018/05/FINAL-REPORT-TO-THE-BOARD-OF-CAMBRIDGE-ANALYTICA-1.pdf

Mao, W., Cui, Y., Chiu, M. M., & Lei, H. (2022), 'Effects of game-based learning on students' critical thinking: A meta-analysis', *Journal of Educational Computing Research*, *59*(8), 1682–1708

Marsh, A., and Lorge, S. (November/December 2012), 'How the truth gets twisted', *Stanford Magazine*, https://stanfordmag.org/contents/how-the-truth-gets-twisted

Martel, C., Pennycook, G., and Rand, D. G. (2020), 'Reliance on emotion promotes belief in fake news', *Cognitive research: Principles and Implications*, *5*(1), 1–20

Matz, S. C., Kosinski, M., Nave, G., and Stillwell, D. J. (2017), 'Psychological targeting as an effective approach to digital mass persuasion', *Proceedings of the National Academy of Sciences*, *114*(48), 12714–19

Matz, S. C., Kosinski, M., Nave, G., and Stillwell, D. J. (2018), 'Reply to Eckles et al.: Facebook's optimization algorithms are highly unlikely to explain the effects of psychological targeting', *Proceedings of the National Academy of Sciences*, *115*(23), E5256-E5257

McCarthy, B. (30 June 2021), 'Misinformation and the 6 January insurrection: When "patriot warriors" were fed lies', *PolitiFact*, Poynter Institute, https://www.politifact.com/article/2021/jun/30/misinformation-and-jan-6-insurrection-when-patriot/

McCaskill, N. (17 February 2017), 'Trump tweets: Press "is the enemy of the American people"', *Politico*, https://www.politico.com/story/2017/02/trump-tweet-media-enemy-american-people-235150

McDonald, J. (30 March 2020), 'No evidence to back COVID-19 Ibuprofen concerns', *FactCheck.org*, https://www.factcheck.org/2020/03/no-evidence-to-back-covid-19-ibuprofen-concerns/

McEvoy, M., and Therrien, D. (26 November 2019), *Investigation report P19-03 PIPEDA-035913 AggregateIQ Data Services Ltd*, Office of the Privacy Commissioner of Canada, https://www.oipc.bc.ca/investigation-reports/2363

McGuire, W. J. (1961), 'Resistance to persuasion conferred by active and passive prior refutation of the same and alternative counterarguments', *Journal of Abnormal and Social Psychology*, *63*(2), 326–32

— (1961), 'The effectiveness of supportive and refutational defenses in immunizing and restoring beliefs against persuasion', *Sociometry*, *24*(2), 184–97

— (1964), 'Some contemporary approaches', in L. Berkowitz (ed.), *Advances in Experimental Social Psychology*, Academic Press(pp. 191–229)

— (1970), 'Vaccine for Brainwash', *Psychology Today, 3*(9), 36–9

— (1996), 'The Yale communication and attitude-change program in the 1950s' (pp. 39–59), In E. E. Dennis and E. Wartella (eds), *American Communication Research: The remembered history*, New York, NY, Routledge

McGuire, W. J., and Papageorgis, D. (1961), 'The relative efficacy of various types of prior belief-defense in producing immunity against persuasion', *Journal of Abnormal and Social Psychology*, *62*(2), 327–37

— (1962), 'Effectiveness of forewarning in developing resistance to persuasion', *Public Opinion Quarterly*, *26*(1), 24–34

Mclaughlin, T. (12 December 2018), 'How WhatsApp fuels fake news and violence in India', *WIRED*, https://www.wired.com/story/how-whatsapp-fuels-fake-news-and-violence-in-india/.

Media Bias/Fact-Check (10 April 2021), Infowars-Alex Jones, https://mediabias factcheck.com/infowars-alex-jones/

Meku, T., Lu, D., and Gamio, L. (11 November 2016), 'How Trump won the presidency with razor-thin margins in swing states', *Washington Post*, https://www.washingtonpost.com/graphics/politics/2016-election/swing-state-margins/.

Melley, T. (2008), 'Brainwashed! Conspiracy theory and ideology in the postwar United States', *New German Critique*, (103), 145–64

Meta (4 April 2018), 'An update on our plans to restrict data access on Facebook', https://about.fb.com/news/2018/04/restricting-data-access/

Montgomery, B. (9 January 2019), 'Proud boy allegedly murders brother with a sword thinking he's killing a lizard', *Huffington Post*, https://www.huffington post.co.uk/entry/proud-boy-allegedly-murders-brother-with-a-sword-thinking-hes-a-lizard_n_5c36042ee4b05b16bcfcb3d5

Morris, A. (15 October 2021), 'It's Not Q. It's You', *Rolling Stone Magazine*, https://www.rollingstone.com/culture/culture-features/qanon-expert-joesph-uscinski-1242636/

Moscovici, S., and Zavalloni, M. (1969), 'The group as a polariser of attitudes', *Journal of Personality and Social Psychology*, *12*(2), 125–35

Motta, M., and Stecula, D. (2021), 'Quantifying the effect of Wakefield et al.(1998) on skepticism about MMR vaccine safety in the US', *Plos One*, *16*(8), e0256395

Murphy, G., Loftus, E. F., Grady, R. H., Levine, L. J., and Greene, C. M. (2019), 'False memories for fake news during Ireland's abortion referendum', *Psychological Science*, *30*(10), 1449–59

Museum of Discovery (2020), *Life Interrupted Exhibit* (March–August 2020), Adelaide, Australia, MOD, https://mod.org.au/exhibits/bad-news-game/

Myers, J., and, M. (15 March 2018), 'Meet the activist who uncovered the Russian Troll factory named in the Mueller Probe', *NPR*, https://www.npr.org/sections/parallels/2018/03/15/594062887/some-russians-see-u-s-investigation-into-russian-election-meddling-as-a-soap-ope

myPersonality database (n.d.), 'The Psychometrics Centre. Cambridge Judge Business School', https://www.psychometrics.cam.ac.uk/productsservices/mypersonality

NAS (20 April 1998), 'Statement of the council of the NAS regarding global change petition', National Academy of Sciences, Engineering, and Medicine, https://www.wired.com/story/how-whatsapp-fuels-fake-news-and-violence-in-india/

National Crime Records Bureau (2019), 'Report on missing women and children in India', Ministry of Home Affairs, Ref. No. 24013/5/2011-ATC. 3 June 2019, https://ncrb.gov.in/sites/default/files/missingpage-merged.pdf

Nemer, D. (25 October 2018), 'The three types of WhatsApp users getting Brazil's Jair Bolsonaro elected', *Guardian*, https://www.theguardian.com/world/2018/oct/25/brazil-president-jair-bolsonaro-whatsapp-fake-news

Newman, E. J., Garry, M., Bernstein, D. M., Kantner, J., and Lindsay, D. S. (2012), 'Nonprobative photographs (or words) inflate truthiness', *Psychonomic Bulletin & Review*, *19*(5), 969–74

Newton, C. (12 May 2020), 'How the "Plandemic" video hoax went viral', *The Verge*, https://www.theverge.com/2020/5/12/21254184/how-plandemic-went-viral-facebook-youtube

Nicas, J. (2 March 2020), 'Can YouTube Quiet Its Conspiracy Theorists?', *New York Times*, https://www.nytimes.com/interactive/2020/03/02/technology/youtube-conspiracy-theory.html

Nisbet, E. C., Mortenson, C., and Li, Q. (2021), 'The presumed influence of election misinformation on others reduces our own satisfaction with democracy', *Harvard Kennedy School Misinformation Review 1(7)*

Nix, A. (19 September 2016), *The power of big data and psychographics*, New York, NY, 2016, Concordia Annual Summit, https://www.youtube.com/watch?v=n8Dd5aVXLCc

Norman, A. (2021), *Mental immunity: Infectious ideas, mind-parasites, and the search for a better way to think*, New York, NY, Harper Wave

Nowak, M., et al. (2 September 2014), 'Determining user personality characteristics from social media networking system communications and characteristics', *US Patent No. US 8,825,764 B2*. Washington, DC, US Patent and Trademark Office

NPR (18 March 2018), 'Spot fake news by making it', *NPR*, https://www.npr.org/2018/03/18/594671289/spot-fake-news-by-making-it

Oliver, J. E., and Wood, T. J. (2014), 'Conspiracy theories and the paranoid style(s) of mass opinion', *American Journal of Political Science*, 58(4), 952–66

Omilusik, K. D., and Goldrath, A. W. (2017), 'The origins of memory T cells', *Nature*, 552, 337–339

Oreskes, N., and Conway, E. M. (2011), '*Merchants of doubt: How a handful of scientists obscured the truth on issues from tobacco smoke to global warming*', Bloomsbury Publishing USA

Orlando, A. (17 May 2021), 'Fake news spread like a virus. These new online games could "vaccinate" people against misinformation', *Discover Magazine*, https://www.discovermagazine.com/mind/fake-news-spreads-like-a-virus-these-new-online-games-could-vaccinate-people

Ortiz, D. A. (14 November 2018), 'Could this be the cure for fake news?', *BBC Future*, https://www.bbc.com/future/article/20181114-could-this-game-be-a-vaccine-against-fake-news

Ortiz-Ospina, E. (2020), 'The rise of social media', Our World in Data, University of Oxford, https://ourworldindata.org/rise-of-social-media

Otgaar, H., Candel, I., Merckelbach, H., and Wade, K. A. (2009), 'Abducted by a UFO: Prevalence information affects young children's false memories for an implausible event', *Applied Cognitive Psychology*, 23(1), 115–25

Paciaroni, M. (2010), 'Visual experiences of Blaise Pascal', in *Neurological Disorders in Famous Artists – Part 3* (Vol. 27, pp. 160–7), Karger Publishers

Pafundo, D. E., Nicholas, M. A., Zhang, R., and Kuhlman, S. J. (2016), 'Top-down-mediated facilitation in the visual cortex is gated by subcortical neuromodulation', *Journal of Neuroscience*, 36(10), 2904–14

Palma, B. (17 January 2018), 'Did a CDC doctor say the flu shot is causing a deadly outbreak?', *Snopes*, https://www.snopes.com/fact-check/did-cdc-flu-shot-causing-outbreak/

— (17 March 2020), 'No, a hair dryer won't stop coronavirus', *Snopes*, https://www.snopes.com/fact-check/did-cdc-flu-shot-causing-outbreak/

Painter, D. L., and Fernandes, J. (2022), '"The Big Lie": How Fact Checking Influences Support for Insurrection', *American Behavioral Scientist*

Pappas, S. (25 January 2017), 'Fake news "vaccine" could stop spread of false information', *Fox News*, https://www.foxnews.com/health/fake-news-vaccine-could-stop-spread-of-false-information

Pariser, E. (2011), *The Filter Bubble: What the Internet is hiding from you*, London, Penguin

— (7 May 2015), 'Did Facebook's big new study kill my filter bubble thesis?', *Medium*, https://medium.com/backchannel/facebook-published-a-big-new-study-on-the-filter-bubble-here-s-what-it-says-ef31a292da95

Pasley, V. (1955), *21 Stayed: The story of the American GI's who chose communist China: Who they were and why they stayed*, Farrar, Straus, & Cudahy

PBS Newshour (27 March 2020), 'In Iran, false belief a poison fights virus kills hundreds', *PBS*, https://www.pbs.org/newshour/world/in-iran-false-belief-a-poison-fights-virus-kills-hundreds

Pegoraro, R. (8 October, 2020), 'The real problem wasn't Cambridge Analytica, but the data brokers that outlived it', *Forbes*, https://www.forbes.com/sites/robpegoraro/2020/10/08/the-real-problem-wasnt-cambridge-analytica-but-the-data-brokers-that-outlived-it/?sh=6a4fcd9326a4

Pennycook, G., and Rand, D. G. (2019), 'Lazy, not biased: Susceptibility to partisan fake news is better explained by lack of reasoning than by motivated reasoning', *Cognition*, 188, 39–50

Pennycook, G., Cannon, T. D., and Rand, D. G. (2018), 'Prior exposure increases perceived accuracy of fake news', *Journal of Experimental Psychology: General*, 147(12), 1865–80

Perraudin, F. (20 November 2019), 'Twitter accuses Tories of misleading public with "factcheck" foray', *Guardian,* https://www.theguardian.com/politics/ 2019/nov/20/twitter-accuses-tories-of-misleading-public-in-fact check-row

Persson, E., Andersson, D., Koppel, L., Västfjäll, D., and Tinghög, G. (2021), 'A preregistered replication of motivated numeracy', *Cognition, 214*, 104768

Pfau, M., Ivanov, B., Houston, B., Haigh, M., Sims, J., Gilchrist, E., . . . and Richert, N. (2005), 'Inoculation and mental processing: The instrumental role of associative networks in the process of resistance to counterattitudinal influence', *Communication Monographs, 72*(4), 414–41

Phadke, V. K., Bednarczyk, R. A., Salmon, D. A., and Omer, S. B. (2016), 'Association between vaccine refusal and vaccine-preventable diseases in the United States: a review of measles and pertussis', *JAMA, 315*(11), 1149–58

Philips, Y. (21 January 2016), 'B.o.B is now rap's leading conspiracy theorist', *DJBooth*, https://djbooth.net/features/2016-01-21-bob-conspiracy-theory

Pilditch, T., Roozenbeek, J., Madsen, J., and van der Linden, S. (2022), 'Psychological inoculation can reduce susceptibility to misinformation in large rational agent networks', *Royal Society Open Science 9,* 211953

'PIPEDA Findings #2019-002' (25 April 2019), 'Joint investigation of Facebook, Inc. by the Privacy Commissioner of Canada and the Information and Privacy Commissioner for British Columbia', *Office of the Privacy Commissioner of Canada*, https://www.priv.gc.ca/en/opc-actions-and-decisions/investigations/investigations-into-businesses/2019/pipeda-2019-002/

Popken, B. (14 February 2018), 'Twitter deleted 200,000 Russian troll tweets. Read them here', *NBC News*, https://www.nbcnews.com/tech/social-media/now-available-more-200-000-deleted-russian-troll-tweets-n844731

Poutoglidou, F., Saitis, A., and Kouvelas, D. (2021), 'Ibuprofen and COVID-19 disease: separating the myths from facts', *Expert Review of Respiratory Medicine, 15*(8), 979–83

Prior, M., Sood, G., and Khanna, K. (2015), 'You cannot be serious: The impact of accuracy incentives on partisan bias in reports of economic perceptions', *Quarterly Journal of Political Science, 10*(4), 489–518

Public Religion Research Institute (27 May 2021), 'Understanding QAnon's Connection to American Politics, Religion, and Media Consumption', PPRI-IFYC. https://www.prri.org/research/qanon-conspiracy-american-politics-report/

Putterman, S. (12 June 2019), 'A video of Mark Zuckerberg shows him talking about controlling "billions of people's stolen data" to control the future', *Politifact*, https://www.politifact.com/factchecks/2019/jun/12/instagram-posts/zuckerberg-video-about-billions-peoples-stolen-dat/

Ramsay, A. M. (1925), 'The speed of the Roman imperial post', *Journal of Roman Studies, 15*(1), 60–74

Rathje, S., Van Bavel, J. J., and van der Linden, S. (2021), 'Out-group animosity drives engagement on social media', *Proceedings of the National Academy of Sciences*, *118*(26), e2024292118

Rathje, S., Van Bavel, J., and van der Linden, S. (13 July 2021), 'Why Facebook really, really, doesn't want to discourage extremism', *Washington Post*, https://www.washingtonpost.com/politics/2021/07/13/why-facebook-really-really-doesnt-want-discourage-extremism/

Raychoudhury, P. (13 July 2021), 'Extremism is bad for our business and what we are doing about it', *Facebook*, https://research.fb.com/blog/2021/07/extremism-is-bad-for-our-business-and-what-we-are-doing-about-it/

Rayne, N. (26 March 2016), 'Robert De Niro Reveals He Pushed for Screening of Anti-Vaccine Movie at Tribeca Film Festival', *People Magazine*, https://people.com/celebrity/robert-de-niro-reveals-he-pushed-for-screening-of-anti-vaccine-movie/

Readfearn, G. (29 November 2016), 'Revealed: most popular climate story on social media told half a million people the science was a hoax', *DeSmog*, https://www.desmog.com/2016/11/29/revealed-most-popular-climate-story-social-media-told-half-million-people-science-was-hoax/

Reber, R., and Schwarz, N. (1999), 'Effects of perceptual fluency on judgments of truth', *Consciousness and Cognition*, *8*(3), 338–42

Reverend Raphael Warnock, 'Get Ready' Campaign 2020 (5 November 2020), *Washington Post*, https://www.washingtonpost.com/video/politics/campaign-ads-2020/reverend-raphael-warnock-get-ready-campaign-2020/ 2020/11/05/00731660-e441-41be-aa94-838c69e069e2_video.html

Rhodes, S. C. (2022), 'Filter bubbles, echo chambers, and fake news: how social media conditions individuals to be less critical of political misinformation', *Political Communication*, *39*(1), 1–22

Rich, J. (2010), 'Deception, lies, and economy with the truth: Augustus and the establishment of the principate' in A. J. Turner., J. H. Kim On Chong-Cossard, and F. J. Vervaet (eds), *Private and Public Lies: The Discourse of Despotism and Deceit in the Graeco-Roman World*, Leiden, Netherlands: Brill Academic, (pp. 167–91)

Richard, F. D., Bond Jr, C. F., and Stokes-Zoota, J. J. (2003), 'One hundred years of social psychology quantitatively described', *Review of General Psychology*, *7*(4), 331–63

Riedel, S. (2005), 'Edward Jenner and the history of smallpox and vaccination', in *Baylor University Medical Center Proceedings* (Vol. 18, No. 1, pp. 21–5), Taylor & Francis

Robertson, L., and R. Farley (23 January 2017), 'The facts on crowd size', *Fact Check.org*, https://www.factcheck.org/2017/01/the-facts-on-crowd-size/

Romano, A. (4 January 2022), 6 January anniversary poll: 'Share of Trump voters who believe 'Biden won fair and square' falls to 9 per cent amid declining trust in US democracy', *Yahoo! News*, https://news.yahoo.com/jan-6-anniversary-poll-share-of-trump-voters-who-believe-biden-won-fair-and-square-falls-to-9-percent-amid-declining-trust-in-us-democracy-100017416.html

Roose, K. (29 March 2019), 'YouTube's Product Chief on Online Radicalization and Algorithmic Rabbit Holes', *New York Times*, https://www.nytimes.com/2019/03/29/technology/youtube-online-extremism.html

— (8 June 2019), 'The making of a YouTube radical', *New York Times*, https://www.nytimes.com/interactive/2019/06/08/technology/youtube-radical.html

Roose, K., Isaac, M., and Frenkel, S. (24 November 2020), 'Facebook struggles to balance civility and growth', *New York Times*, https://www.nytimes.com/2020/11/24/technology/facebook-election-misinformation.html

Roozenbeek, J., and van der Linden, S. (2018), 'The fake news game: actively inoculating against the risk of misinformation', *Journal of Risk Research*, *22*(5), 570–80

— (2019), 'Fake news game confers psychological resistance against online misinformation', *Nature Humanities and Social Sciences Communications*, *5*(65)

— (2020), 'Breaking Harmony Square: A game that "inoculates" against political misinformation', *Harvard Kennedy School Misinformation Review 1*(8)

— (2021), 'Inoculation theory and misinformation', NATO Strategic Communications Centre of Excellence, ISBN: 978-9934-564-49-9

Roozenbeek, J., Basol. M., and van der Linden, S. (11 January 2019), 'WhatsApp wants researchers to tackle its fake news problem—here's our idea', *The Conversation*, https://theconversation.com/whatsapp-wants-researchers-to-tackle-its-fake-news-problem-heres-our-idea-107415

Roozenbeek, J., Schneider, C. R., Dryhurst S., Kerr, J., Freeman, A. L., Recchia, G. . . . and van der Linden, S. (2020), 'Susceptibility to misinformation about Covid-19 around the world', *Royal Society Open Science*, *7*(10), 201199

Roozenbeek, J., Maertens, R., Herzog, S. M., Geers, M., Kurvers, R. H., Sultan, M., and van der Linden, S. (2022), 'Susceptibility to misinformation is consistent across question framings and response modes and better explained by myside bias and partisanship than analytical thinking' *Judgment and Decision Making*, *17*(3), 547–73

Roozenbeek, J., Maertens, R., McClanahan, W., and van der Linden, S. (2021), 'Disentangling item and testing effects in inoculation research on online misinformation: Solomon revisited', *Educational and Psychological Measurement*, *81*(2), 340–62

Roozenbeek, J., Traberg, C. S., van der Linden, S. (2022), 'Technique-based inoculation against real-world misinformation', *Royal Society Open Science 9*, 211719

Roozenbeek, J., van der Linden, S., and Nygren, T. (2020), 'Prebunking interventions based on the psychological theory of "inoculation" can reduce susceptibility to misinformation across cultures', *Harvard Kennedy School Misinformation Review 1*(2)

Roozenbeek, J., van der Linden, S., Goldberg, B., Rathje, S., and Lewandowsky, S. (2022), 'Psychological inoculation improves resilience against misinformation on social media', *Science Advances 8*, 10.1126/sciadv.abo6254

Rosenberg, M., Confessore, N., and Cadwalladr, C. (17 March 2018), 'How Trump Consultants Exploited the Facebook Data of Millions', *New York Times*, https://www.nytimes.com/2018/03/17/us/politics/cambridge-analytica-trump-campaign.html

Rousis, G. J., Richard, F. D., and Wang, D. Y. D. (2020), 'The Truth Is Out There: The Prevalence of Conspiracy Theory Use by Radical Violent Extremist Organizations', *Terrorism and Political Violence*, 1–19

Rowling, J. K. (2005), '*Harry Potter and the Half Blood Prince*', London, Bloomsbury

Ruck, D. J., Rice, N. M., Borycz, J., and Bentley, R. A. (2019), 'Internet Research Agency Twitter activity predicted 2016 US election polls', *First Monday 24*(7)

'Russian active measures campaigns and interference in the 2016 U.S. election', 116th Congress (10 November 2020), Select Committee on Intelligence United States Senate. Report 116–290. https://www.intelligence.senate.gov/publications/report-select-committee-intelligence-united-states-senate-russian-active-measures

Sagarin, B. J., Cialdini, R. B., Rice, W. E., and Serna, S. B. (2002), 'Dispelling the illusion of invulnerability: the motivations and mechanisms of resistance to persuasion', *Journal of Personality and Social Psychology*, *83*(3), 526–41

Said-Moorhouse, L. (30 January 2016), 'Neil deGrasse Tyson fires back at B.o.B with epic mic drop', *CNN*, https://edition.cnn.com/2016/01/29/entertainment/neil-degrasse-tyson-bob-flat-earth-twitter-spat/index.html

Saleh, N., Roozenbeek, J., Makki, F., McClanahan, W. P., and van der Linden, S. (2021), 'Active inoculation boosts attitudinal resistance against extremist persuasion techniques – A novel approach towards the prevention of violent extremism', *Behavioural Public Policy*

Sample, I. (20 February 2018), 'Bad News: The game researchers hope will "vaccinate" public against fake news', *Guardian*, https://www.theguardian.com/

technology/2018/feb/20/bad-news-the-game-researchers-hope-will-vaccinate-public-against-fake-news

Sanders, L. (26 May 2020), 'The difference between what Republicans and Democrats believe to be true about Covid-19', *Yahoo News/YouGov*, https://today.yougov.com/topics/politics/articles-reports/2020/05/26/republicans-democrats-misinformation

Schaffner, B. F., and Luks, S. (2018), 'Misinformation or expressive responding? What an inauguration crowd can tell us about the source of political misinformation in surveys', *Public Opinion Quarterly*, 82(1), 135–47

Schein, E. H. (1956), 'Some observations on Chinese methods of handling prisoners of war', *Public Opinion Quarterly*, 20(1), 321–7

— (1956), 'The Chinese indoctrination program for prisoners of war: a study of attempted "brainwashing"', *Psychiatry*, 19(2), 149–72

Schick, N. (2020), *Deep Fakes and the Infocalypse; What you urgently need to know*, London, Octopus Publishing Group Ltd

Schwarz, N., Newman, E., and Leach, W. (2016), 'Making the truth stick and the myths fade: Lessons from cognitive psychology', *Behavioral Science & Policy*, 2(1), 85–95

Science Friday (27 January 2017), *Building an immunity to fake news*, https://www.sciencefriday.com/segments/building-an-immunity-to-fake-news/

Scott, K. (1933), 'The political propaganda of 44–30 BC', *Memoirs of the American Academy in Rome, 11,* 7–49

Seibt, S. (23 February 2022), 'Ukraine crisis: A low-cost disinformation campaign aids Putin's playbook', *France 24*, https://www.france24.com/en/europe/2022 0223-ukraine-crisis-a-low-cost-disinformation-campaign-aids-putin-s-playbook

Seth, A. (2021), *Being you: A new science of consciousness*, Faber & Faber

Shaffer, C. (31 July 2017), '"Last Week Tonight": John Oliver on Alex Jones's InfoWars Business Model, Health Products', *Newsweek*, https://www.newsweek.com/john-oliver-alex-jones-last-week-tonight-infowars-644240

Shaw, J., and Porter, S. (2015), 'Constructing rich false memories of committing crime', *Psychological Science*, 26(3), 291–301

Shellenbarger, S. (21 November 2016), 'Most students don't know when news is fake, Stanford study finds', *Wall Street Journal*, https://www.wsj.com/articles/most-students-dont-know-when-news-is-fake-stanford-study-finds-1479752576

Shepard, R. (1998), 'Carl Iver Hovland in Office of Home Secretary', (ed.), *Biographical Memoirs* (Vol. 73, pp. 230–61), *National Academies Press*

Sifuentes, J. (20 November 2019), 'The Propaganda of Octavian and Mark Antony's Civil War', *World History Encyclopedia*, https://www.worldhistory.org/article/1474/the-propaganda-of-octavian-and-mark-antonys-civil/

Simchon, A., Brady, W. J., and Van Bavel, J. J (2022), 'Troll and divide: the language of online polarization', *PNAS Nexus*, *1*(1), pgac019

Similarweb (n.d.), Infowars.com, December 2021, https://www.similarweb.com/site/infowars.com/#traffic

Simon, F. M., and Camargo, C. Q. (2021), 'Autopsy of a metaphor: The origins, use and blind spots of the "infodemic"', *New Media & Society*

Skurnik, I., Yoon, C., Park, D. C., and Schwarz, N. (2005), 'How warnings about false claims become recommendations', *Journal of Consumer Research*, *31*(4), 713–24

Sky News (10 June 2020), 'Coronavirus: Father of three who searched for 5G conspiracy theories online jailed for arson attack on phone mast', https://news.sky.com/story/coronavirus-father-of-three-who-searched-for-5g-conspiracy-theories-online-jailed-for-arson-attack-on-phone-mast-12002914

Smith, A., Toor, S., and Van Kessel, P. (7 November 2018), 'Many turn to YouTube for Children's Content, News, and How-To Lessons', *Pew Research Center*, https://www.pewresearch.org/internet/2018/11/07/many-turn-to-youtube-for-childrens-content-news-how-to-lessons/

Smith, T. W. (1995), 'A review: The Holocaust denial controversy', *Public Opinion Quarterly*, *59*(2), 269–95

Solsman, J. E. (10 January 2018), 'YouTube's AI is the puppet master over most of what you watch', *CNET*, https://www.cnet.com/news/youtube-ces-2018-neal-mohan/

Song, H., and Schwarz, N. (2008), 'Fluency and the detection of misleading questions: Low processing fluency attenuates the Moses illusion', *Social Cognition*, *26*(6), 791–9

Sorkin, A. (writer) and Reiner, R. (director), (1992), *A Few Good Men*, Columbia Pictures

Soto, C. J. (2019), 'How replicable are links between personality traits and consequential life outcomes? The life outcomes of personality replication project', *Psychological Science*, *30*(5), 711–27

Spring, M. (15 July 2020), 'Wayfair: The false conspiracy about a furniture firm and child trafficking', *BBC,* https://www.bbc.co.uk/news/world-53416247

Srivastava, K. (2021), 'Fake covid vaccines boost the black market for counterfeit medicines', *BMJ 375*, n2754

Stahl, L. (22 April 2018), 'Aleksandr Kogan: The link between Cambridge Analytica and Facebook', *CBS News*, https://www.cbsnews.com/news/aleksandr-kogan-the-link-between-cambridge-analytica-and-facebook/?intcid=CNM-00-10abd1h

State vs Rader, 62 (Or. 37, 1912), https://cite.case.law/or/62/37/

Stella, M., Ferrara, E., and De Domenico, M. (2018), 'Bots increase exposure to negative and inflammatory content in online social systems', *Proceedings of the National Academy of Sciences*, *115*(49), 12435–40

Stewart, A. J., and Devlin, P. M. (2006), 'The history of the smallpox vaccine', *Journal of Infection*, *52*(5), 329–34

Strandberg, K., Himmelroos, S., and Grönlund, K. (2019), 'Do discussions in like-minded groups necessarily lead to more extreme opinions? Deliberative democracy and group polarization', *International Political Science Review*, *40*(1), 41–57

Sumpter, D. (2018), *Outnumbered: From Facebook and Google to fake news and filter bubbles – the algorithms that control our lives*, London, Bloomsbury

Sunstein, C. (2001), *Republic.com*, Princeton, NJ, Princeton University Press

Sunstein, C. R. (1999), 'The law of group polarization', *University of Chicago Law School, John M. Olin Program in Law and Economics Working Paper* (91)

Surowiecki, J. (2005), *The wisdom of crowds*, New York, Anchor Books

Swami, V., Coles, R., Stieger, S., Pietschnig, J., Furnham, A., Rehim, S., and Voracek, M. (2011), 'Conspiracist ideation in Britain and Austria: Evidence of a monological belief system and associations between individual psychological differences and real-world and fictitious conspiracy theories', *British Journal of Psychology*, *102*(3), 443–63

Swift, A. (15 November 2013), 'Majority in the US still believe JFK killed in a conspiracy', *Gallup*, https://news.gallup.com/poll/165893/majority-believe-jfk-killed-conspiracy.aspx

Swire, B., Berinsky, A. J., Lewandowsky, S., and Ecker, U. K. (2017), 'Processing political misinformation: comprehending the Trump phenomenon', *Royal Society Open Science*, *4*(3), 160802

Tajfel, H., and Turner, J. C. (1979), 'An integrative theory of intergroup conflict', in W. G. Austin and S. Worchel (eds), *The Social Psychology of Intergroup Relations* (pp. 33–47), Monterey, CA, Brooks/Cole

Tappin, B. M., and Gadsby, S. (2019), 'Biased belief in the Bayesian brain: A deeper look at the evidence', *Consciousness and Cognition*, *68*, 107–14

Tappin, B. M., Pennycook, G., and Rand, D. G. (2021), 'Rethinking the link between cognitive sophistication and politically motivated reasoning', *Journal of Experimental Psychology: General*, *150*(6), 1095

Taylor, K. (2006), *Brainwashing: The science of thought control*, Oxford, Oxford University Press

Thirumurthy, P., and Jayarajan, S. (11 May 2018), 'False Whatsapp messages on child abduction trigger violence in TN, killing two', *The News Minute*, https://

www.thenewsminute.com/article/false-whatsapp-messages-child-abduction-trigger-violence-tn-killing-two-81074

Thornton, B. (2000), 'The moon hoax: Debates about ethics in 1835 New York newspapers', *Journal of Mass Media Ethics*, *15*(2), 89–100

Timberg, C. (10 September 2021), 'Facebook made a big mistake in data it provided to researchers, undermining academic work', *Washington Post*, https://www.washingtonpost.com/technology/2021/09/10/facebook-error-data-social-scientists/

Tolosana, R., Vera-Rodriguez, R., Fierrez, J., Morales, A., and Ortega-Garcia, J. (2020), 'Deepfakes and beyond: A survey of face manipulation and fake detection', *Information Fusion*, *64*, 131–48

Tong, C., Gill, H., Li, J., Valenzuela, S., and Rojas, H. (2020), 'Fake News Is Anything They Say!' – Conceptualization and Weaponization of Fake News among the American Public', *Mass Communication and Society*, *23*(5), 755–78

Törnberg, P. (2018), 'Echo chambers and viral misinformation: Modeling fake news as complex contagion', *PLoS one*, *13*(9), e0203958

Traberg, C. S., and van der Linden, S. (2022), 'Birds of a feather are persuaded together: Perceived source credibility mediates the effect of political bias on misinformation susceptibility', *Personality and Individual Differences*, *185*, 111269

Traberg, C. S., Roozenbeek, J., and van der Linden, S. (2022), 'Psychological inoculation against misinformation: Current evidence and future directions', *Annals of the American Academy of Political and Social Science 700*(1), 136–51

Tufekci, Z. (10 March 2018), 'YouTube, the great radicaliser', *New York Times*, https://www.nytimes.com/2018/03/10/opinion/sunday/youtube-politics-radical.html

Tversky, A., and Kahneman, D. (1983), 'Extensional versus intuitive reasoning: The conjunction fallacy in probability judgment', *Psychological Review*, *90*(4), 293–315

UK Parliament (28 March 2018), *Evidence from Christopher Wylie, Cambridge Analytica whistleblower*, London, Digital, Culture, Media, and Sport Committee, https://committees.parliament.uk/committee/378/digital-culture-media-and-sport-committee/news/103673/evidence-from-christopher-wylie-cambridge-analytica-whistleblower-published/

United Nations (12 October 2020), *Want to learn how to spot and resist misinformation? New game by @GOVUK and @Cambridge_Uni can help you understand the strategies used to create & spread misinformation, and how to tackle them* [tweet]. Twitter. https://twitter.com/un/status/131437099752564 3264

United States vs Philip Morris USA Inc. et al, 9F. Supp. 2d 1 (D.D.C. 2006)

University of Cambridge (18 February 2021), 'Cambridge psychologist helps Facebook fight climate change misinformation', Cambridge, https://www.cam. ac.uk/research/news/cambridge-psychologist-helps-facebook-fight-climate-change-misinformation

— (20 February 2018), 'Fake news "vaccine": online game may "inoculate" by simulating propaganda tactics', Cambridge, https://www.cam.ac.uk/research/ news/fake-news-vaccine-online-game-may-inoculate-by-simulating-propaganda-tactics

Uscinski, J. E., and Parent, J. M. (2014), *American Conspiracy Theories*, Oxford, Oxford University Press

Uscinski, J. E., Enders, A., Klofstad, C., Seelig, M., Drochon, H., Premaratne, K., and Murthi, M. (2022), 'Have beliefs in conspiracy theories increased over time?', *PloS One*, *17*(7), e0270429

Van Bavel, J. J., Rathje, S., Harris, E., Robertson, C., and Sternisko, A. (2021), 'How social media shapes polarization', *Trends in Cognitive Sciences*, *25*(11), 913–16

Van Bavel, J., and Packer, D. (2021), *The Power of US: Harnessing Our Shared Identities for Personal and Collective Success*, New York, NY, Little Brown

van der Linden, S. (2013), 'What a hoax', *Scientific American Mind*, *24*(4), 40–3

— (2015), 'The conspiracy-effect: Exposure to conspiracy theories (about global warming) decreases pro-social behavior and science acceptance', *Personality and Individual Differences*, *87*, 171–3

— (2016), 'A conceptual critique of the cultural cognition thesis', *Science Communication*, *38*(1), 128–38

— (10 April 2018), 'Psychological Weapons of Mass Persuasion', *Scientific American Mind*, https://www.scientificamerican.com/article/psychological-weapons-of-mass-persuasion/.

— (2021), 'The Gateway Belief Model (GBM): A review and research agenda for communicating the scientific consensus on climate change', *Current Opinion in Psychology 42*, 7–12

— (23 December 2021), 'The best way to deal with Covid myths this Christmas? Pre-bunk rather than debunk', *Guardian*, https://www.theguardian.com/ commentisfree/2021/dec/23/covid-myths-christmas-vaccines-virus-missinformation

van der Linden, S. L., Clarke, C. E., and Maibach, E. W. (2015), 'Highlighting consensus among medical scientists increases public support for vaccines: evidence from a randomized experiment', *BMC Public Health*, *15*(1), 1207 van der Linden, S., Leiserowitz, A., and Maibach, E. (2018), 'Scientific agreement can neutralize politicization of facts', *Nature Human Behaviour*, *2*(1), 2–3

— (2019), 'The gateway belief model: A large-scale replication', *Journal of Environmental Psychology*, *62*, 49–58

van der Linden, S., Leiserowitz, A., Rosenthal, S., and Maibach, E. (2017), 'Inoculating the public against misinformation about climate change', *Global Challenges*, *1*(2), 1600008

van der Linden, S., Maibach, E., Cook, J., Leiserowitz, A., and Lewandowsky, S. (2017), 'Inoculating against misinformation', *Science*, *358*(6367), 1141–2

van der Linden, S., Maibach, E., Cook, J., Leiserowitz, A., Ranney, M., Lewandowsky, S., . . . and Weber, E. U. (2017), 'Culture versus cognition is a false dilemma', *Nature Climate Change*, *7*(7), 457

van der Linden, S., Panagopoulos, C., and Roozenbeek, J. (2020), 'You are fake news: political bias in perceptions of fake news', *Media, Culture & Society*, *42*(3), 460–70

van der Linden, S., Panagopoulos, C., Azevedo, F., and Jost, J. T. (2021), 'The paranoid style in American politics revisited: An ideological asymmetry in conspiratorial thinking', *Political Psychology*, *42*(1), 23–51

Van Kessel, P. (4 December 2019), '10 facts about Americans and YouTube', *Pew Research Center*, https://www.pewresearch.org/fact-tank/2019/12/04/10-facts-about-americans-and-youtube/

van Prooijen, J. W., and Douglas, K. M. (2017), 'Conspiracy theories as part of history: The role of societal crisis situations', *Memory Studies*, *10*(3), 323–33

van Prooijen, J. W., Ligthart, J., Rosema, S., and Xu, Y (2022), 'The entertainment value of conspiracy theories', *British Journal of Psychology*, *113*(1), 25–48

Vegetti, F., and L. Littvay (2022), 'Belief in conspiracy theories and attitudes toward political violence', *Italian Political Science Review*, *52*(1), 18–32

View, T. [@travis_view] (10 January 2019), *I was looking at the "likes" on the Youtube page of Buckey Wolfe, the QAnon follower who is accused of killing his brother. I want to share the trajectory of his Youtube likes in this thread* [tweet], Twitter https://threadreaderapp.com/thread/1083437810634248193.html

Voigtländer, N., and Voth, H. J. (2015), 'Nazi indoctrination and anti-Semitic beliefs in Germany', *Proceedings of the National Academy of Sciences*, *112*(26), 7931–6

Vosoughi, S., Roy, D., and Aral, S. (2018), 'The spread of true and false news online', *Science*, *359* (6380), 1146–51

Wabnegger, A., Gremsl, A., and Schienle, A. (2021), 'The association between the belief in coronavirus conspiracy theories, miracles, and the susceptibility to conjunction fallacy', *Applied Cognitive Psychology*, *35*(5), 1344–8

Wakefield, A. (director), (2016), *Vaxxed: From Cover-up to Catastrophe* (film), Del Bigtree

Wakefield, A. J., Murch, S. H., Anthony, A., Linnell, J., Casson, D. M., Malik, M., … and Walker-Smith, J. A. (1998), 'RETRACTED: Ileal-lymphoid-nodular hyperplasia, non-specific colitis, and pervasive developmental disorder in children', *The Lancet, 351* (9103), 637–41

Walker, C., O'Neill, S., and de-Wit, L. (2020), 'Evidence of Psychological Targeting but not Psychological Tailoring in Political Persuasion Around Brexit', *Experimental Results, 1* e38

Walter, N., and Tukachinsky, R. (2020), 'A meta-analytic examination of the continued influence of misinformation in the face of correction: How powerful is it, why does it happen, and how to stop it?', *Communication Research, 47*(2), 155–77

Wang, W. C., Brashier, N. M., Wing, E. A., Marsh, E. J., and Cabeza, R. (2016), 'On known unknowns: Fluency and the neural mechanisms of illusory truth', *Journal of Cognitive Neuroscience, 28*(5), 739–46

Weinberger, S. (19 September 2005), 'You can't handle the truth', *Slate*, https://slate.com/news-and-politics/2005/09/psy-ops-propaganda-goes-mainstream.html

Wenz, J. (22 February 2021), '"Mars, fascinating". Why a garbage video went viral before NASA could release the real one', *Inverse*, https://www.inverse.com/science/fake-mars-video

Will Be Wild [podcast] (3 June 2022), 'The War on Pineapple', *On the Media*, https://www.wnycstudios.org/podcasts/otm/segments/war-pineapple-on-the-media

Williams, M. N., Marques, M. D., Hill, S. R., Kerr, J. R., and Ling, M. (2022), 'Why are beliefs in different conspiracy theories positively correlated across individuals? Testing monological network versus unidimensional factor model explanations', *British Journal of Social Psychology*

Williamson, E. (2022), *Sandy Hook: An American Tragedy and the Battle for Truth*, New York, NY, Dutton

Willis, M. (director) (2020), *Plandemic: The Hidden Agenda Behind Covid-19* (documentary), Elevate Films

Wilton Park (2017) #FakeNews: innocuous or intolerable? *WP 1542*, https://www.wiltonpark.org.uk/event/wp1542/

Wineburg, S., McGrew, S., Breakstone, J., and T. Ortega (2016), 'Evaluating Information: The Cornerstone of Civic Reasoning', Stanford Digital Repository, https://purl.stanford.edu/fv751yt5934

Wineburg, S., McGrew, S., Breakstone, J., and T. Ortega (2017), 'The Challenge That's Bigger Than Fake News: Civic Reasoning in a Social Media Environment', *American Educator*, *41*(3), 4–9

Wise, A. (17 November 2020), 'Trump fires election security director who corrected voter fraud disinformation', *NPR*, https://www.npr.org/2020/11/17/936003057/cisa-director-chris-krebs-fired-after-trying-to-correct-voter-fraud-disinformati?t=1642285331596

Wodinsky, S. (24 June 2021), 'Researchers produce obvious study on dunking because they're nerds', *Gizmodo*, https://gizmodo.com/researchers-produce-obvious-study-on-dunking-because-th-1847165088

Wong, J. C. (15 November 2019), 'Twitter's political ad ban to limit micro-targeting putting pressure on Facebook', *Guardian*, https://www.theguardian.com/technology/2019/nov/15/twitter-facebook-ad-ban-micro-targeting

Wong, J. C. (29 January 2020), 'One year inside Trump's monumental Facebook campaign', *Guardian*, https://www.theguardian.com/us-news/2020/jan/28/donald-trump-facebook-ad-campaign-2020-election.

Wood, M. J., Douglas, K. M., and Sutton, R. M. (2012), 'Dead and alive: Beliefs in contradictory conspiracy theories', *Social Psychological and Personality Science*, *3*(6), 767–73

Wood, T., and Porter, E. (2019), 'The elusive backfire effect: Mass attitudes' steadfast factual adherence', *Political Behavior*, *41*(1), 135–63

World Health Organization (23 September 2021), 'What is Go Viral?', https://www.who.int/news/item/23-09-2021-what-is-go-viral

Wylie, C. (2019), *Mindf*ck: Inside Cambridge Analytica's Plot to Break the World*, New York, NY, Random House

Yesilada, M., and Lewandowsky, S. (2022), 'Systematic review: YouTube recommendations and problematic content', *Internet Policy Review*, *11*(1), 1–22

Yoder, K. (25 July 2019), 'Frank Luntz, the GOP's message master, calls for climate action', *Grist*, https://grist.org/article/the-gops-most-famous-messaging-strategist-calls-for-climate-action/

YouGov (4 April 2018), *What the world thinks*, https://today.yougov.com/opi/live_survey_results/6147e107-0a97-11e8-b216-d9ff14e72543/question/cecf46a6-0a97-11e8-bd7b-c532039a14a0/toplines/

Yougov–Cambridge Centre (n.d.), *YouGov-Cambridge Globalism Study* (2019–20), https://yougov.co.uk/topics/yougov-cambridge/survey-results

Yousuf, H., van der Linden, S., Bredius, L., van Essen, G. A., Sweep, G., Preminger, Z., van Gorp, E., Scherder, E., Narula, J., and Hofstra, L. (2021), 'A media intervention applying debunking versus non-debunking content to combat vaccine misinformation in elderly in the Netherlands: A digital randomized trial', *The Lancet EClinicalMedicine 35*, 100881

YouTube for Press (n.d.), https://blog.youtube/press/

Youyou, W., Kosinski, M., and Stillwell, D. (2015), 'Computer-based personality judgments are more accurate than those made by humans', *Proceedings of the National Academy of Sciences, 112*(4), 1036–40

Zarocostas, J. (2020), 'How to fight an infodemic', *The Lancet, 395* (10225), 676

Zarouali, B., Dobber, T., De Pauw, G., and de Vreese, C. (2020), 'Using a personality-profiling algorithm to investigate political microtargeting: Assessing the persuasion effects of personality-tailored ads on social media', *Communication Research*

Zhang, B., van der Linden, S., Mildenberger, M., Marlon, J. R., Howe, P. D., and Leiserowitz, A. (2018), 'Experimental effects of climate messages vary geographically', *Nature Climate Change, 8*(5), 370–4

Zollo, F., Bessi, A., Del Vicario, M., Scala, A., Caldarelli, G., Shekhtman, L., . . . and Quattrociocchi, W. (2017), 'Debunking in a world of tribes', *PloS One, 12*(7), e0181821

Zuckerberg, M. (5 May 2018), 'A blueprint for content governance and enforcement', *Facebook*, https://www.facebook.com/notes/751449002072082/

Zweiback, A. J. (1997), 'The 21 "Turncoat GIs": Nonrepatriations and the political Culture of the Korean War', *Historian, 60*(2), 345–62

ACKNOWLEDGEMENTS

If I need to thank anyone, it's my wonderful wife, Breanne. Without her help and support over the years, this book project would have never made it. She's my inspiration and her brutally honest feedback helped me communicate both my ideas *and* statistics in a way that's not only more accurate but also more accessible. Our beautiful daughter, Gavriella, was born during the pandemic. Her constant smiling and laughter were a source of great inspiration while finishing this book. At barely a year old, she's already my toughest critic.

I can't be thankful enough to my absolutely brilliant agent, Will Francis, at Janklow & Nesbit, who introduced me to the world of literary publishing. I am so lucky to have found an agent who shared my passion and vision for the book. Will not only helped me better articulate and formulate my ideas but was in fact crucial in shaping the proposal that ultimately became this book. On that note, I am indebted to my colleague Sarah-Jayne Blakemore for introducing me to Will in the first place, as without her advice, I would probably still be agonizing over how to write this book. I am tremendously grateful to my fantastic editors: Louise Haines at 4th Estate/HarperCollins and Jessica Yao at W. W. Norton. It was a great match from the outset and I loved working with such hands-on and enthusiastic editors. Not only did they help me convey the science in a way that hopefully prevents the reader from falling asleep, they were incredibly detail-oriented too: from ancient Rome and the British legal system to critical questions about the research and finding better ways to explain what it all means and why we should care about it. I couldn't have asked for more attentive and insightful editors. They helped me be a better writer. Many thanks to Kate Johnson also for her brilliant copyediting and correcting my errors. Any that remain are completely my own.

I want to thank my dear mentors Tony Leiserowitz and Edward Maibach for starting this research with me and encouraging me to explore it further. They are some of the kindest, most brilliant, and meticulous scientists I know and from whom I have learned so very much. In turn, I must thank Jon Roozenbeek, with whom I have conducted much of the later research discussed in this book and without whom much of it would probably not have happened. Jon's brilliant ideas, humour, passion, commitment, and thousands of conversations about this topic have undoubtedly shaped my thinking in a powerful way: he is a force of nature, a true renaissance man, and a wonderful colleague. I would also like to thank and credit Ruurd Oosterwoud, his team at *Bad News*, and Gusmanson Design for their pivotal role in designing the games and for making them freely available for research and education. I thank Luke and his team at Lens Change for his fantastic work on the animated videos.

Although he likes to 'lurk in the shadows', a special thank you goes to Fred Lewsey at the Cambridge Office of Communications who completely understood our research goals and whose efforts were absolutely pivotal in making the interventions an international success. I am also grateful to the massive support from Cambridge University who made this research possible. I would like to thank the whole Cambridge Social Decision-Making Lab (both past and current members) and especially Melisa Basol, Rakoen Maertens, Cecilie Traberg, Steve Rathje and Patrick McClanahan – all phenomenal young scholars whose remarkable research programmes are featured in this book and I hope to have done them the justice they deserve.

I must credit Stephan Lewandowsky and John Cook – two amazing long-standing collaborators. Our lines of research have always converged and our joint work has influenced and inspired many of the ideas presented in the book. I am also deeply grateful to my colleagues Alex Freeman and David Spiegelhalter for the many insightful conversations about transparent evidence communication and the dark arts of persuasion. I have learned a lot from our work together over the years.

Josh Compton at Dartmouth College has been a tremendous source of inspiration for my theorizing and research on inoculation theory. I'm super thankful to Bob Cialdini and my colleague John Jost at NYU for sharing their insights with me about Bill McGuire's early work and ideas. So many other wonderful colleagues have inspired and supported insights in this book through personal conversations and research, including Matthew Goldberg, Lee de Wit, Jon Simons, Costas Panagopoulos, Jay Van Bavel, Ragnar Lofstedt, and Jamie Druckman. I also thank Gordon Pennycook and Dave Rand for the many – and sometimes adversarial exchanges – on the topic of misinformation.

I am grateful to Beth Goldberg at Google Jigsaw, the whole communications team at the UK Cabinet Office, our partners at GEC, Homeland Security, the FCO, WhatsApp and Facebook, the World Health Organization, NATO, and the United Nations for supporting our research. I thank Mike Cherenson from New Jersey for always sharing fantastic examples of inoculation and for introducing me to the Public Relations Society of America. I thank the ESRC, the American Psychological Association, the Gates Foundation, and the European Commission for supporting our work.

I am thankful to each and every participant in our studies and interventions, including the valuable feedback you give us, which undoubtedly has made our work better.

I thank my family and amazing mother, Veronica, for always being my biggest supporter in life and for teaching me how to pursue my dreams.

This book is for Rogier Modderman – one of my oldest friends who suddenly passed during the pandemic. Although no longer with us, his thoughts live on in this book.

I thank Luka Bareis – who always knew I would write a book someday. I am happy that the wave function finally collapsed. I thank Gareth Cook, my editor at *Scientific American* for giving me the first opportunity to write for a wider audience all those years ago.

To all of my friends and colleagues over the years; but *most* of all, to my high school teachers, who were sure I would never amount to anything. This one is for you.

Sander van der Linden, *Cambridge, 24 June 2022*

PICTURE CREDITS

Kanizsa triangle p. 19, Fibonacci, CC BY-SA 3.0 via Wikimedia Commons http://creativecommons.org/licenses/by-sa/3.0/

Inauguration p. 31, © Reuters, https://www.washingtonpost.com/news/power post/wp/2017/03/06/here-are-the-photos-that-show-obamas-inauguration-crowd-was-bigger-than-trumps/

Asch experiment p. 37, Fred the Oyster, CC BY-SA 4.0 via Wikimedia Commons https://creativecommons.org/licenses/by-sa/4.0

'CONSPIRE' p. 61, John Cook

'Der ist Schuld am Kriege!' p. 64, German Library, https://creativecommons.org/publicdomain/zero/1.0/legalcode

Coin p. 86, Classical Numismatic Group, Inc., CC BY-SA 3.0 via Wikimedia Commons, http://creativecommons.org/licenses/by-sa/3.0/

Graph p. 104, Esteban Ortiz-Ospina (Our World in Data, Oxford University), https://ourworldindata.org/rise-of-social-media

Zuckerberg graphic p. 111, courtesy of Meta, https://m.facebook.com/nt/screen/? params=%7B%22note_id%22%3A751449002072082%7D&path=%2F notes%2Fnote%2F&_rdr

Bar graph p. 177, copyright held by an unknown person

Sander van der Linden and Jon Roozenbeek, p. 208 © Dan Parry

Screenshots pp. 213 and 215, Gusmanson/Tilt Studio, www.getbadnews.com

Airplane image p. 216, Alan Wilson, CC BY-SA 2.0 via Wikimedia Commons https://creativecommons.org/licenses/by-sa/2.0

Screenshots pp. 235 and 237, Gusmanson/Tilt Studio, www.goviralgame.com

Screenshots pp. 242–243, Gusmanson/Tilt Studio, www.harmonysquare.com

Father's Day image p. 244, courtesy of Meta, https://www.snopes.com/fact-check/fathers-day-protest-photo/

Tweet p. 244, NBC News, https://i.redd.it/asnbyyp4l1941.jpg

Infographic p. 249, Jigsaw

INDEX